LAWYERS AND FIDELITY TO LAW

LAWYERS AND FIDELITY TO LAW

W. Bradley Wendel

PRINCETON UNIVERSITY PRESS • PRINCETON AND OXFORD

Copyright © 2010 by Princeton University Press
Published by Princeton University Press, 41 William Street,
Princeton, New Jersey 08540
In the United Kingdom: Princeton University Press, 6 Oxford Street,
Woodstock, Oxfordshire OX20 1TW

press.princeton.edu

Library of Congress Cataloging-in-Publication Data

Wendel, W. Bradley, 1969–
Lawyers and fidelity to law / Bradley W. Wendel.
    p. cm.
Includes bibliographical references and index.
ISBN 978-0-691-13719-3 (alk. paper)
1. Legal ethics–United States. I. Title.
    KF306.W458 2010
    174'.30973—dc22   2010005087

British Library Cataloging-in-Publication Data is available

This book has been composed in Electra LT Std and Avenir

Printed on acid-free paper. ∞

Printed in the United States of America

10 9 8 7 6 5 4 3 2 1

For Liz

Contents

Acknowledgments

Many of the ideas in this book can be traced back to the time spent working toward a J.S.D. degree with a concentration in legal philosophy at Columbia Law School, where I was extremely fortunate to have Kent Greenawalt, Jeremy Waldron, and Bill Sage as advisors. Their intellectual guidance and support made my time at Columbia a real watershed in my development as a scholar. Some of the arguments put forward here can be traced to my doctoral dissertation, but the main outlines of this work developed later. However, I am certain I would not have thought about these issues in the same way without their suggestions and criticism, and I am greatly indebted to the feedback they offered on drafts of my dissertation.

Early in the process of writing this book, I decided to proceed by presenting draft chapters at law school faculty work-in-progress workshops. One practical result is that much of the book ended up being written in hotels, airport departure lounges, airplane seats (thank goodness for elite frequent flier status), and visitor offices at various schools. I am substantially indebted to my family for putting up with my frequent absences as I took this project on the road. More substantively, the writing process was one that truly benefited from the existence of a community of scholars. I tried out early versions of arguments, presented half-baked ideas, and learned from the engaged criticism of specialists and nonspecialists on literally dozens of occasions. As I was working on this book, I kept a piece of sage advice taped to the wall above my computer, from Anne Lamott's wonderful book of advice for writers, *Bird by Bird*: "For me and most of the other writers I know, writing is not rapturous. In fact, the only way I can get anything written at all is to write really, really shitty first drafts." Collectively, I owe a great deal of gratitude for tolerating, and helping me improve, those drafts to the organizers of and participants in workshops at Akron, Arizona, Boston College, Cornell, Denver, Duke, Georgetown, Houston, St. John's, St. Louis, San Diego, Suffolk, Texas, Villanova, Washington and Lee, Washington University, Willamette, and at the Australian National University Research School of Social Sciences. Bits of the argument that ended up in the book were also presented as freestanding papers in workshops at Dalhousie, Nevada–Las Vegas, Queen's (Ontario), a Cornell Law School faculty retreat, the Yale Legal Theory Workshop, legal ethics conferences at the Universities of Auckland, Canterbury (New Zealand), Exeter (UK), Fordham and Hofstra Law Schools, the 100th anniversary celebration of the Law Society of Alberta, and the first "legal ethics shmooze," held at Fordham Law School. I also presented an overview of the argument in the book as a keynote address at the Third Annual Legal Ethics Conference on the Gold Coast in Australia; considerable thanks are due to the organizers of that conference for their kind invitation, and to Deborah Rhode and David Luban for a vigorous public debate at the conference.

While the workshopping process as a whole was essential to the evolution of the arguments in this book, I have to single out a number of people for special thanks. These scholars made particularly valuable suggestions and clarifications, engaged in extended discussions of these ideas, pressed objections, insisted that I deal with problems, and refused to let me get away with saying silly things. Although any enumeration risks omission, I can recall particularly valuable contributions made by Greg Alexander, John Bogert, Jules Coleman, Roger Cramton, Sarah Cravens, Dave Caudill, Tim Dare, Mark Drumbl, Bob Gordon, Jim Henderson, Kate Kruse, Doug Kysar, David Luban, David McGowan, Yasutomo Morigiwa, Trevor Morrison, Donald Nicolson, Christine Parker, Gerald Postema, Jeff Rachlinski, Deborah Rhode, Tanina Rostain, Ted Schneyer, Emily Sherwin, Steve Shiffrin, Pat Shin, Bill Simon, M.B.E. Smith, Jane Stapleton, Mark Suchman, Dennis Tuchler, Duncan Webb, Chris Whelan, Jack Wilson, David Zaring, and Ben Zipursky. Special gratitude is due to Steve Pepper for detailed written comments on the legal interpretation materials and extended spirited conversations about this problem. Alice Woolley must be singled out for extra-special thanks for slogging through drafts of each chapter in near-final form, providing uncompromising but always constructive criticism, and insisting that I improve numerous arguments. Many of the attempts to answer objections raised by these colleagues became lengthy discussions here, and I am confident I would not have appreciated the importance of these issues if they had not been pressed so effectively. Of course, none of these can be held responsible for any remaining errors, which no doubt are legion.

A substantial intellectual debt, accrued starting from the very beginning of this project, is owed to my friend, former colleague, and international boondoggle companion Greg Cooper, with whom I co-taught a seminar on legal ethics at Washington and Lee for four years. It is not much of an exaggeration to say that this book would not exist if we hadn't had so much fun teaching that class, participating in the annual Legal Ethics Institute at W&L, and thinking about these issues. Many of the central ideas in this book have their origins in seminar readings and class discussions, and were refined through hours of discussions, sometimes in preparation for class, sometimes in the Palms in Lexington or in a pub in some foreign country, with the accompaniment of quality local beer. I also learned a great deal from the students in our seminar, who had a knack for zeroing in on the weak parts of arguments and refusing to accept simplistic answers. Finally, I am grateful to the distinguished scholars—William Simon, David Luban, Arthur Applbaum, Steven Lubet, Daniel Markovits, Tim Dare, Gerald Postema, and Bob Gordon—who have agreed to serve as keynote participants in the Legal Ethics Institute over the years. The Institute truly is a unique experience, bringing together practicing lawyers and judges, academics, and undergraduate and law students for an intensive weekend-long workshop, and my thinking about legal ethics has been profoundly influenced by my participation in it. Students in my legal ethics seminar at Cornell have been similarly helpful in their persistent questioning of the arguments in many classic legal ethics papers and in my own work.

I am most fortunate to have benefited from the support of the administration at Cornell Law School, particularly Dean Stewart Schwab. In addition to permitting me to take a research leave in the fall of 2007 for the purpose of completing the first draft of this book, Stewart has also been extraordinarily generous with travel funding, enabling me to present many of the arguments in the book at academic conferences around the world. I also appreciate the research assistance provided by our outstanding librarian, Claire Germain, my library liaison Matt Morrison, and the staff of the Cornell Law Library.

I am grateful to a number of people at Princeton University Press who helped this book become a reality. Ian Malcolm's early enthusiasm and continued patience and good humor were invaluable assets to this project. Mike McGee provided excellent editorial suggestions and Heath Renfroe expertly managed the production process. It is customary to thank one's anonymous referees, but in this case both Daniel Markovits and Arthur Applbaum identified themselves, and it is to them I owe considerable thanks for their extensive feedback, which improved the book immeasurably as compared with the penultimate draft manuscript. Arthur Applbaum's report in particular contained an abundance of the kind of sympathetic but rigorous tough-love criticism that was needed to motivate a final revision, resulting in a much tighter and more rigorous finished product. All authors should be so fortunate to have such a dedicated reader. I know both reviewers continue to disagree with much in the book, but I hope these points of contention do not obscure the extent to which I have been assisted by their criticism.

The most important debt of all is owed to my wife, Elizabeth Peck, who has encouraged and believed in me, not only during work on this project, but going all the way back to when I was a lowly graduate student and, before then, a lawyer with the crazy idea of going into legal academia. Without her constant presence, support, and love, I cannot imagine having accomplished anything of importance over the last 18 years. This book is but a small sign of Liz's significance in my life, and it is an honor to dedicate it to her.

LAWYERS AND FIDELITY TO LAW

Introduction

In the United States it is hard to commit large-scale wrongs without the involvement of lawyers. Sure, you can rob a bank or shoot someone, but the really big stuff—accounting gimmickry leading to the collapse of Fortune 50 companies, fraudulent schemes to defraud the Treasury out of billions of dollars in tax revenue, and the defiance of human rights exhibited by the United States in the aftermath of the September 11th attacks—almost always occurs with either the active involvement or the acquiescence of intelligent, sophisticated, elite lawyers. When these scandals become publicly known, commentators on newspaper op-ed pages, television news programs, and weblogs ask with genuine or mock surprise: "Where were the lawyers?"[1] The answer is of course that they were right in the thick of things, so the next question that inevitably follows is, "What is wrong with lawyers' ethics?" A tacit assumption often underlying this question is that lawyers' ethics is a branch of ordinary, common, everyday morality—ethics for people *as people*, not as occupants of defined social roles. Occasionally defenders of lawyers do try to argue that the ethics of lawyers is different, but this has a way of coming off as elitist, as if the bar is demanding special privileges to violate the rights of others without coming in for moral criticism as a result. When two law professors defended the advice given by executive branch lawyers on the treatment of detainees, which apparently had the effect of permitting torture in some circumstances, they called the memos outlining the legal case for torture "standard fare, routine lawyerly stuff."[2] Not surprisingly, this did not sit well with people who believed that lawyers' ethics ought to closely track ordinary-person ethics. Since we know, as regular decent folks, that torture is a grave moral evil, surely there must be something terribly wrong with a system of professional ethics that regards advising on the permissibility of torture as routine.

One way to reach this conclusion is to rely on the horribleness of torture, in the same moral terms that any sensible human being would recognize. If it is a moral failure of the highest order to inflict suffering on a helpless person, then it is at least a serious secondary wrong to provide legal advice to a government that is contemplating the use of torture. Lawyers can be faulted for advising their clients that torture is legally permissible, without attempting to dissuade them on moral grounds. Alternatively, they may be faulted for concluding that anything so plainly a violation of moral norms could ever be legally permitted. Similar arguments could be raised against lawyers who helped Enron structure transactions that concealed the true financial condition of the company, leading to its collapse and the losses of thousand of jobs and hundreds of millions of dollars of investors' wealth. For any high-profile legal ethics scandal, there seems to be a way to describe the lawyers' conduct straightforwardly in moral terms, leading ineluctably to the conclusion that lawyers deserve the labels of liars, cheats, and even torturers. Having worked within a professional role is no excuse—lawyers can be blamed for the harm they assist in because they remain persons, bound by ordinary morality, even when acting in a professional capacity. Critics of the legal profession thus urge lawyers to take personal moral responsibility for their actions, or to aim directly at achieving justice, when they represent clients, either in litigation or in transactional or advising matters.[3]

This book approaches this problem in a very different way. It is about political legitimacy, not justice or ordinary morality. Political legitimacy is the property that political arrangements have when they deserve the respect and allegiance of citizens, even if citizens disagree with particular laws or regard them as unjust. Legitimacy is a normative notion, having to do with the relationship between state power and citizens. The aim of this book is to ground the duties of lawyers on considerations relating to democratic law-making and the rule of law, so that the ethical value of lawyering is located in the domain of politics, not ordinary morality. This book defends an ethical position that should be familiar to practicing lawyers, with one important difference. Practicing lawyers, and many legal scholars claim there are good moral reasons why a lawyer is justified in acting on the lawful interests of her client, notwithstanding the interests of nonclients that would otherwise give someone a reason for acting in another way. The theory of legal ethics I will set out here places fidelity to law, not pursuit of clients' interests, at the center of lawyers' obligations. Law deserves respect because of its capacity to underwrite a distinction between raw power and lawful power, so that it becomes possible for the proverbial little guy to stand up to the big guy, and say, "Hey—you can't do that to me!" Law enables a particular kind of reason-giving, one that is independent of power or preferences. Citizens can appeal to legal entitlements, which are different from mere interests or desires, because they have been conferred by the society as a whole in some fair manner, collectively, in the name of the political community. This is an appeal to the political legitimacy of entitlements, and only indirectly to morality, because citizens accept for moral reasons the legitimacy of laws enacted through fair procedures. Unlike the dominant tradition in academic legal ethics, it is not an appeal directly to ordinary morality, justice, or the public interest.[4]

Popular discourse about the law includes a significant strand of approval of law-breaking, if done in the service of justice. This is true even of lawyers, who are often portrayed in novels and films as morally bankrupt to the extent they comply formalistically with the law, and heroic to the extent they are willing to bend the rules in pursuit of substantive justice.[5] Lawyers know that people who deal with the law often experience it as an irritant or an obstacle in the way of something the client would very much like to do. Business lawyers in particular are accustomed to being criticized as deal-breakers, impediments to exploiting some lucrative opportunity. "So what if the law technically says we can't do such-and-such," clients sometimes say. "Your job is to figure out ways to do what we want."[6] Implicit in this stance is the idea that the law is not entitled to respect *as such*, but has only instrumental value for citizens. If there is some possibility of getting caught and punished, then a prudent person will follow the law, but if clever lawyers can figure out a way to escape detection, gum up the enforcement process, or otherwise avoid legal penalties, then legality alone does not supply a sufficient reason not to engage in this evasion.

A similar attitude toward lawyers and legality has been evident in the defense of the Bush Administration's conduct of the so-called war on terror by lawyers accused of wrongdoing. When one of the principal legal architects of the Administration's response, John Yoo, said that the U.S. Supreme Court's *Hamdan* decision "made the legal system part of the problem, rather than part of the solution to the challenges of the war on terrorism,"[7] he was reflecting the attitude that the law is only instrumentally valuable, and if it stands in the way of accomplishing some important policy goal, then it should be nullified. Yoo is actually quite candid about this, saying that "law is not the end of a matter; indeed, it is often the beginning."[8] In his view, lawyers should be blamed for making a fetish of legality—"look[ing] to the law as if it were a religion or a fully articulated ethical code ... relieving us of the difficult job of making a choice."[9]

Although it is true that law does not end debate in moral terms about a matter, and people may engage in public criticism, protests, civil disobedience, and other acts designed to change the law, Yoo's stance cannot be the ethics of *lawyers*. If the concept of legality means anything, it is that there is a difference between the law and what someone—a citizen, judge, or lawyer—thinks ought to be done about something, as a matter of policy, morality, prudence, or common sense. While citizens may resent the law and resist its application in some cases, lawyers are charged with an obligation to treat the law with respect, not merely as an inconvenient obstacle to be planned around. The observation that one can make a fetish of legality tends to resonate because it may appear that in calling upon lawyers to respect the law, I am defending an ethical system suitable only for sheep, not autonomous moral agents who are expected to take responsibility for their actions. In a reasonably well-functioning democratic political order, however, the law is not the imposition of some alien power, but a collective achievement by people who share an interest in living alongside one another in conditions of relative peace and stability. It is the product of procedures that enable citizens to resolve disagreements that otherwise would remain intractable, making it impossible to work together on common projects. To use John Yoo's example, the September 11th terrorist attacks created a host of major policy-making challenges, such as: how privacy concerns should be weighed against the need for law enforcement officials to acquire information (reflected in the Patriot Act and the NSA's warrantless wiretapping program); whether detainees alleged to have been associates of al Qaeda should be treated as prisoners of war for the purposes of applying the Geneva Conventions; and what kinds of interrogation techniques could be used by the military, the CIA, and law enforcement personnel, particularly where there was some possibility of learning information that could prevent future terrorist attacks. The important thing, as I will argue, is that these questions be resolved through public, reasonably accessible procedures that enable citizens to reach a provisional settlement of these controversies, to enable cooperative action in response to some collective need.* Relying on autonomous moral reasoning and deliberation will only perpetuate an intractable debate. This claim stands in contrast with the assumption (sometimes explicit, sometimes unstated) that a theory of lawyers' ethics must be based on an obligation to pursue substantive justice. One of the aims of this book is to rehabilitate the idea of legitimacy as a normative ideal for lawyers, and to direct lawyers to work within a system that is designed, to a large extent, to supersede disagreements over what substantive justice requires.

The effect of shifting the evaluative frame of reference from ordinary morality and justice to considerations of political legitimacy is to change the terms of the normative criticism of lawyers. In the case of lawyers advising on the

---

* Settlement of society-wide or relatively more local normative controversy is not the same thing as the resolution of litigated disputes, whether by trial or agreement of the parties (which, somewhat confusingly, American lawyers refer to as "settlement" of the litigation). One of the functions of law is to resolve particular controversies between specific parties through judicial or administrative proceedings. Two citizens may disagree over whether a contract for the delivery of chicken refers to broiling chickens or stewing chickens, whether a barge company was at fault in an accident for not employing additional crew members, or whether an employer's conduct constitutes sexual harassment. The settlement function I appeal to here is a larger-scale phenomenon. It supersedes diffuse disagreement over normative issues by replacing the contested individual moral and political beliefs of citizens with a shared social position.

law regulating torture, the perspective shifts from that of ordinary morality, in which the grave evil of torture is the primary consideration, to a political perspective in which we can understand the applicable law as an attempt by domestic and international lawmakers to balance competing interests in humanitarian values and the need for national security. The criticism of Bush administration lawyers who advised on the permissibility of torture is therefore not that they are accomplices to the moral wrong of torture, but that they are primarily liable for unethical conduct as abusers of the law. This would be a hollow criticism if there were no moral reasons to respect the institutions, procedures, and professional roles that constitute the legal system. One of the central tasks of this book is therefore to establish that the legal system is worthy of our respect.[10]

The strategy for doing so is to rely on political normative considerations relating to the ethics of citizenship in a liberal democracy. At its foundation, the argument rests on what John Rawls calls the burdens of judgment—that is, the indeterminacy in practice of our evaluative concepts, due to empirical uncertainty and moral pluralism.[11] Recognition of the burdens of judgment is long overdue in legal ethics, which has tended to assume unwarranted clarity in moral reasoning and to avoid facing up to the problems of pluralism and disagreement.

Ethical pluralism is not the same thing as skepticism or relativism; rather, it is a claim about what is objectively true, concerning the structure of value.[12] Ethical reasons are not arbitrary or subjective. They are related to the sorts of interests, capacities, and needs that people have, the bad consequences they try to avoid, and the ends they seek.[13] These interests, capacities, and ends are diverse, and not susceptible of being reduced to some kind of over-arching master-value that specifies what it means to lead a fulfilling, ethical life. Value conflicts may occur within a single conception of the good life or they may represent opposition between rival visions of human flourishing. Entire cultures may be differentiated in part on the basis of how they prioritize competing values.[14] These different rankings of value are one of the things that sets cultures apart, even though they may be concerned with the same sorts of normative considerations at a high level of abstraction, such as life, health, honest, loyalty, and so on. (Note, too, that diverse cultures can coexist within a single polity, as in the contemporary United States.) In a society characterized by value pluralism, reasonable citizens in a democracy must be prepared to propose and accept fair terms of cooperation, but they may have deep and intractable disagreements at the level of comprehensive moral doctrines. One may hope, as Rawls does, for an overlapping consensus on certain public reasons,[15] but one of the principal arguments offered here is that we can depend on very little consensus, beyond agreeing that certain lawmaking and law-applying procedures are tolerably fair and therefore legitimate. Still, governance through fair democratic procedures is something worth respecting, and lawyers do something valuable by working within a system that maintains legitimate procedures for establishing a stable basis for coexistence and cooperation.

The aim of this book is to provide moral and political arguments for a version of what is generally called the Standard Conception of legal ethics.[16] As we will see, the version defended here may differ sufficiently from the Standard Conception to represent a kind of third way between that conception and its competitors.* The Standard Conception consists of two principles that guide the actions of lawyers, and a third principle that is supposed to inform the normative evaluation of the actions of lawyers.

1. *Principle of Partisanship*: The lawyer should seek to advance the interests of her client within the bounds of the law.
2. *Principle of Neutrality*: The lawyer should not consider the morality of the client's cause, nor the morality of particular actions taken to advance the client's cause, as long as both are lawful.
3. *Principle of Nonaccountability*: If a lawyer adheres to the first two principles, neither third-party observers nor the lawyer herself should regard the lawyer as a wrongdoer, in moral terms.

The difference between the Standard Conception, as usually understood, and the position defended in this book is that I argue that lawyers should act to protect the legal *entitlements* of clients, not advance their interests. The law does not merely set boundaries on what lawyers permissibly may do on behalf of clients; rather, it is what empowers lawyers to do anything at all for clients. The law creates the attorney–client relationship that gives lawyers certain powers to act for others, and also sets limitations on the lawful use of those powers. For example, lawyers *as lawyers* can bind their clients to contracts, must keep their clients' confidences, and must not advise them to violate the law. Ordinary persons—say, friends or family members—have neither these powers nor these restrictions to the same extent. As a descriptive matter, however, the question still remains: Why does the legal system, and the lawyer–client relationship within it, give reasons for lawyers to do something that may

---

* I am not committed to a name for the position defended here, or even to the notion that a label is required, but since fidelity to law, not client interests, is a principal difference between this view and the Standard Conception, the position here might be referred to as the fidelity to law conception, the entitlement view, or something similar.

be contrary to ordinary morality? The argument given here must therefore show why the legal system deserves the allegiance of citizens, so that lawyers will be seen to play a justified role in society.

The book is an exercise in applied moral and political philosophy, but my hope is that it will also speak in terms that make sense of the way practicing lawyers conceive of the ethical value of their profession. The chapters that follow elaborate on these points; they are organized roughly around the three principles that make up the Standard Conception and the modifications I believe are necessary to defend a philosophically sound theory of legal ethics, in which fidelity to law is the central obligation of lawyers.

Chapter 1 is a critical overview of the state of play in the academic legal ethics debate. The central question addressed in this book is often framed in terms of role-differentiated morality—that is, the claim that occupying a social role provides an institutional excuse for what would otherwise be wrongdoing, as considered by the standards of ordinary morality. The problem with this way of looking at things is that it assumes it is possible to construct a baseline case that is similar in all morally relevant ways, but for the presence of a social role. The notion of ordinary morality and its relation to political institutions and roles turns out to be harder to pin down than is generally believed, because obligations in ordinary morality are sensitive to context, and one contextual factor may be acting in a professional role. It may therefore seem that roles, including professional roles, are illusory, or that at most they serve as a shorthand way of summarizing a cluster of ordinary moral rights and obligations. One of the principal arguments of this book is to the contrary, that roles do real normative work by excluding consideration of reasons that someone outside the role would have to take into account. This does not mean that acting in a role is "amoral ethics," as it has sometimes been called.[17] Lawyers work within a set of institutional roles and practices that requires moral justification, but at a higher level of generality. Ethical justification for lawyers is not case-by-case, but systemic and institutional in nature.

More broadly, the argument here is that the ethics of the lawyer's role requires respect for a distinctive set of values—those that are an aspect of citizenship in a complex pluralistic society, in which the lives of individuals are comprehensively regulated by political institutions, and for good reason. Lawyers are people, too, but in their professional capacity they are best understood as playing a small but significant part in the maintenance of these institutions in good working order. This chapter frames the overall argument of the book, that the norms associated with the lawyering role have significant moral weight, which are derived from a freestanding morality of public life.[18] Theoretical legal ethics has made a conceptual wrong turn by trying to use the toolkit of

7

ordinary ethics to address the problems of lawyers, who are better analogized to political officials than to ordinary moral agents. A regime of public ethics, including the ethics of lawyers, cannot simply begin with ordinary moral values such as autonomy or human dignity, and proceed straightforwardly to the derivation of duties based on these values. Instead, the ethical considerations that inform lawyers acting in a representative capacity are, at root, a function of both the reasons why the law is worthy of respect by all citizens, and the special relationship between lawyers and the value of legality.

The Principle of Partisanship is the subject of chapter 2. American lawyers love the Principle of Partisanship. Ask any gathering of lawyers about the ethics of their profession and you will hear all about the obligation of "zealous advocacy." (Sometimes lawyers will actually complete that little maxim, "...within the bounds of the law." The last bit turns out to matter a great deal.) The principal argument of this chapter is that the law does not merely set the limits on permissible advocacy, but constitutes the lawyer's role. Whether they are asserting positions in litigation, structuring transactions in light of legal considerations, or advising their clients on compliance with the law, the legal entitlements of clients empower lawyers to do anything at all. A client may have extra-legal interests, but these do not convey authority upon an agent to act in a distinctively legal manner on behalf of the client. By "distinctively legal manner" here I mean that legal entitlements are claims of right, as distinct from assertions of interest and from the ability to obtain something using power, trickery, or influence. The Standard Conception as generally understood does not make this distinction. The lawyer's job is to zealously protect the client's interests, using means that are not unlawful, but that is not the same as the directive to protect the client's legal entitlements.

A wide range of practices familiar to lawyers can be criticized on the entitlements view defended here. In addition to being competent and diligent representatives of client interests, lawyers must also manifest recognition that the law is legitimate—that is, worthy of being taken seriously, interpreted in good faith with due regard to its meaning, and not simply seen as an obstacle standing in the way of the client's goals. Lawyers wrongly believe that they are permitted or required to exploit legal loopholes, mistakes by opposing lawyers or the court, or other institutional malfunctions. My claim, by contrast, is that lawyers must advise clients on the basis of genuine legal entitlements and assert or rely upon only those entitlements in litigation or transactional representation that are sufficiently well grounded.[19] Naturally, it is difficult in many cases to differentiate between a loophole or malfunction, on the one hand, and a genuine legal entitlement on the other. The aim of this chapter is not to provide definitive answers to the question of what the law permits in particular cases, although I will consider some classic cases like *Spaulding v. Zimmerman*. Rather, the point is to suggest that this is the debate we should be having. If a lawyer manipulates the law to obtain an unjust result, the proper basis for ethical criticism is the failure to exhibit fidelity to law, not the resulting injustice. It may seem like an odd decision to begin a book about legal ethics with a repudiation of the call for lawyers to assume direct responsibility for justice or the public interest. If legal ethics is best understood in terms of fidelity to law, however, the distinctive professional obligations of lawyers are intimately bound up with the value of respect for the law and the legal system.

In order for this line of criticism to work as an ethical stance, fidelity to law must be an appealing ethical ideal. Law must represent some kind of social achievement to be worthy of the loyalty of citizens and lawyers. Chapter 3 argues that, insofar as it matters to lawyers acting in a representative capacity, the function of the law is to provide a reasoned settlement of empirical uncertainty and normative controversy, and a basis for cooperative activity, in what Jeremy Waldron refers to as the "circumstances of politics."[20] The circumstances of politics are the initial conditions of (1) a shared interest among members of a society or group in establishing a common framework for cooperative action, (2) despite disagreement over what that framework should be, yet (3) with a recognition that any procedures that are used for resolving disagreement must permit the competing positions to be heard and treat participants with as much equality of respect as is compatible with the need to reach at least a moderately stable provisional settlement. Procedures that meet a threshold standard of fairness permit people to reach a reasoned settlement of what would otherwise be intractable disagreement. The law is therefore legitimate to the extent it responds adequately to the needs of citizens in the circumstances of politics.

There still appears to be a gap, however, between legitimacy and authority (i.e., the justified claim to create obligations). Legitimate laws can be unjust. Less dramatically, it is not difficult to think of examples of otherwise legitimate laws that represent nothing more than successful rent-seeking by some powerful lobby, the result of congressional earmarks for some representative's home district, or a giveaway to a favored industry. Calling for fidelity to something valueless like the Sonny Bono Copyright Extension Term Act,[21] which retroactively grants heightened intellectual property protection to companies like Disney, who presumably had sufficient *ex ante* incentives to create their works, seems to miss the ethical point entirely. Surely the value of law is instrumental only, and what matters is something else, like the freedom of clients to pursue their projects without interference, or the substantive justice of client ends.

To regard professional duties in this way, as aiming directly at justice or other moral notions such as efficiency or autonomy, would essentially vitiate the capacity of the legal system to supersede disagreements about these values. The point of law is to create a more or less autonomous domain of reasons, rooted in the community's procedures for resolving conflict and settling on a common course of action. In order for the law to function in this way, the obligations of lawyers must be understood as grounded in the "artificial reason of law" and not ordinary moral reasons or considerations of substantive justice. The legal system and the institutional roles and practices associated with it contribute to social solidarity and mutual respect. I am not arguing that the whole of ethical life is constituted by compliance with the law, or even that a society characterized by the rule of law is inevitably better, in moral terms, than one less legalistic. Rather, the point is that, to the extent the law has moral worth, and the value of legality is understood in this way, the role of lawyer is a morally respectable one. Lawyers do something good to the extent they support the functioning of a complex institutional arrangement that makes stability, coexistence, and cooperation possible in a pluralistic society. Legality is not the only good, but it is a good. In order to contribute to the realization of this social good, however, it is necessary that lawyers regard the legal system, and their client's legal entitlements, as creating reasons that override considerations that would otherwise apply to persons not acting in the same professional capacity.

The implications of this position are developed in chapter 4. One is that lawyers should not refer back to ordinary moral considerations when deciding how to act on behalf of a client. Going back to what I take to be an example of a stupid law, the Copyright Term Extension Act, a lawyer representing a client who sought to make use of material under copyright would not be entitled to interpret the Act as a nullity, or something that ought to be planned around and evaded, just because it was a blatant sop to a few powerful companies. Citizens differ over what justice, efficiency, and the public interest require, so permitting or requiring lawyers to take these moral considerations into account would have the effect of undoing the legal settlement, which was necessitated by the existence of this kind of disagreement in the first place. In addition, because it is impossible to design any set of procedures that is immune to capture by some industry group or highly organized minority of the electorate, even laws that are generally regarded as foolish or wasteful are also entitled to respect. If citizens and lawyers could refuse to obey these laws, it would open a whole new arena of disagreement, this time over whether procedures were sufficiently representative, transparent, accessible to all citizens, and so on.

The law in that case has as much claim to the respect of lawyers as a law that was wiser, or struck a fairer balance among competing interests.

This is not to say that lawyers should not be free to challenge unjust, wasteful, or stupid laws using the procedures established by the legal system. The law recognizes civil-rights lawsuits, impact litigation, class actions, constitutional tort claims, lobbying, and many other vehicles for pressing arguments for legal change. Using the legal system to challenge unjust laws is one of the most noble things that lawyers do. There is a significant difference, however, between using legal procedures to challenge unjust laws and subverting them. The obligation of fidelity to law stands in contrast to the position of many legal ethics scholars that ethical lawyers are those who act directly on considerations of morality and justice, rather than the legal entitlements of clients.

Another implication of the obligation of fidelity to law is that the space for the exercise of ordinary moral discretion ought to be understood as somewhat narrow, when a lawyer is acting in a representative capacity. The law governing lawyers permits counseling clients, and even accepting or rejecting clients, on the basis of ordinary moral considerations.[22] That does not mean, however, that the lawyer's role should be understood primarily in ordinary moral terms. Lawyers are not best understood as friends or wise counselors to their clients, but as quasi-political actors, who in their professional representative capacity deal with the coercive force of the state. The attorney–client relationship is not best analogized to a friendship or counseling relationship, but should be seen as the way citizens learn about, assert, protect, and structure their affairs around legal entitlements. As a result, the moral discretion that is built into the lawyer's role should be exercised with respect to political and legal values. Some legal ethics scholars worry that this will be alienating or dehumanizing for lawyers, but it is unclear why the lawyer's role should be saddled with the burden of responding to the full range of human problems that clients bring with them. Lawyers contingently may be friends or counselors in addition to serving as expert legal advisors, but those additional roles are optional from the standpoint of the political justification of the lawyer's role. Legality is fundamentally a political value, which depends on a complex institutional system sustained by people acting within prescribed roles. There is moral value in doing one's part to support a socially valuable institution, but it is a distinctive kind of value, not one that can readily be analogized to ordinary moral notions like friendship or loyalty.

There is, accordingly, a potential gap between the things people value in their capacity as moral agents and the political values underpinning the lawyer's role. William Simon begins *The Practice of Justice* with the provocative claim that "[n]o social role encourages such moral aspirations as the lawyer's, and no social role so consistently disappoints the aspirations it encourages."[23] However, the priority of political considerations in the justification of the lawyer's role does not mean that ordinary morality is effaced entirely. Chapter 5 therefore considers the idea of tragedy—inevitable moral wrongdoing—in legal ethics. This has been called the problem of "dirty hands," which sounds a bit melodramatic, but the basic idea is that there can be "actions which remain morally disagreeable even when politically justified."[24] A lawyer's obligation of fidelity to law may, for example, require her to keep information secret which, if disclosed, could avoid harm to another person. Or, she may be required to counsel a client to comply with a law she regards as unjust, or to assist a client in doing something that violates the moral rights of others. In these cases, the lawyer may be faced with what has been termed a *moral remainder*, resulting from the subordinated-but-not-erased claims of ordinary morality.[25]

The possibility of moral remainders is not a reason to despair, because the remaining claims of morality do not lead only to a crisis of conscience or a lingering sentiment of guilt or shame. Rather, lawyers who feel the pull of ordinary morality, while acting in politically justified roles, may be more likely to deliberate carefully about whether good lawyering really requires some harmful action.[26] One might also argue that moral remainders give rise to a retrospective obligation to make atonement in some way,[27] perhaps by working against injustice in the system in areas that do not effect the representation of one's clients. Lawyers who experience a nagging sense that their job lacks a foundation in something meaningful and valuable may seek to orient their professional lives around a value or commitment that is particularly salient to them, personally speaking. In any event, although it is not an endemic feature of the practice of many lawyers, the possibility of dirty hands and moral remainders is an aspect of legal ethics that should be given its due, and must be taken into account if we take seriously the idea of a distinctively political morality of lawyering. It is, I submit, a better candidate for inclusion in a theory of legal ethics than the existing Principle of Nonaccountability, which claims to efface the perspective of ordinary moral agency. The dirty-hands perspective is necessary, on the other hand, to ensure that the response to the persistence of moral agency is not to deny the obligation of fidelity to law, and attempt to replace that duty with a directive to act directly on the grounds of ordinary moral considerations.

The last piece of the substantive argument in the book is found in chapter 6. This chapter takes up a question that hovers in the background of all that has been discussed previously, but eventually has to be faced directly. That issue is how the law can be said to have a determinate meaning in particular cases. The claim defended here is that lawyers are obligated to counsel clients on their legal entitlements, to take positions in litigation and transactions on the grounds of client entitlement, not interests. Further, this obligation of fidelity to law outweighs ordinary moral considerations, when a lawyer is acting in a representative capacity. Most readers will have an intuition, however, that this is too neat, and that it begs important questions against those who believe that the materials of the law (cases, statutes, regulations, and interpretive conventions) leave a great deal of flexibility, which lawyers may use to advance the interests of their clients without having transgressed the bounds of the law. Indeed, one reason critics of the Standard Conception appeal to ordinary moral considerations may be that they worry that the law may be so manipulable that an obligation of fidelity to law is inherently unworkable. If a sufficiently clever lawyer can interpret all but the clearest law as not applying to her client's (or her own) situation, then the law cannot effectively constrain lawyers in their pursuit of client ends.[28] Thus, the critics argue, if ordinary morality is also no constraint, then we are left with nothing but the unbounded pursuit of client interests as the foundation of lawyers' duties.

One response to this problem, discussed throughout the book, is the contextualization of lawyers' duties. This response assumes that the law is moderately indeterminate—that is, that there may be a range of interpretations that will be deemed reasonable, and some that will be regarded as creative, aggressive, or tendentious. What a lawyer may do with this moderate indeterminacy is a function of the setting in which the lawyer is representing the client. Debates in legal ethics often revolve around the resolution of disputes through court trials and pre-trial litigation. Indeed, the usual argument offered by lawyers to deflect moral blame for their actions trades on the adversary system, which is said to provide an institutional excuse for what would otherwise be moral wrongdoing.[29] In my view, however, litigation is a special case, because lawyers are permitted to assert the *arguable* legal entitlements of clients, leaving it up to the workings of the adversary system to evaluate whether the lawyer's position is plausible.[30] In transactional and advising context, there is no institutional mechanism, comparable to adversary briefing, oral argument, and appeal, to ensure that the lawyer's proposed interpretation of law is the correct one. Thus, lawyers have less latitude to rely on strained or arguable interpretations of the applicable law. The difference between the litigation and counseling contexts is that, in litigation, lawyers share responsibility with other institutional actors for ensuring that the law is not distorted or misapplied. Thus, lawyers have what feels like a heightened obligation of fidelity to law in non-litigation representation, but in reality the obligation is the same—it is just not shared with coordinate institutional actors.

This contextual approach will not be responsive to a critic who thinks the underlying problem is radical indeterminacy in the law. If the law can really be made to say anything at all, then it would be futile to urge lawyers to exhibit fidelity to law. But no one believes that the law is radically indeterminate; at least no sensible participant in the legal system acts as if the law is radically indeterminate.[31] Lawyers make arguments to courts, criticize judges for making mistakes in their application of law, advise clients about their prospective legal liability, and urge that the law be changed. Judges write dissenting opinions criticizing their colleagues for getting the law wrong, not merely making the wrong call as a matter of policy. Senators grill nominees to the federal bench about their willingness to apply the law "as written" and not impose their own policy preferences. Law professors grade students on their understanding of law, and believe with justification that their exam grades are not arbitrary. All of these practices presuppose that the law can bear some objective meaning, and this can be used as a standpoint from which to criticize an actor for having gotten the law wrong.[32]

In other words, there is a craft of making and evaluating legal arguments. This craft is what lawyers learn in law school and continue to refine as they gain experience in practice. While lawyers can give explanations of how it works, if pressed, essentially making and criticizing these sorts of arguments is just what lawyers *do*. If we want to know whether an interpretation is sound, there is really no way to avoid rolling up our sleeves, so to speak, and digging in to the legal reasoning. And while the making and critique of legal arguments will not yield perfect determinacy, and only one right answer in hard cases, they will narrow the range of reasonable interpretations and exclude many would-be readings of the law as distorted, abusive, tendentious, or otherwise not supportable.

To some extent, it is the nature of a craft that it resists being theorized in non-craft terms. Consider a classic example, familiar to all students of Anglo-American jurisprudence, of a municipal ordinance prohibiting "vehicles" in the park. Does it apply to ambulances, bicycles, skateboards, and an Army tank installed as a war memorial?[33] The question "what is a vehicle?" can be answered only if one asks the further question "For what purpose does it matter that we classify something as a vehicle or not?" Resorting to purpose, however, only compounds the ambiguity. Many legal rules and standards serve multiple, sometimes conflicting purposes. The "no vehicles" statute may be aimed at reducing noise, protecting the safety of pedestrians, or preventing pollution. Complicating matters further, purpose is not the only key to a statute's meaning—the express language of the statute may be in conflict with its purpose, and there may be other indications, such as legislative history and context, that cut against the interpretation suggested by the apparent purpose, even if there is only one. Analogical reasoning helps if one can argue that the tank is like or unlike a car or truck in relevant respects; however, judgments of relevant similarity are notoriously difficult to formalize, because "the criteria of relevance and closeness of resemblance depend on . . . the aims or purpose which may be attributed to the rule."[34]

Nevertheless, I want to argue that ethical lawyering means doing well at exactly this sort of thing. There are better and worse ways to go about interpreting and applying the law. For example, while we may be unsure whether the statute prohibiting vehicles in the park applies to a baby stroller, a jeep on a war memorial, or an ambulance rushing to the aid of a heart attack victim in the park, we do know that if the statute means anything, it means you cannot drive a souped-up sports car through the park. A prominent critic of the Bush administration lawyers who drafted the torture memos argues, similarly, that if the legal prohibitions on torture mean anything, they must apply to prohibit the technique known as waterboarding, in which a detainee is subjected to a horrifying near-death drowning experience.[35] Waterboarding is the souped-up sports car of the prohibitions on torture. If one's legal conclusion is that causing someone to experience the physical sensation of imminent death is not torture, then something in that argument has gone off the rails. It is time to abandon whatever interpretive principles led you to that conclusion, which cannot possibly be the right one, in light of the obvious purpose and overall rationality underlying the prohibition on torture. This approach to ethical criticism takes seriously the internal point of view of a lawyer participating in the craft of making and evaluating legal arguments. It is not an external critique, on the grounds of the wrongfulness of torture in ordinary moral terms. That is the distinctive perspective of the ethics of fidelity to law.

This book aims to bridge the gap between academic philosophy (moral, political, and legal) as it might apply to the ethics of lawyers and the circumstances of actual practicing lawyers. Sophisticated lawyers have long wished for a "jurisprudence of lawyering" which integrates theories of the nature and content of law with legal ethics.[36] Methodologically, the argument in this book is an attempt to secure "wide reflective equilibrium" between theoretical considerations and the actual norms followed by conscientious lawyers in their professional lives.[37] The method of reflective equilibrium, in general, seeks to provide coherence among people's considered moral intuitions and a set of moral principles. Simplifying somewhat, *wide* reflective equilibrium begins with the judgments about which a person is relatively confident (i.e., those that are made in a calm reflective frame of mind) and the looks at alternative sets of moral principles that fit with these intuitions, aiming at settling on the best set of principles as a moral theory, taking into account various background theories (including conceptions of human nature, principles of political justice, etc.) that support these moral principles.[38]

Most scholarly accounts of legal ethics begin with moral theories, derive principles from these theories, and apply them to the situation of practicing lawyers. Philosophers are understandably frustrated by the rote incantation of "zealous advocacy within the bounds of the law" as an all-purpose justification for what appears to be patently immoral activity. On the top-down analysis of philosophers, lawyers' role obligations are usually found wanting, from a moral point of view. On the other hand, lawyers begin with the intuition that their role is justified and they have good moral reasons to respect role obligations, such as keeping confidences and vigorously advocating for their clients' positions. These intuitions tend to be rather durable, and when lawyers learn about theories that seem to imply they are engaging in moral wrongdoing, they generally respond that those theories must be faulty. At the risk of caricaturing the prevailing position in theoretical legal ethics, it sometimes seems as though it is great mystery why society tolerates what is effectively a criminal gang in its midst. The result is an impasse between lawyers who believe they are participants in a practice worthy of respect and theorists who find the practice wanting at a foundational level. The methodology of wide reflective equilibrium attempts to take both points of view seriously.

Autobiographically, I approach this project as a former litigator who found a great deal of value and satisfaction in the job of a practicing lawyer, as well as someone with graduate training in philosophy who now makes a living taking a more detached perspective on legal practice. Some lawyers may see the discussion of political philosophy and jurisprudence as a lot of razzle-dazzle without much relevance to the situation of practicing lawyers. Patient readers might be persuaded that the academic philosophy does matter in the real world, and indeed that theoretical legal ethics scholars and practicing lawyers have something to learn from each other. At the very least, a lawyer who was interested in the deep ethical questions about her profession—the justification for things we do as lawyers, as against the claims of ordinary morality—will likely be led to ask the questions considered here, about the relationship between legality and moral agency. Similarly, philosophically minded readers may come away with some appreciation for the complexity of applying law in practice, which lawyers intuitively perceive to be a central aspect of legal ethics. Only by incorporating both perspectives, the practical and the theoretical, is it possible to understand the distinctive nature of the ethics of the legal profession. From that dual perspective, the aim of what follows is to establish that the basic duty of all lawyers is to act with fidelity to law.

Chapter One
The Standard Conception, For and Against

1.1 Introduction: Law, Morality, Ethics, and Legal Ethics

As human beings, we are all subject to the demands of morality. By "morality," I do not mean anything mysterious. Morality refers simply to the standards of right and wrong that we apprehend and apply in our lives, as a basis
for making decisions and as a justification for our actions. We appeal to morality when we attempt to explain and defend our actions against a demand for
justification, particularly in cases in which our actions have had an impact
on the interests and concerns of others. Someone who has been harmed in
some way may ask, "Why did you do that?" The answer, "Because it was in my
interests and I had the power to do so," is generally regarded as an inadequate
justification, and thus not a moral reason. (If you believe morality really does
just come down to the strong doing whatever they want, then we have a meta-
ethical disagreement, which is beyond the scope of this book.) The attempt to
justify one's actions in moral terms must appeal to reasons that can be shared
by those whose interests are affected. Although the subject of moral inquiry
can be broader than this, encompassing matters such as character, integrity,
and how one should live a good life, at its root morality is about the imme-
diate practical question of how one should act rightly, on grounds that are
adequately justified, given that the interests of others are at stake.[1] To put the
point in terms of the perspective of an observer, morality is about justifying
the praise and blame we ascribe to others, on the basis of their actions or their
character; a person who does not have a moral justification for her actions is
subject to moral criticism by others. This may take some concrete form, such
as shunning or ostracism, but it more commonly is manifested in attitudes of
disapproval. People who say "What a jerk!" when they observe others telling
lies, taking advantage of others, or weaseling out of an obligation are implicitly
engaging in moral criticism.

Legal ethics is the concern of lawyers seeking a justification for their actions, which appeals to standards of right and wrong that can be shared by the
people whose interests are affected by lawyers and the legal system. It is also the
point of reference for those who would criticize lawyers for acting wrongly.[2]

Nothing is more familiar than the charges that lawyers are a rather sleazy lot. This criticism comes in a variety of forms, from op-ed pieces in the newspaper, to campaign speeches by politicians, to endlessly repeated lawyer jokes.[3] Beyond that, it is probably a rare lawyer or law student who has not been harangued by an acquaintance at a party or by a seatmate on a long flight about the legal profession. Criticism of lawyers encompasses a bewildering variety of themes: greed, including the closely related theme of overcharging clients; serving the fat cats at the expense of the little guy; preying on the misfortunes of others; being prone to lying and cheating on behalf of clients, and also to sometimes lie to clients; hyper-aggressiveness in litigation, or clogging up the legal system with frivolous disputes; being a drag on productive activities— writ small this is the familiar criticism that lawyers are deal-breakers; writ large it is the lament that lawyers impose costs on productive activities, rather than producing anything of value themselves; and of course the familiar claim (which many lawyers would cheerfully concede) that criminal defense lawyers help guilty people escape punishment, sometimes by obfuscating the truth at trial, other times by taking advantage of procedural technicalities to secure acquittals. To sum it up neatly, the public seems to believe that "the lawyer's skill is the instrument by which justice is defeated; or, if justice prevails, it is because of a lawyer's craftiness rather than for a respectable reason."[4]

The subject of academic legal ethics is nothing more than the attempt to respond to these accusations in a rigorous way. The claim developed in this book is that the best justification for the duties of lawyers, as we understand them, is grounded in the value of legality, or the rule of law. That is, legal ethics is not fundamentally an application of ordinary ethics in a particular context; rather, it is a *political* normative system that is informed primarily by the capacity of the law to enable people to treat one another as equals, live together, and cooperate, despite deep and persistent disagreement about morality and other matters. The idea of political morality is a complex one, but the basic idea is that there may be properties of a political or legal system that give us reasons to act in a certain way with regard to that system. We may have reasons to respect, support, uphold, or even obey the directives of a set of institutions and procedures that are designed for the purpose of sustaining our lives in communities, alongside other persons. Political morality must be a part of morality writ large, in the sense of all of the values, virtues, and ideals that inform human life. At the same time, however, it is distinct in important ways from the morality of ordinary life. Principles of political morality may not be derived in a relatively straightforward way from general moral considerations; rather, political morality may be uniquely adapted to the circumstances of social life.[5] The conception of legal ethics I will defend here is a part of political morality, relying on values and ideals such as citizenship and communities.[6] This does not mean that legal ethics is isolated from ordinary morality, only that it is concerned, fundamentally, with the problem of how social conflict can be resolved and cooperation made possible through legal procedures and institutions.

Lawyers often use the term "legal ethics" to refer to the rules of professional conduct promulgated and enforced by public institutions.[7] Philosophers would be baffled to hear lawyers say things like, "That may be unethical, but it isn't wrong." That phraseology can be explained, however, by the use of the term ethics to denote the rules of professional conduct under which lawyers practice. In the United States, the highest court in each state has the inherent authority to regulate the practice of law within the territorial jurisdiction of the state; these courts issue rules governing matters like fees, advertising, conflicts of interest, and confidentiality. These rules in turn are enforced by some kind of administrative agency, often loosely referred to as the bar association of State X.[8] Lawyers are also regulated by the generally applicable law of agency, torts, contracts, evidence, procedure, criminal and constitutional law, and, if applicable, specialized law such as tax and securities regulation. Taken together, the entire law governing lawyers is sometimes also called legal ethics, particularly in the United States where instruction in "the history, goals, structure, values, rules, and responsibilities of the legal profession and its members" is mandatory in nationally accredited law schools.[9]

While legal ethics in this sense is obviously important to lawyers who are interested in keeping their licenses to practice, or avoiding liability to clients or third parties, it is not the subject of this book. Rather, the focus here is on what lawyers sometimes call "ethics beyond the rules," or "real ethics," not the regulation of the legal profession. To avoid confusion, I will never use the term ethics to refer to rules of professional conduct or other aspects of the law governing lawyers.[10] Instead, this book will focus on legal ethics in the sense of reasons that must be given by way of justifying one's actions, as against a demand for justification by another person whose interests are affected.

This demand for justification was stated with admirable clarity by Charles Fried, who asked, "Can a good lawyer be a good person?"[11] Fried's question highlights the possibility that the demands of the lawyer's role may create a conflict with ordinary morality. Implicit in this way of framing the issue is the assumption that the professional role creates genuine obligations, not just conventions or pragmatically justified norms.[12] Conventions, such as "rules" of etiquette, do have some force. However, conventions do not have the weight of moral obligations, which purport to be binding on agents no matter what else is the case. It would not do to say that something is "the way things have always been done around here" in response to a claim that an action violates the moral interests of others. A convention is, at best, something that should be taken into account when making an all-things-considered judgment. The normative weight of a pragmatically grounded norm vanishes when the interests on the other side of the ledger are morally significant. Fried's question presupposes that professional roles create duties that really are duties, and should be followed in all but exceptional circumstances, not merely considerations that are taken into account in practical reasoning. Understood in this way, professional obligations require a lawyer "to put to one side considerations of various sorts—and especially various moral considerations—that would otherwise be relevant if not decisive."[13] It is this exclusionary character of the lawyer's role that creates genuine duties, but which also leads to the charge that lawyers are inhabiting a simplified moral universe without justification.[14] The aim of this book is to defend the notion of a professional role that excludes ordinary moral considerations, but which is related in the appropriate way to general morality.

1.2   Ordinary and Professional Moralities

Talking about the exclusionary character of professional morality of course requires that we are clear on the baseline of ordinary morality, which is purportedly excluded by duties specific to the professional role. The modifier "ordinary" on morality is intended to capture the idea of moral principles that apply to us simply as people, as moral agents full-stop, not as occupants of social roles or institutions.* Ordinary morality is to be contrasted with the obligations that may arise for occupants of social roles. Thus, the fundamental question in theoretical legal ethics is often described as the problem of role-differentiated morality. Social roles are characterized by obligations related to those roles, which prescribe actions that may be contrary to the demands of ordinary morality. Describing the problem in this way, however, risks begging the question one way or the other. We need to be clear on what is meant by both ordinary morality and the notion of roles and role-specific duties. Somewhat counterintuitively, it is possible to understand the notion of ordinary morality better by first considering the way roles can function in ethical reasoning.

One way to understand a role in normative terms is as a shorthand way of describing a cluster of obligations, permissions, and aspirations that apply by

---

* I use the term "ordinary" morality here, but the terms "general," "common," and "personal" morality are also prevalent in the literature on theoretical legal ethics. See, e.g., Dare (2009); Luban (1988); Postema (1980).

virtue of standing in a particular kind of relationship with others.[15] I make lunches for my kids in the morning, lend my neighbor my snowblower, serve on law school committees, attend church on Sundays, and so on, for reasons that are apparent to anyone who is familiar with the nature of the relevant social institutions—families, neighborhoods, workplaces, religious communities, and so on. As Joseph Raz puts it: "certain offices carry with them certain responsibilities, and ... these establish what counts as 'thinking as a [...]' "[16] It would be possible to spell out these reasons in detail, but there would be little point in the exercise, except to demonstrate one's grasp of the moral requirements that are summed up by the shorthand of "thinking as a [...]." The role, and associated role-specific obligations (which may be in the form of rules), are all merely summaries of obligations that exist apart from the role. The obligations of the role are accordingly *transparent* to moral analysis. In academic legal ethics, as opposed to the self-understanding of the legal profession, the dominant theoretical paradigm is a fairly high degree of role transparency. The reasons lawyers give to justify their actions are translated into ordinary moral reasons, and analyzed as such. In the preceding cases, the arguments would proceed on the basis of ordinary moral considerations such as fairness, reciprocity, and the duty of promise-keeping (in the first case); human life and health, fairness and corrective justice (in the second case); and dignity and privacy (in the third case).

Some social roles, however, appear to involve not a nexus of ordinary moral reasons, but specific obligations that are different in kind from, and potentially conflict with, what would otherwise be the moral requirements that would apply to someone differently situated.[17] These role-specific considerations all make a claim that other reasons should not have priority in the analysis of the rightness or wrongness of the lawyer's actions. They either exclude otherwise applicable moral reasons, or at least are thought to outweigh them in most cases.[18] Whatever metaphor one uses—exclusion, trumping, outweighing, etc.—the idea is that reasons associated with a role are reasons not to act on other reasons, those that would apply to a similarly situated agent not acting in that role.* They are what Raz would call second-order reasons—that is, reasons not to act on reasons.[19] The reason it is difficult to get clear on the relationship between ordinary moral considerations and the duties associated with a social role is that one requires a reason to act on *any* principle that claims to impose obligations, and if those obligations affect the interests of

---

* As we will see in chapter 3, professional roles can best be understood as creating very weighty, seldom-overridden reasons for action that are nevertheless not strictly exclusionary. For now, the important idea is that professional roles create reasons not to refer to what would otherwise be the (first-order) reasons applicable to a similarly situated nonprofessional.

others, a moral reason is required. What is really going on with the idea of role morality and the nontransparency of roles is the claim that there are some second-order moral reasons to follow the obligations of a role, to the exclusion of what would otherwise be the moral reasons that would apply in the absence of the role.

To be sure, lawyers often make these sorts of arguments in a question-begging way. Merely reciting one's professional role-specific obligations is not sufficient to respond to the charge that following these obligations is wrong from a moral point of view.[20] By comparison with the role of lawyer, consider a recognized social role that creates strong role-specific obligations—for example, the role of wiseguy in an organized crime family. As described by Nicholas Pileggi (and memorably translated onto film by Martin Scorsese), occupying the role of wiseguy means inhabiting a thickly normative world, regulated by rules and standards, passed on by socialization into the practice, and reinforced by sanctions.[21] Wiseguys never rat on their friends, they pay tribute to higher-ranking members of their organization and avoid harming protected members, they can have girlfriends as long as they continue to outwardly act like family men, and so on. There is no doubt that these duties are genuine obligations *qua* wiseguy. It should be obvious, however, that these role-specific obligations do not create obligations *qua* moral agent, sufficient to justify acting in ways that would not be permitted by ordinary morality. Within the system of wiseguy norms, if one is "crossed, denied, offended, thwarted in any way, or even mildly annoyed, retribution was demanded,"[22] but the demand for violent retribution that is a part of the normative world of wiseguys does not create a moral permission to beat up or kill another person in response to a trivial insult. The reason these role-specific duties fail to create moral obligations is that the role of wiseguy lacks the connection to the wider normative world of human values and interests that would be required to justify the role itself in moral terms.

The admittedly hackneyed comparison between lawyers and wiseguys is meant to show that, while roles and the duties associated with them take shape within larger practices, these practices must be justified on the basis of some moral good that the practices achieve.[23] The question then arises why this is not simply the "nexus" view previously described, which holds that the concept of role is merely a shorthand way of referring to otherwise existing moral obligations, as they are specified in a particular social context. The problem with the nexus view, as applied to legal ethics, is that it may be insufficiently sensitive to the institutional or political context in which lawyers practice. One way of understanding the "ordinariness" of ordinary morality is that it is fundamentally non-institutional in character.[24] When we say that people ought to honor values such as dignity and truth in their relations with one another, we imagine that these relations are unmediated by structures of government, either state government or something less informal, belonging to the institutions of civil society. When the interests of people come into conflict, morality provides resources for figuring out whose interests should take precedence, but the setting one generally presupposes is some kind of small-scale interaction, which one imagines might be resolved through reasoning and dialogue. In the case of larger-scale disagreement, institutions provide ways of handling conflict in a way that does not depend directly on the ordinary moral values at stake. Legal institutions in particular have virtues that are related to impartiality, the fairness of the procedures they provide for dealing with conflict, and their capacity to treat people with equal dignity and respect. As soon as relations among persons are governed by something more formal, it is natural to look to the properties of those institutions as a source of values and reasons.

One of the central questions in theoretical legal ethics is whether the toolkit of moral concepts that should be brought to bear on the analysis is the same toolkit used elsewhere in moral philosophy, or whether it is tied to professional roles, institutions, or values in some distinctive way. One of the principal arguments in this book is that legal ethics is part of a freestanding political morality, which gains its structure and obligatory force from the situation of compliance with morality in communities. This does not mean these values are unrelated to ordinary morality, only that they may not be reducible in a straightforward way to ordinary moral considerations. The relationship, rather, is indirect, with ordinary moral values going into the justification of a set of institutions, practices, and associated normative ideals.[25] For example, the political-moral notion of an individual as a *citizen* implies reciprocity and rough equality in the way one is treated by state actors and institutions. The political theory of John Rawls begins with this kind of distinctive political idea: "The philosophical conception of the person," Rawls writes, "is replaced in political liberalism by the political conception of citizens as free and equal."[26] Political freedom, in turn, can be understood as a specific kind of freedom, namely collective self-governance.[27] Similarly, legality (or the rule of law) suggests a number of evaluative criteria, including impartiality and the commitment by the government to be bound by generally applicable rules.[28] There is an irreducible aspect of public-ness to this way of understanding the rule of law. Thus, it is not clear that it can be translated into ordinary moral terms without significant distortion, even though all of the animating ideas—justice, equality, reason-giving, and so on—are cognizable within ordinary morality. Moreover, it may be part of the structure of political institutions and practices that participating in them necessarily requires excluding consideration of ordinary moral reasons.[29] This idea of exclusionary reasons is fundamental to the idea of role morality defended here, particularly in chapter 3.

The relationship between ordinary and role morality can be illustrated with a hypothetical based on a well-known case. The XYZ Company manufactures an intrauterine contraceptive device that is alleged to have caused thousands of injuries to users, including infections leading to hysterectomies, sterility, and death.[30] The manufacturer has been besieged by both groundless and meritorious claims. In general, its practice has been to settle the valid claims for a fair amount, but to contest vigorously the doubtful cases. There is no question that the product's unsafe design could cause injuries to users of the product in some cases. As the manufacturer rightly points out, however, the injuries could be exacerbated in some cases by certain kinds of sexual activity. Accordingly, the judge supervising pre-trial litigation in the consolidated nationwide product liability action has allowed inquiry into claimants' sexual history, as long as the questions are "reasonably likely to lead to the discovery of admissible evidence." In American civil procedure, these questions occur in depositions, which are sworn examinations before a court reporter but outside the presence of a judge. In his ruling on the plaintiffs' motion for a protective order, the judge indicated that he is disinclined to supervise depositions closely, expects that the defendant's lawyers will "respect the letter and the spirit of the discovery rules," and trusts that "the lawyers will conduct themselves ethically" in the depositions.

In the course of defending these actions, the manufacturer has noticed that aggressive questioning of women about their sexual practices tends to motivate many of the claimants to settle early, for comparatively small sums. Thus, in cases it believes to be without merit, the manufacturer has directed its lawyers to probe the sexual histories of the women maintaining the claims. The lawyers conducting the depositions have learned that they can linger over the subjects for a long period of time, ask many different varieties of the same question, use explicit terminology, and focus on particularly embarrassing details, such as extramarital affairs. Lawyers representing the women may object, but not terminate the depositions without risking sanctions. Defense lawyers even have what they privately refer to as the "dirty questions list," which includes specific, graphic questions about plaintiffs' hygiene and sexual practices. The result of that mode of questioning is generally to humiliate the witness and sometimes to intimidate her into settling the case for less than she otherwise would be able to obtain by way of settlement or judgment.

In moral terms, how should we evaluate the conduct of the lawyers representing XYZ Company?[31] The case seems to be easy to analyze in ordinary moral terms. Surely no one would contend that men are permitted to ask embarrassing, intrusive, humiliating questions about the sexual practices of women with whom they are barely acquainted. But this seems like an unnaturally abstract way to evaluate the conduct.[32] Surely one would want to ask who these men and women are, and for what purpose the men are asking the intrusive questions. If the parties are social acquaintances, it would be—at the very least—creepy for the man to question the woman about her sexual practices. If the man intended to humiliate the woman with his questioning, we would criticize him in moral terms for assaulting another person's dignity. In the hypothetical case, however, the man is a lawyer representing a product manufacturer in a lawsuit in which the conduct of the plaintiffs may be a defense to liability. At least in the adversary system of dispute resolution, lawyers for the contending parties are allowed to ask questions, under oath, to determine what lawyers call "the facts" of a case. Finding out the facts may involve intrusive questioning, but if the inquiry is designed to uncover relevant information, one can hardly blame the lawyer for continuing the questioning, despite the discomfort it may cause the plaintiffs.*

Asking embarrassing questions about a stranger's sex life is rude and intrusive, but depositions of plaintiffs in a product liability lawsuit are not simply an encounter between strangers. In daily life, the women would be free to terminate the conversation, but in this case they have been required by subpoena to attend the depositions and answer questions. Although this fact might justify a

---

* Note that the questioning in this instance may still be wrongful, even if the adversary system and the pre-trial discovery process are justified in general terms. The federal rules of civil procedure, and most state rules, provide that the parties may obtain discovery only of matters that are relevant to their claims or defenses. Fed. R. Civ. P. 26(b)(1). Thus, if there is no conceivable connection between the plaintiffs' conduct and their injuries, the questioning would be beyond the scope of permissible discovery. In addition, courts may prohibit discovery "to protect a party or person from annoyance, embarrassment, oppression, or undue burden or expense." Fed. R. Civ. P. 26(c). A court considering a party's request for such a protective order would consider the likely significance of the matter inquired into, and compare its evidentiary value with the harm (embarrassment, undue burden, etc.) suffered by the party. It is important to point out this feature of the rules of civil procedure, because many cases that seem to pose the problem of role-differentiated morality do not, in fact, pose law-versus-morality conflicts. The conduct in question may be flatly prohibited by law. If that is the case, there would be no claim that a good lawyer should engage in it, quite apart from what a good person would do. See Dare (2004); Schneyer (1984). My own view of this case, for what it is worth, is that the defendant had no genuine entitlement in most cases (absent a specific reason to believe the questioning will develop evidence of product misuse through unsafe sexual practices) to ask the most humiliating questions of the plaintiffs. The lawyers behaved unethically by conducting the aggressive depositions, not because the questions were creepy and humiliating, but because there was no legal entitlement to ask questions solely for the purpose of intimidating the women.

conclusion that the questioners should take even more care not to humiliate the women (because they cannot voluntarily terminate the questioning), the reason that the depositions are compulsory is related to a voluntary act by the plaintiffs of filing a lawsuit. Surely they knew that litigation is unpleasant, and assumed the risk of some unpleasantness in order to have the chance of recovering damages from XYZ. As Harry Truman's aphorism goes, if you can't stand the heat, stay out of the kitchen. Granted, calling the process "voluntary" ignores the prior wrongdoing by XYZ. The company's sale of a defective product, which allegedly caused grievous harm to many people, arguably gives rise to a moral duty of corrective justice. This duty, at a minimum, requires fair treatment of alleged victims as part of an orderly process of determining whether compensation is owed. This duty of fair treatment arises as a result of the specific context of a set of procedures for the just resolution of disputes. It is related to the ordinary moral notion of fairness, but has a specific source in the dispute–resolution procedures we have adopted.

This is what is meant by freestanding values. The claim is not that they are unrelated to ordinary morality,[33] but that they depend to such a significant extent on the institutional context that some political considerations bear only a family resemblance to cognate ordinary moral notions. The scope of permissible humiliation in ordinary moral life is very different from what we are willing to tolerate in connection with a legal proceeding aimed at establishing an obligation to pay damages as the result of an injury sustained by the plaintiff. The main argument in this book is that in the majority of cases, a fully worked-out moral analysis of what a lawyer ought to do will conclude that the lawyer has an obligation of fidelity to law that precludes reasoning on the basis of ordinary non-institutional moral values. The upshot is that justified social roles are relatively nontransparent to moral analysis.[34] That does not mean the occupants of social roles are immune to criticism. The nontransparency of roles and the priority of role-specific reasons for action simply channel permissible normative critiques in certain ways. For example, it may be the case that an entire social role is not entitled to moral respect. The wiseguy example is a caricature, but it is meant to highlight that the constitutive rules of a role must be established with due sensitivity to pre-role moral obligations. A role that prescribes violent retribution for trivial insults is so contrary to what morality would require of any socially tolerated activity that it should not be regarded as a source of moral obligations. Thus, it is conceivable that the practice of lawyering may be constituted in such a way that participating in the role does not create superseding moral obligations. If the legal system deserves our respect, however, lawyers may appeal to it as an excuse for what would otherwise be deemed wrongful conduct.

William Simon objects to this way of looking at professional roles, arguing that it privileges a long-run view of justice over the short-run injustices that may result, even within a generally just legal system. Defenders of role-differentiated legal ethics, he claims, "assert that it produces a higher level of justice in the aggregate and the long run," and portray specific injustices as "sacrifices that have to be made in order to avoid greater injustices."[35] As we will see throughout this book, one of the standard rhetorical moves in legal ethics is to contrast the significant injustice (in moral terms) that would result from following the law in a particular case with the relatively insignificant harm to the overall system of justice-administration that would result from disobedience. As David Luban observes:

> [A]n occasional lapse from zealous representation of a particularly dangerous and repulsive criminal defendant would not do much damage to criminal defense as a whole, and might do a lot of good .... [T]he marginal harms to the system that result from violating one's professional duty typically are slight in a single case. On the other side of the ledger, the marginal benefits of following [ordinary] morality rather than professional duty may be great.[36]

The default perspective in theoretical legal ethics is to privilege the analysis of the justice of particular cases over the justice of institutions and procedures, considered at a high level of generality. Thus, one way to understand the overall aim of this book is to defend a conception of legal ethics that justifiably maintains a long-run, or institutional, perspective on things, and resists being drawn into case-by-case analysis of what morality, or justice, requires in a particular situation.

Here is another example from one of the classic cases in legal ethics, illustrating the difference it makes in whether legal ethics takes an ordinary or institutional perspective. Borrower runs a small business.[37] Needing a loan to tide him over in a cash crunch, he borrows $5,000 from Lender, his neighbor. Borrower executes a simple promissory note agreeing to repay Lender beginning on a certain date. The date passes and Lender never asks for the money back. Seven years pass, and the economic situation of the parties reverses dramatically. Borrower's small business has flourished and was acquired by a much larger company; he is now a highly compensated executive with that company. Lender has fallen on hard times—he lost his job, had his house foreclosed upon by the bank, and is now in desperate need of money to meet medical expenses. A friend of Lender who is a lawyer agrees to represent him for free, in an attempt to recover the $5,000 plus interest that Borrower owes him. Borrower, who could write a check for $5,000 and hardly notice the difference in his bank account balance, directs his lawyer to oppose Lender's claim, using "any lawful means." The applicable statute of limitations provides that an action to recover on a debt must be filed within six years of the debtor's default. (One purpose of the statute is to prevent litigants from taking unfair advantage of the lapse of time, by waiting to file claims until evidence has been lost and the memories of witnesses have grown stale.) Procedurally, the effect of the statute of limitations is to serve as a complete defense to a claim for payment on a debt. Borrower's lawyer accordingly files a motion to dismiss the lawsuit as time-barred, which the trial judge granted.

Consider the analysis in ordinary moral terms. If you were told that A borrowed money from B, but subsequently refused to pay it back, your reaction would probably be that A had done something wrong. Why? Because in our daily lives we recognize that promises can create obligations, and people act wrongly when they break their promises without a good reason. If you were told further that A had subsequently become wealthy and could easily afford to repay the debt to B, who badly needed the money, you would likely express even stronger condemnation of A—"What a jerk!" The reason for the stronger negative evaluation may be that in addition to the obligation created by A's promise, the disparity in wealth between the parties creates an additional obligation of fairness, or that A's failure to perform his promise has worse consequences than the failure to repay a debt to a creditor who has plenty of money. Applying these ordinary moral reasons to the analysis of Borrower's lawyer's decision to plead the statute of limitations, it seems difficult to avoid the conclusion that Borrower is cheating somehow—evading his legitimate obligation to Lender—and that Borrower's lawyer is helping him cheat.[38]

This analysis misses the distinctiveness of the institutional context. Granted, failing to repay a legitimate debt is cheating or chiseling, but pleading the statute of limitations feels different somehow, because the defense to the claim for repayment is part of a system that has been established to adjudicate the legitimacy of the obligation. Calling Borrower's obligation "just," and thus criticizing his lawyer in moral terms, may be putting the cart before the horse by assuming the debt is justly owed, when that is exactly what the legal system needs to determine. The *legal* justice of the obligation in this case is a function not only of Borrower having agreed to repay Lender, but of Lender having followed certain formal procedures to establish a legally enforceable claim to repayment. It is the goal of much of the rest of this book to establish that lawyers, when they act in a professional capacity, should be concerned only with the legal justice of their clients' situations. This does not mean there may not be good moral reasons for Borrower to repay the debt here, only that these moral reasons have only limited relevance to what the lawyer is permitted or required to do on behalf of her client. The ethics of lawyers acting in a professional capacity is different from the ethics of ordinary people.

1.3   The Standard Conception

When it comes to the ethics of the legal profession, the perspective of most critics relies on ordinary moral considerations. Lawyers, however, have their own view of what is ethically permissible, and it is very different from the idea that they should simply act as ordinarily morally reflective people would. This working ethical theory of lawyers has been labeled the "Standard Conception" of legal ethics or the "Dominant View" (I will use the former term here) to emphasize its status as the default position.[39] The elements of the Standard Conception are generally understood to be:

1. *Principle of Partisanship*. The lawyer must act out of exclusive concern with the legal interests of clients. She is permitted to disregard the interests of affected third parties and the public interest, if it would be in the client's interests to do so, and if the law permits the violation in question of the third party or public interest. Although the lawyer may counsel the client that disregarding the interests of another is morally wrong, if the client insists on taking the action (and again, if it is legally permitted), the lawyer is obligated either to do it, or to withdraw from representing the client if withdrawal can be accomplished without prejudicing the client's interests.

2. *Principle of Neutrality*. Nor may the lawyer let her own moral convictions stand in the way of doing something that she otherwise would regard as wrong, if the client instructs her to do so. Ordinary moral values are excluded from the lawyer's practical reasoning and from the retrospective evaluation, by the lawyer herself or by others, of the lawyer's actions. Citizens should not be denied entitlements secured by the legal system solely because a lawyer finds that person's objectives unjust. The lawyer may—and indeed, in many cases must—refuse to pursue an objective that is unlawful, but may make this judgment on the basis of considerations internal to the law, not extra-legal moral reasons.

3. *Principle of Nonaccountability*. The third principle is not really a prescription for lawyers to follow, but a rule of inference that third-party observers should respect. The Principle of Nonaccountability means that, as long as the lawyer acts within the law, her actions may not be evaluated in ordinary moral terms.[40] People should not call lawyers sleazy just because they represent sleazy clients, or do nasty things on behalf of clients. An observer evaluating the actions of lawyers representing clients should be limited to approving or

disapproving the lawyers' actions as a matter of lawyering craft. It is impermissible to step outside the practice of lawyering, and appeal to standards that are not part of the professional normative domain.

A frequently discussed case illustrates the working of the standard conception in practice: A lawyer in a small town learns from his client the location of the hidden bodies of two teenagers who had disappeared on a camping trip, murdered, as it turns out, by the lawyer's client.[41] The entire community is living in terror of further attacks and the parents of the missing children are anguished, but the lawyer nevertheless keeps both the location of the bodies and his client's involvement secret. From the standpoint of professional role obligations, this is an easy case. A lawyer must keep secret anything she learns in the course of representing her client, even if disclosure of confidential information would alleviate great suffering.[42] On the other hand, as a matter of ordinary morality, surely a decent person would feel troubled to be causing so much harm by keeping the secret of a dangerous murderer. One of the lawyers in the hidden bodies case admitted as much, saying of the parents: "I caused them pain, I prolonged their pain .... There's nothing I can say to justify that in their minds. You couldn't justify it to me."[43] The lawyers in the hidden bodies case followed the prescriptions of the Standard Conception to the letter, representing their client effectively despite believing he was "a piece of scum."[44] They received plenty of moral criticism from other members of their community, and in fact were socially and professional ostracized for their work on the case. However, they believed they were justified in their actions, and the opprobrium unwarranted—hence, others mistakenly failed to respect the Principle of Nonaccountability.

As the description of the hidden bodies case suggests, the Standard Conception is not some ivory tower construct, but represents the beliefs about many, if not most, practicing lawyers about the relationship between law and morality. In an empirical study of ethics in large law firms, conducted by several prominent legal sociologists, lawyers showed a remarkable knack for translating just about every would-be moral issue into a question of tactics and prudence.[45] Asked about a hypothetical case involving a defective product manufactured by the client that might fail and cause injuries (like the example given earlier), one lawyer's suggestion that the case presented a moral issue was met by a narrow definition of role obligations, offered by another lawyer: "[The client] can go talk to his minister if he wants moral advice. That's not why he's coming to you."[46] This is consistent with the Principle of Partisanship—lawyers must concern themselves with furthering the client's interests, which may include refraining from unethical tactics likely to backfire and cause trouble for the client later in the litigation,[47] but are not required, or even permitted, to consider moral issues in their own right.

Significantly, central to the lawyers' version of the Principle of Partisanship is the view that client *interests*, as opposed to the legal entitlements of clients or the moral judgment of lawyers, are paramount in determining what actions lawyers should take on behalf of clients.[48] The Principle of Neutrality shows up in practice as a pervasive sense that adversary litigation is not a practice within the domain of morality but is an artificial stylized practice—a game with rules that can be manipulated within limits.[49] Finally, according to the Principle of Nonaccountability, as long as lawyers play by the rules of the game, however, the moral implications of their practice can safely be ignored.[50]

The Standard Conception, as it is usually understood, elevates client interests to a position of primacy. The position defended here insists that the legal entitlements of clients, not client interests, should be paramount for lawyers. One of the fundamental principles of the law governing lawyers is that lawyers, as agents of their clients, have an obligation to "proceed in a manner reasonably calculated to advance a client's lawful objectives, as defined by the client after consultation."[51] In practice, however, lawyers tend to aim at advancing their clients' objectives, full-stop, rather than pursuing only their clients' *lawful* objectives (i.e., their entitlements). This is where lawyers go wrong in their ethical theories, but the critics of the Standard Conception also err. Regarding the Principle of Neutrality, critics place too much emphasis on ordinary moral considerations, to the detriment of the political values associated with the rule of law, as the basis for lawyers' practical reasoning. The theory of legal ethics in this book will not be justified in terms of ordinary morality, but will rely on freestanding political evaluative considerations. In order to differentiate this justification from those that have usually been offered for the Standard Conception, the remainder of this chapter will consider the defenses that have been offered for the Standard Conception, in ordinary moral terms, and the corresponding critiques based on ordinary morality. With this debate in the background, for the remainder of the book we can consider the arguments for a freestanding professional ethics for lawyers.

1.4 Traditional Justifications for the Standard Conception and Moral Critiques

1.4.1 *Client Autonomy*

Stephen Pepper's "first class citizenship" model is the clearest and best case that has been made for grounding role-differentiated morality on a foundation of individual autonomy.[52] His argument is solidly within the political liberal tradition, emphasizing as it does the value of free and unconstrained

31

choices by citizens. Specifically, it relies on the importance of the moral value of autonomy. Although many conditions exist for the realization of the ideal of autonomy in one's life,[53] Pepper focuses on the removal of one particular barrier to the exercise of autonomy, namely coercion by the state. The structure of a liberal legal system should allow as much freedom as possible for individuals to define and act on their own conceptions of the good, subject only to the restraints on liberty that are necessary to secure a similar measure of liberty for others. The law affects individual autonomy in two ways—first, by providing tools (such as rules setting out the conditions for making enforceable contracts, wills, and the like) that citizens can use to structure their affairs and interactions with others, and second by clearly demarcating the rights of others, so that citizens can plan their actions around the possibility of state penalties.[54]

In Pepper's view, it would be a good thing if the law and legal institutions were set up to maximize autonomy, because "increasing individual autonomy is morally good."[55] If the law is morally valuable because it increases autonomy, then lawyers partake of this positive moral value when they represent clients seeking to exercise rights given to them by the law. If the law provides a right to X, then apart from the morality of X considered apart from the law, the fact that there is a legal entitlement to X is a good thing. Thus, lawyers can claim to be doing good in moral terms when they represent clients who wish to do X, where they have a legal right to do so. Putting the same point in negative terms, if a citizen has a legal right to do X, and the liberty to do X or not is intrinsically valuable, then a lawyer who refuses to assist her client in securing the right to do X acts contrary to a moral value. The upshot is that, for any act performed by a lawyer on behalf of a client, it is morally permissible if it can be described somehow as "enhancing autonomy." Because Pepper understands providing access to law as inherently autonomy-enhancing, his theory has the result of creating a general moral permission that is quite broad in scope.

The problem with Pepper's argument, if it is understood in ordinary moral terms, can be illustrated by plugging in specific acts for the generic "X" in the previous reconstruction. Considering the hypothetical cases discussed earlier, persons (or artificial legal persons like corporations) arguably have the legal right to plead procedural defenses, such as the statute of limitations, to avoid paying debts they willingly contracted; to play games with the discovery process (as long as they avoid violating specific rules of civil procedure) to delay the resolution of lawsuits, or even to try to make the litigation process so unpleasant that plaintiffs settle early; and to keep secret information learned in the course of representing clients. Pepper wishes to argue that these instances of legally permitted (or required) actions acquire moral value because they represent exercises of autonomy by citizens, but this move would conflate the morality of the action with the morality of autonomously having chosen it.[56] Pepper writes that "[d]iversity and autonomy are preferred over 'right' or 'good' conduct,"[57] but it is hard to see, if it is a morally lousy thing to refuse to pay back money I borrowed, how the moral evaluation of my conduct changes if the legal system permits me to refuse to pay back the debt. I now have the freedom to choose to pay the debt or not, without facing legal sanctions, but the ability to escape legal sanctions does not confer moral value on the refusal to pay the debt, unless in some sense anything that is legally permitted is morally right.[58] A similar argument can be made regarding keeping information secret that could prevent serious harm if disclosed, or vigorously contesting liability in a civil action in a way that leads to the humiliation of the plaintiffs. It cannot be the case that having been autonomously chosen is a sufficient condition for judging something to be morally right, or even permissible. Autonomous action is "valuable only if exercised in pursuit of the good."[59] From the standpoint of the moral evaluation of agents, autonomous choices are evaluated as good or bad with reference to independently existing values.[60]

This is a powerful criticism, as long as one believes that legal ethics is essentially a branch of moral philosophy—that is, that the values that inform lawyers' actions in their representative capacity are the values of ordinary morality. In that case, David Luban would be right that it is impossible to rest an ordinary moral justification on autonomy alone:

> [S]ome things legally right are not morally right, and so in any such argument we must ask how the rabbit of moral justification manages to come out of the hat. And the answer, I believe, is the one we expected: rabbits don't come out of hats unless they have been put in the hats to begin with .... Pepper, I believe, assumes that the morality is already in the law, that in an important sense anything legally right *is* morally right. That however, cannot be...[61]

Luban's objection would be well taken if Pepper's reliance on autonomy were intended to pull an ordinary moral rabbit of justification out of the hat. Since I think that is what Pepper was trying to do,[62] Luban's criticism has real bite.

It may be possible to reformulate an argument like Pepper's, so that the rabbit is not ordinary moral justification but some kind of special justification in terms of values that are a property of a well-functioning legal system, not of ordinary morality. This would be a freestanding political conception of legal ethics, as opposed to one which is derived from a moral conception.[63] Pepper hints at this sort of justification when he talks about the negative value of interfering with clients' exercise of autonomy. In his view, lawyers acting in a representative capacity must not do anything to *decrease* the autonomy of their clients, relative to the level of autonomy that is provided by the law, because to do so would be to deprive the client of something to which he or she is entitled under the law, on the basis of an idiosyncratic value judgment of the lawyer. This is true even if the lawyer believes interfering with the client's exercise of this legal right is morally justified, as in the statute of limitations case. Pepper's concern is that this kind of moral gatekeeping by lawyers replaces the rule of law with "an oligarchy of lawyers,"[64] who may disagree with the prior political judgment concerning the rightness or wrongness of the client's actions. For lawyers, therefore, there may be an obligation within political ethics not to interfere with the autonomy of their clients. Because this obligation flows from the lawyer's role in the legal system, it applies even if the underlying legal right of the client is devoid of moral value.

Leaving aside the observation that a client wishing to pursue any given project could probably find a lawyer who would not interfere with it, perhaps it would not be such a bad thing if lawyers blocked their clients' access to the law on moral grounds. Luban argues that there would be nothing wrong with lawyers being simply another "informal filter" on people pursuing legally permissible projects.[65] Social ordering relies on informal pressures, such as the disapproval of friends and neighbors, to a much greater extent than it relies on formal legal sanctions. The reason most of us refrain from doing nasty things is that we worry about what other people will think. Luban says that a lawyer's refusal to assist a client in carrying out a legally permissible but morally wrongful project is no different from "these other instances of social control through private non-cooperation."[66] This is the "Lysistratian prerogative," named for the play by Aristophanes in which the wives of Athenian soldiers conspired to end the Peloponnesian War by withholding sex from their husbands until they agreed to make peace. In that play, the public good of peace was secured not by a political decision, but by private acts of non-cooperation by the soldiers' wives. If lawyers are similarly well positioned to dissuade their clients from committing moral wrongs, they should be permitted to try, and if they are permitted to try, then they are subject to moral criticism for *not* trying in appropriate cases.

There is a significant difference, however, between social relationships and the allocation of entitlements in a political system, and that is that political relationships are... well, political. Although that sounds like a banal point, it can be difficult to pin down exactly what is the heart of the normative difference between personal and political associations. One might emphasize the nonvoluntary nature of the professional relationship. If one friend refuses to assist another in a nefarious project, the refusal is likely on the basis of a reason shared by the other friend, but in any event the friends are free to part ways and find other cooperative partners who are more agreeable. In a political relationship, by contrast, one party would unfairly coerce the other if she made decisions respecting the other's public, political rights on the basis of reasons not shared by the subject of these decisions, where there is no viable exit option. The lawyer–client relationship is legally voluntary in the sense that the parties are not literally stuck with one another, except in the relatively unusual case of court-appointed counsel, but as a practical matter it can be difficult and costly for a client with a recalcitrant lawyer to locate substitute counsel.[67] This is the most salient distinction, however, because the cost of abandoning long-standing social relationships (to say nothing of family relationships) is bound to be greater than the cost of finding a new lawyer. True, these costs do not have market prices attached to them, but surely it is more costly to someone, in the sense of being a significant bad event, to turn his or her back on an old friend who gave inconvenient moral advice. Thus, rather than focusing on the voluntary or involuntary nature of entry into or exit from relationships, it may be better to ask why, within certain kinds of relationships, we would prefer the parties to advise one another on the basis of a restricted set of reasons. When we do, we can reconstruct Pepper's autonomy-based defense of the Standard Conception, on distinctively political lines.

The political argument from client autonomy relies on distinctively political values such as liberty, equality, and the rule of law, rather than on the ordinary moral value of autonomy. This version of the argument is implicit in Pepper's ideal of first-class citizenship.[68] However, instead of relying on the ordinary moral notion of autonomy, the political reconstruction of the argument from client autonomy emphasizes the value in not having one's freedom of action limited in the name of society as a whole, except on the grounds of publicly available, impartially applied rules.[69] This can be seen by imagining a version of the *Lysistrata* in which the rulers of Athens decreed that it would be illegal for women to sleep with men who opposed the Peloponnesian War. This "noncooperation" would be different in kind from the sex strike in Aristophanes's play, not only because of its mandatory nature, but also because directives of political rulers, made in the name of all citizens collectively, must be made on the basis of reasons that all members of the society can share. In a pluralist democracy, these shared reasons are procedural—citizens agree to resolve their substantive differences (e.g., over whether to wage war with Sparta) by entrusting the resolution of disputes to certain procedures that treat the views of all citizens with at least some minimum level of respect. There is no similar requirement of formal procedural justice in private relationships like friendship, again not only because these relationships are voluntarily entered into, but also because friends or family members are likely to share a thicker set of substantive values, and are therefore less likely to need to rely on procedural mechanisms to reach agreement.[70]

In the public domain, the rule of law demands that "the power of the state should never be exercised against individual citizens except in accordance with rules explicitly set out in a pubic rule book available to all."[71] In turn, the value of the rule of law is held to be independent of the moral worth of the legal entitlements available to citizens.[72] The reason for this independence is the key to understanding why the moral value of autonomy—or any ordinary moral value—cannot be the basis for the duties of lawyers. Legality is important because it enables people to live together in a relatively peaceful stable society, despite deep and persistent disagreement about moral ideals, values, and conceptions of the good life.[73] This disagreement is not necessarily rooted in selfishness or ignorance, let alone a view that morality is a matter of taste or preference, but in a genuine plurality of worthy ideals and forms of life, to which people might reasonably subscribe. People who wish to coexist and cooperate in light of this ethical pluralism have reason to establish and respect a system by which general rules of conduct can be adopted and enforced, without regard to whether all who are affected by the rules can agree that they are in accordance with the demands of justice.

In addition, the law protects the freedom of individuals to choose, to the extent compatible with the interests of others, to live according to ideals that may not be shared by others. Legal officials, including lawyers representing clients and advising them about their entitlements, would interfere with this end if they acted according to their own conception of justice, not the position embodied in the law. If a lawyer's advice was that a client should not do such-and-such, because the lawyer believed (possibly even rightly) that it is morally wrongful, the lawyer would in effect replace the systemwide settlement of moral controversy with one of the contested moral views whose existence necessitated the legal settlement in the first place. Besides being a kind of arrogance or disrespect for competing viewpoints, the lawyer's advice is a political wrong, in light of the social value of the framework for cooperation created by the law. The lawyer acts as though her own beliefs about what others should do are entitled to greater respect than the social view on the matter, reached through adequately fair procedures.

Lawyers are not political actors for all purposes. Most obviously they are not paid out of public funds, nor are they subject to civil service rules and other protections available to government employees. In addition, lawyers are permitted to allocate their services on the basis of ability to pay and to turn away prospective clients for reasons that would be impermissible if given as reasons by a true government agent. Doing so does not interfere with the rights of prospective clients except in the rare "last lawyer in town" scenario in which no other lawyer is available to represent the client. The point of the term "political" is simply to highlight the connection between the ethical obligations of lawyers and a scheme of rights and duties enacted in the name of society as a whole. When a lawyer acts on the basis of non-public reasons, even if the effect is not to coerce a would-be client into giving up an entitlement, the lawyer still lacks a justification that can be given in the appropriate terms. The things lawyers do for clients must be justified on the basis of the legal entitlements of clients, not the interests or preferences of clients or lawyers.

1.4.2   *Partiality to Clients and the Value of Dignity*

One striking aspect of the Standard Conception is its lack of concern for the ends of the legal system as a whole. Instead of concerning herself with justice or the public good, the lawyer cares only about her client's interests, the interests of society as a whole be damned. Putting the criminal defense lawyer's point of view bluntly, Alan Dershowitz says, "When defense attorneys represent guilty clients—as most do, most of the time—their responsibility is to try, by all fair and ethical means, to *prevent* the truth about their client's guilt from emerging."[74] This principle partiality was even more forcefully expressed by the English barrister defending Queen Caroline against what were, in effect, allegations of adultery, in the early nineteenth century:

> An advocate, in the discharge of his duty, knows but one person in all the world, and that person is his client. To save that client by all means and expedients, and at all hazards and costs to other persons, and amongst them, to himself, is his first and only duty; and in performing this duty he must not regard the alarm, the torments, the destruction which he may bring upon others.[75]

This speech of Lord Brougham has been quoted so frequently that most legal ethics teachers have probably committed it to memory. However, Brougham made his statement in the context of a parliamentary debate, not a judicial proceeding, and the speech was intended as a veiled political threat to King George IV. Given the extraordinary circumstances of the case, it can hardly be argued that the Brougham speech has any general applicability; it certainly does not describe the prevailing norms of the English Bar in 1820.[76] Nevertheless, it has come to be understood to encapsulate, in a particularly vivid way, the Principle of Partisanship.

In the law governing lawyers, the Principle of Partisanship, understood also as the value of loyalty to one's client, is often protected by rules prohibiting conflicts of interest, self-dealing, or other breaches of fiduciary duty. As the 1969 ABA Model Code put it, "[t]he professional judgment of the lawyer should be exercised ... solely for the benefit of [the lawyer's] client, and free of compromising influences and loyalties. Neither [the lawyer's] personal interests, the interests of other clients, nor the desires of third persons should be permitted to dilute [this] loyalty."[77] The current Model Rules proscribe representation that would be adverse to the interests of current and former clients in certain matters, regulate business transactions with clients, and prohibit other instances of self-dealing, such as romantic relationships with clients.[78] In ethical terms, as distinct from the law of lawyering, the value of loyalty leads lawyers to claim a moral permission to favor the interests of one person, the client, over the interests of all others who might conceivably make claims on the lawyer's care and concern.[79] The question is whether that preference can be justified.

The values of partiality and loyalty are not unknown in ordinary morality.[80] Being able to form relationships and attachments is constitutive of our character as persons, and therefore of the very possibility of having concerns, values, and moral reasons at all.[81] We are therefore entitled to reserve some area of special concern for those persons with whom we stand in particularly close relationships. We must see them as unique, not as instantiations of some impartial value like utility or human dignity. In fact, if a person looked for some impartial moral principle to legitimize the decision to save a loved one instead of a stranger, when only one person could be saved, we would criticize the actor for having "one thought too many."[82] People are not abstractions, but unique, non-fungible sources of value. A humane system of morality would permit, and indeed require, people to act directly on deep attachments to other persons that cannot be explained by, or reduced to, impartial considerations.

Charles Fried has used an argument like this in an attempt to justify the lawyer's exclusive concern for her client's interests. Lawyers are often criticized because "the ideal of professional loyalty to one's client permits, even demands, an allocation of the lawyer's ... resources in ways that are not always maximally conducive to the greatest good of the greatest number."[83] Clients seek legal advice not because they want to do what is morally right, all things considered, but because they want to "avoid their obligations in justice" and "procure ... advantages ... at the direct expense of some identified opposing party."[84] In a brilliant bit of rhetorical jujitsu, Fried turns this criticism around to make all of these seemingly disagreeable results into professional virtues for lawyers. It is true that lawyers help their clients avoid obligations in justice, and harm third parties, but this is only to be expected if we are morally permitted to give priority to the interests of those with whom we are in close personal relationships.[85] Fried locates the source of ethical value in every person's appreciation of his or her unique significance, which does not simply merge into the interests of humankind as a whole.[86] It follows from the distinct value of concrete individual persons that we should be entitled to reserve a special area of concern for others, notwithstanding the claims of others to a share of our time, concern, and resources. If the lawyer–client relationship is understood in this way, as a kind of "limited-purpose friendship," the lawyer will have a moral permission to ignore, or at least give less weight to the interests of others.[87]

Critics have had a field day poking fun at Fried's friendship metaphor. William Simon rightly observed that if one party to an intimate relationship has paid money to spend time with the other, we would call it prostitution, not friendship.[88] Less polemically, the distinguishing feature of a true friendship is that friends value the interests of the other for the sake of the other as an individual person as such, not because that person belongs to some class that is generally entitled to concern.[89] The whole point of the argument from the uniqueness of persons is that they cannot be reduced to being bearers or instantiations of impartial value, but lawyers value clients only insofar as they have legal problems within the lawyer's area of expertise and can pay their bills. Fried also ignores the element of time and shared history in constituting the value of friendship.[90] The gulf is simply too great between the case of the interwoven identity of friends, who take one another's interests as their own because in a sense they literally do share these interests, and the case of strangers who agree to work together on a matter of mutual convenience and profit. Finally, even taking the friendship relationship for granted, friends are not privileged to do nasty things for each other just because they are friends.[91] We may be permitted to reserve some special concern for others, but that surely does not license unlimited concern for a close relation, at the expense of others. Moreover, lawyers do things to their clients that friends should not do to other friends, such as stop helping them when they run out of money.[92] In brief, the friendship metaphor only works for Fried because he has loaded up the definition of friendship in advance so it turns out that friends look a great deal like lawyers. Critics have accordingly proposed a different metaphor—lawyer as bureaucrat, who treats clients and third parties as nonpeople (or, one might say, as merely occasions for the recognition of legally protected interests).[93]

I think a better reading of Fried's argument reveals that his friendship metaphor is really beside the point. His concession that a lawyer is a *limited-purpose* friend shows that the image of lawyer as friend is meant to be provocative, but should not be taken literally (it was intended as a metaphor, after all). Rather, the role of "legal friend" is created by the legal system to recognize and protect the underlying value which also figures prominently in friendship—namely, the intrinsic value of individual persons. "It is because the law must respect the rights of individuals that the law must also create and support the specific role of legal friend."[94] In other words, the same sorts of liberal political considerations we encountered previously, in the discussion of autonomy, inform the role of lawyer as limited-purpose friend. The lawyer and client need not be actual friends—and indeed, a relationship which is fundamentally aimed at vindicating an interest that all members of a class (such as citizens, or potential clients) share cannot be a friendship in the traditional Aristotelian sense.[95] The important thing is that the client is entitled to a kind of protection that friends may, in some cases, give each other, which is to have the interests of an individual taken seriously, as against the claims of the wider collectivity.[96] The anti-utilitarian thrust of Fried's argument is much more important than the friendship metaphor:

> [O]nce the [attorney–client] relation has been contracted, considerations of efficiency or fair distribution cannot be allowed to weaken it .... The relation must exist in order to realize the client's rights against society, to preserve that measure of autonomy which social regulation must allow the individual.[97]

The lawyer should not be seen merely as a scarce resource, to be allocated in whatever way maximizes overall social welfare, but should be seen as the protector of the rights of individuals. Rights, in turn, may be traceable to the value of autonomy or, alternatively, to a different value such as human dignity.

Interestingly, David Luban, who trenchantly criticized the defense of the Standard Conception based on the value of autonomy, has endorsed a modest version, at least in the context of criminal defense, grounded on the value of dignity.[98] Conflating autonomy and dignity is a mistake, he argues, because autonomy is a property of individual persons, as a metaphysical matter,[99] while dignity is a property of relations among persons. Although in ordinary usage dignity may denote a quality that some people have, as a moral value it refers to a way people deserve to be treated. Treating someone with dignity means recognizing her subjectivity.[100] Persons should not be understood as bearers or instantiations of impartial value, but as sources of value in their own right. Because we regard ourselves as intrinsically valuable, and would object to being used merely as a means to some impartially justified end, we acknowledge that others are similarly valuable.[101] Luban therefore argues that dignity is grounded in human subjectivity, it requires "honoring [someone's] being, not merely their willing,"[102] and thus constitutes a source of ethical value.

Relying on dignity as a property of the relations among persons suggests a possibility that will be pursued in depth in this book—namely, that legal ethics should be understood as part of the morality of communities. The issue Luban explores is really not how one person should treat another with dignity, because that probably does not include absolute duties of confidentiality and highly aggressive adversarial advocacy, but how *the state* should treat its citizens with dignity. In the context of criminal defense, it means that accused persons should be afforded the opportunity to tell their own story, in their own terms, and that lawyers should not refuse the client's request to conduct the defense in a particular way, and should not treat people "as though their own subjective stories and commitments are insignificant."[103] The value of dignity also provides a rationale for the privilege against self-incrimination, which humiliates people by forcing them to participate in the process of punishing themselves.[104] I think Luban's account of dignity is on the right track, but I would go farther in maintaining that dignity, insofar as it matters to legal ethics, is a property of individuals in communities, as citizens of societies, rather than being a property of individuals as unadorned moral agents, without obligations as citizens.

Focusing on dignity as an aspect of the morality of living together in communities shows how dignity and autonomy are distinct values, and how Luban's approach to legal ethics differs from Pepper's. Both Pepper and Luban can plausibly claim not to be invoking the notion of role-differentiated morality at all, because both are simply telling lawyers to act on an ordinary moral value, either autonomy or dignity. But this is where Pepper runs into difficulties, because the mere fact of some action having been autonomously chosen does not invest it with moral value. A person who makes a free, uncoerced, genuinely autonomous decision to do something stupid or harmful will still have done something stupid or harmful; we do not praise that person's actions just because they were uncoerced. Moreover, the concept of autonomy does not provide guidance for resolving conflicts between competing claims of autonomy. Many political conflicts involve incompatible assertions of rights to be able to do something. Freedom of speech conflicts with freedom from harassment and hateful messages; one's freedom is restricted at airport security lines to protect the right of other passengers to travel safely; intellectual property rights interfere with the claimed rights to share digital music and video files, to have access to inexpensive medications, and so on. Thus, lawyers who act directly on the value of autonomy still need a justification for interfering with the rights of others. Because Luban locates the value of dignity in relations among people, rather than as a property of humans themselves, the obligations he derives for lawyers from this foundational value are better tailored to the problems encountered by the clients of lawyers, whose legal problems arise from their interactions with others.

However, several problems still exist regarding the reliance on dignity as a foundational value in legal ethics. First, dignity is a property of actual human persons, not entities such as corporations and government agencies. It is unclear what it would mean to treat a bank or the Environmental Protection Agency with dignity. (From this it might follow that organizations are not entitled to the same quality of lawyering as natural persons, but this seems odd, given that the law provides many avenues for natural persons to act through entities, presumably because this allows natural persons to pursue their goals more efficiently.[105]) Second, while the value of dignity works well as an explanation and justification of several existing practices within adversarial litigation, particularly criminal defense, it is less useful in an account of non-litigation representation. Taking the subjectivity of a client seriously is well and good as a principle of trial advocacy, where an impartial trier of fact has to decide which of several competing stories represents the truth about something. When lawyers are counseling clients about compliance with the law, however, the client's subjectivity is less important than the obligation created by the law. A client may believe—in sincere subjective good faith—that the law is wrongheaded, but the lawyers' job is nevertheless to bring the client into compliance with legal requirements. Finally, just as autonomy versus autonomy conflicts bedevil Pepper's theory of legal ethics, Luban must deal with the possibility of conflicts between incompatible assertions of dignity. Respecting the dignity of one's client may mean interfering with the dignity of others. Consider the product liability hypothetical, in which taking the defendant's story seriously may require asking humiliating questions of the plaintiffs. In order to resolve a dignity versus dignity conflict, some other value would need to be deployed to break the tie. That value could not be partiality to one's client because, as we have seen, partiality must be justified on the basis of some other value. Relying on dignity as the underlying value would create a vicious circle.

A more promising approach is to ground legal ethics on the value of fidelity to the law. The idea of human dignity plays a role in this conception of legal ethics, but dignity is protected indirectly. The idea is that a political community can be characterized as one in which individuals are treated with due respect for their dignity—that is, treated as full and equal citizens—if there is a tolerably just legal system that establishes a framework of legal rights and duties that citizens can use as a basis for regulating their interactions with one another. Luban is not averse to this general way of thinking about dignity in the context of political institutions. In an important paper on Lon Fuller's jurisprudence, Luban notices something interesting in Fuller's well-known definition, that law is "the enterprise of subjecting human conduct to the governance of rules," namely that Fuller is defining law in terms of an activity, not truth conditions for a legal proposition.[106] This activity is the job of various officials and quasi-officials, including judges and lawyers. Moreover, it is a *purposive* activity, and carries along with it standards of excellence, and criteria of success and failure.[107] What is the purpose of doing law (i.e., subjecting human conduct to the governance of rules)? Fuller's answer, which Luban adopts, is that proceeding in this way reflects a moral decision, to treat citizens with dignity insofar as one governs their activities.[108] There are, accordingly, moral constraints on the activities of lawmakers and law-interpreters. "[I]nstitutions, particularly legal institutions, although they are entirely human creations, have moral properties of their own ... that are connected only indirectly to general morality."[109]

This idea of institutions having moral properties, connected only indirectly to general morality, is the basis for the distinction between role-based obligations and ordinary morality. An understanding of a political value like dignity or equality (and thus of professional roles supported by that value) emerges from reflection on the question, "What would it mean to establish a *community* among such beings?" A community, and the institutions by which it governs itself, must take account of the intrinsic value of all its members, their capacity for reflection, and also the need to establish grounds upon which competing claims to scarce resources can be evaluated. A regime of legality, in contrast with tyranny or even benevolent managerial direction, manifests respect for citizens as autonomous agents, as well as trust in their capacity for self-governance.[110] Thinking responsibly about one's moral relation to others is a distinctive process when one is situated in a community. Treating someone with dignity within a community means giving significant weight to political institutions that have been set up to regulate rival conceptions of the moral relations between individuals. It does not entail the sort of unrestrained partisanship exemplified by the quote from Lord Brougham earlier, but entails instead the diligent effective representation of a client with respect to her legal entitlements.[111] This indirect protection for the dignity of citizens is close to the foundation of a conception of legal ethics emphasizing fidelity to law.

1.5 Simon's Legalist Critique of the Standard Conception

William Simon's critique of the Standard Conception (which he calls the Dominant View) appears to proceed from the same premise relied upon here—namely, that legal ethics should be understood as fundamentally structured by political considerations, not ordinary moral values. He rejects the two defenses of the Standard Conception considered earlier here, in terms of client autonomy and the moral value of loyalty or partiality to the client. Rather than demanding that lawyers justify their actions in terms of moral considerations such as autonomy, dignity, and loyalty, Simon demands that they justify themselves in terms of *justice*. The normative principle he would have lawyers follow is: "Lawyers should take those actions that, considering the relevant circumstances of the particular case, seem likely to promote justice."[112] He rightly observes that the rights and obligations of lawyers are derivative of the legal entitlements of clients. This is subtly different from Pepper's view that the fundamental goal of the legal system is to safeguard the liberty or autonomy of citizens.[113] The trouble with linking lawyers' duties with client autonomy, as opposed to legal entitlements, is that the client's claim of autonomy to take some action may conflict with the claim to autonomy of another person to take an incompatible action. Indeed, much of the common law is structured around competing claims of rights asserted by the parties to a dispute. Nuisance cases provide a clear example—one party's claimed right to operate a cement plant interferes with the rights of the plant's neighbors to be free from dirt, noise, and vibration from the plant[114]—but the law of torts generally involves a claim by the plaintiff that some right of hers was violated by the defendant, who claims a right to engage in the conduct that caused the plaintiff's injury. Because of this opposition between incompatible claims of right, Simon argues that the law does not secure as much autonomy as citizens may desire, but only "a just measure of autonomy,"[115] compatible with the interests of others. Justice, not autonomy, is therefore in the normative driver's seat for Simon.

Unfortunately, justice turns out to be an exceedingly difficult term to pin down in Simon's theory. Generally speaking, one can distinguish among varieties of justice. A familiar distinction is between distributive and corrective (or retributive) justice, and theorists like Rawls have given renewed prominence to questions of distributive (or social) justice (i.e., how major social and political institutions ought to be structured to distribute rights, resources, and opportunities).[116] For the purposes of understanding Simon's approach to legal ethics, the crucial conceptions are of procedural, substantive, and legal justice. Procedural justice means most obviously compliance with the preexisting rules of a legal system, but since rules can be assessed as more or less procedurally just, it must also mean something like the right balance between specifically procedural virtues, such as efficiency and accuracy in fact-finding.[117] Substantive justice refers to the congruence between the outcome of a legal proceeding and the requirements of morality.[118] Legal justice, on the other hand, refers to an outcome that is supported by the relevant law. Legal justice means that would-be legal norms are, in fact, validly enacted laws, and also that the correct interpretation of those norms supports a conclusion that a party is legally entitled to something. One must be careful here, because the law establishes procedural and substantive entitlements. An individual has a substantive entitlement to enjoy the use of her property free from the interference of others, as well as the procedural entitlement to have disputes about the applicability of that right determined by a fair process.

These distinctions imply the possibility of conflicts among conceptions of justice. Many procedural entitlements have the effect of interfering with substantive moral values such as desert or truth. Consider the statute of limitations example discussed previously. In terms of the moral value of desert, justice favors the creditor; in terms of the procedural values of finality and accuracy in adjudication, however, justice favors the debtor who can assert the statute of limitations. Thus, the result in the statute of limitations case, permitting the debtor to avoid repayment, may be regarded as procedurally and legally just, but substantively unjust. It is understandable that legal ethics theorists want to avoid this result. If lawyers follow the Standard Conception, there seems to be a gap between the requirements of morality and the obligations of one's professional role. A connection must still be established between legal justice (which may be less confusingly called legal *validity*) and morality. It is well understood that this is a problem for the Standard Conception, but ironically it turns out to be a problem for Simon as well, unless the notion of justice that is central to his theory is something other than legal validity.

Simon's theory of legal ethics is aimed at "minimiz[ing] the lawyer's participation in injustice."[119] The question is, of course, from what kind of injustice Simon wants to extricate the lawyer. In places, Simon equates justice with "legal merit,"[120] or legal validity. If he understands legal ethics as fundamentally a matter of avoiding legal injustice, then it is hard to see how his position is different from a sensible moderate version of the Standard Conception.[121] Of course, it is useful to remind lawyers that the Standard Conception, appropriately understood, does not permit manipulation and abuse of the law.[122] But Simon sees himself as doing something much more radical than encouraging lawyers to respect the law. His project is to reorient legal ethics around a distinctive jurisprudential position, one which demolishes a formalistic, mechanical style of reasoning and replaces it with a non-categorical, flexible, "contextual" approach.[123]

A better reading of his work as a whole is, therefore, that when Simon talks about justice, he means to refer to substantive justice, quite apart from the legal merits of a party's position.[124] His examples of lawyers participating in injustice are often cases, such as nondisclosure of confidential information, in which the legal merits of the client's position would be substantively unjust.[125] This raises the question: How does a lawyer determine when the client's position is substantively just? The answer is quite an undertaking, reminiscent of the task confronting Ronald Dworkin's ideal judge Hercules when he decides cases. A Simonian lawyer should consider the distribution of legal resources, and whether her talents could be better used by more deserving clients[126]; the substantive meaning of a legal entitlement, and not just its formal plausibility[127]; whether the client's legal entitlements are important or "fundamental," as compared with the interests of non-clients[128]; the competence of coordinate institutions within the legal system, the reliability of their decision-making procedures,[129] and the likelihood that they will make decisions that track the substantive justice of the client's position.[130] Lawyers who engage in this contextual, noncategorical process of decision-making will therefore aim more directly at the realization of justice, and not simply punt the responsibility for doing justice to the impartial procedures of adversarial adjudication, or to the legal system as a whole.

If lawyers are called upon to aim directly at justice, and if this end is understood as substantive justice, then it seems that Simon is calling upon lawyers to act directly on ordinary moral values, with little concern for the legal entitlements of clients. Upon closer examination, Simon actually turns out to be a moral critic of the Standard Conception, despite claiming to reject "the common tendency to attribute the tensions of legal ethics to a conflict between the demands of legality on the one hand and those of nonlegal, personal or ordinary morality on the other."[131] The moral critique comes in by way of all of the discretionary judgments a lawyer is called upon to make about the relative merit of the client's projects, the importance of procedural values (institutional competence and so on) in relation to other evaluative considerations, whether rights are "fundamental" or purposes "problematic," and so on. A great deal of fiddling with the jurisprudential part of the theory is required, in order to ensure that all of these considerations are deemed "legal" values, not moral ones. When push comes to shove, however, it is clear that morality, not legality is in the driver's seat. Simon even calls upon lawyers to consider exercising powers of nullification.[132] While nullification of legal norms in pursuit of substantive justice may be reluctantly tolerated by the legal system in places, a core value of legality cannot be the readiness to dispense with formal law whenever it appears to conflict with substantive justice. Simon appeals to the discourse of legality because it makes it psychologically easier for lawyers and law students to do the right thing,[133] but at root his theory is no different from Luban's or other morality-based objections to the Standard Conception.

In response to this line of criticism, Simon tries rather gamely to deny that he is calling upon lawyers to engage in open-ended moral reasoning, rather than exhibiting fidelity to the law. He tries to square this circle by relying heavily on Ronald Dworkin's theory of law. Dworkin claims that legal merit and substantive justice are extensionally equivalent in any given case, because legal validity depends on coherence with principles of political morality that are presupposed by, and lie at the foundation of, the legal system. He argues that, *pace* Hart,[134] it is impossible to formulate a content-independent rule of recognition without reference to moral criteria, because moral argumentation is necessary to establish the existence and validity of law in hard cases.[135] However, he denies that a judge is engaging in all-things-considered moral reasoning when she makes a decision with reference to the society's political morality. A judge must base her decision on principles that can be shown to be consistent with past political decisions made by other officials (judges and legislators) within a general political theory that justifies those decisions.[136] Dworkinian principles are controversial in the sense that they cannot simply be "read off" the law in a straightforward way, without arguing that they are justified on the basis of the normative political theory.[137] A judge "must decide which interpretation shows the legal record to be the best it can be from the standpoint of substantive political morality."[138] It is crucial for Dworkin that a judge never step outside existing law and make new law, for to do so would be to retroactively confer new rights on the parties.[139] Thus, he insists that judges engaging in normative arguments about the consistency of past political decisions with the society's fundamental principles of morality are engaging in the interpretation of existing law, not the creation of new law.

Dworkin may insist that judging is really about interpretation, not all-things-considered moral reasoning, but one would still expect there to be a great deal of disagreement on the political questions that Dworkin sees as inextricably bound up with judging. For Dworkin, the task of a judge is to find an interpretation of the governing cases and statutes that will show the existing law of the community in its best light.[140] Since "best" here means "normatively best, in terms of ethical ideals," we would expect judges to differ in hard cases on the interpretation that shows the community's law in its best light. Even in a simple tort case judges might differ on whether the best law for the community is one that emphasizes individual responsibility or the commitment of the community to safety. Dworkin recognizes the possibility of disagreement, and candidly admits that part of the justification of a judicial decision may be the judge's own moral commitments, which may not coincide with the moral commitments of other judges or of affected citizens. A judge's decision must fit with existing precedents, and "the actual political history of his community will sometimes check his other political convictions," but once a possible interpretation passes a threshold of fit, the judge must apply "[h]is own moral and political convictions" to say what the law of the community is.[141] Even if judges are all reasoning with respect to *this* law of *this* community, the demand that they justify decisions in terms of a normatively attractive political ideal opens the door to disagreement over what the content of law ought to be. In this "protestant" conception of judging,[142] judges are invited to apply their own moral ideals. Thus, when Simon appeals to Dworkin's jurisprudence to deny that lawyers are engaging in ordinary moral reasoning, it is important to remember that Dworkin has opened the door fairly wide to the application of ordinary moral considerations, under the guise of legal interpretation. A number of Simon's case cases reveal that moral ideals about justice, not fidelity to existing law, should be paramount in legal ethics.[143]

The remainder of the book will attempt to sustain the claim that lawyers have a good reason to care about legal justice, but not substantive justice. Thus, legal ethics is not about "ethics" as it is ordinarily conceived. Rather, it is an aspect of the political value of legality. The next chapter considers what legal ethics would look like if a lawyer understood herself as obligated to act on the basis of her clients' legal entitlements, not her clients' interests or her own views about what substantive justice requires.

Chapter Two

From Partisanship to Legal Entitlements:

Putting the Law Back into Lawyering

2.1   Lawyers as Agents

The Standard Conception of legal ethics consists of two principles of action for lawyers: Partisanship and Neutrality. Partisanship is generally understood as the maxim that a lawyer should act to vindicate the interests of clients. The primary objective of this chapter is to establish, as the first aspect of a conception of legal ethics centered on fidelity to law, that the legal *entitlements* of clients, not client interests, ordinary moral considerations or abstract legal norms such as justice, should be the object of lawyers' concerns when acting in a representative capacity. When representing clients, lawyers must respect the scheme of rights and duties established by the law, and not seek to work around the law because either they or their clients believe the law to be unjust, inefficient, stupid, or simply inconvenient. The obligation of respect means that lawyers must treat the law as a reason for action as such, not merely a possible downside to be taken into account, planned around, or nullified in some way. This obligation applies even if it would be very much in the client's interests to obtain a result that is not supported by a plausible claim to a legal entitlement.

Critics of the Standard Conception often stigmatize freestanding role-based normative systems as narrowing the range of reasons that a professional may consider in deliberating about how to act.[1] While the Principle of Neutrality does have this effect (the reasons for which will be considered in the next chapter), my claim is that the ideal of partisanship, properly understood, represents a commitment within political morality to the value of legality. Legality may be seen as narrower than morality in general, but as I will argue, it also represents a distinctive way for citizens to live together and treat each other with respect, as equals. Thus, rather than inhabiting a "simplified moral world,"[2] lawyers actually inhabit a world of demanding ethical obligations of fidelity to law. The Standard Conception, therefore, should be modified so that the Principle of Partisanship is understood as requiring lawyers representing clients to protect the legal entitlements of their clients, not merely to seek to advance their interests. Talking about obligations such as loyalty and partisanship is unobjectionable, as long as it is understood that the object of the lawyer's commitment is not obtaining whatever the client wants, but what the client is legally permitted to have. In this modification of the Standard Conception, which is grounded on fidelity to law, lawyers still have obligations of loyalty and partisanship which run to clients, but which are constituted by the legal entitlements of clients.[3] Legal ethics is therefore not primarily an excuse for immoral behavior but a higher duty incumbent upon occupants of a professional role.

Lawyers who represent clients act to protect legal entitlements by asserting them in litigated disputes or negotiations, counsel their clients on what the law permits, and structure their clients' affairs with reference to the law. As this term will be used here, a legal entitlement is a substantive or procedural right, created by the law, which establishes claim-rights (implying duties upon others), privileges to do things without interference, and powers to change the legal situation of others (e.g., by imposing contractual obligations).[4] Familiar examples of substantive legal entitlements include privacy interests that are protected by statutes and common-law rights against wiretapping, public disclosure of private facts, illegal searches by law enforcement officers and the like; real property rights that protect against trespass, encroachments, and seizures of property by the state without the payment of compensation; intellectual property rights that prohibit the appropriation of valuable ideas; and common law tort rights that seek to deter accidental injuries by providing remedies for those who have been harmed through the negligence of others. Entitlements may be created by courts, legislatures, administrative agencies, or by citizens themselves, using legal tools for private ordering, such as wills, trusts, contracts, partnerships, and corporations.

Substantive legal entitlements have the effect of defining the boundaries between the competing interests of citizens. To take a simple example, if one landowner wants to operate a feedlot for cattle next to his neighbor's residential housing development, these activities are mutually incompatible.[5] The neighbors will appeal to conflicting rights that are inherent in the notion of being a property owner. Property is often explained in terms of the metaphor of a "bundle of sticks," with each stick being a right of some sort—to exclude other users, to transfer the land to others, and to make productive use of one's land. The trouble is, these claims of right conflict, and some resolution is required to avoid a standoff. The parties may bargain to an acceptable solution, but in the absence of an agreed-upon resolution, these conflicting assertions of interests can be resolved by either common-law adjudication of a nuisance claim (e.g., holding that the feedlot is a nuisance, which creates an entitlement in favor of the residential property developer) or legislation (e.g., specifying that land in the area may be used for agricultural purposes, which creates an entitlement in favor of the feedlot owner). Much of the law can be understood in this way, by establishing a framework of entitlements that marks off the boundary between the permissible range of potentially incompatible interests asserted by citizens.

In addition to substantive entitlements, the law also establishes procedural entitlements, which regulate the manner in which substantive entitlements are investigated and adjudicated. For example, a lawsuit must be commenced with pleadings which are formally served using specified procedures. This process ensures that someone who is made a defendant in a lawsuit has notice of the claims being asserted against him, and an opportunity to defend himself. The rules of evidence also create procedural entitlements, which ensure that substantive rights and obligations are adjudicated in an orderly way, on the basis of admissible evidence only, and without unjustified interference with the rights of the litigants or of third parties. The hearsay rule, for example, prevents the introduction of evidence that is generally deemed unreliable, while the rule against introducing evidence of a party's insurance coverage seeks to prevent the jury from acting out of bias against "deep pocket" insurance companies. Procedural rules may also be designed to protect more substantive interests. For instance, the rule against admitting evidence of a subsequent remedial action taken by a party is intended to avoid creating a disincentive to modify products or change safety procedures out of fear that these changes will be admitted at trial to show wrongdoing.

Legal entitlements should not be confused with the legal *merits* of a case, if by "merits" one means a judgment about guilt or innocence, liability or non-liability, or some similar factual and legal conclusion. Legal entitlements may conflict, and the job of a lawyer or judge may be to make a judgment about how a conflict among entitlements should be resolved. That resolution is what is commonly meant by the merits of a lawsuit. The possibility of conflicting substantive and procedural entitlements is familiar from criminal litigation, in which important dignitary interests of the defendant are protected by procedural entitlements against abuse by state officials. These entitlements, in turn, are backed up by remedies that may have an impact on the determination of the guilt or innocence of the accused. For example, the remedy for a wrongful search of the defendant's premises may be exclusion of the wrongfully obtained evidence from trial. If that evidence is crucial to the prosecution's case, the exercise of the defendant's procedural entitlement may result in a verdict of acquittal. Non-lawyers sometimes decry this result as getting the defendant off on a "loophole" or a "technicality," but the exclusionary rule is not a technicality—it is an important remedial doctrine that supports the constitutional right of all citizens to be free from overly zealous law-enforcement activities. It is therefore an entitlement within the meaning of this theory of legal ethics.

One of the fundamental principles structuring the law governing lawyers is that a lawyer's role is defined and bounded by the client's legal entitlements. To put it another way, the lawyer is an agent for a principal, the client, and as such can have no greater power than that possessed by the client. In legal terms, an agent is someone empowered to act on behalf of another. Because of the agency relationship between lawyer and client, the lawyer's decision-making authority is structured and limited by the client's legal entitlements. As an authoritative summary of American law puts it, a lawyer has a legal obligation to "proceed in a manner reasonably calculated to advance a client's lawful objectives, as defined by the client after consultation."[6] This duty may require a lawyer to argue the client's legal position in litigation, counsel the client on what the law requires and permits, or structure a transaction to avoid legal penalties or take advantage of legal benefits. But in any event, when a lawyer is acting in a representative capacity, her legal obligations are constrained by the client's legal entitlements. Acting on any other basis, such as ordinary moral reasons or the interests of clients, would exceed the lawful power of the lawyer as agents. It would be *ultra vires*, in the language of agency law, and thus a legal nullity.

A corollary of the principle that the client's legal entitlements structure the attorney–client relationship is that lawyers may not permissibly assist clients in legal wrongdoing. The lawyer disciplinary rules state that lawyers may not "counsel a client to engage, or assist a client, in conduct that the lawyer knows is criminal or fraudulent,"[7] and agency law provides that the lawyer retains inherent authority, which cannot be overridden at the instance of the client, to refuse to perform unlawful acts.[8] The lawyer may not assist the client in illegality, because the lawyer–client relationship is created by the legal system for a particular purpose, which is to enable clients to receive the expert assistance they need in order to determine their legal rights and duties. As the United States Supreme Court noted, discussing the attorney–client privilege, a relationship of trust and confidence between a client and an attorney is necessary "to encourage full and frank communication between attorneys and their clients and thereby promote broader public interests in the observance of law and administration of justice."[9] On the other hand, lawyer–client communications are not privileged *ab initio* if the client consults a lawyer for the purpose of committing a crime or fraud.[10] These legal principles show that society tolerates lawyers (albeit sometimes grudgingly) because lawyers contribute to a process by which people can regulate their interactions with one another with reference to legal entitlements. Take away the idea of legal entitlements and lawyers would literally cease to exist as a distinct profession. Thus, whatever lawyers do for their clients must be justified on the basis of their clients' lawful rights, permissions, and obligations.[*]

This approach to legal ethics depends to a great extent on the determinacy of law. If the law differentiates individual or group interests or preferences from socially-established rights, there must be something about the process of law-making and law-application that enables lawyers to figure out when their clients are appealing to an actual legal entitlement, as opposed to merely asserting what they wish to be the case. Clients and lawyers sometimes talk as though the law can be made to mean pretty much anything a clever lawyer wants it to mean. I am not really worried about this caricatured version of legal realism here. A more serious objection is that the law cannot be made to mean anything at all, but even so, there is a range of reasonable interpretations that the law might bear, and it is an important aspect of legal ethics to determine what a lawyer should do within that zone of reasonableness.

The full version of this argument will be developed in chapter 6, but the response in brief is that there is a difference between trying to figure out what the law actually is, and acting in accordance with what one believes the law ought to be. Where the law is unclear, citizens and lawyers may be aiming at a moving target, they may see only through a glass darkly, or some other metaphor may better capture the idea that legal judgments are not always capable of being made with a great deal of precision. Nevertheless, it is possible to distinguish aiming at the law from trying to get around it (which requires, ironically, that one have the law fairly clearly in view, to know how to evade it).[**] It is permissible, of course, to make arguments about what one believes the law ought to be, but these are formally different from statements about what the law actually permits or requires. This observation about this formal difference

---

[*] As discussed later, in the section on zealous advocacy, protecting the legal entitlements of clients does not require, and in many cases may not justify, the kinds of scorched-earth litigation tactics for which lawyers are rightly criticized. Tim Dare and Ted Schneyer have both emphasized that the law of lawyering, *properly understood*, does not require or permit lawyers to be attack dogs. Dare (2004); Schneyer (1984). It is a separate question, also discussed later in this chapter, whether it is merely a fortunate coincidence that the law governing lawyers requires fidelity to law, or whether it is a constraint on any morally acceptable set of norms governing the legal profession that they require fidelity to law.

[**] Compare Harry Frankfurt's distinction between lies and bullshit, in Frankfurt (2005). Lying is necessarily parasitic upon belief in the existence and knowability of the truth. A liar seeks to persuade others of something that the liar believes not to be true. Bullshit, by contrast, is indifference to the truth. The lawyers who structured the transactions underlying the Enron collapse and the OLC lawyers who drafted the torture memos were engaged in lying, because they knew what the law was and sought to evade it. Those who claim that the law is radically indeterminate, including some defenders of the Enron and OLC lawyers, are bullshitting.

leads to a point about the institutional structure of litigation and non-litigation representation. Lawyers representing clients in litigated matters have some leeway to assert arguable legal interpretations, leaving it up to opposing counsel to challenge these positions, and to the court to make a decision about the best interpretation of the law.[11] However, litigation is a special case, in which lawyers share responsibility for other institutional actors for getting the law right. In counseling and transactional representation, by contrast, the lawyer is frequently the only actor who has any power to render a judgment about what the law permits. That is not to deny that there is a range of meanings that the law can reasonably be understood to bear—within that range, there is nothing wrong with the lawyer adopting a view that is consistent with her client's interests. At the same time, however, lawyers are not permitted to adopt positions outside the range of reasonable interpretations, simply because it would be advantageous to their clients if they did so.

2.1.1 *Legal, Not Moral, Rights*

As discussed at the beginning of this chapter, with the simple example of the feedlot and the residential housing development, one of the most important functions of the law is to supersede uncertainty and disagreement and provide a resolution of competing claims of right, so that citizens can coexist and work together on mutually beneficial projects. The law may accomplish this by creating entitlements directly, or by providing means for citizens to create their own private ordering by agreement. Without the coordinating function of the law, disagreement would make it much more difficult for citizens to cooperate on common undertakings. Reasons abound for disagreement, including self-interest, strategic behavior, and empirical uncertainty. Because the subject of legal ethics has primarily been concerned with the moral obligations of lawyers, and these are often thought to depend directly on ordinary moral considerations, this book focuses principally on the problem of reasonable disagreement over morality.. However, that should not be taken to exclude other reasons for disagreement, such as factual uncertainty or asymmetric information. The law also serves to stabilize and coordinate the interests of citizens in light of disagreement of a more mundane sort as well.

Moral disagreement arises for many reasons, as we will see further in chapter 3. The most important is value pluralism. Even if there is broad agreement at a high level of abstraction on the significance of an ethical value, there may be a great deal of internal complexity in the structure of that value, or it may contain competing, possibly incompatible conceptions of the concept.[12] As a result, people are likely to disagree in good faith about how to specify an abstract ethical value as a concrete maxim of action. Consider the moral value of equality. Practically everyone would agree that equality is an authentic ethical ideal, at some level of generality. As soon as we attempt to specify what equality requires in particular cases, however, all manner of disagreement breaks out. Does distributive justice require only equality of access to opportunities, or equality of outcomes? Is it fair to give preferences to members of traditionally disadvantaged groups in hiring, university admissions, and so on, in order to help rectify historical wrongs? How much must employers accommodate the disabilities of employees, and what counts as a disability? A second source of ethical disagreement is that human experience, and the goods and values associated with it, is sufficiently complex that it is impossible to reduce all of these goods and values to some higher-order master value that can be used to rank and prioritize competing ethical considerations.[13] There are many different ends people may pursue, and still be recognized as fully rational, and fully human; there are multiple *objectively valuable* things that individuals and cultures may regard as fulfilling and worthy objects of attainment.[14] The attainment of one of these ideals often requires the subordination or abandonment of others.[15] Third, competing values may be formally different, in that some pertain to things we have reason to care about from an impersonal perspective (i.e., consequences), while others depend on seeing ourselves as in some way the source of value (agent-relative reasons, such as deontological considerations).[16] Finally, even if we can reach agreement on how an ethical maxim should be specified on the basis of more general values, a great deal of judgment may still be required to ascertain how that maxim ought to be applied in light of all the relevant circumstances, and people may disagree in good faith at the level of exercising this judgment.[17] Taken together, these sources of disagreement constitute the burdens of judgment, which make politics necessary.[18]

As a result, law is necessary in a society not because of "the stupidity and incompetence of its members, their infirmity of purpose and want of devotion to the group, their selfishness and malice, [and] their readiness to exploit and 'free ride',"[19] but the impossibility of using reason alone to achieve a consensus view among all members of society on what morality requires in a given case. As Isaiah Berlin has argued, human history teaches us to be extremely wary of any claim to political legitimacy and authority that is founded upon a claim that the rulers have accurately discerned the "true" nature of their subjects.[20] "In the ideal case, liberty coincides with law[;] autonomy with authority,"[21] but this is true only if human beings have only one true purpose, and "the ends of all rational beings must of necessity fit into a single universal, harmonious pattern."[22] Berlin's striking observation is that the worst tyrannies and the most utopian hopes for human salvation through government shared the Platonic belief that there is only one rationally appointed order for human life.[23]

It would be a dramatic overstatement to say that permitting lawyers to act directly on their perception of the public interest or moral truth would lead to tyranny.[24] However, it may nevertheless be the case that actions grounded in a lawyer's beliefs—even sincere good-faith beliefs—about morality are lacking in legitimacy, with respect to the client. Remember that lawyers are agents of clients. As such, they are empowered to take actions to advance the client's lawful objectives. Although there is nothing wrong with discussing with the client whether the client's objectives are prudent, the lawyer's central role is to evaluate whether the client is legally entitled to pursue some objective. The lawyer's professional expertise, power, and value to the client are all related to the lawyer's knowledge of the law, not of the wisdom or moral worth of the client's objectives. Clients may disagree with a law on its merits, and believe it to be ill-conceived, wasteful, stupid, or even morally repugnant, but insofar as they seek to act under a claim of legal justification, they are obligated to act in accordance with the law. This must be the case if the law is to fulfill its function of enabling cooperation in the face of deep and persistent disagreement. Because the power of lawyers derives from the legal entitlements of clients, lawyers must be guided by law, not by the moral reasons the law supersedes.

One might nevertheless object that, whatever is true about moral pluralism in general, none of the cases discussed here involve questions about which good-faith disagreement is possible. Surely the gratuitous humiliation of the plaintiffs in the product liability case, or the refusal to pay one's justly owed debts, is morally wrong. However, the law properly interpreted might, for good moral reasons, create an entitlement to engage in what the lawyer sincerely believes to be morally wrongful conduct. The first reason for this is the possibility of disagreement considered earlier. The lawyer and client might simply disagree in good faith over the justice of some action. In addition, there may be moral reasons for the law to recognize legal entitlements to engage in moral wrongdoing. In tort law, for example, there is no duty to rescue a stranger in peril, even if the rescue could be accomplished easily, without any risk to the rescuer.[25] Similarly, there is an entitlement, as a matter of constitutional law, to engage in offensive speech and conduct; a person can publish a parody advertisement suggesting that a prominent religious leader had sex with his mother in an outhouse,[26] or march in a neo-Nazi rally in a town populated by Holocaust survivors,[27] without legal penalty.

In cases that involve legal entitlements to engage in wrongdoing, there are frequently countervailing moral values associated with procedural ideals or considerations of institutional competence. Some cases of the priority of procedural considerations are familiar to every law student. Tort law does not impose a duty to rescue, for example, because of concerns about the incentives it might create, and the difficulty in administering standards that require people to expend effort and resources on behalf of others. In the constitutional cases, the entitlement to engage in offensive speech and conduct reflects fears about the power of the state to define orthodoxies of belief, and to suppress critical speech or the activities of unpopular minorities.[28] Interfering with the neo-Nazi march may suggest, by implication, that people are generally permitted to interfere with unpopular and odious speech, to the detriment of a political culture that thrives on dissent and the protection of unpopular minorities.

This pattern of procedural values conflicting with substantive moral considerations also informs the cases we have been considering. The statute of limitations is grounded in the right to have official decisions made pursuant to fair procedures. It responds to concerns that, over time, the recollection of witnesses may grow stale, and documents may be lost, so that there is an increasing likelihood of an erroneous adjudication of liabilities. Similarly, in the product liability case, the entitlement to conduct relatively unregulated discovery is based on the importance of uncovering all potentially probative evidence. Judges who micromanage the discovery process not only waste their own time, but potentially interfere with a line of inquiry that could lead to the discovery of admissible evidence. While aggressive lawyers can exploit unsupervised discovery to inflict psychic costs on their opponents, it still may be that, on balance, it is better to leave the process relatively unstructured and outside the control of judges.

The resolution of all of these cases appeals to the possibility of disagreement over moral issues as a way of understanding the role of the legal system and, derivatively, of lawyers. From that, it is a straightforward inference to specific duties on the part of lawyers. The reason lawyers should be neutral partisans, providing loyal client service notwithstanding their own moral objections, is that the law has prioritized competing moral considerations (both substantive and procedural) and done so in a way that is more respectful of competing viewpoints than the lawyer's unilateral decision-making process would be. The claim here is not that courts and legislatures are superior to individuals in moral deliberation, but that they are better at taking into account a wider range of positions on the matter.

This inference is somewhat more attenuated, however, where the disagreement in question pertains to matters of fact, not law. The most important source of disagreement in the product liability case is not whether the judge should grant a protective order, it is over whether the product in question was defective and whether the plaintiffs' conduct played a causal role in their injuries. Various procedural entitlements, such as the attorney–client privilege, the work-product doctrine, and rules of evidence forbidding inquiry into certain matters, cannot be justified as a way to enable citizens to live together despite intractable *moral* disagreement. It is hard to see how the argument for the legitimacy of the legal system underpins many of the practices of lawyers representing clients in litigation. After all, much private litigation involves law that is well settled, with the uncertainty pertaining to the facts. A great deal of civil litigation practice thus involves attempting to shape the factual record in ways that favor the interests of one's client, through artful investigation, discovery tactics, motions practice, and examinations of witnesses.

It is true that none of the political values supporting the legal system would go unserved if lawyers were not required to take a partisan stance with respect to the facts of disputes. Thus, the justification for duties of loyalty and partisanship in civil litigation is largely pragmatic, and contingent in the context of the adversary system.* An ethical principle, or a provision of the lawyer disciplinary rules, requiring lawyers to assert only genuine entitlements in litigation, and to correct for factual mistakes by their adversaries, would be susceptible to gaming. Imagine that lawyers were ethically obligated to disclose facts if the opposing lawyer failed to serve a properly focused interrogatory or request for production during discovery. A lawyer could sandbag her opponent by pretending to make a mistake, hoping to learn additional information that the opponent would otherwise not be inclined to produce. Moreover, this ethical obligation would unsettle the allocation of responsibility established by the discovery rules, which places the burden on the requesting party to draft a narrow targeted request. Similarly, strategic decisions may also reveal private information, so a lawyer may try to avoid committing to a particular theory of the case until late in the discovery process, when it is too late for the opponent to counteract effectively.

As long as the parties retain control over the claims and defenses they assert in the litigation, the game-theoretic structure of the interactions between opposing counsel require that the ethical obligations we impose on lawyers be

---

* Criminal defense is different, because of the importance of the defendant's procedural entitlements, such as the presumption of innocence, the requirement that the state prove its case beyond a reasonable doubt, the privilege against self-incrimination, and the privacy and dignitary interests protected by constitutional doctrines governing police investigations. The role of the criminal defense lawyer is more strongly partisan than any other lawyer's role, because in the American system at least, it is believed that this is the best way to protect these important constitutional rights.

sensitive to the possibility of strategic behavior. The rules of the adversary process, including rules of pleading, discovery rules, and rules governing motions practice, represent a balance among considerations of efficiency, fairness, respect for the privacy interests of litigants, and the desire to resolve disputes accurately on the merits. Thus, even though a given dispute may turn only on the facts, not the law, permitting or requiring litigators to take a partisan stance with respect to the facts of a dispute is still justified on the grounds that the legal system has established a framework for the orderly resolution of disagreement.

2.1.2 Rights, Not Power

Lawyers often talk as though the bounds of their role obligations are given by client interests rather than legal entitlements. In any principal–agent relationship, however, the agent's rights and obligations are derivative of those of the principal. Someone who retains a broker to sell property conveys legal authority to the broker to transfer only whatever title the owner has. Similarly, a lawyer's professional role is defined with reference to the rights and duties vested in the client by the law. Lawyers may lawfully do for their clients only what their clients lawfully may do. The lawyer's professional role also excludes any permission on the part of the lawyer to try to exploit "arbitrariness, whimsy, caprice, 'nullification,' and the like."[29] A lawyer may be able to get away with some action that goes beyond her client's entitlements, but this would lack significance as a lawful act, and thus not be something that can properly be said to be within the role of lawyer (as opposed to some other kind of advisor, like a mob *consigliere*).

This is such an obvious point that it is hard to understand why lawyers sometimes fail to appreciate it. But it may be the most pervasive feature of the normative framework of practicing lawyers that they proclaim an obligation to defend their clients' *interests* within the law, rather than vindicating their clients' legal entitlements. The difference between "interests within the law" and legal entitlements may seem like a semantic nicety with no theoretical significance, but in fact it reveals a vast gulf between attitudes of fidelity to the law and indifference to the law except as a potential source of sanctions to be avoided. Entitlements are what the law, properly interpreted, actually provides, while working "within the law" seems to suggest something broader and looser—equivalent, perhaps, to "whatever one can get away with." The question of whether the lawyer's obligation ought to be oriented toward client interests or entitlements may therefore be resolved in part by considering basic jurisprudential issues regarding the nature of the law.

Philosophers debate the nature of the concept of law for many reasons, but one of the most important is to distinguish legitimate exercises of authority from raw power. A gunman demanding your wallet is different from the government requiring you to pay taxes on your income, even though in both cases you have less money and you would be subject to unpleasant consequences for failing to comply with the demand. In the terms made prominent by H.L.A. Hart, you may feel *obliged* to give up your wallet to the gunman, but the state claims to create an *obligation* to pay taxes.[30] Hart's recognition of the distinction between an obligation and being obligated creates the possibility of a style of justification that constrains the exercise of power. In colloquial terms, the essence of the rule of law is the ability of the little guy to say to the big guy, "You can't do that to me."[31] The big guy can be the state, a large corporation, or a well-connected individual—anyone or anything that, in the absence of law, would be able to do basically whatever it wanted. A regime of laws means, however, that the little guy can actually stand up to the big guy. As the historian E. P. Thompson argued, rather than being merely an instrument used by the ruling class to secure its domination, the law also enables the subjects of power to challenge its legitimacy. "[A]s long as it remained possible, the ruled—if they could find a purse and a lawyer—would actually fight for their rights by means of law."[32] The whole point of the law is that it creates a standpoint from which it is possible to criticize the exercise of power. Power just *is*—those who possess it can do nasty things to other people. *Lawful* power, by contrast, incorporates the dimension of *ought*—those who are subjects of legitimate authority have a reason to do what the authority asks of them, apart from the fear of being subjected to unpleasant consequences.

Powerful actors sometimes incorrectly appeal directly to the prerogatives of power as a justification. President Andrew Jackson reportedly said, of a Supreme Court decision with which he disagreed, "Justice Marshall has made his decision; now let him enforce it."[33] Jackson subsequently evicted the Cherokee Indians from their land that had been guaranteed them by treaty, despite the decision of the Court upholding their right to remain on the land. Jackson is also alleged to have told his Attorney General in the course of an argument about the dis-establishment of the national bank: "You must find a law authorizing the act or I will appoint an Attorney General who will."[34] Similarly, Arkansas Governor Orval Faubus precipitated a dramatic confrontation (and a constitutional crisis) when he ordered state troops to surround Central High School in Little Rock, to prevent the enrollment of African-American children at the school, as ordered by the Supreme Court.[35] Most attempts by the big guys to deprive little guys of legal rights are not so openly defiant of the law. But they all do reflect what might be called the Holmesian bad man stance with respect to the law, after the notorious definition of law proposed by Holmes.[36] Holmes equated the content of law with predictions of how legal officials would decide cases, and dramatized this definition by imagining a "bad man" who cared only about avoiding the legal penalties that might be attached to his conduct.[37] On this account, the law does not impose limitations as such on citizens. Instead, knowledge of the law merely enables people—at least lawyers, who are experts in ascertaining the content of the law—to predict when the state will do something unpleasant, like lock people in jail or enforce a monetary judgment. Further, it is an implication of Holmes's position that the only reason people have for action, namely maximizing the satisfaction of their preferences, is antecedent to and independent of the law. This bad man approach, in which client interests and power are the only constraints on what lawyers may do, cannot function as a theory of law or of legal ethics because it eliminates the dimension of obligation, which is essential to justification.

To make this point clearer, it may be helpful to begin by setting up a caricatured version of legal realism as the position I am arguing against. On this simplistic legal realist definition of law, "the law says you must do such-and-such" is understood as being equivalent to some formulation like, "if you do not do such-and-such, the sheriff will seize your property or throw you in jail."[38] This definition of law has many flaws. Hart subjected it to devastating criticism in *The Concept of Law*, pointing out that identifying the law with predictions about how officials will decide cases (1) does not have the conceptual resources to explain the normativity of law, or why officials would feel any need to pay attention to legal norms, (2) offers no coherent explanation of how legal judgments can be mistaken, and (3) cannot account for the perspective of a deliberating official, who presumably could not act on the basis of a prediction of what she might decide.[39] Simple legal realism would even be unable to distinguish, conceptually, between bribing one's way out of a conviction and being acquitted of a crime.[40] It is no good to respond that the bribe is illegal, because if a crook manages to bribe or intimidate his way out of the bribery charges, then given the simple realist definition, the original bribery was not illegal. This kind of naive legal realism thus eliminates lawfulness as a conceptual category altogether.

Following Hart, my suggestion is that the distinction between a legal right or permission, on the one hand, and getting away with something, on the other, is a matter of regarding the law as intrinsically reason-giving—in Hart's terms, acknowledging legal obligations from the internal point of view.[41] If a person is concerned merely to act and to avoid sanctions, then she may adopt any attitude whatsoever toward the law, but she cannot claim to have acted lawfully without accepting the law as a reason for action as such. Legality as an explanatory or justificatory concept simply drops out of the picture unless one regards the law as intrinsically reason-giving. From a detached, external point of view, someone may say, "Gee, look at that—I managed to avoid being thrown in jail," but from that perspective it is incoherent to say, "I acted lawfully."

Hart was keenly concerned to avoid a definition of law that collapses legal obligation into the threat of sanctions. He vigorously attacked the Austin-Bentham command-sanction conception of law on many grounds, the most significant of which is that reducing all legal commands to threats backed by force fails to account for the possibility of accepting norms from the internal perspective. In addition to "bad" citizens, who obey the law only out of fear of punishment, there may also be "good" citizens, who believe that legal norms are weighty, or even conclusive of practical reasoning with respect to some matter.[42] The good citizen looks to the law for guidance, and regards legal directives as reasons for action, apart from any consideration of whether he will be punished for failing to comply with the law. The good citizen regards the law as a source of reasons, while the bad citizen's reasons are essentially unaltered by the law, except insofar as the law is another source of negative consequences like being deprived of liberty or property. The bad citizen regards the law as something like a force of nature, which can be studied and hopefully avoided, but which does not alter the citizen's practical reasoning by providing new reasons for action. The bad citizen is already concerned with avoiding harm, and the law presents merely another kind of harm to be avoided. The practical reasoning of the good citizen, by contrast, is altered in a different way by the law, because she regards it as a reason for action that did not exist independently. From her internal point of view, the good citizen accepts the law as creating new justified demands.

In Hart's jurisprudence, it is conceptually necessary that judges regard the rule of recognition from the internal point of view. Significantly, however, in his focus on the perspective judges must take toward the law, Hart says relatively little about the perspective citizens must take. Perhaps there can be a society in which there exist some good citizens and some bad ones, in the sense we have been using "good" and "bad," and the society can still be one that is law-governed, as long as officials adopt the internal point of view when pronouncing on legal norms. It is clear, on Hart's account, that citizens *may* take the internal point of view, but he does not argue that they *must*. Indeed, he admits that "private citizens ... may obey each 'for his part only' and from any motive whatever."[43] A society in which only judges accepted the law from the internal point of view might be "deplorably sheeplike,"[44] but there is no reason why a society composed predominantly of bad citizens or passive sheeplike subjects could not be said to have a legal system, as long as judges viewed the law from the internal perspective.

Hart's only explicit argument regarding citizens' attitudes in *The Concept of Law* is that command-sanction theories of law, as well as American legal realism (represented by Holmes, among others), are theoretically deficient in that they lack the conceptual resources to account for the possibility of citizens taking the internal point of view.[45] It may be the case, however, that Hart stopped short of where his theory would logically end up, and that good reasons exist to require citizens to regard the law from the internal point of view, at least insofar as they seek to act lawfully.[46] That reason is, roughly, that it would be incoherent to claim to act legitimately when one exploits the legal system, by "simultaneously living within its shelter and breaking its restrictions."[47]

Modestly extending Hart's position, I believe that the perspective of the good citizen is constitutive of genuine legal compliance. The argument trades on what is necessarily involved in claiming that one is acting lawfully. Anyone who claims to care about having her actions described as lawful, as opposed to "something I got away with," is thereby committed to viewing the law as creating reasons for actions as such. The linchpin of this expressivist argument is the purpose for which a citizen engages with the law. She may be interested only in describing and predicting certain patterns of behavior among fellow citizens, in which case it is perfectly appropriate to take an external perspective on the law. If she is interested in acting lawfully, however, her practical reasoning necessarily proceeds from the internal perspective. The internal perspective is mandated by the conjunction of *action*, as opposed to observation (for which an external perspective would be adequate) and the evaluation that an action is *lawful*, as opposed to merely something that one can get away with.[48] If this relationship holds, then acting under law while regarding the law from an external point of view would be on a par, normatively speaking, with robbing a bank and successfully asserting an alibi defense, or bribing a prosecutor to drop charges. The actor would have managed to avoid sanctions, but the evaluation of the action would be that it was wrong from the standpoint of a relevant normative framework, that of legality.

The appeal to the discourse of legality is natural when one wishes to assert not only that one wants something, or has the power to obtain it, but that it is *right* that one have it. For something to be a legal right, it must be an aspect of a legal system, which is necessarily connected with the interests and values of a society, not the individual.[49] Legality is the normative domain in which citizens seek to transform brute demands into assertions of rights.[50] This transformation necessarily commits one to a certain pattern of explanation and justification. This is the case for participants in any practice, whether players in a game, initiates of a religious vocation, political officials, or in this case citizens who seek the ascription of lawfulness for their actions.[51] Participating in social practices entails accepting the authority of internal practice-dependent regulative standards as guides to behavior, and accepting the legitimacy of criticism based on those standards. These regulative standards are not arbitrary, but have their origin in some ultimate state of affairs or value that is the aim of the social practice of which they a part. The regulative standards of the practice has authority for a participant because of the participant's voluntary act of agreeing to participate in the practice.[52] It would be a conceptual error for participants to regard the norms of a practice from a detached quasi-scientific perspective, because to participate in a practice means to aim at the end for which the practice is constituted, and doing this requires conformity to the internal regulative standards of the practice. Thus, the "bad man" perspective on any practice is ruled out by the act of avowing that one is a participant, rather than an observer.[53]

In addition, the picture of rational actors maximizing their utility and viewing the law as only a source of sanctions runs counter to empirical evidence. Studies have shown that people are likely to comply with legal prohibitions that do not reference *malum in se* acts if they believe the authority they are dealing with has the legitimate right to regulate their behavior.[54] Another puzzle for rational choice accounts of compliance is the very fact of observed compliance. If individuals and organizations were really rational actors, it would seem that "the regulatory legal environment may exert its largest effects not by motivating compliance, but rather by motivating evasion."[55] Yet, there is a great deal of evidence that citizens believe themselves to be obligated to comply with the law, and make a good faith effort to determine what the law requires (even while they may reinterpret it), rather than simply trying to evade it.[56] Ironically, it is *lawyers* who tend to exhibit less concern for the law as such. For example, lawyers interviewed as part of an American Bar Association study of litigation ethics "exhibited little sense of moral duty to the well-being of the larger legal system," and "seemed to perceive little chance that their pragmatic gaming would undercut the administration of justice."[57] The real Holmesian bad men turn out not to be ordinary citizens, as Holmes thought, but the professionals entrusted with the duty of maintaining the legal system in good working order.

Of course, the Holmesian bad man attitude is not always manifested as clearly as President Jackson defying Justice Marshall to enforce his order. It tends to show up, instead, in the guise of more sophisticated techniques of evasion, such as obfuscating questionable transactions with confusing disclosures, which was the strategy followed by crooked managers at Enron; relying on the "audit lottery" to avoid having tax filing positions tested by the IRS or using techniques like netting gains and losses in partnerships to avoid revealing the extent of losses to the IRS; inserting invalid provisions or extremely one-sided (and thus unlikely to be enforced) terms into standard-form contracts, knowing that many consumers will not challenge them in litigation; and resisting enforcement actions with such vigor that government officials are unable to sanction violations.[58] Even though these techniques may not appear openly contemptuous of the law, they stand on no better ethical foundation than Jackson's defiance. There is no way to give a justification of any of these techniques in terms of the client's legal entitlements. Indeed, the point of many of them is to avoid having the client's legal entitlements verified by an impartial decision-maker. The only justification that could be offered for these various entitlement-avoiding techniques would be based solely on client interests and, as we have seen, client interests alone must be distinguished from claims of legal right.*

This is not to suggest that ascertaining the content and scope of client entitlements is a straightforward matter. The simplest or clearest legal rule can often be ambiguous. Thus, one cannot consider the lawyer's duties of loyalty and partisanship without facing the jurisprudential problem of legal determinacy and the ethical issues surrounding the manipulation of law by lawyers. One feature of many of the recent legal ethics scandals, at least in the United States, is the apparent view of the lawyers involved that the law can be made to mean pretty much whatever the client wants it to mean. If that is true, the problem may not be so much that lawyers are manipulating the law, but that there is no law to manipulate. To put it less hyperbolically, the law on any given point may bear a range of good-faith interpretations, so that one lawyer would be justified in concluding that it is permissible for the client to do something, while another would be equally justified in concluding that the law prohibits the same action.

The following section is a survey of some of these issues, which seeks to establish two basic points. First, there is distinction between a legal entitlement

---

* This sort of reasoning is not just a hypothetical possibility, as revealed by investigations into some high-profile scandals. For example, a senior tax advisor at the accounting firm KPMG argued in an internal e-mail message that the firm should not comply with IRS requirements that required the registration of certain tax shelters, because the penalties for noncompliance with the registration requirements were much less than the potential profits that could be earned from marketing the shelters. The partner included an explicit cost-benefit calculation showing that the maximum penalty for noncompliance would be $14,000 per $100,000 of fees earned by the firm. See United States Senate, Permanent Subcommittee on Investigations, Committee on Governmental Affairs, "U.S. Tax Shelter Industry: The Role of Accountants, Lawyers, and Financial Professionals" (2003), pp. 13, 28.

and something else — either a strained interpretation or the result of some kind of institutional malfunction. For any given area of law, there is a core area of agreement in interpretive judgments, which represents an ideal synthesis of the applicable materials, such as cases, statutes, and principles of interpretation. There need not be only one best interpretation, but any interpreter would recognize, as an ideal, that "[t]he objective of legal reasoning [is] to find the view of the law that best reconciles the relevant body of text, principle, and precedent."[59] The second point is that, if a lawyer intends to rely on something other than the best interpretation that can be constructed from the applicable body of legal materials, she must be prepared to offer a justification for deviating from the ideal. That justification is given, in many cases, by the institutional context. Lawyers representing clients in litigation, for example, can rely on less well-supported interpretations — that is, those farther from the core — because there are other institutional actors, including opposing counsel, the trial judge, and appellate courts, that work together to ensure that bogus legal interpretations do not become entrenched. It is a mistake, however, to assume that the same interpretive freedom that applies in litigation is an aspect of the role of lawyers acting as counselors or transactional planners.

2.2   Legal Ethics as Interpretation

2.2.1   *Loophole Lawyering*

Many legal ethics problems, which seem to present a conflict between legal entitlements and moral values, actually raise legal-interpretive questions. Once the interpretive issue is resolved, the moral issue dissolves. In general, this can be called the problem of "loopholes" in the law. The idea of exploiting loopholes is a staple of the popular criticism of lawyers, but it is important to be careful in defining these and other cognate terms. Members of the public sometimes complain about criminal defense lawyers "getting the defendant off on a technicality," where the reason for the acquittal, or dismissal of charges, was to remedy the violation of a constitutional right held by the defendant. The problem perceived by observers is that the result of the proceeding did not track the substantive guilt or innocence of the defendant — in other words, whether he actually did the act of which he was accused. But the purpose of a trial is not only to ascertain guilt or innocence, but to do so within a framework of procedural entitlements that are designed to safeguard important values such as the privacy and dignity of all citizens, and to protect against abuse of state power. These procedural entitlements are no less part of the law, and no less a part of the legal justice of the matter, than the determination of factual guilt or innocence. While one might criticize the existence or content of a particular procedural entitlement, perhaps on the grounds that it ties the hands of law enforcement personnel or is not necessary to protect values like privacy or dignity, the possibility that the entitlement is ill-considered does not make it a loophole.

Similarly, procedural entitlements are available to parties in civil litigation which may have the effect of defeating the resolution of issues related to the substantive entitlements of the parties. Again, there are good reasons for the legal system to recognize certain procedural entitlements. The statute of limitations, for example, serves the dual purpose of ensuring that trials are not conducted on the basis of stale evidence and also of permitting citizens to form stable expectations that, at some point, their right to something will not be challenged. Legal ethics scholars sometimes talk about the "merits" of a case, and when that term is used, it is important to query whether merits includes the correct resolution of interpretive questions related to procedural entitlements. The lawyer in a case like the statute of limitations hypothetical may take an action that vindicates her client's procedural entitlement, but defeats resolution of the substantive merits of the opponent's position. This is consistent with the lawyer's obligation of fidelity to law, because the legal system includes both substantive and procedural entitlements, and because the lawyer has a legal duty, as an agent of her client, to assert her client's legal entitlements, whether substantive or procedural.

A much subtler kind of loophole is created where the client wants the lawyer to do something in reliance on an interpretation that the governing legal texts do not support. Here is an extended example, modified slightly from a real but unpublished case:

Louis is an outside lawyer for Matewan Mines, which for many decades has operated a coal mine in West Virginia.[60] Matewan is required to pay benefits under a federal statute to particular classes of miners who had been employed by Matewan and who have become totally disabled due to pneumoconiosis, commonly known as "black lung disease." As the preamble to the statute observes, black lung disease is a serious occupational health hazard for coal miners, and few states provide disability benefits:

> It is therefore the purpose of this [statute] ... to ensure that ... adequate benefits are provided to coal miners and their dependents in the event of their death or total disability due to [black lung disease].[61]

For the companies, black lung claims are expensive, and a significant administrative headache, and Matewan wishes to avoid paying them whenever possible. Lately, Matewan has been facing increased competition from foreign mining companies, who are not required to pay benefits to miners suffering from black lung disease; thus, its profits have been gradually dwindling relative to foreign competitors, leading to some consternation among shareholders. The board of Matewan is worried that if its profits decline any further, the company may be taken over by a multinational conglomerate, possibly leading to a loss of jobs in the area.

Cole Minor was employed by Matewan for all of his working life. Thus, the injury "arose out of the course of his employment" as required by the statute. Last year he had a chest X-ray that revealed he was suffering from black lung disease and had a lesion on his lung that measured 1.5 cm. Under the governing statute and regulations, the presence of the 1.5-cm lesion created a legal presumption that Cole was "totally disabled" and therefore eligible for benefits. Matewan therefore began paying benefits of $760 per month to Cole. Cole's doctor was concerned that the disease might spread rapidly, so she put Cole on the list for a lung transplant. Two months ago, Cole was approved for a transplant and successfully underwent lung transplantation surgery. His rapid recovery from the surgery was due in part to powerful (and expensive) drugs used by his treating physicians to prevent Cole's body from rejecting the new lung.

Upon learning of the operation, a representative of Matewan had a creative idea. He called Louis's law firm, which represents the company, and demanded that the lawyers file a motion to terminate Cole's benefits, on the ground that his disability had ended. Without the 1.5-cm lesion, the client representative reasoned, Cole would not be permitted to take advantage of the statutory presumption of disability, and would be required to establish disability through a lengthy process involving several medical examinations and hearings before an Administrative Law Judge. In the meantime, the company would save the cost of paying the black lung benefits. Of course, in the meantime Cole could die if he were unable to obtain the anti-rejection drugs because his benefits had been terminated. The client representative was determined to terminate benefits. "Look, mining is a dangerous occupation," he said. "We take reasonable precautions, but we're not obligated to eliminate all risks. We're also not obligated to pay benefits to every person who's ever worked for us. Cole has recovered—he's not disabled—just look at the statute." Louis responded that the most reasonable interpretation of the statute and regulations is that the 1.5-cm lesion is simply one way, among many, of establishing total disability. It would not follow, Louis argued, that the absence of the lesion established the absence of disability. Upon questioning by the client representative, however, Louis conceded that the motion might be granted. "It's a pretty weak legal argument," Louis said, "but probably not utterly lacking in any plausibility. The Administrative Law Judges around here are pretty sympathetic to the mining companies, and might grant the motion as long as there's some non-frivolous ground."

The argument that the removal of the 1.5-cm lesion reverses the presumption of disability may pass the proverbial straight-face test, but most reasonable lawyers would reject it as the best (or even a pretty solid) interpretation of the statute and regulations. The law can be made to say that the miner is not disabled, but it takes some twisting and manipulation to make it say that. The ethical problem this raises can be stated plainly: Why shouldn't lawyers be allowed to engage in this sort of creative interpretation? Isn't that what lawyers do? It is certainly a long-standing feature of the folklore about lawyers that they can make the law fit their clients' interests. King Louis XII of France allegedly observed that, "Lawyers use the law as shoemakers use leather; rubbing it, pressing it, stretching it with their teeth, all to the end of making it fit their purposes."[62] The problem identified by the king is that the law as actually interpreted and applied by lawyers has come apart from the law as it *should* be interpreted and applied.[63] As noted at the beginning of this chapter, the principal ethical obligation of lawyers is to advance their clients' lawful interests—their entitlements. The legal entitlements of clients constrain what they may do, and since lawyers are agents of clients, a client's entitlements likewise constrain the actions her lawyer permissibly may take.

Using legal entitlements as the constraint on client and lawyer behavior presupposes that there is at least some moderate determinacy in the law—that is, some way of differentiating between a genuine legal entitlement and a sham of some sort. This raises a jurisprudential issue, namely how to define the yardstick against which a legal interpretation is measured so that an interpretation may be evaluated as a windfall or a loophole, and a lawyer's application of the law may be criticized as abusive, manipulative, or otherwise a violation of the lawyer's duty of fidelity to the law. Chapter 6 will take up the question of *how* it is possible that the law can be moderately determinate. For now, however, we need to work with the idea of *moderate*, as opposed to complete, determinacy. The law does not lend itself to binary judgments. While a person cannot be sort of pregnant, it is possible for a legal interpretation to be sort of well supported. Lawyers are accustomed to thinking in this way, even if they do not always communicate their doubts to clients, so that the conclusion of legal research and analysis might be, "I'm pretty sure you can do that," or "You can give it a shot, but I expect it won't work."

This is not to say that the law is radically indeterminate.[64] Some interpretations of law that might be offered by a judge or lawyer are so utterly lacking in plausibility that they are deemed frivolous. This strikes me as simply a fact about the way lawyers make and evaluate legal arguments—some interpretations of the law just won't do, no matter how they appear to fit with a formalistic reading of the applicable legal texts. No competent observer of the legal system would deny these conclusions, even though there may be some superficial plausibility to the arguments. If it is true that some interpretations of law are utterly lacking in plausibility, then a theory of legal interpretation must account for that fact, rather than becoming preoccupied with the abstract question of how language can ever constrain judgment.[65] It is the case, however, that relevant legal sources do, to some extent, *underdetermine* interpretive judgments.[66] If the law was perfectly determinate, there would be no plausibility dimension to interpretive judgments, only right or wrong answers. Underdetermination by law means there is a range of legally acceptable outcomes which is narrower than the domain of all possible outcomes, but it does not mean unique solutions exist to questions requiring the interpretation of law.[67]

In addition to underdetermination by authoritative legal sources, cases also abound in which lawyers may be able to get away with a certain amount of trickery or exploitation of the rules merely because of incompetence or lack of enforcement resources on the part of judges and others who monitor the actions of lawyers. The black lung hypothetical was designed to suggest both the possibility of a loophole in the governing regulations and incompetence by the administrative law judge who considered the motion to terminate benefits. The first possibility, involving legal uncertainty, is an interesting and difficult problem for lawyers. The second is simply abusive. Being able to hoodwink a lazy or inept judge into accepting a bogus interpretation of law does not make the position any less bogus. If it is possible to conclude, for example, that the black lung benefits statute and regulations do create an entitlement to benefits, then the lawyer's obligation of loyalty and partisanship permits the lawyer for the mining company to go no farther than the company's entitlement permits. In this case, the correlative entitlement of the mining company is to pay no more than the benefits provided for in the statute and regulations, but it is not to terminate benefits entirely, merely because an incompetent judge can be made to accept a spurious argument.

It should be noted that there is a dynamic element to legal interpretation.[68] A position that may have been bogus at one time, which could only have been adopted by a judge who was not the brightest star in the judicial firmament, may nevertheless subsequently become "the law" for the purposes of the lawyer's obligation of fidelity to law. It is an implication of the legal positivism defended here that the validity and content of law is a matter of its social sources, not its wisdom, efficiency, or justice. A judge who makes a stupid decision nevertheless creates law, and subsequent interpreters, including lawyers advising clients on their entitlements, are no less bound to respect that law because it is stupid. Conversely, a better interpretation of the law may be only inchoate at time t_1, and may lack sufficient support in the relevant social sources until there has been some evolution toward a new position at time t_2. An example familiar to American lawyers is the rejection of the privity of contract requirement as an element of the tort liability of product manufacturers. Judge Cardozo's *MacPherson* decision for the New York Court of Appeals is arguably best understood not as a radical change in the law, but an elaboration and distillation of several lines of doctrinal change that had been leading to the rule announced by Cardozo. At some point, t_n, the relevant social sources warranted Judge Cardozo's decision. It may be possible to debate whether t_n had arrived at the time *MacPherson* was decided.[69] The important point is that this is exactly the debate we should be having. The question lawyers and judges should care about is whether a judgment at some point in time is warranted by existing law or by a good-faith argument for its extension, modification, or reversal. The important point is that this is a legal interpretive argument, not an ethical one in ordinary moral terms.

The ethical principle for lawyers defended here is that loyalty to clients *within the law* requires lawyers to interpret the law, assert positions, plan transactions, and advise clients on the basis of reasons that are internal to the law. Relying on extra-legal considerations like the justice or efficiency of a law is not permitted. While the law changes and evolves, and may do so in response to concerns about its justice, wisdom, and the like, fidelity to law requires lawyers to aim at recovering the best understanding of the existing law, and to act on that basis. However, it is also important to emphasize that obligations to clients must be understood in context. A lawyer may be constrained to act only on the basis of her best judgment about how the law should be interpreted, if the lawyer is acting in an advisory capacity. In litigation, by contrast, a lawyer may have greater freedom to rely on interpretations that are not as well supported. This freedom is not unlimited, even in litigation, and in some cases a lawyer may be required to exercise interpretive judgment and conclude there is no legal entitlement that can be asserted with a sufficient degree of plausibility. In that case, the lawyer would be ethically prohibited from taking that position in litigation. In any event, the analysis of an act as permissible or impermissible turns on whether one could make a good-faith argument that the lawyer is asserting an entitlement of her client, either as a position in litigation or as the basis for taking some action under a claim of legal right.

2.2.2 Mistakes, Institutional Malfunctions, and Windfalls

Many problems in legal ethics involve some kind of breakdown in the normal functioning of the legal system, which creates an opportunity for exploitation in a way that does not seem to track what would be the allocation of client entitlements in a well-functioning system. Consider the famous case of *Spaulding v. Zimmerman*.[70] Simplifying the facts somewhat, Spaulding and Zimmerman were involved in a car accident. Spaulding filed a lawsuit against Zimmerman, alleging that Zimmerman was negligent and this negligence was the cause of Spaulding's injuries. As part of the post-accident litigation, Zimmerman's lawyer required Spaulding to submit to an independent medical examination at which a doctor hired by Zimmerman examined Spaulding to make sure he was not exaggerating his injuries. This doctor diagnosed an aortic aneurysm—a dilation and weakening of a major blood vessel, which might rupture if not repaired surgically—of traumatic origin, which meant it very likely resulted from the car accident. Zimmerman's lawyer immediately realized the significance of this information. Spaulding's own physician who treated him after the accident had missed the aneurysm, and Spaulding's lawyer was therefore preparing the case for trial or a negotiated settlement on the assumption that his damages were relatively modest.

Inexplicably, Spaulding's lawyer failed to request a copy of the medical examination report from Zimmerman's lawyer, as he was entitled to do under the civil discovery rules.[71] This failure is what sets up the ethical dilemma for Zimmerman's lawyer. Disclosing the aneurysm would eliminate the lurking risk of Spaulding's death, but would drive up Zimmerman's damages, perhaps over the limits of his liability insurance policy. Zimmerman's lawyer would have been required to turn over the medical examination report in response to a request from Spaulding's lawyer, but in the absence of that request, Zimmerman's lawyer would be required by the duty of confidentiality to keep the report secret unless Zimmerman himself permitted it to be disclosed.[72]

Of course, this is a wrenching ethical dilemma for Zimmerman's lawyer, but notice how the whole problem hinges on two professional mistakes— Spaulding's treating physician missing the aneurysm and Spaulding's lawyer forgetting to request a copy of the medical examination report. If either of these mistakes had not been made, the litigation would have been conducted with knowledge of the full extent of Spaulding's injuries, and Zimmerman would have had to pay the greater damages to which Spaulding was legally entitled. This case is therefore not representative of an interesting and deep conflict between legal entitlements and ordinary moral responsibilities. Mistakes are not uninteresting on their own, but it is difficult to generalize from them to conclusions about the whole of legal ethics. The most that can be said of a general nature about *Spaulding* is that it illustrates the potential for complex systems to occasionally malfunction, and the obvious point that such breakdowns can result in the arbitrary allocation of good and bad consequences. Because these benefits and burdens of institutional malfunctions are random, with respect to the reasons underlying the institutional structure, I refer to would-be entitlements such as Zimmerman's ability to withhold information about the aneurysm as legal *windfalls*.

Windfall cases are a recurring pattern in legal ethics.[73] Most, like *Spaulding*, involve situations in which the client's interest lines up with an apparent legal entitlement, which, upon closer examination, arguably turns out not to be a legal entitlement at all, but is merely the product of some kind of accident or institutional malfunction. One should not be too quick to conclude, however, that mistakes vitiate legal entitlements in all cases. In *Spaulding*, the defendant would have a right, under agency law and the professional disciplinary rules, to insist that the lawyer not disclose confidential information. Confidentiality in this case is a genuine legal entitlement. It is true that the defendant's right to confidentiality is limited by procedural rules that provide for disclosure of information that would otherwise be confidential. Like many rules of procedure, the rule governing discovery of medical examination reports requires some action by opposing counsel to trigger that party's entitlement. William Simon has forcefully argued, regarding the lawyer's duty of confidentiality, that the client has a legitimate interest only in the measure of confidentiality that the law actually provides for. It is no betrayal of the client for the lawyer to disclose information in which the client never had a legally protected confidentiality interest, such as communications with the lawyer in furtherance of a crime or fraud.[74] Similarly, in *Spaulding*, one might argue that Zimmerman had no reasonable *ex ante* expectation that his lawyer would not have to disclose the report from Spaulding's independent medical examination.

In this case, the negligent failure of the plaintiff's lawyer to request the medical examination report is importantly different from the case of a client consulting a lawyer for the purpose of committing a crime or fraud. Technically speaking, the rules governing confidentiality give the lawyer discretion to disclose information to prevent, rectify, or mitigate certain client frauds.[75]

More conceptually, the legal system includes meta-principles such as default rules about which parties bear the risk of mistakes by other institutional actors. There are accordingly reasons internal to the legal system—not ordinary moral reasons—to believe that Zimmerman's lawyer is not required to take corrective action in response to the plaintiff's lawyer's failure to request the medical examination report. Many procedural entitlements, such as the plaintiff's right to see a copy of the medical examination report, are not self-executing, but require action by the lawyer for the party claiming that entitlement. The reason for requiring this action is that it may or may not be in the party's best interests to assert the entitlement. Lawyers have discretion to refuse to make use of procedural entitlements, and it would be asking too much of opposing counsel to discern whether the non-assertion of a right is a mistake or a tactical judgment made by the lawyer.

There may be good reasons, relating to the effective functioning of dispute-resolution procedures, to refrain from imposing ethical obligations on lawyers not to take advantage of mistakes by opposing counsel. For example, the content of ethical obligations must be sensitive to the possibility of strategic behavior by lawyers. Something that may look on its face like a mistake may actually have been done for tactical reasons.[76] While one should not make too much of this concern—sometimes mistakes are just mistakes—in a system that allows a great deal of control by the lawyers over the means by which their clients' objectives are accomplished, there must be some latitude for lawyers to take their opponents' actions at face value, and not attempt to discern whether they are the result of a mistake or whether the opposing lawyer had some good reason for the action.

One could waffle back and forth indefinitely on *Spaulding*; it is a hard case, which is why it has become a classic in legal ethics. In fidelity-to-law terms, *Spaulding* is hard because it involves the conflict between two legal entitlements. The plaintiff had a genuine entitlement to see a copy of the medical report and the defendant had a genuine entitlement to insist that his lawyer keep confidential all information relating to the representation unless he gave informed consent to disclosure or an exception to the duty applied. In my judgment, the plaintiff's lawyer's mistake does not vitiate the plaintiff's entitlement to obtain a copy of the report. At the same time, however, the defendant's lawyer must respect his client's entitlement to keep the report confidential unless the client consents to disclosure.

The parties' legal entitlements are in equipoise, which suggests a couple of possible responses. First, the defendant's lawyer may wish to be more aggressive than would otherwise be permitted in trying to persuade his client to give informed consent to disclosing the report. Zimmerman's lawyer could emphasize the terrible outcome if Spaulding's aneurysm were not treated, and seek to persuade Zimmerman that the only right thing to do, morally speaking, is to disclose the report. Second, Zimmerman's lawyer may decide to disclose even without informed consent, and take his lumps if Zimmerman seeks sanctions against the lawyer. In effect, this approach would shift responsibility to an official adjudicative body to resolve the conflict between the parties' entitlements. There would be a risk for Zimmerman's lawyer, of course, but it may be one worth bearing considering the potential cost to Spaulding. For my own part, I find the possibility of non-disclosure intolerable for moral reasons, but if Zimmerman refuses to give informed consent to disclosure, the best course of action would be for his lawyer to disclose anyway and run the risk of professional discipline. A six-month license suspension for disclosing client confidences would be a serious harm to Zimmerman's lawyer,[77] but it is one that he may be morally obligated to incur in order to avoid the harm to Spaulding.

The product liability hypothetical from chapter 1 may also involve a windfall if the judge in the case had been careless or lazy. The ethical problem in the hypothetical is that the lawyers representing the manufacturer were able to ask harassing questions of the plaintiffs because the judge supervising the litigation failed to enter a protective order forbidding the questioning, as the lawyers for the plaintiffs had requested. It is true that discovery is generally allowed into matters that are relevant to the claims or defenses of any party, but a trial judge may, for good cause, restrict discovery into relevant matters.[78] One of the grounds recognized in the rules of civil procedure for restricting discovery is to protect a party from "annoyance, embarrassment, oppression, or undue burden,"[79] which certainly seems to cover the humiliating questions asked by defense counsel. However, the trial court *may* grant this relief if sought; the judge is not obligated to enter a protective order. Thus, while the defendant does not have an *ex ante* legal entitlement to ask the questions, the plaintiff does not have an *ex ante* legal entitlement to avoid the questioning. The legal permissibility of the questioning is a matter committed to the discretion of the trial judge, so the assignment of entitlements is conditional on the trial court's decision. Once the judge ruled on the plaintiff's motion for a protective order, the defendants did have a genuine legal entitlement to question the plaintiffs about their sexual history.

To this it might be responded that the judge made a mistake by not granting the protective order, and this mistake creates the windfall. If the judge might reasonably have concluded that the questioning should be allowed—that is, it was within his discretion to rule in this way and not to grant the protective order—then the defendant had an entitlement to ask the "dirty questions." On the other hand, the judge might have denied the plaintiffs' motion for a protective order out of laziness or disinclination to supervise the depositions closely, in which case the would-be entitlement would be aptly characterized as a windfall. The procedural virtue of finality requires that judicial decisions be accepted at face value. This means lawyers should not be empowered or required to second-guess the reasons for a judicial decision, except through formal channels such as a motion for reconsideration or an appeal. If the judge had discretion to grant or deny the plaintiffs' motion for a protective order and was permitted to consider a wide variety of reasons for and against the motion (including the simple disinclination to get involved in micro-managing discovery disputes), then the decision disposes of the permissibility of asking the questions. In that case, the decision would not be a windfall at all, but a genuine entitlement.

The fact that the trial judge has discretion to rule one way or the other on the motion means only that the judge's decision is less likely to be reversed on appeal; it does not necessarily mean the defense lawyers had no ethical obligation to make a judgment about the permissibility of asking the dirty questions.[80] In the law, there can be a right without a remedy. In this case, the plaintiffs may have a legal right not to be subjected to gratuitously humiliating questioning even though they may not have an effective remedy if the trial court rules against them on the motion for a protective order. Lawyers make these sorts of judgments all the time. If a hypothetical reasonable impartial lawyer considering the case would conclude that there is no basis for asking the questions, then the defense lawyers have done something unethical by engaging in the questioning, even if the trial court does not enter a protective order.

We can imagine a variation on the product liability hypothetical in which the distinction between a genuine entitlement and a windfall is clearer from the lawyer's *ex ante* point of view.[81] Suppose the parties had litigated the plaintiffs' motion for a protective order and the trial court had ruled that there were thirty questions that could be asked of the plaintiffs, pertaining to their sexual history. These questions, and no more, would be deemed reasonably calculated to lead to the discovery of admissible evidence. Now suppose that the defendant's medical expert, after reviewing the questions, informed the defendant's lawyer that it was possible to ask the questions in a certain order, so that the first five questions would do most of the work of sorting out plaintiffs against whom a plausible defense could be asserted. If a particular deponent answered "no" to the first five questions, the remaining twenty-five would not lead to the discovery of evidence that would bear on the resolution of that particular case. In a few other cases, the remaining twenty-five questions would be useful, according to the expert, but not in cases with negative answers to the first five. (We can further assume that the remaining twenty-five questions are the really humiliating ones, dealing with specifics of high-risk sexual practices.)

Notice how this variation on the problem removes the issue of the defense lawyers' intent, which could otherwise be used as an evasion of the ethical problem. On the original version, the lawyers could make a kind of argument from double effect (i.e., claiming that the humiliation of the plaintiffs was merely collateral damage, and they were actually intending to discover admissible evidence). On the thirty-questions variation, with respect to the plaintiffs who answered no to the first five questions, there is no basis for claiming that the aim of the lawyer was not to humiliate the women. The entitlement created by the trial court's order is only an apparent entitlement in the cases with negative answers to the first five questions. Furthermore, because there is no possibility of gaming the judge's order (that is, lawyers for the plaintiffs cannot sandbag the defendant's lawyers if the defendant's lawyers are permitted to ask the first five questions in each deposition), there is no *ethical* reason to permit the defendant's lawyers to ask the twenty-five humiliating questions in most cases. A lawyer asking the twenty-five humiliating questions, in a case in which the defendant's own expert said the information would be irrelevant, could not claim to be doing anything other than exploiting an opportunity, created by the generality of the trial court's order, to inflict gratuitous humiliation on these women.

In all of these cases, there may be some room for disagreement at the margins. We can play around with the hypotheticals to create more or less uncertainty, and to make the interpretive judgments by lawyers more difficult. The important point, however, is that the ethical permissibility of actions taken by lawyers—a line of questioning pursued at a deposition, the decision to file a motion as part of a litigation strategy, and so on—is a function of whether the client has a legal entitlement to take that action. This is just as true in litigation as in counseling and transactional representation. The remainder of this section will consider the contextualization of lawyers' duties, which may create *greater* ethical obligations on lawyers representing clients in non-litigated matters. One should not conclude from this, however, that anything goes for litigators. When the client's entitlements run out, the lawyer's permission to act is similarly limited.

2.2.3   A Note on "Zealous" Representation

Lawyers quite properly understand themselves as having demanding obligations of client service, including following their clients' instructions, keeping confidences, and delivering legal services in a competent and diligent manner. Curiously, American lawyers at least tend to include in their normative self-understanding an obligations to provide "zealous" representation, which gives competence an oddly affective dimension. The term "zealous" appeared in the ABA's Model Code of Professional Responsibility,[82] which has since been superseded in virtually every U.S. jurisdiction by the Model Rules. The modifier "zealous" does not appear in any of the legally enforceable obligations of the current Model Rules, although the Preamble to the Rules does continue to recognize that "[a]s advocate, a lawyer zealously asserts the client's position under the rules of the adversary system."[83] Nevertheless, if one were to ask practicing lawyers to justify actions in the hypothetical cases that appear to violate ordinary moral obligations (i.e., pleading the statute of limitations, filing the motion to terminate benefits, or aggressively questioning the plaintiffs about their sexual practices), the argument would more often than not make reference to the duty of zealous advocacy.[84]

The enduring popularity of this notion in the thinking of lawyers is noteworthy, because it seems to prescribe an affective state, as opposed to an action, and as a general rule lawyers do not think of legal obligations in terms of emotions and attitudes.[85] It would be an unusual lawyer who advised a client that the duty of reasonable care in tort law required the client to feel a sentiment of concern for third parties; the lawyer's advice would rather be that the client had to take such-and-such a precaution, and that would be the end of the matter. My hunch is that lawyers are attracted to the idea of zealous advocacy because it simplifies their normative universe to a considerable extent, by resolving ethical dilemmas in favor of the client's interests. It only does so, however, by begging all of the important questions about how the obligation of zealous representation is to be weighted against the obligation to respect the law, which is also a feature of the lawyer's role.

It would be an unqualified intellectual advance if the expression "zealous advocacy" disappeared forever from legal ethics. Its overuse seems to encourage two significant conceptual mistakes. First, lawyers tend to forget the second half of their little mantra. The ABA Code said that lawyers should represent their clients zealously *within the bounds of the law*. As the Restatement provides, the lawyer's basic duty is to "proceed in a manner reasonably calculated to advance a client's lawful objectives, as defined by the client after consultation."[86] The reference to the client's *lawful* objectives shows that the client's legal entitlements, not the client's autonomy, moral commitments, or the lawyer's own moral projects, are the yardstick against which the lawyer's duties should be measured. In other words, the Model Code underscores the agency-law position taken here, which is that the lawyer's basic duty as an agent for her client is to act competently and diligently on behalf of the client, but only to the extent that the client's interests are recognized as legal entitlements. Even in litigation contexts the lawyer's obligation is to pursue the client's legal entitlements by lawful means, not to be unboundedly zealous. The law governing lawyers in litigation recognizes numerous limitations on zealous representation, including the prohibition on presenting frivolous legal arguments in federal and state rules of civil procedure,[87] and duties of candor to the tribunal in the lawyer disciplinary rules.[88] Although in some areas of practice, such as the representation of indigent criminal defendants by grossly overworked public defenders, lawyers may be rightly accused of being insufficiently zealous,[89] by far the more pressing problem for legal ethics is the lack of respect by lawyers for the bounds of the law, defined in any sensible way.

As Tim Dare has argued, given the existence of a complex, somewhat esoteric system of laws, it makes sense to create an occupational group for the purpose of enabling citizens to avail themselves of whatever rights are granted under the law.[90] Thus, lawyers have an obligation of "mere zeal" to assist their clients in asserting and planning their affairs around these legal rights. This obligation can be justified in the same way that the legal system as a whole is justified, on functional grounds, as enabling people to cooperate despite the diversity of views about what we should do as a community.[91] However, lawyers seem to think that if mere zeal is justified, then they may also be permitted or required to exercise "hyper zeal," which is the pursuit of every advantage that can be obtained for the client by legal means.[92] Lawyers are often criticized for excesses of zeal, but it is important to bear in mind that much of this conduct is prohibited by the law governing lawyers. For example, lawyers may attempt to discredit the testimony of a truthful witness, but they are not permitted to do so using innuendo and baseless inflammatory arguments designed to prejudice the jury.[93] A lawyer who did the latter would have violated the obligations of her role, rather than being in a situation of conflict between role obligations and ordinary morality.

Notice the crucial jurisprudential distinction implicit here, between legal rights and "what the legal system can be made to yield"—what I have been referring to as the distinction between entitlements and windfalls or loopholes. As Dare rightly insists, "not every lawful advantage that can be obtained through the law is a legal entitlement."[94] This strikes some lawyers as deeply confused. What else could a legal entitlement be, if not that which can be obtained through legal procedures? As noted earlier, this is a serious jurisprudential mistake, because it commits one to the view that there is no such thing as a legal error, a decision obtained through bribery or corruption, or a whimsical decision having nothing to do with the scheme of rights and duties established by the law. For the same reason, the Principle of Partisanship as understood within the Standard Conception as creating a permission, or imposing an obligation, to engage in hyper-zealous representation is not a jurisprudentially coherent view.

As noted previously, a thorough understanding of the law of lawyering shows that lawyers are not permitted to seek "every lawful advantage" that may be obtained for a client. What if the law were different? Imagine that a state followed the proper procedures for amending its rules of professional conduct, and enacted a new Rule 0.1:

> All lawyers, whether representing clients in litigation, advising, or trans-actional contexts, have a duty to zealously advance all the interests of their clients within the bounds of any straight-faced interpretation of the law.[95]

Would that new rule change the normative landscape for lawyers in that state? The answer may sound like a technical quibble, but it is important: the rules of professional conduct are only one aspect of the law governing lawyers, and do not exhaust the obligations of lawyers. As Susan Koniak has argued, the organized bar often has one normative vision of the role of lawyers, but courts, legislatures, and administrative agencies may have quite a different one.[96] Consider the Kaye Scholer matter, for example, in which the federal Office of Thrift Supervision entered an asset freeze order against a law firm that had helped its client, Lincoln Savings, resist an investigation of financial improprieties.[97] The response of the organized bar was to assert the familiar "libertarian-litigator's view of the lawyer's role,"[98] corresponding to the Standard Conception's Principle of Partisanship and to the hypothetical Rule 0.1 quoted earlier. That vision was ultimately trumped by the vision of federal regulators, who contended in effect that lawyers representing clients in non-litigation contexts must serve as gatekeepers and refrain from assisting clients in transactions that undermine the purpose of banking regulations. The bar can only push so far for its view that an aggressive tendentious advocacy mind-set is permissible in all lawyering roles before encountering serious resistance from other parts of the legal system. In the end, the law governing lawyers is the product of the tension between the bar's mentality of zealous advocacy and the position of other institutions, which insist on fidelity to law.

The Kaye Scholer case suggests another reason to wish for the elimination of the expression "zealous advocacy" from lawyers' working vocabulary, which is that lawyers often over-generalize from the paradigm of adversary litigation and contend that they have essentially the same obligations when representing clients in non-litigated matters. * Ironically the Model Code, which was frequently criticized for assimilating all lawyering activities to adversarial litigation, actually recognizes quite plainly the importance of context in fixing lawyers' obligations. "Where the bounds of law are uncertain, the action of a lawyer may depend on whether he is serving as advocate or adviser."[99] According to the Model Code, taking an aggressively partisan stance toward the law would be appropriate only (if at all) in adversarial litigation, and only where the lawyer has a good faith belief that her interpretation of the law is supported by existing norms or by a reasonable argument for extension, modification, or reversal of existing law.[100] In adversarial litigation, this highly partisan stance toward the law may be justified by the effect on the tribunal of opposing partisan presentations: "[T]he advocate, by his zealous preparation and presentation of facts and law, enables the tribunal to come to the hearing with an open and neutral mind and to render impartial judgments."[101] The Model Code goes on to say that an attorney as adviser is bound to render a professional opinion as to the applicability of law, interpreted from the point of view of an impartial tribunal.[102] Even under the organized bar's most litigation-centric set of rules, in many cases lawyers cannot accurately understand themselves as advocates at all in any normatively significant way, let alone zealous ones. Lawyers who fail to understand this are setting themselves up for serious legal sanctions.

2.2.4 *Legal Uncertainty and Lawyering Roles*

The central argument in this book is that the legal system, considered as a whole, must respond to the needs of citizens for a stable but moderately flexible framework for coordinated action in the face of uncertainty and disagreement. Within the system as a whole, however, various responsibilities may be parceled out to actors occupying different roles. In other words, the legal system may employ direct or indirect strategies for ensuring that the overarching systemic ends of settlement, fairness, and flexibility are realized. A simple illustration of this division of labor is the distinction between the roles of prosecutors and defense lawyers. In the American legal system, prosecutors are conventionally understood as having obligations to pursue justice, not merely aim at convicting as many defendants as possible. A prosecutor who reasonably believes that there is insufficient evidence to support a conviction must

---

* Unfortunately, even official statements on legal ethics sometimes encourage lawyers counseling clients to think of themselves as litigation advocates, despite the absence of institutional checks on overly aggressive interpretations of law. See, e.g., ABA Standing Comm. on Prof'l Ethics, Formal Op. 85-352 (July 7, 1985), the ABA's opinion on advising clients on tax returns.

drop the charges and must turn over potentially exculpatory evidence to the defendant in advance of trial.[103] Defense lawyers, on the other hand, are permitted to argue for inferences inconsistent with the guilt of their clients, even if they believe (or even know) their client is factually guilty of the offense charged, and may also rely on the defendant's procedural entitlements, such as the right to be free from unreasonable searches and seizures, to obtain dismissals of charges against clients they believe or know to be guilty. This division of labor is commonplace and generally taken for granted by lawyers (if sometimes viewed with suspicion by the public), but it conforms to a less well-appreciated pattern. All lawyers' duties, I will argue, are moderately context-specific, while being structured at a high level of generality by the settlement function of the law.

Although lawyers in popular culture and the public imagination are often portrayed defending accused criminals or at least representing individual clients in disputes with others, a great deal of lawyering work does not take place in the context of litigated disputes. An unfortunately common theoretical error is to assume that the lawyer's attitude toward the law, and their understanding of what legal compliance entails, should be invariant across the different contexts in which lawyers represent and advise clients.[104] Many lawyers in private practice spend their time counseling clients about compliance with legal requirements, assisting clients in structuring and closing transactions, designing risk-management strategies, or negotiating with regulators or private parties. Government lawyers may prosecute criminal cases, pursue civil enforcement actions, implement regulations governing some activity, or advise government agencies on the legal permissibility of some course of action. It would be surprising if the lawyer's relationship with the law should be constant across all these contexts. To a surprising extent, however, lawyers talk as though there is a monolithic "lawyer's attitude" that is invariant among different practice settings. That invariant attitude is that compliance with the law means nothing more than avoiding the violation of unambiguous legal prohibitions. If there is any uncertainty in the law, the lawyer is permitted to advise the client that the conduct is permissible. Up to the point at which conduct—either the client's or the lawyer's—clearly crosses an unambiguous boundary, the lawyer's job is to push right up to the boundaries of the law. This is the vision of their professional role that lawyers often encapsulate under the maxim of "zealous representation within the bounds of the law."

Here is an illustration of what is meant by the difference in attitudes or stances toward the law. William Hodes, a respected expert on the law governing lawyers, reports that he was teaching as a visiting professor at an American law school when a retired judge came to address the students about legal ethics. The judge told the students that legal ethics means that a lawyer must "find the line between what is permitted and what is not, and stay far, far to the good side of that line." Hodes later told his students that the judge was all mixed up on that point:

> You must try to find the line between what is permitted and what is not, and then get as close to that line as you can without crossing over to the bad side. Anything less is less than zealous representation—which already leaves you on the bad side of the line. Whatever distance is left to travel up to that elusive line is territory that belongs to the client and has been wrongfully ceded away.[105]

The problem with Hodes's stance toward the law is that it presupposes a notion of compliance that is far from self-evidently valid. As a counterexample to Hodes, imagine a college professor who wonders, "How much may I flirt with my student before it counts as harassment?"[106] We would say of someone who tries to walk right up to the boundary of actionable harassment, without actually crossing the line and suffering legal penalties, that he simply misunderstands what it means to respond appropriately to legal anti-harassment rules. Even if he manages to avoid legal sanctions in a particular case, he has still not truly "complied" with the law. Compliance in this case entails an attitude of respect for the law as setting standards of conduct, quite apart from the bad consequences that state institutions may attach to deviating from those standards. It also requires an effort to recover the meaning of the operative term "harassment," as opposed to exploiting any indeterminacy that may exist in the legal definition.

This is not to deny that in some lawyering contexts, it is permissible to push right up to the boundaries of the law. That is what criminal defense lawyers, and to a lesser extent civil litigators, quite properly regard as the appropriate stance toward the law. That stance is permissible, even a virtue, in these contexts because it is one way the legal system remains open to considering the perspectives of citizens that have been suppressed by existing legal norms.[107] In order to have the capacity for change and evolution, the legal system needs, as an input, the partisan stances of the opposing litigants, who may take positions at odds with existing law. It is a serious mistake, however, to generalize from the special context of litigation to other settings. The image of pushing against the boundary of the law (admittedly my metaphor, not Hodes'), suggests that some other actor will be pushing back. In Hodes's example of witness coaching, however, the conduct in question occurs in private, unobserved by opposing counsel or the trial judge. No one can push back on the line, because no one else knows what the lawyer is doing. If the lawyer herself does not undertake to comply with the actual requirement of law, as opposed to doing whatever she can get away with, the law will create no meaningful reason for action in that case. Thus, the most important feature of the lawyer's role that varies by context is the permissibility, or not, of asserting relatively creative or aggressive legal positions.

This does not mean that the law must remain static, and that it unfairly privileges the status quo, to the disadvantage of marginalized citizens. The law governing lawyers creates some latitude for lawyers who represent clients opposed to existing legal regimes. The federal civil procedure rule proscribing frivolous filings requires that claims be adequately grounded in the law, but it specifically permits lawyers to make good-faith arguments for the extension, modification, or reversal of existing law.[108] Thus, the lawyers who argued *Brown v. Board of Education* were in no sense ethically precluded by *Plessy v. Ferguson* from pursuing that litigation. Lawyers who pursue a professional tradition dedicated to resisting injustice are a recognized, and much lauded aspect of the professional tradition in all common-law countries.

There are two crucial things to notice about this, however. First, the lawyers representing African-American parents in the school desegregation litigation were litigators—lawyers working within the adversary system to establish or defend their rights. The second point is that the lawyers we valorize for resisting oppression nevertheless work *within* the law to establish new rights or extend existing ones. They are not saboteurs or guerilla warriors against the law. At some point, if a lawyer becomes sufficiently radical that she does not believe it is possible to work within the law, and do her part to maintain the legal system in good working order, she is no longer entitled to claim that she is acting as a lawyer. Instead, she must be deemed to have opted out of that social role and into another, such as radical or even revolutionary.* The lawyer's obligation to respect and uphold the law prohibits attempts to nullify or evade the law on the grounds it is unjust or wrongheaded. Claiming to work as a *lawyer* while simultaneously claiming no obligation of fidelity to law would be self-undermining. The role of lawyer, as distinct from other social roles (such as lobbyist, activist, or radical), is constituted by a relationship between the role occupant and existing positive law.

---

* A less dramatic, and indeed perfectly mundane kind of opting out occurs whenever a lawyer ceases to act in a representative capacity on behalf of clients. Nothing in this theory of legal ethics would imply that lawyers, acting as ordinary private citizens, cannot engage in lobbying, organized efforts at law reform, and even protests and civil disobedience as a way of resisting unjust laws.

The problem of legal injustice presents two conceptually distinct problems. On the one hand, a problem of interpretation may exist. The client's legal entitlements may appear to permit injustice, but upon closer inspection it may turn out that the client is not actually entitled to do what it wants to do. (The problem of the so-called "torture memos," considered in chapter 6, has this structure.) On the other hand, there may be cases in which legal injustice cannot be interpreted away. There was no doubt that the positive law of the United States in the early twentieth century, interpreted in good faith by competent lawyers and judges, included the principle of "separate but equal." The law also contained resources which enabled a process of evolution that led to the decision in *Brown* repudiating legal segregation, but if a lawyer had been working for a Southern school district in 1910, a moderate sensible view of the legal landscape would have been that there was no legal mandate to operate integrated schools. In that case, the lawyer would face the problem of legal injustice squarely, and would be forced to consider whether her role as a lawyer, and the value of legality, were sufficient reasons to continue to represent the school district and to act on the basis of its legal entitlement to operate segregated schools. The following chapter considers these reasons in detail, and concludes that, in most cases, lawyers should act with reference to their clients' legal entitlements, not ordinary moral considerations.

Chapter Three
From Neutrality to Public Reason
Moral Conflict and the Law

3.1   Legality and Legitimacy

Chapter Two observed that lawyers should assert their clients' entitlements in litigation; counsel clients on what actions are lawful, given their entitlements and those of others; and structure their clients' affairs using legal techniques like contracts and wills. Contrary to the Principle of Partisanship, the arguments of the last chapter aimed to establish that the legal entitlements of clients, not client interests, fix the boundaries of lawyers' duty of loyalty to their clients. Lawyers believe, further, that in the course of providing effective representation to their clients, they should consider *only* their clients' legal entitlements, and not reasons given by ordinary morality. The fact that something is a lousy thing to do, morally speaking, does not warrant a lawyer's refusal to assist the client in doing it, if the client has a legal entitlement to perform the act. For example, in the statute of limitations case, Borrower may have a moral obligation to repay the loan, but Lender does not have a legal entitlement to recover the money. The legal entitlement therefore acts as either an exclusionary reason in the practical reasoning of the lawyer, or as a very weighty reason that should be overridden by the value of the justice of Lender's claim. The lawyer's role-based obligation is to assert Borrower's legal entitlement in litigation, if Borrower insists on taking advantage of it, regardless of any moral qualms the lawyer may have about taking that position. Within the Standard Conception, this is known as the Principle of Neutrality.

Critics of the Principle of Neutrality question whether the existence of a legal system, professional roles within the system, and a framework of legal entitlements can alter the bedrock fact of moral agency.* A person remains a

---

* It is impossible to avoid a potentially confusing overlap in terminology here. As I argued in chapter 2, in terms of the common law of agency, lawyers are agents of their clients. That means they are legally obligated to carry out their clients' lawful instructions, refrain from self-dealing* and other breaches of the duty of loyalty, keep client confidences, and so on. This chapter is

moral agent even when acting in a role; people and actions within roles remain subject to moral evaluation.[1] Being a person *simpliciter* is prior to being a person-in-role; one's moral agency persists, notwithstanding the potentially competing demands of social roles. Critics maintain that, although in the ordinary run of things, legal entitlements mostly overlap with moral rights and permissions, in the interesting cases in which they conflict, moral obligations are always trump. Thus, even if duties of loyalty and partisanship are justified, there can be no moral justification for the Principle of Neutrality. Lawyers may have duties of effective client representation, but these must always be pursued within the constraints of ordinary morality. If vindicating a client's legal entitlement—whether by asserting a position in litigation or counseling the client on that basis—involves moral wrongdoing, then the lawyer is morally obligated to do less than what loyalty to the client would otherwise require.

The critique of Neutrality grounded in the persistent moral agency of lawyers is a powerful one. In response, it is not enough for lawyers merely to assert that their role requires such-and-such. There also must be some reason to believe that this obligation has moral significance, and a further reason to believe that obligation should have priority over ordinary moral duties—that is, an argument must establish the exclusionary effect of role-based obligations. The claim in this chapter is that considerations associated with the value of legality and the rule of law provide reasons for lawyers to act with fidelity to law, rather than acting on the basis of the moral and nonmoral considerations that would otherwise apply in the absence of the lawyer–client relationship.

The argument here requires first establishing the legitimacy of the legal system. A legal system is legitimate if a citizen ought to respect the laws it enacts, even if she disagrees with the substance of the law.[2] A legitimate law is one which *by right* creates obligations on citizens, such as the obligation to respect the law. Legitimacy is different from substantive justice in important ways. In a democracy, laws can be legitimate not because they are just, but because they have been enacted using procedures that satisfy criteria of fairness, representativeness, and so on. Legitimate laws may be substantively unjust, as long as the injustice is not sufficiently severe or pervasive to call into question

---

concerned with the *moral* agency of lawyers, who remain persons with moral responsibilities even while acting in a representative capacity. The question considered here is whether moral agents ought to understand themselves as legitimately subject to political obligations, resulting from their role as legal agents of clients, that might conflict with what would otherwise be moral obligations, arising from their moral agency as persons. Which of the senses of the word "agent" is intended should be clear from the context of the discussion.

the fairness of the system. The conception of legitimacy I will argue for here is a fairly thin, procedural one, but it is grounded in the normative attractiveness of democracy.[3] The basic idea is that in a society of free and equal citizens, each with his or her own view of what should be done in the name of society as a whole, no one's view can prevail all the time. Substantive injustice is not self-evident in a pluralist society; people disagree about what outcomes are substantively unjust. Given this disagreement, the only way for a law-making and law-applying process to manifest respect for the equality and dignity of all citizens is to create duties that are independent of the content of legal norms. Democratic equality is therefore the most important value in politics.

In an account of legal ethics derived from this view of politics, substantive criteria of justice play little role in assessing the legitimacy of the legal system and the laws it enacts. The reason for this, developed in Section 3.2, is that legitimacy depends on some position being enacted in the name of the community as a whole. When the members of a community reasonably subscribe to diverse moral points of view, the legitimacy of the institutions created to govern that community must somehow transcend these matters about which people disagree. Rawls believes that reasonable citizens may subscribe to a diversity of reasonable comprehensive doctrines, but from within those comprehensive doctrines they may be able to endorse a political justification for a fair scheme of cooperation.[4] The argument here, by contrast, is primarily procedural rather than substantive—that is, less dependent upon the justice of the outcome of procedure and more focused on the fairness of the procedure itself.[5] Given the fact of reasonable pluralism, we cannot expect much consensus on substantive principles of justice; moral pluralism drives a wedge between substantive and procedural criteria of legitimacy.[6] The best we can hope for is a conception of legitimate procedures for making, interpreting, and applying laws. For this reason, the duties of lawyers must be oriented toward respect for the law itself, not ordinary moral considerations. Even if a lawyer believes that a particular law is unjust, or that the law as applied to her client's situation will produce an unjust outcome, she nevertheless has a reason to respect the law and not work around it.

If the legal system is legitimate, further argument is still required to establish that its legitimacy gives reasons for lawyers to respect laws that are enacted by this system.[*] In other words, there must be something about a

---

[*] By "respect," I do not have in mind only obeying the law, particularly criminal statutes, but a broader notion of conducting one's affairs with due regard for the legal entitlements of others. A person fails to respect the law, for example, when she refuses to honor a contractual obligation, or commits a tort without justification. Also, as discussed in chapter 6, a lawyer disrespects the law when she relies on abusive or manipulative interpretation in advising clients about their legal

legitimate legal system that is independently worthy of respect, apart from the substantive justice of outcomes. As Section 3.3 will argue, when we act as members of a political community, we seek to act under a claim of right that is established in the name of the community as a whole. When we say we have a publicly recognized right to do something, we are not just asserting that we have the raw power to do it, or can bamboozle others into not interfering with us. Rather, the claim is that the community itself has taken a normative stance with respect to the matter, and has decided that citizens may assert a permission to act in a particular way. Speaking in terms of the community taking a position sounds obscure, but it is really just a metaphorical way of saying that a society has instituted procedures for resolving disagreements and establishing a framework for coexistence and cooperation. If those procedures are tolerably fair, they provide a way for citizens to transform their claims on each other from brute demands into cooperatively established entitlements.[7] Making reference to these legal entitlements can be seen as a way of expressing respect for the equality and dignity of other citizens. The procedures of the legal system therefore constitute a means for living together, treating one another with respect, and cooperating toward common ends, despite moral diversity and disagreement. The values of dignity and equality therefore underwrite the claim of the legal system to have a right to the respect of citizens, as distinguished from mere *de facto* power. Because lawyers are agents of their clients, they have no special dispensation from the obligation of their clients to respect the law. Thus, the fundamental ethical obligation of lawyers is fidelity to law.

3.2 The Circumstances of Politics

The starting point for any theory of public ethics, including legal ethics, is recognition that we have to work out a way to live alongside one another and resolve disagreements about normative or empirical matters through means other than violence and coercion. As the seventeenth-century legal theorist Hugo Grotius observed, we are quarrelsome but socially minded creatures by nature; we each seek our own advantage, but we have a desire for peaceable society with one another.[8] In more modern terms, the problem is that a society made up of free and equal people will be characterized by a wide diversity of

---

entitlements or those of others. The obligation of respect may require less than the obligation of obedience, in some cases. For example, it may be consistent with the obligation of respect to ignore a law that is generally regarded as anachronistic.

89

moral and religious outlooks, and because these disagreements will in many instances be reasonable, it will be impossible to secure a stable and just society using reason alone, including reason about justice.[9] All moral agents and human societies recognize as basic a set of goods, including life, knowledge, play, aesthetic experience, friendship, practical reasonableness, and a relationship between humans and the divine.[10] However, agreement on the existence and importance of an abstract ethical value (life, say, or equality) may conceal a great deal of internal complexity in the structure of that value; it may contain competing, possibly incompatible conceptions of the concept.[11] Thus, people are likely to disagree in good faith about how to specify an abstract ethical value as a concrete maxim of action.[12]

Jeremy Waldron has referred to our predicament as the circumstances of politics. The circumstances of politics has three aspects: (1) the perceived need for a stable framework of cooperation among people in a society (2) who disagree over the grounds of that framework or system of norms, and (3) who recognize one another as equals and acknowledge a moral obligation to treat fellow citizens and their opposing views with respect.[13] Several theoretical responses to the circumstances of politics might bear on legal ethics in different ways. One response would be to seek to improve institutions and procedures so politics may be more deliberative—that is, better responsive to diverse points of view and better capable of fostering engagement among citizens.[14] A legal ethics of deliberative democracy would emphasize the lawyer's role as a facilitator of citizen participation in government, and exalt the lawyer's creative law-making capabilities. A different theoretical response to disagreement would seek areas of agreement, and attempt to build a justification for political institutions on such consensus as may exist in pluralistic society. The basis of a just and stable society cannot be comprehensive moral, religious, or philosophical doctrines. Despite their differences, however, citizens may agree *for moral reasons* on certain political principles.[15] These political principles may be invoked as a justification for norms enunciated, and potentially enforced using coercive means, in the name of the community as a whole. A legal ethics of public reason would direct lawyers to act on the basis of these shared values. Under either of these approaches the test for the legitimacy of laws and political institutions is at least to some extent substantive. Outcomes must be just in order to be deemed legitimate, and therefore lawyers can be criticized for complicity in injustice if they do not respect the demands of justice and morality.

The position defended here takes a third approach to the problem of disagreement. It emphasizes the connection between legitimacy and democracy, particularly the capacity of democratic institutions and procedures to treat citizens as equals, entitled to an equal measure of respect no matter what their substantive views about justice and morality.[16] Democratic political institutions should be deemed legitimate if they are adequately (not ideally) responsive to citizen demands for participation. Laws that are the product of these political institutions are legitimate if they are enacted using adequately (again, not ideally) fair procedures.

This is admittedly a thin basis for solidarity, but it likely is the best we can do. (One might paraphrase Winston Churchill's quip about democracy being the worst form of government, except for all the others.) Reserving allegiance only for substantively just institutions and laws would mean denying any reason to respect the political infrastructure of actual, as opposed to ideal societies.[17] To take examples from the contemporary American scene, electoral politics is skewed by the influence of wealthy donors, both corporate and individual, and policy-making is affected by interest-group lobbying; the ability of many citizens to participate in the political process is limited by disparities in wealth and the inability to organize into effective coalitions; differentials in wealth and power are reinforced by structural features such as inequality in primary and secondary education and the practical inaccessibility to middle-income families of elite higher-education institutions; women, people of color, sexual minorities, and people with disabilities face persistent discrimination, both explicit and tacit, which reinforces inequality in the political, economic, and social realms; and for the poorest and most disempowered citizens, the state is not perceived as a means of engagement at all, but as an alien force they experience, if at all, through intrusive policing and bureaucratic indifference.[18] This sounds pretty grim, but a similar list could be generated for any moderately decent democratic society that actually exists. The ethics of lawyering does not depend on ideal conceptions of justice; rather, it is all about doing the best we can, through legal procedures, to respond to the situation of people who disagree but nevertheless need to live alongside one another in conditions of relative peace and stability.

The aim of politics is to enable people to live together peacefully, cooperate on mutually beneficial projects, and to acknowledge the claims of others to be treated with respect and dignity. Laws and a legal system are essential parts of the political order of a society, because they establish the possibility of a particular kind of evaluation, in terms of some act of state of affairs being lawful. Being lawful means more than simply conforming to the will of a person or institution that possesses power. It means, instead, being validated in a particular, often complex way by procedures that have been put into place to enact norms that conform to requirements such as generality, publicity, and prospectivity.[19] One of the principal claims of this book is that the normative attractiveness of the lawyer's role depends on the normative attractiveness of legality. If it sounds good to you that a society maintain institutions and procedures for the purpose of constraining powerful actors, both public and private, then you might be inclined to see value in the role of the lawyer. Legality is not the only value, of course, and it will be important to take up the relationship between the value of legality and morality generally, and to set limits on the authority of laws enacted using democratic procedures. (That will be the task of Section 3.3.) This section will first elaborate the idea of the circumstances of politics, and the value of law as a response to this human predicament.

3.2.1 *Disagreement and the Need for Settlement*

Political conflict is the result of reasonable pluralism.[20] Politics often appears unattractive, and is readily stigmatized as being riven with lobbying and rent-seeking by "factions" or "special interests"(notice how these terms are used instead of "others with whom we disagree"). These features of politics are not necessarily the result of greed, corruption, stupidity, or malice, although in some cases they may be. Rather, they are often the byproduct of good-faith disagreements. The influence of wealth on electoral politics is due, in part, to a political commitment (enforced by a line of Supreme Court cases) to a strong principle of freedom of expression, which includes the right of citizens to use money as a way of participating in politics.[21] Income inequalities are the result, in part, of a pervasive free-market, anti-regulation ideology that proponents believe is justified on the capacity of markets to make more efficient allocation decisions and avoid the unintended negative consequences of well-intentioned government regulation. The point here is not to present an apologia for American society, but to point out the difficulty of relying on substantive criteria of legitimacy. Political ethics, including legal ethics, must have something to say about the duties of citizens and officials in a non-ideal world,[22] and one characteristic of non-ideal ethics is that it must be suited to practical application in cases where people disagree about what ought to be done. As John Rawls argues, reasonable citizens who recognize each other as free and equal, and seek a basis for coexistence and cooperation must recognize what he calls the burdens of judgment, which show why people may be fully rational and acting in good faith, and nevertheless disagree about matters of morality or justice.[23]

Rawls stresses that the need for politics arises from the fact of *reasonable* pluralism, not pluralism as such.[24] A great deal of normative weight rests on the word "reasonable," because there is no requirement that a just society tolerate unreasonable comprehensive doctrines, such as those held by white supremacists or violent religious fanatics. Rawls says that reasonable comprehensive doctrines are those which reasonable citizens affirm, but again that merely shunts the analytical weight onto the term reasonable. In my view, reasonable pluralism means a diversity of comprehensive doctrines that respect certain baseline constraints on what counts as an ethical view. For example, one might say that at a minimum, ethics is concerned with avoiding certain evils:

> There is nothing mysterious or "subjective" or culture-bound in the great evils of human experience, re-affirmed in every age and in every written history and in every tragedy and fiction: murder and the destruction of life, imprisonment, enslavement, starvation, poverty, physical pain and torture, homelessness, friendlessness.[25]

Ethics may also be founded on basic human goods, such as life, health, relationships with others, and so on.[26] Or, one might take a more functionalist tack and argue that any adequate morality must take account of the role of morality, which is to enable people to live together, in light of their basic human needs and capacities.[27] In any case, morality is not "just a matter of opinion," as students in introductory ethics classes sometimes assert. Human needs, goods, and capacities really are as they are described, and the recognition of our common humanity gives us reasons to act in certain ways, given those needs and capacities. An ethical position that respects these human needs and capacities, and aims to avoid great evils, is a reasonable one and is entitled to respect by one's fellow citizens.

Disagreement among citizens threatens their common interest in living together and realizing the benefits of cooperation. One might talk about a *"felt need among the members of a certain group for a common framework or decision or course of action on some matter,"*[28] but it is not necessary to rely on assumptions about the psychology of the parties. Citizens in fact have an interest in peaceful coexistence, whether or not they feel particularly well disposed toward others, or motivated to find a basis for cooperation. Facts about motivation are not necessary to establish that one has a reason to do something. If what look like psychological assumptions are to be made here, they are more in the nature of foundational premises about human nature, such as those made by Hobbes, who assumed that "[t]he passions that incline men to peace are fear of death, desire of such things as are necessary to commodious living, and a hope by their industry to obtain them."[29] A common *interest* in peaceful coexistence and a stable framework for cooperative activity is compatible with feelings of animosity between neighbors. In fact, in the absence of a certain amount of friction, the need for a procedural resolution of disagreement would not arise in the first place. The assumption here is that people, by nature, share an interest in forming a relatively stable and peaceful society with others, even those with whom they disagree. We share this interest even though we may be more or less self-interested, or may even be in competition with others; the framework of a common society is something that each individual considers worth maintaining as a means to her own objectives.[30]

The need for a stable framework to enable cooperation is sometimes referred to as a coordination problem, although this should not be taken to invoke the sense of that term as it is used in game theory. In game theory, a coordination problem arises when it is important that players settle on one course of action, but it does not matter to the players which is chosen, as long as that solution is followed by others. The standard example of a coordination game is whether a society should require cars to drive on the right or left side of the road.[31] Neither the right side nor the left side has any real pre-social significance, but the possibility of chaos on the roads demands that drivers settle in advance on one or the other. By contrast, in the circumstances of politics it matters a great deal to citizens (the "players") which option is chosen. Consider two examples, which illustrate the difficulty of settling on a common course of action in light of the fact of reasonable pluralism. These are the sorts of coordination problems to which the legal system responds.

First, imagine that a university wishes to adopt admissions policies that are aimed at admitting a class of incoming students that is racially diverse, both because it believes diversity has educational benefits and in order to help rectify the effects of discrimination against historically disadvantaged groups.[32] Some citizens believe that this policy violates the moral value of equality, which should be understood as prohibiting government and private actors from taking race into account when deciding how to allocate various goods, including scarce places in the university's entering class. They believe all racial classifications are improper, regardless of the motive for employing them. It would be unfair, the university's critics contend, to disadvantage white students in the application process if the justification were remedying discrimination in which this generation of white students could not have been implicated.

Supporters of the university's policy respond that the concept of equality has both formal and substantive aspects, and race-conscious admissions policies can further substantive equality, even if they appear to operate on a formally unequal basis. It would be futile, they argue, to attempt to remedy the effects of race-based discrimination using only race-neutral means.[33] Structural racism, which the university's policy is aimed at ameliorating, can in some cases do as much harm as individual subjective racism. And in any event, the morally prohibited variety of racial discrimination is only targeting members of a given group out of racial animus. Opponents reply, however, that discrimination is discrimination, and should always be morally condemned, whether it is motivated by belief in racial inferiority or by a laudable desire to remedy social inequality.

Second, suppose a hospital is considering how it should respond to some recurring ethical problems that arise in the care of terminally ill patients. In particular, it must establish guidelines for withdrawing life support and possibly even assisting patients in ending their own lives—dying with dignity, as some patients' advocates put it.[34] The hospital's deliberations attract a great deal of public attention, and citizens urge the hospital to adopt policies that respect the moral values of human life, human dignity, and autonomy. Not surprisingly, however, they disagree over how those values should be understood and prioritized in particular cases.[35] All agree that human life has value, but disagree over whether biological life alone is valuable, so that a patient in a permanent vegetative state should be maintained on life support, or whether some quality of life measure is needed to evaluate whether a life is worth living. Mere biological life accompanied by severe and dehumanizing suffering may be worse than death from the patient's point of view. However, there is further controversy over what criteria of quality of life should be used, with doubts expressed over whether criteria can be articulated with sufficient precision to avoid deeming the lives of mentally handicapped people to be of "low quality" for these purposes.

When it comes to physician-assisted suicide, the disagreement becomes even sharper. Many citizens are concerned that voluntary euthanasia will be a "wedge" or a slippery slope, and that physician-assisted suicide can lay the groundwork for eventual state-sanctioned eugenics programs. Others respond that wedge arguments are not persuasive where there is a clear moral distinction between cases, and that doctors know the difference between helping someone die with dignity and executing newborns with severe disabilities, aged people whose medical care consumes a great deal of public resources, or other "unwanted" people. Critics of voluntary euthanasia respond that if the quality of life of a terminally ill patient is judged to be low, or if the value of life is deemed to be outweighed by other interests, then there would appear to be no reason not to enlarge the scope of morally permitted killings, with disastrous consequences. Hovering in the background of these debates is the question of the moral permissibility of abortion, and all of the participants are aware that the policies they choose in the end-of-life context will have implications for the abortion debate.

These cases are not pure coordination problems, because citizens perceive value not only in adopting some policy, but in getting it right—that is, having it track substantive moral values such as truth or justice. Importantly, however, we cannot resolve the question of what it means to get something right by appealing to substantive moral values, because disagreement about morality is exactly what has created these intractable public-policy problems. Rawls argues that substantive and procedural criteria of justice are related, because a procedure is fair only if it gives the correct (just, fair, true, etc.) result most of the time.[36] Insisting that fairness depends on substantively correct outcomes leaves us without any content-independent way to assess the legitimacy of procedures used to resolve disagreements such as the ones just canvassed. The university and the hospital need a way of establishing a basis for making decisions, going forward, which takes into account the reasons given by the parties who disagree about the content of the guidelines, but which supersedes these reasons and provides a new basis for making decisions. The parties thus have dual aims of getting it right, as a matter of morality, and settling on a single definitive position that represents the view of the relevant community concerning what is to be done about the matter. The circumstances of politics arises from the collision of these two aims. People would prefer to get it right, but recognizing that others disagree about what the right outcome would be, they are willing to accept a position reached using fair decision-making procedures.[37]

In order for people to be in the circumstances of politics, their disagreements cannot be so comprehensive or basic that they cannot be said to be in a common society with one another. The conception of legal ethics set out here is limited to lawyers practicing in a more or less just society. This is not to say that all citizens should be assumed to be reasoning in good faith and following what they take to be their moral obligations in all cases. I do mean to exclude societies marked by such extreme division that waging war on one's neighbors is a real alternative to cooperating peacefully. The obvious example of this kind of society is present-day Iraq, with its bitter and violent sectarian divisions. It may happen in the future that Shiites and Sunnis come to see each other as fellow citizens with whom peaceful coexistence is desirable, but in the present situation Iraqis cannot be said to be in the circumstances of politics. I also mean to exclude societies run by moral monsters, such as Nazi Germany. The settlement-based argument for the obligation to respect the law does not support a moral obligation to respect Nazi laws—not because they are not "laws" according to some source-based criteria of validity, but because the laws were adopted through procedures that ensured the oppression of a sizeable group of citizens and because the laws commanded actions that were grave moral evils.[38]

There are, of course, citizens of what are generally taken to be reasonably just societies who believe that those societies' laws are substantively morally evil or were adopted through procedures that ensured the oppression of some minority. Unless the majority is engaged in such brutal oppression of a minority that citizens cannot be said to be in the circumstances of politics with one another, the substantive injustice of a law is not a basis for conscientiously objecting to the duty to respect the law. Law is what makes a viable and lasting community possible in the kind of society we inhabit, characterized by a diversity of religious and ethical viewpoints. That very diversity makes inevitable deep and intractable disagreements about whether particular laws are just. The kind of epistemological humility reflected in tolerance for opposing moral points of view can also be seen as an ideal for government, so that we recognize obligations to one another, mediated through the political institutions of our society, despite substantive disagreements.

Disagreements that make the law necessary are not only about justice and morality. In fact, much of the law serves to resolve disagreements of a purely empirical nature. Many disputes between citizens do not turn on whether something is just, right, or fair in general, but whether the facts (understood in light of the applicable law) create an obligation to do something. For example, the parties in the product liability hypothetical in chapter 1 may agree that if a manufacturer's defective product caused an injury to a consumer, the manufacturer would have an obligation, sounding in corrective justice, to pay compensation. Assuming that the parties agree on this normative question, however, there is still a disagreement over whether, in this particular case, the injury was caused by a defect in the product or by something else, such as the plaintiff's risky behavior. Agreement at the level of general principles of justice does not entail agreement at the level of application to specific cases. Manufacturers and consumers are still in the circumstances of politics with respect to each other, even if the disagreement between them is purely empirical in nature. Generalizing from this case, there may be many issues about which there is mostly empirical disagreement. Many pharmaceutical products and medical devices, as well as industrial emissions and other pollutants, are regulated (or left unregulated) despite some factual uncertainty concerning the dangers they pose. Because this uncertainty cannot be resolved using generally accepted scientific techniques, and yet it is necessary to determine whether and under what conditions these activities may be allowed, the circumstances of politics arises for citizens in these cases, just as it would in cases of pure normative disagreement.

3.2.2 *Rough Equality and Tolerably Fair Procedures*

In the circumstances of politics, people are unable to establish a stable basis for cooperative activity with reference to comprehensive doctrines of the good, or substantive theories of rights. They do, however, conceive of themselves and others as equals, as fellow citizens, presumptively entitled to be treated with respect.[39] Recognition of the equal political liberty of citizens who disagree creates a basic constraint on any method that is used to resolve conflict.[40] For Hobbes, this is a practical constraint—we all seek to increase our power to protect ourselves from the depredations of others, while knowing that others are also trying to acquire more power. I would go further, however, and contend that the equality of one's fellow citizens is a *moral* constraint on the procedures adopted to settle disagreement.[41] Many ways exist to resolve a society-wide controversy, which would not represent the same kind of achievement in terms of treating citizens as presumptive equals whose moral beliefs are entitled to respect by others. One option would be to turn power over to a strongman who simply imposes his will on citizens by fiat. Historical experiences with Tito in the Balkans and Saddam Hussein in Iraq show that it is possible to quell conflict in this manner, but not in a way that warrants the respect and allegiance (as opposed to the acquiescence) of citizens. Installing a dictator lacks normative attractiveness because, although it does accomplish a settlement of conflict and brings about some social goods like peace and stability, it does so at the expense of failing to give as much consideration as practicable to the competing views of citizens about what the content of the settlement should be.

The constraint of equality requires us to give an equal voice to participants in a political debate, so that the resulting legal settlement reflects the view of everyone, as much as possible. Equality is reflected in legality because "all those affected have to be able to feel that they have done as well as they could reasonably hope to."[42] This would plainly be an idealization if it relied on the actual motivations and attitudes of the participants. But interests and values, not motives and sentiments, are the foundation of the law's claim to authority.[43] If citizens are in fact entitled to equal respect, then it would count in favor of the authority of law that it enables citizens to treat each other as equals, with respect, in the context of social disagreement. The deep moral ideal here is broadly Kantian; it is the notion that "however much we may disagree with others and repudiate what they stand for, we cannot treat them as merely objects of our will."[44] We accept this constraint on our dealings with others because we recognize them as being human like ourselves, in their capacity to have beliefs and ideals, deliberate on how to live, and to act on reasons.[45] Resolving disagreements using force is ruled out by this moral constraint on how people can treat one another, so the next step is to try dialogue. By hypothesis, however, reasoned persuasion has also failed. Thus, members of society might reasonably opt for the use of procedural mechanisms to transcend the disagreements that divide them, and to establish a framework for coordinated action. It may be hopeless to try to resolve disagreements by reasoning alone, but perhaps all could agree it would be fair to submit the issues to a vote or to a decision by an impartial adjudicator.

Of course, it is open to any of the citizens (and to any observer of this process) to object to the procedures used to enact laws resolving the issues. As suggested previously, however, the legitimacy of procedures is not based on optimizing fairness but on doing as well as possible given the need for both equal respect and finality.[46] The process need not satisfy conditions of "an ideally conducted discussion"[47] in order to be legitimate. Rather, a sufficient condition for legitimacy is a political order that does *well enough* at permitting affected individuals to influence political decisions. In a non-ideal domain such as politics, all that is necessary for a law to be legitimate is that it was enacted using procedures that enable citizens to participate in the process of lawmaking as well as can be expected in a large-scale, diverse, decentralized society.[48] Utopian conceptions of politics that depend on ideally fair procedures or insist on substantively just outcomes as a condition of legitimacy fail to recognize that there is value in a system that enables citizens to at least participate in an orderly process of establishing a claim of right in the name of the community as a whole, as an alternative to powerful citizens simply dominating others.

IMPERFECTIONS IN PROCEDURES

It is impossible to read the newspaper and maintain any kind of idealistic view of the lawmaking process. It is conventional wisdom that legislative procedures are flawed by defects such as "deal-making, logrolling, interest-pandering, pork-barreling, horse-trading, and Arrovian cycling."[49] In the U.S. Congress, for example, legislative leaders select committee chairs who will do the leadership's bidding; the minority party is often frozen out of the committee process, in which bills are drafted and amendments proposed; the leadership in both houses can use the conference-committee process, by which Senate and House bills are reconciled, to add or delete provisions without full debate;

savvy legislators can employ procedural means to stall or derail legislation they disagree with; and legislation is notoriously larded with "earmarks" or appropriations for the home districts of representatives, which are in the interest of no one except residents of that district.

A couple of representative anecdotes should suffice to illustrate the problem. During the first term of the George W. Bush administration, an article in *The New Republic* described the effort of a first-term Democratic representative to secure a full vote of the House of Representatives on a proposed amendment to a piece of legislation.[50] The Rules Committee, controlled 9-4 by Republicans, refused to permit consideration of the amendment to the bill. (As another Democratic House member put it, the committee's action does not just go to fundamental issues, but whether Congress should *debate* fundamental issues.[51]) Beyond the episode described in the article, the House Republican leadership, particularly Majority Leader Tom DeLay, was well known for using hardball parliamentary tactics to push legislation through the chamber, without debate or opportunity for amendment, regardless of whether their action had the support of a majority of representatives. In one notorious episode, DeLay held open the voting on the Medicare prescription drug bill until 6:00 a.m. so that Republican leaders could persuade—some might say coerce—a few dissenting members of their party to vote in favor.[52] Even worse, DeLay promised one holdout, Nick Smith, that he would endorse his son in a congressional race if Smith would change his "no" vote to "yes," but threatened to work against Smith's son if Smith continued in opposition.[53]

Whatever one thinks of the merits of the legislation produced by these shenanigans, it is difficult to characterize the process as respectful consideration of competing points of view and of the persons who participate in the disagreement. In these cases, DeLay and the chair of the Rules Committee were acting peremptorily, contrary to what should be the realization of each citizen in the circumstances of politics that "his is not the only voice in the society and that his voice should count for no more in the political process than the voice of any other rights-bearer."[54] In addition to criticizing the law-making process in ethical terms at the micro-level, some feature of the political process as a whole might be the basis for claiming that a given law is illegitimate. For example, one might contend that the system of financing election campaigns is so badly skewed toward wealthy donors, particularly large corporations, that any statute passed by an elected legislature is potentially subject to objection on the grounds that the interests of individual citizens were not represented in the legislative process.[55] Similarly, one might argue that the current redistricting system fails to redress historical grievances against racial minorities. Others might respond that the Supreme Court has gone too far in allowing race even to be considered as a factor in redistricting. Nevertheless, most of the legislation and common-law decisions produced by the political institutions of modern democracies are legitimate by the standards of non-ideal political theory.

The reason for treating these procedures as legitimate despite their defects is twofold. First, it is hard to devise a process for handling complex lawmaking tasks that is not susceptible to a certain amount of crass partisanship, manipulation, and abuse. Even in a legislature generally characterized by mutual respect and civility, it will occasionally be necessary for a majority to impose its preferred resolution of a matter on the minority, and it is entitled to do so simply because it is the majority (subject of course to limitations in the Bill of Rights and requirements of procedural due process). While the procedural maneuvering described in *The New Republic* article sounds unsavory, in a 435-member body that routinely produces 3,000-page appropriations bills, it is necessary to impose some limits on debate and the offering of new amendments. These limits can be abused in order to suppress dissent, but it is necessary to give legislation produced by these procedures presumptive legitimacy in order to avoid becoming mired in disagreement over whether a particular procedural maneuver was abusive or justified. If a piece of legislation could be judged illegitimate if the debate and amendment procedures were not maximally respectful of competing points of view, then legislation would not be able to perform its function of enabling coordinated social action in the face of disagreement. Taking opposing viewpoints as seriously as possible is an ideal of the democratic process,[56] but it cannot be a necessary condition of democratic legitimacy that the legislative process be maximally respectful of the views of dissenters. At some point the majority is entitled to say, "we have heard enough," and move on.

Second, all of these evaluative terms (partisanship, abuse, etc.) are ascriptions about which people can disagree in good faith. Fairness is an important virtue of procedures, but so is finality. Procedures that enhance fairness, such as giving members of the minority party an opportunity to propose amendments to legislation, may undercut the interest in finality as a measure is laden with competing amendments. The United States Senate is famously protective of deliberation, and therefore fairness, but it is also notoriously inefficient. Practices such as the filibuster and permitting a single Senator to place holds on judicial nominees (known as "blue slips") arguably overvalue fairness at the expense of finality. Similarly, procedures such as earmarks that appear to create opportunities for engaging in pork-barrel politics may be justified in terms of enhancing the representativeness and democratic responsiveness of the legislature. An earmark may be decried as pork, but one person's pork is another's effective government response to some pressing local issue that would otherwise be swamped by the debate over an issue that is, for some reason, more broadly politically salient.[57]

Given the plurality of procedural virtues that a lawmaking body might seek to realize, such as efficiency, deliberation, finality, and fairness, it is not surprising that reasonable people might disagree over the rules that should regulate the activities of this institution. By implication from the existence of reasonable normative disagreement, if procedures had to be sufficiently fair that no one could believe that there was anything unfair about them, there would be no way for a society to use the legal system to bootstrap itself out of the circumstances of politics. Thus, if agreement on the fairness of procedures were a necessary condition of legitimacy, the lawmaking process would never be able to settle conflict and establish a provisional basis for coordinated action. The same argument can be made, *mutatis mutandis*, about macro-level fairness concerns in connection with campaign finance and the like.

Of course, one might point out that there is a plurality of reasonable conceptions of legitimacy, with a significant amount of disagreement remaining over what pedigree we should require of laws before they are deemed legitimate.[58] The only way to resolve this second-order disagreement is to set the threshold very high for a finding of unfairness that is sufficient to undermine the citizens' shared interest in resolving social disagreement using the procedures of formal law. (That is the reason I used the terms *rough* equality and *tolerably* fair procedures as the section title.) To put it another way, the any criterion of procedural fairness that serves as a necessary condition of legitimacy must be very thin. There is a risk that this procedural conception of legitimacy will be so thin that it applies to truly awful governments, which used fair procedures to enact terrible laws—the Nazi regime in Germany being the obvious historical illustration. It is tempting to respond that if something were truly beyond the pale of what would be tolerated in a civilized society, it is highly unlikely that a moderately fair and well functioning legal system would ever give it legal recognition.

SUBSTANTIVE INJUSTICE

The problem is that in the Nazi case, as well as in notorious examples of injustice in American history, the laws in question were not regarded as being utterly beyond the pale in the society. Indeed, they were enthusiastically supported by substantial majorities of the population. But just as moral philosophy can be excessively fixated on highly aberrational hypotheticals, such as being stuck in a lifeboat with another person and only enough water for one, or waking up to find oneself tethered by the kidneys to a famous violinist, legal philosophy can become too preoccupied with *Dred Scott, Plessy,* and *Korematsu.* "To design a system of authority around *Dred Scott* (or Nuremberg), rather than around the views of contemporary politicians about abortion or school prayer, is to make a decision-theoretic choice that is far from obvious."[59] The Jim Crow regime in the southern United States from the period following Reconstruction through the civil rights movement in the 1950s and '60s did not satisfy even minimal standards of treating dissenting views with respect and not suppressing disagreement, at least with respect to issues that affected African-Americans. In that regime, African-American citizens were treated merely as objects of the will of the majority.

It does not follow from these examples of defects in legitimacy that every respect in which the current system falls short of an ideal renders the directives that are its product illegitimate. As noted earlier, it would be an unusual limiting case—conceivable, but not a regular occurrence—for people to believe reasonably that the political system is so pervasively biased against them that none of the resulting laws are legitimate with respect to them. A more likely situation is that of a perception of localized injustice. For example, members of sexual minority groups (gays, lesbians, bisexual, and transgendered persons) may believe that the political process has been captured by citizens whose irrational bigotry renders them unable to decide fairly on matters of concern to these groups, such as same-sex marriage and same-sex partner adoption rights. The question therefore arises, whether it is possible to cure localized injustices through practices of legal interpretation that permit citizens to contest the meaning of the applicable law, and to assert, from the standpoint of justice, that the "official" version of the law is wrong and should be understood differently. This possibility will be considered in chapter 6. If it is not possible to interpret the law correctly to reach the just result, then it may be the case that the local injustice must be tolerated by lawyers even while it is resisted by citizens. (If the citizen is the lawyer's client, then the lawyer is in the unenviable position of telling her client that the law does not coincide with the client's interests.) The ethics of lawyers may be more demanding than the ethics of ordinary citizens and may impose a heightened obligation of respect for the law in certain cases.

Critics of pure procedural criteria of legitimacy object that surely some substantive constraints must be placed on political procedures to ensure the justice of outcomes. As Rawls argues, we would not deem legitimate a legal system that recognized "slavery and serfdom, religious persecution, the subjection of the working class, the oppression of women, and the unlimited accumulation of vast fortunes..."[60] A somewhat glib response to this objection is that, in fact, the American legal system countenances many instances of what one might refer to as the subjugation of the working class (laws that make union organizing highly burdensome, for example), religious persecution (the Supreme Court's prohibition on prayer in public schools, as seen through the eyes of some religious fundamentalists), the oppression of women (for instance, the legal permissibility of much pornography), and that American political institutions certainly tolerate the accumulation of vast fortunes.

Although this response is a bit facile, because the legal system does not accept the worst violations of these substantive principles of justice, it should be clear by now that the problem of reasonable pluralism makes it difficult to employ concepts like subjugation, oppression, and persecution without showing that proponents of the law in question are not being reasonable. The truth in the glib response stated earlier is that there may be reasonable positions on both sides of a dispute. As against the claim, for example, that the legal permissibility of pornography contributes to the oppression of women, there is a long history in the United States at least, of judicial decisions protecting unpopular, even reprehensible expression for reasons relating to distrust of state power and official orthodoxies of belief.[61] We should be very hesitant to proclaim a law illegitimate because it appears unjust by our lights. In the domain of politics, a citizen must think of her "own uncompromising convictions about justice as just one set of convictions among others" and be "willing to address, in a relatively impartial way, the question of what is to be done about the fact that people like [herself] disagree with others in the society about justice."[62]

There must be a limit to this toleration, of course. The liberal political theory of Rawls would extend toleration only to view about which disagreement is reasonable, not to dissenting views as such.[63] Unfortunately, Rawls has little to say to illuminate this distinction. Reasonable comprehensive doctrines, he writes, are those that are not merely the expression of self- or class interests. Furthermore, it counts as evidence of a position's reasonableness that it is freely affirmed by citizens without the necessity of the view being imposed by coercive state power.[64] Beyond that, however, there seems to lie only a formal criterion of reasonableness: that a reasonable comprehensive doctrine is one that recognizes the criterion of reciprocal and general justification[65] (i.e., that one must be prepared to meet a demand for justification with a reason that can be accepted by the affected person). "[M]oral reasons must be intersubjective-general, discursively redeemable, *shared* reasons."[66] The injustice of limiting cases like the Jim Crow regime is inherent in the inability of those laws to be justified to affected citizens in terms they can accept. The substantive injustice of Jim Crow was treating African-Americans as less than fully equal citizens whose interests did not matter as much as those of white citizens. A comprehensive doctrine that treats others as less than human can be ruled out as unreasonable, and laws grounded solely on such a doctrine would lack legitimacy. These limiting cases are rare, however, and lawyers should be wary of assuming that their own belief in the injustice of a law is a sufficient reason to regard it as illegitimate.

3.3   Moral Reasons and Legal Obligation

In legal ethics, the conventional wisdom is that there is no *prima facie* obligation on the part of citizens to obey the law, and thus lawyers do not have an obligation of fidelity to law.[67] Lawyers, on this view, have no obligation to treat the law as a reason as such when giving advice to clients, because citizens do not have a moral obligation to obey the law. Thus, the law can only serve as a pragmatic constraint on what lawyers do on behalf of their clients. Getting caught violating the law and being subject to official penalties is unpleasant, and lawyers can help their clients avoid these bad consequences. But this is not a moral reason, only a prudential one. There can be no moral obligation for lawyers to counsel their clients on the basis of what the law requires, because clients themselves have no moral obligation to obey the law. The upshot of this position is either that lawyers have an obligation to regard client interests as the most important source of reasons for action (the usual way of understanding the Standard Conception), or that lawyers should act directly on considerations of ordinary morality (the usual way of criticizing the Standard Conception). In order to move beyond this framing of the debate, it is necessary to justify the claim that the law creates reasons for citizens.

Robert Paul Wolff offers an example to illustrate the difference between acting for good reasons at the behest of someone else and regarding that person as an authority—that is, as a person whose directives can create reasons for action:

> [I]f I am on a sinking ship and the captain is giving orders for manning the lifeboats, and if everyone else is obeying the captain *because he is the captain*, I may decide that under the circumstances I had better do what he says, since the confusion caused by disobeying him would be generally harmful. But insofar as I make such a decision, I am not *obeying his command*; that is, I am not acknowledging him as having authority over me.[68]

There may be good reasons to follow the directives of another, but the centrality of autonomy to moral responsibility requires that we never follow these directives *because* they come from someone else. To do so would be to give up the things that constitute us as persons. For something to constitute a reason means it withstands reflective scrutiny. Reflection is closely related to normativity, in that we reflect from the standpoint of having a conception of oneself, under which it makes sense to do something.[69] The interests of others can be taken into account by considering whether the reasons we rely upon in reflection would be acceptable to those who are affected by our actions.[70]

Rational self-governance is therefore fundamental to both the creation of value and the ascription of moral responsibility. Morality presupposes that people can give reasons for their actions, and acting on the basis of someone else's reasons is an abdication of an essential precondition of moral agency. As Wolff's example shows, we can do what someone tells us, but only if we independently conclude, after reflection, that there are indeed good reasons to do what that other person tells us to do. For this reason, from the point of view of an autonomous person, "there is no such thing, strictly speaking, as a *command*."[71] The only reasons to follow the captain's command are reasons that would exist whether or not the captain gave an order—namely, the importance of an orderly evacuation to saving as many lives as possible. The captain does not create those reasons; his command merely facilitates people in doing what they already have reason to do.

What is true of the captain's orders is also true of legal commands, which potentially interfere even more with the exercise of responsible moral agency by threatening citizens with coercive sanctions if they fail to comply. Wolff is a philosophical anarchist—that is, someone who believes that the law can never create reasons—but many political philosophers take a more moderate stance, claiming that the law creates new reasons for action only under certain, fairly restrictive conditions.[72] If the law commands something that is already a moral requirement, like refraining from harming others, then citizens have an obligation to do what the law demands, but that is because the action commanded is already a requirement of morality. The law may also "concretize" moral requirements,[73] for instance by specifying that the moral requirement to act reasonably to protect the safety of other users of highways requires, in certain cases, that one not exceed a certain defined speed. Additionally, there may be cases in which the law secures a fair scheme of cooperation, which requires that those benefiting from the scheme do their part to support it, and not free-ride on the cooperation of others. Apart from these cases, however, traditional arguments from consent, tacit consent, fairness, and associative obligations have been found wanting as the basis for a general obligation of obedience. Few, if any, acts by citizens of modern democracies can plausibly be taken as giving voluntary informed (actual or tacit) consent to be bound by the law, and most citizens do not voluntarily accept benefits, most of the time, from just schemes of cooperation, so that an obligation to obey could be grounded on reciprocity considerations or the need to prevent free-riding.[74]

The section immediately following (§ 3.3.1) argues that there is a general obligation to respect the law. As noted earlier, this is not quite as strong as an obligation to *obey* the law. There can be political obligations other than the obligation of obedience of the law.[75] In the circumstances of politics, it is impossible to establish a basis for cooperation and coexistence without using a procedural mechanism to settle disagreement. All citizens have an interest in living together and working on common projects, and doing so on the basis of rights that others will accept as legitimate. This means that citizens have an obligation to one another to act in a way that is respectful of moral pluralism, which means acknowledging that others may disagree in good faith about what rights people should have. Citizens comply with this obligation by acting on legal norms, which have been established by institutions and procedures entrusted with the responsibility of settling on a position, in the name of the community as a whole, regarding what should be done in a particular situation. Section 3.3.2 deals directly with the question of the strength of the reasons created by the legal system. Joseph Raz argues that it is a conceptual necessity that the law claims authority, and that legal authorities create exclusionary reasons for action.[76] Although I follow the general Razian account of the authoritative nature of law, I will argue that the law creates presumptive, not conclusive obligations.

3.3.1   *Obligation, Authority, and Exclusionary Reasons*

Arguments that have been leveled against the standard grounds for an obligation to obey the law—consent, tacit consent, fairness, and so on—have convinced many philosophers that law does not create general moral obligations, even if in some instances it may underwrite relatively discrete and localized obligations. In other words, one may deny that the law possesses legitimate authority. Possessing authority means that someone or something has a right to command action, and that right carries with it a correlative duty on the part of subjects of authority to obey these directives.[77] Authorities change the normative situation of their subjects by creating "oughts"—when an authority commands that someone perform action A, then the subject has at least a *prima facie* reason to do A.[78] The example of the captain is intended to show the tension between moral agency and authority. Following the captain's commands because he is the captain appears to involve an abdication of responsibility,

107

what Jean-Paul Sartre would call acting in bad faith.[79] Significantly, however, if one follows the captain's commands because the captain has proven in the past to be a reliable guide to safe nautical practices, and one has an interest in staying safe on the sea, then it might not be irrational, or an abdication of responsibility, to follow the captain's commands.

This observation suggests a way in which the authority of law can be defended on the basis of reasons that citizens have in any event, prior to any legal norms coming into existence. This is the solution proposed by Joseph Raz.[80] Raz holds that the only acceptable moral justification for regarding anything or anyone as an authority is that it enables a person to do better at something which he already has a good reason to aim at, as compared with the person trying to get by on her own, without the benefit of the authority.[81] This is known as the Normal Justification Thesis. This claim is rooted in reasons that an agent already has for acting, and relies on the capacity of an authority (a person or impersonal institution like the legal system) to enable the agent to do better at realizing the ends she already has a reason to pursue.

The Normal Justification Thesis sounds obscure, but an analogy with the authority of experts makes clear how it works.[82] Suppose I want to make a good beef stock for use in a consommé or sauce. I am a reasonably competent cook, and could muddle through the job, but imagine that I have food-loving friends coming over for dinner and I want this batch of beef stock to turn out to be really good. I would do better at realizing that end if I consulted the instructions in Jacques Pépin's compendium of cooking techniques than if I tried to work out the procedure on my own. I know that Pépin is a much better cook than I could ever hope to be, and that over the course of his long career he will have learned everything there is to know about the fundamentals of classical culinary techniques. Regarding Wolff's "abdication of responsibility" critique, the important thing to note is that I am not acting in bad faith or subordinating my will to Pépin, because in following his directives I am acting on the basis of reasons that are my own—namely, the desire to make a good beef stock. I am not following Pépin just because he is a highly respected chef, but because I am aware that I have reached the limits of what I can accomplish on my own, and that another person (namely Pépin) can help me do better at achieving some goal that is authentically my own.[83]

The expert analogy can only go so far, however, because much expert authority is theoretical only. The directives of a theoretical authority, such as Pépin and his book of classical cooking techniques, provide information about the balance of reasons that exists independently of the authority's utterances.[84] Regardless of what anyone has to say about the matter, a careful cook has reasons to roast the bones, keep the water at a bare simmer, and skim off the scum that rises to the top of the pot when making quality beef stock. No master chef or compilation of recipes can alter the balance of reasons that exists; the best the authority can do is alter the probabilities that a subject of authority will get the balance of reasons right.[85] Theoretical authorities are useful to people who are interested in getting the balance of reasons right, but they do not preempt the reasoning of agents who are trying to work out, on balance, what they ought to do. Even if someone might defer across the board to a theoretical authority, this deference is only weakly warranted by considerations of convenience or information costs. Perhaps someone is such a novice cook that she would never succeed in making anything if she went against Jacques Pépin's instructions, but as she gains experience, she may be justified in going her own way in certain instances. It is always open to the subject of theoretical authority to make reference to the underlying reasons and act directly on them.[86] The most that a theoretical authority can do is give good reasons for a *belief* that something is the case; it does not bear directly on the question of what one ought to do.

By contrast, practical authorities, including the law, claim to alter the normative situation of their subjects.[87] These authorities claim to create reasons for action, not merely reasons for belief, and according to Raz, these reasons preempt the underlying reasons that would otherwise apply to the subject of authority.[88] Rather than working through the balance of underlying reasons, perhaps with the guidance of an expert, the subject of practical authority must regard the directives of the authority as binding, as a conclusive reason for action. Recall that the justification for regarding anything as an authority is that following its directives enables a person to do better at what she already has reason to do. All authorities "mediat[e] between people and the right reasons which apply to them,"[89] but practical authorities can only enable people to better comply with reasons by replacing what would otherwise be reasons for action, as opposed to adding to the balance of reasons on one side or the other. This sounds counterintuitive, or even incoherent, but there are some familiar situations in which deference to the directives of another is the best way to realize one's ends.[90] Weakness of will is one example, where it may be possible to accomplish some goal only by making an advance commitment to obey the instructions of someone else whose will is presumed to be steadier. Similarly, there may be situations in which deciding on the appropriate course of action causes so much anxiety or takes so much time that someone would be justified in permitting a trusted person (like a family member) to make the decision for her.*

---

* The authority of experts may run out in certain cases, for particular subjects of the authority. For Raz, authority is a three-place relationship between an authority, the subject, and a domain of

The justification for political authority can be generalized from another case, this time based on a well-known example of Raz's, which illustrates the function of legal authorities in achieving settlement and solving coordination problems. Imagine that a dispute arises between two parties to a longstanding commercial relationship.[91] Suppose one of the parties is a distributor of machine parts designed and manufactured by the other party. The manufacturer believes the distributor has misappropriated trade secrets that relate to the manufacturing process, and is selling its own line of parts in violation of the distributorship agreement. The distributor responds that the technology at issue is not covered by trade secret protection, that the side distribution of its own parts is not a violation of the terms of the agreement, and that the manufacturer is tortiously interfering with contracts entered into by the distributor. Resolution of even this fairly simple dispute would involve numerous issues of fact, contract interpretation, and law. The relevant jurisdiction's law of contracts, trade secrets, and tortious interference with contract frame the legal issues; the language of the contract and the course of dealing of the parties sets the parameters of the private agreement to distribute the parts; and the actions of the parties (Did the distributor sell parts of such-and-such description to this party?) are disputed as issues of fact. Each of the parties has a view about the right way to interpret the contract and the applicable law, and the facts upon which the dispute has arisen. But as each tries to persuade the other of the correctness of its view, the parties realize that reasoning alone will be insufficient to resolve the dispute. The parties are at an impasse, but assume further that they both perceive an opportunity for gains from the continuing relationship. They desire that the mutually beneficial relationship continue, but need to get beyond the dispute in order for that to occur. Thus, they agree to submit the dispute to an arbitrator and regard the arbitrator's decision as a binding resolution of the dispute.

As Raz points out, the arbitrator's decision has significant features. First, the decision is useful to the parties only if it is binding regardless of whether, in the view of the parties, it is correct on the merits.[92] The authority of the arbitrator's decision is therefore said to be *content-independent*.[93] Given the

---

reasons. Raz (1986), p. 28. Some subjects may have more expertise regarding certain reasons than the authority: "An expert pharmacologist may not be subject to the authority of the government in matters of the safety of drugs..." Ibid., p. 74. This observation does not undermine the case for the authority of law because, as Raz notes, the claim to legitimacy of political authorities is rooted in their communal character. Ibid. As I have been arguing here, the law enables all citizens to justify their actions to others on the grounds of rights and duties that have been established in the name of the political community collectively. If that justification holds, it is general across all citizens of the community.

intractability of the dispute (or at least the complexity and costliness of resolving it), there would be no point in submitting the dispute to the arbitrator if each party was entitled to ignore the decision if the decision was mistaken.[94] Second, although the arbitrator's decision replaces the underlying reasons, it must be based on those reasons and not something irrelevant to the resolution of the dispute.[95] The parties want the arbitrator to resolve a dispute on the basis of a view about which party's reasons are the most persuasive, not by arbitrarily choosing a winner. If the arbitrator flipped a coin or decided for the party who paid the largest bribe, the decision would not be legitimate, in that it would not represent a justified exercise of whatever power the arbitrator claimed, and could in fact compel acquiescence in it. Similarly, some kind of Solomonic decision permitting the distributor to sell to only half its former customers would not reflect the reasons the parties had introduced in support of their claims of legal entitlement. The force of the arbitrator's decision—if it is to be regarded as legitimate—derives not from the *de facto* power of the arbitrator to compel obedience, but from the arbitrator's attempt to reflect the balance of underlying reasons in her decision. Raz refers to these underlying considerations as *dependent reasons*, and stresses that although the arbitrator's decision necessarily preempts dependent reasons, its legitimacy cannot be understood apart from the reasons that already apply to the parties.[96]

Finally, and of central importance to Raz's account of authority, the arbitrator's decision is not merely another reason to be added to the balance of underlying reasons that the parties already have for acting.[97] If it is to function for the parties as they intend it to, the arbitrator's order must replace the underlying reasons on which the dispute is based. The decision is a *preemptive* or *exclusionary* reason for the parties to act, in the sense that reasons the parties could have relied upon (such as a view about the way a contract provision should be interpreted) can no longer be relied upon after the arbitrator's decision is given.[98] After the decision is rendered, to the extent the parties are interested in some issue covered by the decision, such as whether the distributor is entitled to make use of certain intellectual property of the manufacturer, the reasons the parties give for action are limited to the arbitrator's decision. "The order clearly permits me to sell machine parts to X," is a permissible reason for the distributor's action, while "selling machine parts to X is not prohibited by the contract," is not a permissible reason.

Raz argues that authoritative reasons must be exclusionary in order for the authority to serve the end for which it is needed by the parties. In the arbitrator example, each party believes it has the balance of applicable reasons right. Unless one of them is acting strategically or in bad faith (certainly a possibility), each would be claiming to have a justification for their position that is grounded in the facts, contract provisions, and applicable law. The existence of the other party, who believes her own claims are equally well justified, creates an impasse. Both parties would like to act in the context of this jointly created commercial relationship, but each finds that the presence of the other, and the disagreement over the right way to evaluate their respective claims of right, stymies their capacity to do anything. Thus, in order to go further, the parties need to appeal to a procedural mechanism that will resolve their disagreement and create a reason for action that supersedes the underlying reasons the parties bring to the dispute. The context of the ongoing relationship not only limits the parties' options, but also creates a constraint on the sorts of considerations they can appeal to in order to get beyond the impasse. As long as there is some reasonable basis for the parties' respective positions, appeals to the rightness of the reasons supporting those positions will be futile. The parties must "retreat to neutral ground," as it were, and find some basis for continued cooperation upon which they can both agree.[99]

Raz's arbitrator example suggests a simple intuitive picture of the authority of law.[100] This is not an invisible-hand explanation suggesting that the law of any community has actually evolved in this way. Rather, the example is intended to be more in the nature of a fable, similar to the stories found in economics textbooks to illustrate the development of money or the banking system. It explains the authority of law not as a matter of its historical pedigree, but on the basis of its normative attractiveness, by bringing into relief what we would lose if we gave up on the concept of legality.[101] The idea is that if people disagree about the course of action that best conforms to the requirements of reason, but nevertheless agree that something needs to be done, the only way to realize their ends may be to defer to the directives of an authoritative person or institution. In doing so, they effectively agree to treat the authority's reasons as *the* reason for doing what ought to be done. In the arbitrator example, the authority of the decision arises from the consent of the parties to be bound by the arbitrator's judgment; in the case of the law, authority arises from the circumstances of politics.

The argument here adds a bit of flavor from John Finnis's modern natural law theory to the Razian account of authority. Finnis begins with the observation that all individuals all subject to the demands of morality—as he puts it, we have to engage in practical reasoning about the relationship between our own well-being and the well-being of others.[102] Although we can agree on the importance of certain basic values at a high level of generality,[103] we have to determine what these moral values mean in terms of concrete practical action. Our reasoning about the demands of morality must be coordinated with that of others—without this coordination, we cannot be said to be acting in a community.[104] When we act in communities with others, and our actions affect the interests of others, we have to think about what morality demands of us as individuals, but also be sensitive to the possibility that others might disagree with our specification of concrete principles for action, and how completing principles should be weighted and prioritized.

This is not a position distinctive to Finnis. Rawls, who differs from Finnis in many respects, emphasizes the burdens of judgment that lead to reasonable disagreement among persons.[105] What is distinctive in Finnis is the idea that an authority is necessary to coordinate the efforts of all citizens to comply with the demands of morality in a political community.[106] If people in a larger-scale community are concerned to comply with the demands of morality, and these demands include (as they must) concern for the interests of others, then citizens in a community face a problem: Each person is concerned with realizing her own interests, consistent with the demands imposed by morality that her actions in pursuit of her own interests not interfere with the interests of others, without justification. There must, therefore, be a means by which the demands of morality are coordinated, so that people are able to act rightly, with justification, in light of the interests of others which give rise to the demand for justification. The law should be deemed legitimate insofar as it enables individuals to act on the common good, where the "common good" is understood as "a whole ensemble of material and other considerations that tend to favour the realization, by each individual in the community, of his or her own personal development."[107] Individual reason alone will not lead to a conclusion regarding what morality requires in a community, because compliance with morality in a community *means* coordinating one's own beliefs about morality with the beliefs of others.

3.3.2 *Presumptive or Conclusive Obligations?*

I have said that I differ from Raz in not holding that authorities create exclusionary reasons for action. The position defended here is that it is enough for the legal system to establish very weighty reasons, which should be overridden only in extraordinary circumstances. The argument here also differs from both Raz and Finnis in being more normative, and less conceptual. Finnis offers a constitutive argument, appealing to the notion of what compliance in communities means as a conceptual matter; importantly, he does not appeal to the good consequences of an authoritative settlement, such as peace or stability.[108] Raz similarly argues that it is a truth concerning the concept of an authority that the directives of authority preempt the reasons that otherwise would apply to the subjects of authority.[109] In contrast to Raz and Finnis, the basis of my argument is a more frankly normative appeal to the value of treating other citizens with respect in the circumstances of politics.

People who disagree can deal with each other in various ways. The least respectful way involves attempting to dominate others by physical force or intimidation. This response to disagreement fairly obviously displays the attitude that others are merely obstacles to realizing the satisfaction of one's desires, not to mention creating the cycle of violence and fear so memorably described by Hobbes. A more respectful way of handling disagreement is to seek to persuade others. An attempt at persuasion appeals to another's status as someone who can be moved by appeals to shared interests and values, thereby displaying recognition of the equality of the participants in the dialogue, at least with respect to the capacity to deliberate on reasons.[110] Suppose, however, that persuasion is ineffective and we are in the circumstances of politics, where people disagree in good faith over the solutions that should be adopted to a variety of pressing problems. In the circumstances of politics, deliberation is insufficient to secure unanimous agreement on a course of action that can be pursued in the name of the whole society.[111] Something else is needed to enable the action that all agree is necessary.

That "something else" should be a procedure that does as well as possible at treating the views of all citizens as presumptively entitled to respect, consistent with the need to eventually resolve the dispute and settle on a common course of action, in the name of the community as a whole. The law enables people to transform brute demands into claims of entitlement. In other words, the legal settlement of normative dispute represents the best we can do, as a society marked by deep and persistent disagreement, to embody equality in our relations with one another, and to act on the recognition of the inherent dignity of all persons. Equality and dignity are the normative underpinnings of this argument, and embodying respect for persons is the source of the obligation to respect the law.

It is true that citizens often experience the law as an irritant, rather than something that deserves allegiance. Popular culture is replete with admiration for lawbreakers, from the Clash defiantly singing "I fought the law and the law won," to the Hollywood cliché of the maverick cop who is willing to break a few rules to catch the bad guys.[112] Less dramatically, people put quarters in parking meters because they would rather not get a ticket, not out of some grandiose conception of the social value of parking regulations. Regardless of one's motivation, however, the law in fact establishes a means of living alongside one's fellow citizens and treating them as bearers of rights. If someone claims that the law does not really create an obligation, she is in effect claiming a kind of superior power over her fellows, an immunity from having to abide by the same rules as others. It is no different than pushing to the front of a queue or using connections to get a child into an elite private school. These are all relatively minor instances of disrespect, in the sense that chaos and disorder are not likely to break out if a few people refuse to abide by the rules, but they are nevertheless affronts to the equality and dignity of others. Think about the reaction one has to queue-jumpers: "Hey, you jerk! What makes you special?" The sense of offense one experiences is connected to the sense of having been treated as less than an equal by the offender.

In contrast with instances of self-help, the law resolves disagreement in a way that takes seriously the claims of other citizens to have their preferences considered impartially, and not to have their voices count for less than others' in determining what should be done in the name of society as a whole.[113] Ignoring the law essentially takes back the respect that was extended to individuals by legal processes, and replaces it with the exercise of raw power, or with the attitude that the individual stands apart from society as a whole and is, in effect, a law unto herself. Refusing to justify oneself to others on the basis of legal entitlements leaves one in the rather embarrassing position of simply expressing bare desires, like a toddler throwing a tantrum. One may comply with the law only grudgingly, as is often the case with annoying intrusions of the law into one's daily life, but even grudging compliance expresses respect for one's fellow citizens. We may valorize disobedience in popular culture, but it cannot consistently serve as a basis for the ethics of citizenship because of the disrespect for others manifested by defiance of the law. Thus, there is an obligation to obey even an unjust law, as long as the law does not exceed some limit of injustice.[114]

Because this is a normative argument, not a conceptual claim like those advanced by Raz and Finnis, the weight of the obligation to respect the law must be established separately. Recognition of the equality and dignity of others, being in the circumstance of politics, and the capacity of the law to transform demands into claims of right create moral reasons to act in a way that manifests respect for the law. Those reasons may have different weights, as follows:

1. A moral reason but, without more, not an obligation to obey the law.
2. A *prima facie* or (stronger) presumptive reason. That is, in the absence of some reason to act otherwise, which rebuts the presumption, there will be an obligation to obey the law.
3. A conclusive reason to obey the law.

Position (1) represents the conventional wisdom in legal ethics.[115] Critics of the Standard Conception argue that lawyers are attempting to pull a moral rabbit out of the hat of the positive duties that define the lawyer's role. But the trick, of course, depends on getting the rabbit into the hat in the first place, and without some moral reason to respect the law, there would be no reason to respect the requirements of a role that are keyed to legal obligations.[116] These critics concede that sometimes there may be a reason to obey the law, but this must be established independently, based on the features of the particular situation, such as the law tracking what is otherwise a moral requirement, or creating a fair scheme of cooperation. There is no general obligation to obey the law, even if there may be an obligation in particular cases.

Logically, position (3) is the conclusion of the Normal Justification Thesis, as applied to the authority of law. For Raz, it is necessarily true that authorities create exclusionary reasons. Rather than making this sort of argument, however, one might offer normative (or maybe better described as functional) arguments, relying on the point of having law in the first place.[117] This argument would begin by asking why it matters that lawyers work within a practice in which legal norms are differentiated from extra-legal moral considerations. The claim in this chapter is that law can perform its function as a distinctive mode of governance precisely because of its independence from contested moral considerations. In a pluralistic society, the law provides a framework for coordinated action in the face of disagreement. "[T]he values associated with law, legality, and the rule of law—in a fairly rich sense—can best be achieved if the ordinary operation of such a system does not require people to exercise moral judgment in order to find out what the law is."[118] The value of legality can best be achieved by directing lawyers (representing either private citizens or government actors) not to act directly on what they perceive to be the requirements of morality or justice, because what morality and justice requires is contested, in good faith, in most interesting cases. The law provides a framework for dealing, as a community, with these problems by enacting a provisional settlement of normative disagreement.

Because this is not a conceptual argument, it makes no claim to be true of all laws, in all places and at all times. Instead, it is a claim about the normative attractiveness of law, based on the values it might secure, in a pluralistic society in which there are tolerably fair procedures available for the enactment of laws. It is therefore implausible to think that it underwrites an absolute obligation of obedience. We are therefore somewhere in position (2), and the remaining question is whether the argument given here justifies a *prima facie* obligation or something stronger, like a presumptive obligation. In either case, the question can be seen in terms of how much must be shown, on the other side of the balance, to justify disobedience. The answer to the question, put in these terms, depends on whether we are talking about the obligations of citizens or of lawyers. Citizens may be permitted to disrespect the law in ways that are prohibited for lawyers. The distinctiveness of the social role of lawyer and its associated rights and duties must be understood with reference to the value of legality. The role of citizen, by contrast, is not so narrowly defined.

In thinking about the obligations of citizens and lawyers, it is important not to become too preoccupied with marginal cases. Although a theory of legal obligation has to have something to say about Nazi law and the Jim Crow regime in the American South (which will be taken up in the next section), a theory of legal obligation *as applied to legal ethics* should have more to say about how lawyers in run-of-the-mill law practice settings should conceive of the significance of client legal entitlements in their representation of clients. Most of the interesting issues for practicing lawyers turn out not to be akin to the situation of citizens in Nazi Germany. Rather, they are often matters of legal analysis and interpretation, and the attitude one should take toward the laws of an essentially decent and just regime. The obligation to respect the law turns out to be contextualized in interesting ways, depending on the specific role of the lawyer and the ambiguity that exists in the law. Rather than talking in general terms about this duty of respect, it is more productive to situate this discussion in the context of various practical problems that lawyers encounter.

For example, the value of legality makes it wrong for lawyers to engage in excessively "creative and aggressive" interpretation of legal norms when advising clients or structuring transactions.[119] Lawyers know that no matter how clear a rule appears to be, there will be some exploitable ambiguity, some room for manipulation. This wiggle room is limited, however, despite the belief prevalent among non-lawyers that the language in which legal norms are embodied is infinitely manipulable, and a sufficiently clever lawyer can make the law mean whatever the client wants it to mean. This attitude is exemplified in the well-known quote from J. P. Morgan, who insisted that he did not "want a lawyer to tell me what I cannot do; I hire him to tell me how to do what I want to do."[120] However, lawyers know, at least if they are being honest with themselves, that words cannot be made to mean anything at all. There are interpretations that fail to pass the proverbial straight-face test, and interpretations that range from "colorable" (meaning there is some support, but not much, for the interpretation), to those on which reasonable minds can differ, to those which most lawyers would agree are well within the mainstream view of well-informed judges and lawyers. As discussed at some length in chapter 2, the permissibility of relying on a more aggressive interpretation depends to a great extent on how much adversarial procedural checking exists, whether in litigation or in some regulatory or transactional setting. The same legal position ("my client is entitled to do X, for the following reasons...") may be permissible in litigation but unacceptable as the basis for prospective legal advice or transactional planning.

Similarly, context plays a role in assessing the relevance of the ordinary moral considerations that would seem to cut against an obligation of fidelity to law. David Luban has written about the case of a prosecutor in the Manhattan District Attorney's office who allegedly threw a case in favor of the defense, because he was personally convinced of the innocence of the accused.[121] The prosecutor, Daniel Bibb, had been asked to conduct an internal investigation of a murder prosecution, and after a two-year review, concluded that two men in prison were innocent. Defense lawyers representing the two men had obtained a court hearing into the possibility that newly discovered evidence would show their innocence. Bibb urged his supervisors to ask the court to set aside the convictions, but the supervisors ordered him to go to the hearing and present the strongest case for the government. Rather than following this instruction, Bibb helped the defense lawyers sort through the new evidence, persuaded reluctant witnesses to testify who could offer testimony helpful to the defendants, told the witnesses what questions to expect at the hearing, and refused to attempt to undermine the credibility of the witnesses on cross-examination. Commenting on the case, Stephen Gillers said Bibb should be disciplined for subverting the government's case. Luban responded that Bibb deserved a medal, not a reprimand.

The debate between Gillers and Luban can be understood as turning on the weight a lawyer should give to ordinary moral considerations when serving in a representative capacity. As Gillers put it, Bibb may be entitled to his conscience, but his conscience permits only withdrawal from the case, not throwing for the defense. Luban, by contrast, believes that the role of a prosecutor incorporates a significant component of ordinary moral decision-making. The role of a prosecutor is to seek justice, not to win at all costs. Luban admits that the positive law governing prosecutors specifies that the "seek justice" maxim should be understood in certain narrow ways, including an obligation not to pursue a prosecution without probable cause, and duties to turn over potentially exculpatory or mitigating evidence.[122] Still, he argues for a substantive ethical conception of the prosecutor's role in which seeking justice means more than merely complying with requirements stated in disciplinary rules and constitutional law. At a minimum, seeking justice means "you shouldn't try to keep people behind bars if you think they didn't do it." Fidelity to law cannot possibly mean actively seeking to keep someone in jail if a lawyer has a sincere well-founded belief that he is innocent.

The weakness in Luban's argument is that it overlooks the institutional context of Bibb's decision. The whole point of institutional decision-making processes is that one person's sincere belief about something is only an input into the process. Bibb's certainty of the innocence of the two defendants is not conclusive of what ought to be done with their cases. A conclusive decision comes only after each actor in the system does its job, presenting what necessarily is a one-sided partisan view of the evidence. The relevant process here is not just the adversary system, in which opposing evidence is presented by defense counsel (who may have secured the reversal of the convictions anyway, without Bibb's assistance), but also includes intra-office review procedures and the chain of command that necessarily facilitates decision-making in large organizations. Significantly, Bibb's supervisors disagreed with him, concluding that there was good reason to believe the two men were guilty. Why should we trust Bibb's belief more than the belief of his supervisors? Presumably they made their decision upon consideration of all of the evidence developed by Bibb in the internal investigation. Bibb can be made to seem like a hero in this case only by stipulating that he made the right analysis of the innocence of the defendants, but that simply begs the question, because the office hierarchy and the internal investigation process are set up for the purpose of reaching conclusions about whether there is enough evidence of guilt or innocence to justify going to trial.

More generally, the valorization of lawyers like Bibb, who act on the basis of their own beliefs about what justice requires, reflects a pervasive distrust of institutions by legal ethics scholars.[123] There is a tendency to presume that if an institutional process has reached one conclusion (e.g., "sufficient evidence of guilt") and an individual actor has reached the contrary conclusion, the individual must be right. No one can deny that institutions can reach unjust results, and can pressure or socialize individuals into doing wrong.[124] The Milgram experiments, Stanford Prison Experiment, and other findings of social psychology demonstrate that people in groups respond to subtle behavioral cues, and unconsciously rationalize away ethical qualms, all in the service of some collective end which may be appalling (such as administering life-threatening electrical shocks). The response to this observation, however, is not to rely more extensively on individual ethical decision-making, because the whole point of these findings is that individual judgment can be corrupted by situational factors. Instead of calling upon people to do the right thing, either explicitly or implicitly by praising lawyers like Daniel Bibb, we should seek more effective regulatory approaches to ensure that institutions do not become corrupt.[125] One may respond that, in the event of some regulatory failure, individual decision-makers may still be in a position to avoid injustice. Whether there may be a better way to safeguard against wrongful convictions is one thing, but it is quite another to say that Bibb should not take personal moral responsibility for avoiding a wrongful conviction if there has been some systemic failing.

Bibb's defenders may respond that his actions were based on his belief about facts, not contested normative concepts like the public interest. Luban, for instance, has long been a vigorous critic of the claim that the adversary system can be justified on its utility at finding out factual truth.[126] Adversarial litigation is often animated by a concern to suppress relevant facts, not disclose them; a great deal of discovery practice in civil litigation is aimed at ensuring that one's adversary does not find out the whole truth. Underfunded parties may lack the resources to conduct a thorough investigation, so not only will they be ignorant of facts within their opponents' knowledge, but they may also be unaware of facts they might otherwise have been able to discover, given more time and money. It is certainly not inconceivable that, in the course of a two-year internal investigation, Bibb was able to learn previously unknown evidence suggesting the innocence of the two defendants. On the basis of this evidence, Bibb believed his office should do something to ensure the acquittal of the defendants.

The crucial elision in this argument comes between the word *evidence* and the inference to conclusions about facts. Assuming Bibb acquired evidence, it still remains to be determined, somehow, whether the defendants are factually guilty or innocent. Because matters of the weight, sufficiency, and credibility of evidence are things about which people can disagree, we have set up various institutional processes for dealing with this disagreement. Adversarial litigation is one such process, but so are intra-office chains of command and review procedures. Institutions such as law firms and prosecutors' offices are set up, in part, with a view toward making reliable decisions about what should be done, in light of the evidence known to the lawyers in the organization. These decisions are often made against a background of good-faith disagreements about the right conclusion to draw from the evidence. In this case, Bibb presented to his supervisors all of the evidence he learned, and the supervisors concluded that there was sufficient reason to continue to believe that the defendants were guilty. There must be some reason to believe that Bibb is more likely to have weighed all of the relevant evidence correctly. Bibb would not be "ducking his moral responsibility" if he had complied with the procedures of his office.[127] Rather, doing the morally responsible thing means respecting the institutional scheme that is set up to accomplish some morally worthwhile end.

The Bibb example is meant to illustrate the overall point of this chapter, which is that a lawyer has a very weighty moral reason to act with reference to client entitlements and work through established procedures, rather than acting on the basis of ordinary moral notions like truth and justice. This obligation of fidelity to law holds in reasonably just well-functioning political systems, and depends on the capacity of the system to enable people to arrange their relationships with each other with reference to rights established in the name of the community as a whole. Acting peremptorily, on one's own beliefs about what justice requires, or drawing one's own conclusions about what the facts are that bear on a matter, exhibits disrespect for the legal system and thus for one's fellow citizens. The lawyer's duty is not absolute, and there may be circumstances in which an injustice is so patent, and the result mandated by the regular functioning of the legal system so intolerable, that no person could, in good conscience, believe that exhibiting fidelity to law is the right thing to do, all things considered. There will, of course, be disagreement about which cases fall into this category, but the important thing for the purposes of this argument is to note that the obligation of fidelity to law is very weighty, and lawyers should regard as exceptional any case of deviation from a result supported by client legal entitlements.

This is a strong claim on behalf of the authority of law, but the relationship between legal and moral obligations is a bit more complicated for practicing lawyers. The reason is that the law incorporates many opportunities for discretionary decision-making, by both citizens and lawyers, which may permit reference to ordinary morality. Being a lawyer is not a matter of blindly obeying the law to the exclusion of morality. The next chapter considers the practical effect of the obligation of fidelity to law on lawyers' moral decision-making, with reference to several problems that recur for lawyers acting in a representative capacity.

Legal Entitlements and Public Reason in Practice

If the arguments up to this point are sound, then the fundamental obligation of the lawyer's role is fidelity to the law itself. The law supersedes moral disagreement and provides a basis, however thin, for social cooperation and solidarity. Lawyers are expected to be faithful agents of their clients, ascertaining and defending their clients' legal entitlements, notwithstanding any moral disagreement they may have with their client. In several important areas, however, including client selection, withdrawal from representation, and client counseling, the law governing lawyers contemplates a role for ordinary moral considerations in the lawyer's decision-making process. In these areas, the lawyer's role is not strictly differentiated from ordinary morality. Lawyers have some moral discretion, even when acting in a representative capacity. Even so, there is an overarching professional idea of fidelity to law that should inform these exercises of discretion.[1] Despite occasional references to ordinary moral reasons, the overall structure of the law demands commitment to legal ideals, at a high level of generality, as opposed to making case-by-case determinations of the justice of clients' causes. This obligation is not absolute, but it is quite weighty, and in most cases will displace the ordinary moral reasons a lawyer would otherwise have for acting. Recognizing a near-absolute obligation changes the analysis of lawyers' duties in important ways. Essentially, lawyers should be seen as having duties more reminiscent of those of public officials, rather than being understood straightforwardly as ordinary moral agents, who just happen to do things on behalf of other persons.

Beyond these pockets of discretionary moral decision-making recognized by the law governing lawyers, many of the problematic cases in legal ethics have a common structure, involving a client with an actual or apparent legal entitlement that would permit the client to do something contrary to ordinary moral values such as justice, dignity, or equality. Not only does the lawyer appear to be a moral wrongdoer for assisting the client in those circumstances, but the law itself appears to be an instrument of wrongdoing, and thus not entitled to respect. What is missed in this line of criticism is that the law can still have value, and this value can structure the lawyer's role so extensively that the ethics of lawyering diverges from ordinary morality. Legality has moral value, and it is this value that underpins the lawyer's role and gives it normative significance. The problems in this chapter are all concerned, in one way or another, with the way this balance between ordinary morality and the moral value associated with the rule of law should be struck for lawyers in practice. The implication of the fidelity to law conception defended here is that the ethics of lawyering is constituted principally by the political obligation of respect for the law, not ordinary moral considerations.

4.1   Disobedience and Nullification

A persistent feature of our thinking about the rule of law and the value of legality is that we remain justified in disobeying substantively unjust laws. In some cases, we believe that morality permits, even requires, various forms of dissent that may be deemed unlawful.

> It will quite often happen that in "a well-ordered society" which is "a fair system of cooperation between reasonable and rational citizens regarded as free and equal," a group of citizens, probably a minority, finds its strongest moral convictions overridden by policies that have been fairly chosen within the basic institutions recognized by the dissenters themselves as fair. The dissenters are not irrational fanatics, and they agree that fair and just institutions ought to be respected and obeyed, except when they engender policies that are for them morally unacceptable.[2]

This is not philosophical anarchism, because the dissenters here concede that just institutions generally ought to be obeyed. The problem is rather that there may be pockets of injustice within an otherwise just legal system. Despite the hope of theorists like Lon Fuller, that following fair lawmaking procedures will result in substantively just laws,[3] there are too many counterexamples of basically just legal systems that nevertheless enact substantively unjust laws, using formally reasonable procedures. In the United States, the Alien and Sedition Acts, the Chinese Exclusion Act, and the Fugitive Slave Act, as well as the Nuremberg Laws of Nazi Germany, were all in compliance with formal standards that are inherent in the concept of legality.[4] A theory of legal ethics must have something to say about when the obligation of fidelity to law runs out in the face of substantive injustice. One possibility is that lawyers should be empowered to disregard unjust laws when representing clients.

As I will discuss, however, most interesting cases in legal ethics do not really implicate civil disobedience or conscientious objection, as those practices are generally understood.

4.1.1 Civil Disobedience and Conscientious Objection

Civil disobedience is the public, non-violent, conscientious violation of a law for the purpose of calling attention to its substantial and clear injustice.[5] The aim of civil disobedience is persuasion—either transforming the political community's values or reminding the community of its existing commitments, from which it has strayed.[6] It accordingly appeals to those political principles actually shared within the community, or those principles to which the community ought to aspire, as opposed to idiosyncratic personal moral reasons.[7] Because civil disobedience is aimed at persuading political officials and one's fellow citizens, it must manifest respect for the basic legal institutions of the society. Martin Luther King's famous defense of civil disobedience calls for breaking unjust laws openly, lovingly, and with a willingness to accept the penalty.[8]

King's directive to disobey "lovingly" may sound odd, particularly abstracted from the religious context from which it grows, but it does focus attention on the attitude conveyed toward other citizens by obedience or disobedience to the law. The idea behind civil disobedience is that justice will better be promoted by violating the law in a particular instance, while nevertheless expressing respect for one's fellow citizens and the basic institutions of one's society. For this reason, it is essential to justified civil disobedience that the actor accept the legal penalties for her violation of the law. Limiting justified disobedience to those who are willing to accept punishment also keeps the scope of disobedience in check, so that it does not threaten the stability of society or its laws generally.[9] Familiar examples of civil disobedience from American history are lunch-counter sit-ins by African-American students to protest Jim Crow laws, and draft card burning to protest the Vietnam war.

Conscientious objection refers to the morally motivated refusal of a citizen to obey a law, on the grounds that it would involve her in moral wrongdoing.[10] It is not a public statement to the community as a whole, made with the aim of persuading other citizens or political officials. Rather, it is essentially a private act. For this reason, it may be based on moral reasons that are not shared by the community as a whole.[11] Conscientious objection is exemplified by the refusal of pacifists to register for the draft, or the refusal by some pharmacists to dispense contraceptive products that they believe would involve them in the taking of human life. The law may or may not accept sincere conscientious motivations as an excuse or a mitigating factor when determining whether punishment is warranted.

A decent tolerant society should recognize some latitude for morally motivated refusal to obey, but only to the extent consistent with the circumstances of politics. That is, people who disagree about matters of conscience still must coexist and cooperate, and require some basis for doing so that establishes a basis for stable legal rights. In many cases, however, it is possible to recognize claims of conscientious objection without destabilizing the common framework of legal entitlements. For example, in a large city with many competing pharmacies, a customer's legal entitlement to obtain prescription contraceptives will not be substantially burdened by the conscientious refusals of a few pharmacists to dispense the prescription; the analysis may be different in an isolated area with only one pharmacist. Similarly, the law governing lawyers contemplates conscientious objection by lawyers, and generally does not require the representation of clients the lawyer deems repugnant, nor the use of morally disagreeable tactics. In a small town in which few lawyers have the relevant experience and skills, this kind of morally motivated refusal may substantially burden the legal entitlements of certain clients. In most cases, however, competition in the market for legal services renders conscientious objection a relatively marginal problem.

As applied to lawyers, the categories of civil disobedience and conscientious objection cover only a small range of cases. These concepts should not be understood broadly as, for instance, "lawyers who, for reasons of conscience of political commitment, act illegally or unethically as part of their 'client service.'"[12] As noted, civil disobedience covers only open public disobedience of the law, accompanied by a willingness to accept punishment. Conscientious objection is permissible only in cases in which lawyers have such a fundamental moral disagreement that it essentially rises to the level of a conflict of interest. (This point will be elaborated on a little further in Section 4.2 of this chapter.) Most of the cases discussed by legal ethics scholars under the rubric of civil disobedience or conscientious objection actually involve something else, like covert evasion of the law or, less dramatically, cases in which the lawyer has *legal* authority not to take some action that she regards as immoral. The following sections consider these cases.

4.1.2 *Legal Permissions vs. Legal Duties*

A simple but important point may be obscured by the analysis of authority and legal obligations. The law in many cases establishes permissions to do something, but not obligations to do it. Moreover, a good deal of law is facilitative, in that it provides the tools for citizens to do something, but otherwise sets few restrictions on what may be done. This is the character of much of the law of contracts, corporations and other business associations, and trusts and estates. Thus, much law cannot be understood as imposing obligations of the form "you must do X"; rather, the law in effect says, "if you want to do X, that is permitted, but it is also permitted not to do X." When the law imposes obligations, it usually excludes other reasons. On the other hand, when the law makes something legally permissible, it leaves the underlying balance of reasons largely unaltered. If someone wants to start a business to sell widgets, the law does not alter the balance of reasons one would have for selling widgets; the law instead makes it easier to raise capital, establish clear expectations, reassure third parties, and so on. These are valuable aspects of legal ordering, but they do not depend on the capacity of the law to create exclusionary reasons. Because the balance of underlying reasons is unaltered by the law in these cases, the evaluation of the actors' decisions in ordinary moral terms is also unaffected by the law.

As an example of the distinction between a legal permission and a legal obligation, consider the statute of limitations case from chapter 1. The statute of limitations is an affirmative defense that may be asserted by a debtor, but is by no means obligatory. Although Borrower is legally permitted to rely on the statute as a basis for dismissing a lawsuit for repayment of the debt, the law does not alter the moral reasons the debtor would have, which would require repayment. Thus, one would be justified in regarding Borrower as a jerk for not repaying the loan. But what about Borrower's lawyer? The Standard Conception insists that the lawyer is not a wrongdoer if she asserts the statute of limitations in a motion to dismiss, at the direction of her client. This conclusion would follow, however, only if the law governing lawyers requires lawyers to abide by their clients' lawful instructions concerning the representation. There is some ambiguity in the disciplinary rules, which often goes unnoticed by non-lawyers writing on legal ethics, concerning the obligation of the lawyer to employ aggressive or offensive tactics on behalf of clients. The disciplinary rule on the allocation of decision-making authority states that a lawyer must abide by the client's decisions concerning the objectives of the representation, but retains discretion to make decisions concerning the means by which they will be carried out.[13] Certain decisions are so important that they are within the area of the client's exclusive authority. These decisions include whether to make or accept an offer of settlement of a civil case, or whether to plead guilty in a criminal case. By analogy, other matters may be sufficiently important that the lawyer ought to defer to the client's wishes.[14] Other decisions, respecting "technical, legal and tactical matters," are within the lawyer's exclusive authority. The lawyer should consult with the client about these tactical decisions, even if the client's informed consent is not necessary to authorize the lawyer to make them.[15]

Thus, if Borrower insists on asserting the statute of limitations, the lawyer first must determine whether the decision is one for the client to make, or whether she has the legal discretion to refuse to comply with the client's request. Given the outcome-determinative effect of asserting the statute of limitations as an affirmative defense, I would contend it should be regarded as a decision within the client's exclusive scope of authority, not one over which the lawyer has discretion. If that is the case, the lawyer's lawful options are to comply with this instruction, seek to dissuade the client, or withdraw from representation (if otherwise permitted).* Borrower has two legal entitlements in this case — one, to assert the statute of limitations as a defense, and the second, to have a lawyer (if one has been retained, there being no right to counsel in civil cases) assist with vindicating this entitlement, by filing a motion to dismiss the lawsuit. Notice that the law does not alter the balance of reasons Borrower would otherwise have for acting. The only effect of the law is to remove the possibility of legal penalties, in the form of a judgment against the debtor, if Borrower refused to pay back the loan. By contrast, the law does significantly alter the balance of reasons that Borrower's lawyer would otherwise have. As a result of entering into a lawyer–client relationship with Borrower, the lawyer has become bound by the law of agency and torts to exercise reasonable care on behalf of Borrower, and to follow Borrower's lawful instructions. It is true the lawyer may be legally permitted to withdraw from the representation, but this should be considered as a last resort, available only in exceptional cases. While working on behalf of Borrower, a lawyer's discretion is limited by applicable law, and thus the law alters the lawyer's practical reasoning in a way it does not affect Borrower's.

One may still question the conclusion that the lawyer should not be blamed in ordinary moral terms for helping Borrower avoid repaying a just debt. The statute of limitations is part of a class of procedural entitlements that sometimes have the effect of defeating the resolution of lawsuits on the merits. (Others include waiver rules for appellate courts, procedural default doctrines in habeas corpus proceedings, preclusive sanctions for various kinds of litiga-

---

* Withdrawal in this case would require permission of the tribunal in which the litigation was proceeding. Model Rules, Rule 1.16(c). Judges tend to be skeptical of motions by counsel to withdraw, believing (often rightly) that they are merely strategic ploys to cause delay in the litigation.

tion misconduct, and rules of evidence law that exclude probative evidence for extrinsic policy reasons.) What I want to suggest here is that the merits of a position may matter differently for clients than for lawyers. Intuitively, one regards Borrower as a wrongdoer in this case because his situation is straightforwardly a choice between paying the debt or avoiding it, albeit through legally authorized means. The lawyer's situation is different, however, because refusing to assist Borrower in asserting a legal entitlement would be to deprive a client of that very thing for which the role of lawyer is constituted. There is moral value associated with the lawyer's role because lawyers contribute to the functioning of a system that has moral value; the system's value, in turn, depends on its capacity to establish a framework for the orderly resolution of disagreement. Notably, the system is concerned with more than the merits of claims. Rule of procedure, for example, are to be "construed and administered to secure the just, speedy, and inexpensive determination of every action and proceeding."[16] Justice is one value among many that are served by the legal system, and lawyers must respect all of these values, to the extent they are embodied in positive legal norms.

Nevertheless, the moral criticism of the lawyer in this case may be based on the sense that, whatever one might say about the value of procedural entitlements in general, *in this case* the entitlement simply defeats substantive justice, with no corresponding benefit in terms of finality, reliability, reduction in expense, or any other procedural virtues. No good comes out of this particular representation, so the lawyer appears to be bootstrapping moral value out of things that are true of the statute of limitations only in very general terms. To some extent, however, the whole point of legal entitlements is that they are relatively insensitive to justice or injustice in particular cases. The classic ideal of the rule of law is that "all persons and authorities within the state, whether public or private, should be bound by and entitled to the benefit of laws publicly and prospectively promulgated and publicly administered by the courts."[17] The requirements of prospective promulgation and impartial administration of laws entail a certain amount of insensitivity to case-by-case injustices, and it's a good thing, too.[18] It is good because it is this quality of the law that enables it to serve as a check on the arbitrary exercise of power, and to enable people to coordinate their actions around claims of right, established in the name of the community as a whole. Because the moral value of the law depends on it being general and prospective, lawyers should understand their obligations not in terms of individual case-level justice, but instead in terms of fidelity to the legal system. The moral quality of actions by lawyers and clients may therefore differ, and we may consistently criticize Borrower for avoiding a just debt, while approving of the lawyer's conduct in filing a motion to dismiss on the grounds of the statute of limitations.

4.1.3 *Lawyering for Change*

It is important to emphasize that the law establishes only a *provisional* settlement that gives due weight to the positions of citizens who disagree with each other. The law creates a structure or a framework of moderate stability, but within this framework disagreement remains possible.[19] The legal system may therefore establish procedures that enable citizens to challenge the existing settlement and accompanying distribution of legal entitlements. Some of these procedures naturally require that citizens work through lawyers. For example, civil rights lawsuits enable citizens to challenge the abuse of state power, and in the process to establish the boundaries of permissible state action. Impact litigation seeks to bring about institutional changes on a large scale, such as school desegregation and prison reform. Some constitutional rights may be asserted against the government by plaintiffs in actions for damages; fee-shifting provisions in some of these statutes create incentives for lawyers to bring these claims.[20] Criminal defense lawyers assert procedural entitlements on their clients' behalf, and the results of these trials and appeals further refine the established rights that individuals can assert against the state. Even ordinary civil litigators, who are ordinarily prohibited from asserting frivolous claims (i.e., those unsupported by a colorable interpretation of existing law), are permitted to make good faith arguments for the extension, modification, or reversal of existing law.[21] Rules prohibiting the in-person solicitation of prospective clients have exceptions for lawyers seeking to assist individuals who are willing to challenge unjust laws.[22] Finally, lawyers are encouraged by professional tradition to represent unpopular clients and to challenge injustice.

Far from acquiescing in the existing settlement, lawyers who use procedures such as these are resisting it, but they are resisting it through legally established means. Once a legal system recognizes the right to bring claims on behalf of disempowered clients, cast in terms of legal rights, lawyers may use these procedures to challenge the existing settlement. "[L]egality, because it provides the legitimating ideology of the powerful, can be an important weapon in the political struggle."[23] Thus, what may seem to be a system that protects the interests of the powerful may be turned on itself, in the service of the powerless. Thus, the concept of legality, and a normatively attractive theory of lawyering, can tolerate, and may even depend upon some degree of oppositional behavior *vis-à-vis* the existing allocation of legal entitlements, but at some point there is a limit beyond which radicalism is impermissible. A thoroughgoing opposition to the law, reflecting the attitude that legality is not entitled to any respect whatsoever, denies the achievement that the law represents. Even if that achievement does not count for much, for some affected citizens, it is something, and the alternative may be much worse.

Daniel Markovits and others have argued that the legitimacy of the legal system must be understood as depending on a political process characterized by shared collective participation, not merely the aggregation of antecedent preferences.[24] On this view, politics must be *jurisgenerative* (i.e., capable of transforming private, and selfish, persons into public-regarding citizens).[25] Political participation must be structured in such a way that it does not simply feed in exogenous preferences as inputs, and produce laws as outputs, according to some aggregation process. Instead, the process must permit citizens to persuade each other, to alter their preexisting preferences, and to work together as a community, in the name of the interests of the society as a whole. Citizens must act non-strategically, be open to persuasion, and be committed to acting from a kind of idealized first-person-plural point of view, as opposed to trying to maximize the satisfaction of their preferences.

As applied to legal ethics, the political legitimacy of the law is a function not only of the process by which it was enacted, but the process by which it is interpreted and applied by lawyers representing clients. This is because the meaning of a legal norm, in order to be intelligible to citizens, must borrow from culturally salient meanings that are created through activities other than merely making and complying with laws.[26] Any time a community constituted by its allegiance to certain sources of ethical value seeks to regulate itself using the reason-giving discourse of law, it is inevitable that the meaning of law will be shaped by the community's existing narratives. So it is nonsensical to talk about law-application as a top-down imposition of legal meaning onto a community which is already possessed of abundant resources for understanding itself in terms of foundational constitutive values. Instead, the law should be understood as an "arena of struggle," or a site of contestation of the meaning of the community's political commitments.[27]

Even granting that the legal system as a whole must respond to the demand for legitimacy, and assuming this means that the legal system must provide meaningful channels for political engagement by citizens, it does not follow that, in any particular case, the lawyer's role ought to be understood as facilitating engagement with a process of legal meaning-making. Individual lawyers representing particular clients may play a roles in an overall institutional division of labor, which has enhancing political participation by citizens as one of its ends. It does not follow, however, that the lawyer's role in every case will be the same, or that it will be identical with the role of the system, considered as a whole. Certain lawyering roles may be best understood as facilitating political engagement. "Cause lawyers" of various stripes aspire to transformative legal practices, not simply taking the economic, social, and political status quo as given.[28] Criminal defense lawyers see themselves as standing with the friendless, fighting for the underdog, and resisting the power of the state, and they may regard themselves more generally as political opponents of a harshly punitive criminal justice system.[29] However, other lawyers handle fairly routine matters on behalf of clients who are not particularly interested in political engagement. Many large institutional clients regard the legal system as an impediment in the way of their desires, or at best a cost to be managed by retained experts, and would find laughable the claim that their lawyers are aiming at political transformation on their behalf.

One should not overgeneralize from these cases, any more than one should overgeneralize from the paradigm of criminal defense representation. Lawyering as a whole need not be a conservative practice, but it also need not always be oppositional. More to the point, individual lawyers need not aim at all of the virtues of a legal system in their practices. Some lawyers may be dedicated to speaking truth to power, or facilitating political engagement by citizens, but others may be content to play a role in routine claims processing or regulatory compliance. Legality is a complex political value, including ideals of both stability and flexibility. A legal system as a whole should be designed with the value of legality in mind, and this value informs the practice of individual lawyers, but each lawyer need not instantiate the system's response in her own system of ethical norms.

4.1.4 *Nullification and Subversion*

An avenue of dissent that is precluded by the obligation of fidelity to law is covert nullification or subversion of a law the lawyer believes to be unjust. The self-styled radical law professor Duncan Kennedy once suggested that progressive lawyers ought to insinuate themselves into powerful organizations and engage in acts of sabotage, with the aim of interfering with unjust exercises of power and destabilizing illegitimate hierarchies. Lawyers should aim to "politicize their work situations" by using "sly, collective tactics ... to confront, outflank, sabotage or manipulate the bad guys and build the possibility of something better."[30] If respect for legality means anything, it is that *this* form of responding to injustice is closed to lawyers acting in a representative capacity. That does not mean that lawyers representing clients whose positions are at odds with the dominant power structure must simply acquiesce in their clients' subordination. But lawyers' struggles against injustice must always be within the law. This is a constraint on the ability of lawyers, as opposed to non-lawyer activists, to oppose injustice using extra-legal means. Unlike activists, however, lawyers can make use of legal means for opposing injustice. Lawyers can argue that their clients have or should have legal rights, even if those rights are presently unrecognized or are underdeveloped by existing law; lawyers can employ procedural means to ensure that their clients are treated fairly, even if the substantive law is not on their side; and lawyers can urge decision-makers to exercise their discretion in favor of their clients' position, however unpopular it is. Significantly, they can do none of these things without a well-functioning legal system. Kennedy's suggestion that lawyers should work to undermine the very thing that makes legal strategies of resistance possible is therefore incoherent. One cannot ethically take advantage of the very institutions one is simultaneously trying to subvert.

A lawyer might reply that she is unconcerned with the effective functioning of the law, which is a problem for legislators, rulemakers, or judges, but not for her or her client. If those "others" were unable to make the law fully effective, so much the worse for them, but it is of no moment to the lawyer or her client. Although it suffers a bit from overuse, the scene in *A Man for All Seasons* in which More defends the Devil's right to hide behind the law remains a powerful defense of the value of legality:

ROPER: So now you'd give the Devil the benefit of law.
MORE: Yes. What would you do? Cut a great road through the law to get after the Devil?
ROPER: I'd cut down every law in England to do that.
MORE: Oh? And when the last law was down, and the devil turned round on you, where would you hide, Roper, all the laws being flat? This country is planted thick with laws from coast to coast, man's laws not God's, and if you cut them down—and you're just the man to do it—do you really think that you could stand upright in the winds that would blow then?
ROPER: Yes, I'd give the devil the benefit of the law, for my own safety's sake.[31]

More's argument, at least as it comes across in this frequently quoted passage, comes across as purely strategic or instrumental. He would give the Devil the benefit of the law, but only because his own future safety might depend on it. This is not necessarily a bad reason to defend the law, and a great deal of respect for the law may be motivated by the recognition that one day it may be useful to take advantage of its protections. A lawyer *must* be concerned about the effective functioning of the law, because without it, neither she nor her client could realize her own interests. The market economy presupposes a background of stable law, custom, and enforcement that enforces private ordering.[32] Even if a lawyer and client were concerned only with pursuing their own narrow self-interest, paradoxically it is only possible to behave self-interestedly within a framework of other-regarding obligations. A lawyer might evade regulatory requirements by some kind of "creative" structuring of a transaction in one case, but cause long-run damage in the form of eroding the capability of the legal system to facilitate the functioning of the kind of market in which the client is participating. The lawyer cannot be indifferent to this long-term damage and still claim to be making an ethical argument about the obligations of her role, because it is in the nature of ethical arguments that they must be generalizable to relevantly similar situations. It may be true that a lawyer could game the system once without causing catastrophic damage, but this would constitute impermissible free-riding on the cooperation of others. Considerations of fairness thus rule out the attitude of indifference to the functioning of the legal system.

Kennedy's rhetoric of guerilla warfare and More's response to Roper may be a bit melodramatic as a way of describing the practices of most lawyers, but the problem of covert evasion is nevertheless one that a theory of legal ethics must address, because it is a feature of many problematic cases. Consider a case discussed by Deborah Rhode and William Simon.[33] A legal services lawyer represents a recipient of public assistance (welfare) benefits. The client lives rent-free with her cousin, but even so is barely able to make ends meet on her state benefits. The lawyer realizes that, under the applicable regulations, the client should be reporting the free lodging as in-kind income at fair market value; if the client does this, her benefits will be reduced by $150. The lawyer wonders whether she should inform the client about the regulatory reporting requirement and, if she does, whether to recommend that the client make a nominal monthly rent payment to her cousin to avoid the obligation to report the receipt of lodging at no cost. (The latter question is really about whether the nominal payment would be a strategy of law-evasion and, if so, whether evasion is morally justified.)

Simon handles this case by arguing that the law, properly interpreted, creates a legal entitlement for the client to receive the full amount of benefits, not reduced to account for the in-kind income. He accomplishes this feat, as previously noted (see § 1.5), by relying on a Dworkinian conception of the content of law, so that an alleged fundamental right to a minimally adequate income outweighs the plain language of the regulation requiring the client to report the free housing. Rhode, on the other hand, encourages lawyers to "make the merits matter," and to assess the merits from a moral standpoint, not solely in terms of the client's legal entitlements.[34] She does not make the Dworkinian move, arguing that the law properly interpreted would include a legal entitlement to the full amount of benefits, not reduced to account for in-kind income. Rather, she observes that "[m]any impoverished clients have compelling claims for assistance that the law fails to acknowledge."[35] In order to assist clients in achieving justice—the entitlements the law morally ought to provide, but does not—a lawyer may be justified in cutting legal corners, employing evasive strategies to get around unjust laws. For example, Rhode seems to approve of little charades like presenting scripted "evidence" of adultery when it was the only statutorily available ground for divorce, and engaging in strategies of selective ignorance, such as making sure to question clients carefully to avoid learning about undisclosed in-kind income. This is the classic "zealous advocacy within the bounds of the law" position, because she insists that lawyers use illegal means, such as perjury or falsifying documents.[36] Subject to that constraint, however, Rhode would have lawyers make an assessment of the morality of their clients' interests, and if the lawyer believes that the client's legal entitlements are not morally just, the lawyer should act directly on the basis of her view of what would be the just outcome. Ironically, although she often criticizes the Standard Conception, in this case Rhode endorses its most problematic aspect, which is ignoring the limits of legal entitlements where the client's interests are to the contrary.

A reader of Simon and Rhode's proposals cannot help feeling that their calls for ethical discretion, and their conception of how lawyers should exercise this discretion, are animated by their political commitments. "An impoverished mother struggling to escape welfare stands on a different ethical footing than a wealthy executive attempting to escape taxes," Rhode states, assuming her readers will agree that this conclusion is self-evident.[37] Simon's examples similarly appear slanted—for example, in favor of a union and against management in a representation election.[38] (Simon's extended example is complex, but his analysis is essentially that the employer's lawyer has an obligation not to take advantage of a procedural mistake by the union, as permitted by the text of a labor-relations statute, because the purpose of the statute is to make local unions representative of the bargaining unit, and the mistake in the election does not affect the representativeness of the union.) In response, one can note the overtly moral arguments that have been made in favor of the conduct of powerful clients. High-ranking officers at Enron believed, in sincere subjective good faith, that their company's business model was so game-changing that it had simply outpaced legal regulation, and that fidelity to anachronistic laws would only hamper necessary innovation in dynamic markets.[39] Because they were willing to accept these arguments about the injustice of being constrained by inflexible regulatory norms, Enron's lawyers were all too willing to rubber-stamp deals structured by their client's officers to evade legal restrictions. Similarly, many lawyers within the executive branch of government in the George W. Bush administration believed that the September 11th attacks created a "new paradigm" of executive power, in which the President had to have unlimited authority to ignore laws that tie his hands in responding to threats to national security.[40] This argument lacked legal support, but it was not an implausible conception of what the public interest required. Government lawyers acting directly on what they perceived to be the public interest were therefore prepared to subvert the law by interpreting it in an implausibly narrow manner.[41] As a result, government officials ordered or permitted the treatment of detainees in a manner that almost certainly constituted legally prohibited torture.

As the next section will explain, there is nothing wrong with having a moral dialogue with one's client about whether to exercise the client's legal entitlements. But this is a long way from the position that the lawyer ought to believe herself to be morally permitted to work around legal prohibitions on the client's conduct, simply because the lawyer believes the law has got it wrong as a matter of justice.

4.2   Morally Grounded Client Counseling

One frequently voiced criticism of the Standard Conception maintains that lawyers who respect role-specific obligations to the exclusion of ordinary moral considerations will inhabit an oversimplified normative universe, understand their role in narrow technocratic ways, and engage in a style of ethical decision-making that bears no resemblance to the practices of moral deliberation and judgment that virtuous moral agents should cultivate.[42] This perspective is said to involve the lawyer and client in an ethically impoverished relationship, in which legal interests alone structure the conversation about what the client ought to do. Lawyers equate their clients' values and projects with legal entitlements only, ignoring the nonlegal dimension of the problems many clients bring to the law office. Clients may have moral problems, which either cannot be reconceptualized in terms of legal entitlements alone, or which create tension with the legal entitlements of clients or others. Lawyers will therefore provide incomplete, unhelpful advice if they focus only on the legal dimension of their clients' situations.

As an illustration of this criticism, consider the work of Thomas Shaffer, who has written with great sensitivity about the ethics of the lawyer–client relationship. He argues that the entire legal discipline of estate planning, for instance, makes sense only against the background of the cultural and moral notion of the family.[43] Without families, there would be no reason that anyone would worry about estate planning. Yet when lawyers encounter ethical dilemmas in estate-planning practice, they tend to fall back on technical legalistic "solutions" to these problems. For example, when a lawyer learns from one spouse that she has wishes contrary to the provisions in the wills prepared jointly with her husband, Shaffer notes that the standard response within legal ethics is to criticize the lawyer for having learned private information from one of two jointly represented clients.[44] This response, however, leaves the family out of the analysis, and assumes that the spouse's interests are reducible to legal interests, which in turn rest on radically individualistic premises. More generally, it misses the moral dimensions of the client's situation.

Scholars who worry about losing sight of the moral dimension of the lawyer–client relationship would have the lawyer see her role in terms of the whole panoply of human interests that the client brings into the office.[45] A lawyer ought to want the client not only to avoid infringing the legal entitlements of others, but to do the right thing in more general moral terms. A lawyer should want this for the same reason as anyone should want this— because we live together in communities and are jointly committed to living ethical lives. Along with his co-author Robert Cochran, Shaffer proposes that lawyers deal with moral issues that arise in the course of representing clients in the same way that friends would deal with moral issues.[46] Here, Shaffer and Cochran have in mind a thicker conception of friendship than the "special purpose friend" metaphor used by Charles Fried to justify the Principle of Partisanship (see § 1.5.2). They emphasize that friends see one another as collaborators in the good, as jointly aimed at right action, for the right reasons. A lawyer–client conversation that begins and ends with consideration of the client's legal entitlements alone cannot possibly constitute a collaboration in the good, because there is much more to the good than respecting the law. Thus, the lawyer should not view the spouse in Shaffer's estate planning example in isolation from the client's own sources of value. For the client, there may be no way to disentangle the moral and legal issues involved in contemplating a disposition of one's property after death. The lawyer, therefore, presents a kind of radically alienating way of thinking about problems when she focuses myopically on the client's legal entitlements, without considering the way the legal and moral problems are inextricable from the client's point of view.[*]

Shaffer and Cochran are not insensitive to the problem of moral pluralism. In fact, since both write partly within traditions of theological ethics, they are particularly aware of the diversity of religious and moral traditions. Their solution is a conception of moral conversation that stresses the equality of the parties: The lawyer's job is to assist the client in bringing her own moral resources to bear on the problem, and the lawyer's own moral resources are offered in a kind of provisional way, to the extent they may be helpful in guiding the client through alternative solutions that the client may not have perceived from their own perspective.[47] In the context of counseling, however, the problem is not really moral pluralism. Despite the diversity of conceptions of the good and persistent disagreement, people generally share enough in the way of a moral vocabulary and middle-level principles of right and wrong to have a productive moral conversation.[48] The concern, rather, is that one of the parties may illegitimately dominate the other in the course of the relationship.

The disciplinary rules of most states permit lawyers to "refer not only to law but to other considerations such as moral, economic, social and political factors," when advising a client.[49] In legal terms, there is nothing *prima facie* impermissible about a lawyer counseling a client that, while she may have a legal entitlement to do something, it is a morally wrongful thing to do. There may nevertheless be situations in which a client could perceive moral advising as an infringement on her autonomy. Sophisticated repeat-player clients, often corporations with in-house legal staff, are unlikely to be intimidated by lawyers they retain. Inexperienced clients, on the other hand, may be in a position of vulnerability with respect to their lawyer, and may tend to be strongly influenced by any advice the lawyer gives, even if the lawyer takes pains to distinguish between moral and legal advice. Moreover, as sociologists of law have shown, lawyers dealing with clients often exaggerate the importance of being an "insider" in the system, and correspondingly downplay the significance of formal law.[50] In the advising process, positive law is often taken only as a start-

---

[*] An empirical study of divorce lawyers and their clients describes the way in which lawyers and clients negotiate their way toward an understanding of the past and an agreement on what should be done in the future. Sarat and Felstiner (1995). Clients use the moralized language of guilt, fault, and responsibility to understand the behavior of their spouse, while lawyers focus resolutely on legal categories and procedures. Lawyers may have an understanding of what they believe is in the client's legal interests, but the clients may describe their interests very differently, in terms that do not translate easily into the language of legal entitlements. The result of this divergence in perspectives is an intricate interaction in which power is mediated by the language used by the parties to describe the nature of their problems and the desired outcome.

ing point,[51] and lawyers emphasize factors like local norms, the personalities of officials, and the extralegal factors that influence judges.[52] Lawyers present themselves as having insider knowledge that is inaccessible even to clients who are otherwise educated, successful, and competent to make important decisions.[53] A client might naturally react to this kind of anti-formalist advice by blurring the distinction the lawyer was trying to make, between legal entitlements and extralegal considerations, which the lawyer had just taken pains to show were important to the resolution of disputes. Thus, lawyers must be aware of the risk that reference to "other considerations," while legally permissible, might cause clients to assume that the lawyer's legal judgment is inextricably dependent upon the cited moral considerations.

There is a significant countervailing risk, which many proponents of morally oriented client counseling emphasize, that a lawyer who is too concerned not to coerce her clients into giving up a legal entitlement may equate the client's ends with her legal entitlements, and not consider the possibility that her client has more important ends that are not identical with what the law permits her to do.[54] The danger exists also for theoretical legal ethics, which sometimes tends to "ignore clients, except as persons who have wicked desires which lawyers can help to satisfy or who have legal rights which morally ought not be secured."[55] It is certainly possible in principle, and seems to be true as an empirical matter, that clients do not always want to take advantage of all of their legal entitlements. For example, in *Spaulding v. Zimmerman* (§ 2.2.2), the plaintiff's lawyer's failure to request the independent medical examination report created a procedural entitlement, permitting the defendant to keep the report confidential. As a result, the defendant had no legal obligation to inform the plaintiff of his life-threatening medical condition. Legal ethics teachers sometimes ask students what they would do if the defendant elected to stand on this right, but it is important to observe that in the real case, the defense lawyers never consulted with their client, apparently deciding on their own not to disclose the information.[56] Had the defendant been consulted, he may very well have elected to warn the plaintiff about his injury, particularly since the Spaulding and Zimmerman families were friends and neighbors in a small, closely knit rural community.[57]

When a lawyer is dealing with a client in a situation like this, it is inevitable that legal, moral, and practical considerations will be all mixed up together, and it would be an implausible, impractical conception of professional ethics that sought to exclude nonlegal factors from the counseling process. Clients may not always make the selfish choice. Zimmerman may not have wanted to risk having his personal assets exposed to a judgment in excess of his insurance policy limits, but he also might not have wanted to keep the full extent of Spaulding's injuries secret, particularly since Spaulding was a family friend and a neighbor.[58] The basic principal–agent structure of the client–lawyer relationship means that clients ultimately have the final word concerning the objectives of the representation.[59] As long as their objectives are lawful, they are free to define them as they see fit. Zimmerman could have chosen "do the right, moral, neighborly thing" as the objective of the representation, just as he could have chosen "minimize my financial exposure by all lawful means." Without consulting the client, a lawyer has no way of knowing what her objectives are, and it would be a significant ethical failing for the lawyer to assume that any client's objectives are merely to maximize financial gains or to engage in any conduct that the law permits.

It should go without saying that whatever advice the lawyer provides the client, it must candidly differentiate moral from legal advice. Assuming there is no likelihood of coercing the client, there is nothing wrong with a lawyer saying, "You want to such-and-such, and you have a legal right to do so. But from the moral point of view, I think it's a pretty lousy thing to do." Not every client may appreciate that sort of advice, but it is permissible, in terms of the ethics of the lawyer's role, for a lawyer to give it. It would be very a different matter, however, if the lawyer attempted to dress up moral advice as a judgment about what the law permits. The risk is not so much that a lawyer would lie outright, although this may happen in some cases. Rather, the risk is that a lawyer's judgment about what is legally permissible will be subtly influenced by her beliefs about what the law *ought* to permit. I have argued that one explanation for the poor quality of the legal advice provided to the Bush administration by lawyers in the Office of Legal Counsel is that the lawyers were true believers.[60] They were strongly committed to a novel vision of presidential power in wartime, which had some support in precedent, but which had never been accepted in the strong form they believed in. The advice they gave was not qualified or identified as having considerably less support than competing legal positions. Instead it was presented as a bland statement of what the law permits.

One response to this critique is that legal advising is never a matter of concluding simply that the law permits or prohibits something. There are areas of uncertainty, arcs of evolving doctrine, positions that might seem farfetched until fleshed out by a talented lawyer, and so on. Moreover, the process of legal interpretation is inevitably influenced by moral judgments, because the law reflects moral values to some extent. Textbook examples include the Eighth Amendment's prohibition on cruel and unusual punishment, the requirement of good faith and fair dealing in contract law, the reasonableness standard in negligence law, and the rule from the regulation of police investigations, that a search may be unreasonable if the procedure "shocks the conscience."[61]

These terms all refer to moral values, which have significance apart from law, and can be used to give content to legal norms. As a jurisprudential matter, however, there is a difference between moral concepts that have been incorporated into the law and those that have not. When making legal judgments, it may not be necessary to ascertain the *truth* of some moral principle (e.g., "solitary confinement is genuinely cruel punishment") in order to determine whether a proposition of law incorporating them is actually part of the law in a given legal system.[62] The incorporation of morality into law may be a social fact, in the sense that one can trace the validity of a proposition of law back to its having been relied upon by an official institutional actor, such as a judge or a legislator, as one of the grounds for a legal judgment. If moral truth is irrelevant to legal validity (with validity understood in terms of social sources), then it is irrelevant whether a lawyer believes some interpretation of law would be better, morally speaking. The moral principle in question is either part of the law or it is not. There is no open question, as part of the process of reaching a legal conclusion, pertaining to the truth of the moral principle.

If moral principles become incorporated into law, they may count in favor of a legal judgment in virtue of there being a social fact of their prior incorporation, not in virtue of their truth. Still, this does not fully answer the objection that the law is indeterminate to some extent. There are many sources of indeterminacy in law other than moral disagreement. Chapter 6 will take up the question of whether there can be enough determinacy in the law to satisfy the functional end of establishing a framework for cooperation that stands apart from matters about which people would otherwise disagree. If the affirmative answer is supportable, and it is possible for legal interpreters acting in good faith to differentiate between a genuine legal entitlement and a manipulation of the law, then it is possible to insist on the point made here, that a lawyer must clearly identify those aspects of her advice that are extra-legal moral or prudential considerations, and not related to the lawyer's legal judgment. Shaffer argues that legal advising is inherently moralized, because discerning the client's interests, which is a precondition to providing legal advice, requires discernment and judgment, which are moral acts.[63] I have no problem describing counseling as involving moral discernment, provided it is understood that it is a particular kind of discernment, which aims at understanding how the client's interests fit in with the scheme of available legal entitlements. The lawyer is not a minister, rabbi, or trusted relative, and while there may be moral concepts incorporated into the law somehow, the lawyer's expertise is generally limited to advising on these moral concepts only insofar as they are incorporated into the law. If Shaffer means that specifically *moral* discernment is required, then we have a real disagreement.

Much of what has been said up to this point about client counseling is uncontroversial. The difficult problem—as with much of theoretical legal ethics—comes in the form of reconciling the lawyer's moral agency with what the lawyer owes in light of the client's legally protected entitlements, where there is some genuine conflict between law and justice. To illustrate this problem, consider Stephen Pepper's discussion of the statute of limitations case.[64] Borrower has no legal obligation to repay the debt, and Pepper says that it would be an impermissible deception for the lawyer to refuse to inform the client of this legal entitlement. This is a reasonable implication of Pepper's view that the lawyer's role is fundamentally about protecting the political value of autonomy, by ensuring that all citizens have access to the law. But he remains troubled by the alternative moral description that is available here, that the lawyer is facilitating injustice. The client may not have a legal obligation to repay the loan, but he has a moral obligation to repay. Pepper then says, somewhat surprisingly, that it would be intolerable if the client is not informed that the client has a moral choice in the matter, and if the client chooses not to do the right thing, the responsibility for the injustice will be the client's, not the lawyer's or the legal system's.[65] The point of requiring this advice seems to be to reconcile the lawyer's autonomy with the client's. As a moral agent, the lawyer has a responsibility not to facilitate injustice. As Pepper puts it, "the lawyer ought to be responsible for ensuring that the client is morally responsible for the conduct,"[66] such as not repaying the debt.

The problem Pepper, Shaffer, and others worry about is that counseling and assisting a client to assert her legal entitlements is morally corrupting in terms of the full range of human moral experience, if it is detached from advice about the client's moral situation. There are more things in heaven and earth than are dreamt of as legal entitlements. Shaffer says, for example, that counseling one spouse in a joint estate-planning representation without considering the spouse's connection to the family would be irresponsible.[67] The lawyer should see her role as counseling the whole client, and the whole client is tied to a family and a "larger moral ecology."[68] There is something strangely un-human about reducing all of the complexities of family relationships to rights and obligations created by formal state law.

While I will gladly concede that a lawyer remains an ordinary moral agent while acting in her role, I do not understand why a lawyer should be *more* than a moral agent, simply because she is in a contractual relationship with another person. In other words, moral counseling is supererogatory—an obligation over and above the ordinary range of moral duties, understood as "what we owe to each other." We owe strangers a duty to refrain from harming them in particular ways, but not a duty to help them become better people, or even to help them to avoid becoming morally corrupt themselves. We owe different obligations to family members and close friends, but these are owed in virtue of the shared history and reciprocal vulnerability that characterizes those relationships. Most lawyer–client relationships, on the other hand, are arm's-length economic transactions. Some are not, of course, but it is significant that many of Shaffer's examples, from literature and real life, involve lawyers and clients who are members of the same tightly knit community, in which other kinds of bonds exist, independent of the lawyer–client relationship. In those cases, there may be an obligation to give moral advice, or at least a strong reason for the lawyer (who is also a friend, neighbor, co-religionist, etc.) to offer moral counseling. In the ordinary lawyer–client relationship, however, there is no greater obligation to provide this kind of advice than there would be as part of any other economic transaction.

Shaffer himself says something intriguing that would appear to reinforce this point. He notes that "working at estate planning is a way to look at death and at property."[69] One might rephrase that slightly and observe that working at estate planning is a way to look at death *through* property. Coming to grips with the inevitability of death is a central human preoccupation, and some people — members of the clergy, novelists, maybe doctors who treat terminally ill patients — may have some relevant expertise that could be used to help people grappling with death. The lawyer's expertise, by contrast, is limited to dealing with death insofar as it affects property relationships with other people. This is not a bad thing. One aspect of death is that it disrupts economic relationships, and people are interested in planning to ensure that their loved ones are provided for after their death. It is useful for a society to have an occupational group that concerns itself with understanding the rules that make this sort of planning possible.

Moreover, there is nothing corrupting about being a member of an occupational group that is dedicated to dealing with one aspect of a full well-lived human life. There is more to life than having healthy teeth, but it is a good thing for society to have dentists, and for someone to be a dentist. Clients probably expect more moral counseling from their lawyers than patients do from their dentists, but in the end both professions are on a par in terms of their expertise in moral counseling, despite the superficial similarity between some moral and legal problems. It is true that lawyers may acquire some additional expertise in moral decision-making through a lifetime's worth of exposure to the human problems of their clients. Even though that may happen in the course of one's professional life, it is incidental to the essential expertise that lawyers bring to their clients' problems, which is facility with the scheme of legal rights and duties that allows people to interact with each other under the community's imprimatur of legality. A lawyer with real moral expertise, familiarity with a client's situation, and enough shared history to earn the client's trust may provide valuable moral advice in that case. This case is the exception that proves the rule, however, because the conditions for concluding that a lawyer is an appropriate moral counselor are absent in so many routine representations.

4.3   Morally Motivated Client Selection

As a matter of the positive law governing lawyers in the United States, lawyers do not have a legally enforceable obligation to serve any given client.[70] The only circumstances under which a lawyer would be required to accept representation is where a court appoints the lawyer,[71] and in those cases that lawyer has previously agreed to have her name added to a roster of lawyers willing to accept court appointments. Moreover, the lawyer disciplinary rules contemplate a substantial role for moral discretion in the selection of clients. Even the rule on accepting court appointments permits the lawyer to opt out of a particular representation on the basis of the lawyer's belief that the client's goals are morally repugnant.[72]

At least on the surface, the American position seems far removed from the British "cab-rank" rule, which requires barristers (but not solicitors) to accept the representation of clients in the order they come through the door, like taxicabs waiting in a queue for passengers.[73] The rule is widely thought to be honored mostly in the breach, because barristers are permitted to refuse representation on a variety of grounds, including incompetence, conflicts of interest, the client's inability to pay, or simply being too busy to take on new cases.[74] But it nevertheless underscores an important normative commitment by the legal profession, to refrain from making moral judgments about clients' ends, and thereby to ensure that access to the law is rationed to all potential clients on a morally neutral basis. In the words of a leading English case:

> If counsel is bound to act for [an unpopular] person, no reasonable man could think the less of any counsel because of his association with such a client, but, if counsel could pick and choose, his reputation might suffer if he chose to act for such a client, and the client might have great difficulty in obtaining proper legal assistance.[75]

The cab-rank rule should be understood as intended to block the evaluative inference that may be drawn by observers, from the client's vicious moral character or actions to the lawyer's moral culpability for assisting the client in dealing with the legal system.

Although there is no binding cab-rank rule in the United States, the best interpretation of the law governing lawyers is that a moral decision not to represent a client should be regarded as an exceptional case. For example, comments to the rule on accepting court appointments set a high bar for opting out of representation on the basis of repugnance. The repugnance exception "applies only when the lawyer's feeling of repugnance is of such intensity that the quality of the representation is threatened."[76] In other words, in many cases the lawyer is required to hold her nose and proceed with the representation, as long as she is capable of providing competent legal services to the client. Similarly, the rule governing termination of the attorney–client relationship permits withdrawal in cases where "the client insists on taking action that the lawyer considers repugnant, or with which the lawyer has a fundamental disagreement,"[77] the right to withdraw is qualified by the requirement that the lawyer ensure the client is not harmed by the withdrawal,[78] and the obligation to continue representation in a litigated matter if ordered by a court.[79] Moreover, the permission to withdraw does not extend to cases in which the lawyer and client merely disagree; it is limited instead to cases of such profound and irremediable inability to work together that no reasonable lawyer could continue the representation.[80] There is also a curious non-rule, which does not impose an obligation to represent but which nevertheless reminds lawyers that "[a] lawyer's representation of a client ... does not constitute an endorsement of the client's political, economic, social or moral views or activities."[81] Finally, the oath of admission in many U.S. jurisdictions includes a promise that the lawyer "will never reject, from any consideration personal to myself, the cause of the defenseless or oppressed."[82] Taking all of this together, one might say that there is a normative cab-rank *principle* underlying the American scheme of rules, despite the absence of an enforceable rule.[83]

Individual lawyers and the legal profession frequently cite this cab-rank principle when lawyers are criticized for representing unpopular clients. Alan Dershowitz devotes a chapter in his book about the O. J. Simpson criminal trial to rebutting charges that he has gone over to the side of evil, after an honorable career of fighting anti-Semitism. He quotes a person who approached him on the street in New York to upbraid him for his representation of Simpson: "I used to love you so much, and now I'm so disappointed in you .... You used to defend Jews like Scharansky and Pollard. Now you defend Jew-killers like O. J."[84] The implication of this sort of criticism, that Dershowitz endorses the goals of his client (killing Jews) may be ridiculous, but it is a familiar theme. It has equivalents in ordinary morality, particularly folk maxims like "You are known by the company you keep" or, more colloquially, "If you lie down with dogs, you'll get up with fleas."

Consider the analogous case of criminal defense lawyer Michael Tigar, who has represented accused Oklahoma City bombing accomplice Terry Nichols as well as Lynne Stewart, the criminal defense attorney charged with helping her client, convicted terrorist Sheik Abdel Rahman, pass messages from prison to his followers. If one wanted to pile on, one could also mention Tigar's representation of John Demjanjuk, accused of being the notorious concentration camp guard known as "Ivan the Terrible." Do these representations mean that Tigar has a soft spot for terrorists and Nazis, and shares their goals of murdering innocent people? Of course not. Reaching that conclusion would be just as stupid as calling Alan Dershowitz an accomplice of Jew-killers.

The reason this criticism is misplaced is not that lawyers have a legal obligation to represent unpopular clients. Dershowitz quotes another letter from his pile of hate mail that observes—quite rightly—that "[y]ou are not compelled to accept a case."[85] No one forced Dershowitz to represent O. J. Simpson, and although Tigar was appointed by the court to represent Nichols, he has voluntarily represented other notorious clients, including Demjanjuk. Rather, by their voluntary actions, these lawyers are expressing fidelity to the legal system and the values it embodies. As Tigar has argued, we do not honor the victims of crimes by permitting other crimes to be committed in the name of the state.[86] In the Nichols case, "[i]t seemed that many people in the government had decided that the stakes were high enough that the rules didn't matter."[87] If the notion of the rule of law stands for anything, it is that the government may not act arbitrarily, but must be constrained by relatively stable rules that apply impartially. Ensuring compliance with the rule of law is not the same as being pro-terrorist, but this is true whether or not lawyers have an obligation to represent any particular client.*

---

* It should be conceded that both the positive law governing lawyers, and theoretical approaches to legal ethics, may be irrelevant if we are concerned about third-party attributions of the client's moral commitments to the lawyer. Survey data show that public complaints about lawyers cluster around themes of greed, aggression, dishonesty, and pursuing frivolous lawsuits that hurt the economy. Galanter (1998). None of the familiar anti-lawyer themes appear to reflect a tendency to stigmatize lawyers by associating them with the moral taint of their clients. In addition, a great deal of literature in social psychology has shown that observers will draw conclusions about the speaker's beliefs, even if they know the speaker has been assigned a side randomly. In one famous experiment, observers attributed pro- or anti-Castro attitudes to speakers who had been assigned to give a speech in support of, or in opposition to, the Cuban leader, even when the observers knew the assignments were random. As David Luban summarizes this literature, "Our

That voluntariness of representation is beside the point is illustrated nicely by a controversy over the *pro bono* representation by lawyers at major law firms of detainees in the American detention center at Guantánamo Bay, Cuba. The detainees were challenging several aspects of the Bush Administration's policies toward them, including the attempt to deny meaningful judicial review of their cases. Angered by the participation of elite lawyers in this resistance to government power, Deputy Assistant Secretary for Detainee Affairs Charles "Cully" Stimson tried to persuade clients of the law firms involved to threaten to withhold business unless the firms agreed to stop representing detainees:

> I think, quite honestly, when corporate CEOs see that those firms are representing the very terrorists who hit their bottom line back in 2001, those CEOs are going to make those law firms choose between representing terrorists or representing reputable firms, and I think that is going to have major play in the next few weeks.[88]

He then proceeded to name the firms publicly, proclaiming it was "shocking" to see these firms doing pro bono work for alleged terrorists.[89] In response, Charles Fried wrote a scathing op-ed piece in *The Wall Street Journal*. Fried said Stimson "showed ignorance and malice," referred to the honorable tradition of lawyers representing the dishonorable, and linked that tradition to the rule of law in a free society, in contrast with "today's China or Putin's Russia."[90] (Note that Fried carefully calls this an honorable tradition, not a legal requirement.) Fried went further, however, and argued that *any* criticism of *any* lawyer's decision to represent a particular client was out of bounds. He noted the "extravagant rhetoric of [left-wing] ideologues" who regularly criticize large law firms for representing large tobacco and pharmaceutical companies. If the political left wants to condemn lawyers for cigarette manufacturers in moral terms, for helping addict children to a deadly drug, and criticize lawyers for big pharmaceutical companies for helping to push health care costs beyond the reach of ordinary Americans, then they have to accept that the political right will criticize voluntary representation of detainees in Guantánamo Bay as tantamount to "helping al Qaeda."

Fried's dilemma is not just a strategic or rhetorical problem for lawyers. It reveals a certain amount of unresolved ambivalence about whether lawyers

---

tendency to infer attitudes from advocacy-behavior apparently leads us to discount almost entirely information about external constraints on what others are advocating." Luban (2007), p. 270. Whether Alan Dershowitz volunteered to represent O. J. Simpson or was appointed very much against his will by the trial judge, observers are likely to draw the facially ridiculous conclusion that Dershowitz endorses the idea of killing Jews.

should be blamed, or praised for that matter, for the clients they represent. Despite being in many ways the most ardent defender of the Standard Conception, Monroe Freedman has argued that lawyers have an obligation to justify, in moral terms, their decision to represent any given client.[91] Referring to Michael Tigar's decision to represent John Demjanjuk, Freedman inferred that Tigar must have asked himself, "What side am I on?" and made a personal moral decision to side with a man who had stood out for his brutality even at Treblinka.[92] Similarly, William Simon has written approvingly of the decision by the elite Washington, D.C., law firm of Covington & Burling to stop representing government-owned South African Airways during the government's apartheid regime.[93] Since Covington has a legal right to represent or not represent any client it wishes, it follows that the firm must make a comparative decision about the "worth" of each client. Simon suggests that this decision was rightly made on the basis of a comparison between the claims and goals of South African Airways and other potential clients. The firm ought to be applauded for giving lower priority to a potential client whose business was deeply implicated in the South African government's system of racial subordination. Freedman and Simon both assume that there is room for moral discretion *within* the professional role, and lawyers can be praised or blamed on the basis of how they exercise that discretion.[94]

The existence of discretion within the role does not mean, however, that a lawyer who represents an unpopular client endorses the client's projects or values. Rather, the lawyer should be seen as endorsing more general political values embodied in the legal system. As Freedman admits, Michael Tigar has good moral reasons for representing John Demjanjuk, which Tigar offered to explain why he accepted Demjanjuk as a client. First, the memory of the Holocaust should not be dishonored by denying even its perpetrators the fullest benefits of legality, and second, that one of the lessons of the Holocaust is government power must always be checked to prevent their abuse.[95] Similarly, the law firms representing detainees (and their clients, including many major corporations) responded with a moral defense based on the values of fairness, due process, and equality before the law, rejecting the suggestion that the firms were trying to "tilt the playing field in favor of al-Qaeda."[96] Notably, these are values associated with legality, not with the client's ends. An important question in legal ethics is thus whether these are the *only* values that may properly be invoked, either in deliberation about which clients to represent, or in subsequent justification of that decision.

The answer to that question must be that the political values associated with legality should have significant weight for the lawyer, and be regarded as reasons for action in all but highly exceptional cases, but that other values from ordinary morality may contribute to a sense of regret or unease. As moral agents, lawyers are subject to the demands of ordinary morality, even when they are acting in a professional role. More colloquially, lawyers are people, too. However, an aspect of the role of lawyer is that it creates obligations that outweigh the demands of ordinary morality in most cases. The lack of an enforceable cab-rank rule creates some complications when a lawyer is deliberating, on the basis of professional values and obligations, about the clients she ought to represent. As I have argued, there is a non-enforceable but nevertheless real cab-rank principle in the American law governing lawyers. Moreover, the Freedman–Tigar debate shows that there are political considerations underlying the legal system, such as the importance of treating even moral monsters with dignity, and the need to check the power of the state. A lawyer should take these sorts of considerations into account when deliberating about what clients to represent. Although Freedman wants to differentiate the client-selection decision from the actions a lawyer must take within an established professional relationship, the evaluative considerations underlying both situations are the same.[97]

This does not mean that a lawyer may not continue to feel the pull of ordinary moral considerations. A vivid illustration of these competing currents of values is provided by the case of Anthony Griffin, who briefly became the lawyer for the Ku Klux Klan.[98] Griffin was an African-American lawyer in East Texas, who had served as a volunteer attorney for the American Civil Liberties Union (ACLU), as well as general counsel for the local chapter of the National Association for the Advancement of Colored People (NAACP), one of the most prominent African-American civil rights organizations, and one which has historically played a central role in the legal struggles for racial equality. The conflict for Griffin arose after the Klan engaged in a campaign of terror against a few black residents who had moved into a previously all-white housing project. The Texas Human Rights Commission sought to compel discovery of the Klan's membership lists, in order to prosecute members for making threats against the black residents. Griffin volunteered to take the case, on the side of the Klan, out of his commitment to the constitutional rights at stake, including the rights of freedom of expression and association. He noted that these were the very rights that had protected the NAACP's membership lists from discovery in the 1960s, when segregationist law enforcement officials in Alabama sought to prosecute members who had participated in demonstrations.

In order to morally evaluate an action, one must describe the actor and his situation. In this case, we can describe Anthony Griffin's decision as either "helping to perpetrate the very racist practices that, in his capacity as

General Counsel for the NAACP, he has fought so long to eradicate"[99] or "preserving the underlying constitutional principles at stake in these cases."[100] Further complicating the task of description is Griffin's identity as an African-American lawyer. Picking up on this aspect of his situation, one might also describe him as "a 'Judas' who sold out the real and concrete interests of black Americans in the name of an ethereal 'principle' that has little relevance to blacks" in this East Texas town.[101] All of these descriptions have some plausibility. Emphasizing one of the descriptions does not eliminate the others; the description in terms of helping to perpetrate racist practices persists, even though the description in terms of protecting constitutional rights is also a fitting one.[102] As Arthur Applbaum has argued, while it may be the case that a practice, such as baseball, does not exist apart from the rules that constitute it, it does not follow that the actions of baseball players can be described only in terms of the rules of the practice. He imagines a group of children playing baseball on the mean old neighbor's lawn, and when the neighbor objects that they are trampling his grass seedlings, the children object, "You don't understand. We are not crushing the seedlings, we are playing baseball."[103] Applbaum's point is that the rules constituting the practice of baseball do not erase the description in non-practice-dependent terms. The pre-practice description persists alongside the description in terms of the rules of the practice, and both descriptions are fitting, or apt, for some purposes.*

The persistence of descriptions in non-practice-dependent terms is manifest in the example of Anthony Griffin, in the form of the criticism that he is a Judas, or that he is helping to perpetuate the racist activities of the Klan. Griffin's argument is essentially that of the children playing baseball—you don't understand; I'm not aiding and abetting racism, I'm protecting constitutional rights. While Applbaum is correct to insist that descriptions in ordinary non-practice-dependent terms persist, that only shows that there are multiple potentially apt descriptions. There is still a further evaluative question in addition to the descriptive question, namely which of these descriptions is the *most* apt. In essence, the client-selection question is whether a third-party observer *ought* to view Griffin under the description of "Judas," or whether the appropriate moral evaluation is framed by the description in terms of the practice. Applbaum is concerned to preempt the inference from the possibility of a

---

* In another helpful example, Applbaum notes that the descriptive accounts "nodding," "telling the bandleader to play the *Marseillaise*," "helping the Resistance," and "pursuing a career as an actor" are all consistent with the facts of Humphrey Bogart acting on the set of *Casablanca*, or Bogart's image projected onto a screen in a showing of the film. Applbaum (1999), p. 78. Someone would describe the same set of facts differently depending on whether she were a student of acting technique, a film historian, or a viewer attempting to figure out the plot of *Casablanca*.

practice-dependent description to a normative conclusion. He worries that defenders of role-differentiated morality are trying to "bypass the hard work of moral argument by suppressing part of the true story."[104] This may be a fair criticism of simplistic assertions of role-based duties. Lawyers sometimes do point to role-dependent descriptions in a conclusory way, as if by repeating the incantation "zealous advocacy within the bounds of the law," they can bypass the hard work of moral argument. Applbaum is right to point to the multiplicity of potentially apt descriptions. Lawyers can be described as moral agents, participants in the economic marketplace, professionals, "officers of the court," and so on.[105] Each one of these descriptions carries some normative baggage with it, so one might try to preempt the hard work of moral argument by capturing the values associated with some description.

A more sophisticated version of the argument does not naively assume that a description in role- or practice-dependent terms "eats up" the descriptions in terms of natural facts or ordinary morality. Baseball is not the game of Applbaum's invention called "acidball" which dissolves all other practice-independent descriptions.[106] Acidball fails to eat up the description of trespassing, but that is true only because we have no reason to recognize implied exceptions to the law of trespass for playing acidball. By contrast, we can appreciate the normative significance of autonomous domains of value, associated with ordinary morality and the problem of living together in communities. Both domains ground apt descriptions of a situation, neither of which purports to eat up the other. The evaluative question is, rather, whether the act in question (representing a client, playing baseball, whatever) is justified, given all of the descriptions that may be given. In this case, Anthony Griffin may conclude that, as a lawyer, the most apt description of his actions is "protecting constitutional rights," and this action is to be commended on that basis. On the other hand, he may conclude that, as a person (or an African-American), the most apt description is "furthering racism," which is an action that must not be permitted. If the arguments given here are sound, then the political evaluative perspective controls the moral evaluation, even though it is possible to view the same situation simultaneously from the point of view of ordinary morality.

The client-selection debate may have the intractable character it has because the positive law governing lawyers in the United States does not specify which of these descriptions should control the evaluation. A true cab-rank system, one with enforceable obligations on lawyers to accept all potential clients, would make it clearer that the role-dependent description of the scenario ("protecting constitutional rights") is the best way to understand what is going on in evaluative terms. The absence of anything other than a general cab-rank principle (as I argued earlier) in the American law of lawyering means that lawyers are not, strictly speaking, required to represent any particular client. The legal permissibility of Griffin turning down the Klan as a client creates enough of an opening for his critics to call him a Judas.[107] If a lawyer has the option to reject a client, then the voluntary decision to accept that client must be based on some reason. It does not follow, however, that this reason must be agreement with the client's beliefs or projects.

Consider the familiar context of criminal defense representation. Public defenders and private lawyers who agree to accept court appointments do not choose individual clients, but they have nevertheless voluntarily agreed to represent clients from a population known to include many violent, dangerous individuals. When asked to justify this decision, lawyers have a fairly predictable response. It goes something like this: "The Bill of Rights to the U.S. Constitution is dedicated to the preservation of individual liberty. Of course, law enforcement and public safety are important, and we should punish people who break the law, but it is essential that people be punished only after they have been treated fairly by the legal system. That is the meaning of the constitutional guarantee of due process of law. It is important to find out the truth at trial (i.e., whether this defendant did the crime of which he or she is accused). But we want to find the truth *fairly*, so we start with a presumption of innocence and require the government to prove its case beyond a reasonable doubt, to a jury of one's peers. We also worry about the abuse of government power, by police officers and prosecutors. In order to protect individuals from the abuse of state power, the constitution also provides citizens with rights against unlawful searches and seizure of property, coerced confessions, misconduct by prosecutors, and cruel and unusual punishment. To enforce those rights, courts have provided for a variety of remedies, such as the exclusion of unlawfully obtained evidence at trial. Sometimes that results in a guilty person being acquitted, but that is the price we as a society sometimes have to pay for the protection of the rights of individuals."[108]

Most lawyers and law students could rattle off something like this in their sleep, but that does not mean it is simplistic. In fact, there is a lot going on in this argument, including the appeal to a moral division of labor between defense lawyers and other actors such as police officers and judges; the balance the legal system tries to strike between values related to substance (e.g., guilt or innocence) and procedure (e.g., the fairness of the process); and perhaps most significantly, the need for lawyers sometimes to do morally disagreeable things in order to contribute to a socially valuable institution. Note that this is not a simple consequentialist argument that if lawyers select clients on moral grounds, unpopular clients will be unable to obtain legal representation. In countless discussions with students, I have heard disavowals of interest in representing tobacco companies, "polluters" (presumably clients in the chemical, energy, or forest-products industries), companies who engage in union-busting and workplace discrimination, and "big corporations" (everyone else). Needless to say, these clients tend to have no difficulty securing representation by elite law firms. Even prospective clients who are exceedingly repugnant and deservingly unpopular as individuals, such as John Demjanjuk (if he was in fact the concentration camp guard "Ivan the Terrible"), the domestic terrorists who committed the Oklahoma City federal building bombing, the Grand Dragon of the Texas Ku Klux Klan, and the police officer accused of forcibly raping Abner Louima with a broomstick, have all found highly competent lawyers to represent them.

This is not to say there are no instances in which unpopular clients have failed to secure legal representation. White southern lawyers, almost without exception, refused to represent plaintiffs in civil rights cases during the 1950s and '60s.[109] There are also a handful of reported cases authorizing increased attorneys' fees awards, on the ground that it was difficult for a client challenging restrictions on abortion services to find representation in certain communities.[110] In general, however, there does not appear to be a pervasive problem of potential clients being turned away on account of their morally disagreeable qualities, as opposed to their inability to pay. It is always difficult to prove a negative, of course, but it is noteworthy that American commentators who favor a norm analogous to the British cab-rank rule seem to be unable to cite data, as opposed to scattered anecdotes, showing that morally motivated refusals to represent have created a pervasive problem of lack of access to counsel. The real scandal of differential access to lawyers is that wealth, not the morality of the prospective client's projects, determines whether a lawyer will be willing to accept the representation.[111] As a result, many lawyers believe their decision to reject a representation on moral grounds is harmless, or at least a marginal contribution to what turns out to be a fairly insubstantial problem.

This marginal cost/benefit argument is irrelevant if the reason to represent any client is understood in terms of playing a role in a system that is justified on the basis of its capacity to enable people to coordinate the demands of complying with morality in a diverse society, characterized by moral pluralism. Consider Simon's example of the law firm deciding whether to represent South African Airways. It seems likely that the firm had other clients whose representation was no more attenuated from considerations of social justice than that of South African Airways. Perhaps these hypothetical other clients were not implicated in the South African system of racial subordination, but they were probably implicated in other moral wrongs, such as reinforcing the

American system of racial subordination, discriminating on the basis of sex or sexual orientation, attempting to undermine labor unions, or causing damage to the environment. Large law firms tend to represent disagreeable clients. In part this is due to the market for legal services—the clients of large firms tend to be large entities with wide-ranging operations, which in the natural course of events come into conflict with a variety of constituencies with claims of being treated unjustly by the large entity. Patterns of normative conflict that are prevalent in society are therefore replicated in the interactions between the entity clients and employees, transactional partners, federal and state regulatory agencies, and others who act on the basis of values with which a large firm lawyer might have a certain degree of sympathy. Thus, a lawyer might choose to represent an unpopular client while justifiably believing that there is some moral value to assisting the client in ordering its affairs with reference to the legal entitlements set up to regulate normative conflict.

Still, there appears to be a substantial gap between a moral *permission* to represent a particular client or industry and a moral *obligation* to represent any given client. One might view this gap as a good thing, as a way to prevent the demands of the professional role from interfering with the lawyer's moral agency to a greater extent than necessary. Some commentators have expressed concern that excessive emphasis on moral neutrality *vis-à-vis* clients could lead to a "bleached out professionalism," in which lawyers are alienated from central constitutive aspects of their identity.[112] The case of Anthony Griffin is particularly difficult because he is not just a lawyer, or a civil rights lawyer, but an African-American lawyer. Similarly, the conclusion of a state anti-discrimination agency, that a female divorce lawyer had committed sex discrimination by refusing to represent men as clients, seems to undervalue the lawyer's commitment to an important aspect of her identity—not only as a lawyer, but as a person.[113]

Cases like these suggest that recognizing an obligation (whether an enforceable regulatory duty or a moral obligation) on the part of lawyers to represent all clients will turn lawyers into fungible service-providing machines, not moral agents. One response to this concern might be to embrace the identity of service provider, and try to give it a moral foundation.[114] A different response would be to recognize a wide scope for moral decision-making at the client-selection stage.[115] (This is, formally at least, the position of the American law of lawyering.) There is a third alternative, however, in which the political values informing the legal system, not ordinary moral reasons, constitute the appropriate frame of reference for client-selection decisions, and the most apt description of a lawyer's decision is be given in those terms. However, ordinary moral considerations persist, and contribute to the "moral remainders" experienced by a person like Griffin, who must subordinate ordinary moral ideals to the requirements of professional ethics.

Casting the client-selection decision in terms of political values means that a lawyer like Anthony Griffin or the matrimonial lawyer who wishes to confine her practice to representing women must be prepared to offer a justification in terms of considerations that can plausibly be located within the legal system. In the Griffin case, the relevant values underlying the legal system include principles of both substantive and formal equality. A lawyer could respect formal equality by defending constitutional rights whether they are asserted by the Klan or the NAACP. On the other hand, a lawyer might choose to respect substantive equality by refusing to lend his assistance to a violent racist organization. Formal and substantive equality are similarly available as potentially justifying values in the matrimonial lawyer case. The important thing is that the values pertain to the legal system in some way, and not be extra-legal moral values. It may happen in many cases that ordinary moral values overlap with considerations that pertain to the legal system. Griffin could easily have decided that his commitment to fighting against racism required him not to represent the Klan. While extra-legal moral or other commitments may have been the motivation, he would not be subject to moral criticism *as a lawyer* as long as there was an available justification that could be cashed out in terms of legal values. In the Griffin case, either decision would have been justifiable, so Griffin had discretion to choose either to represent the Klan or not.

These sorts of permissible exercises of discretion, at a higher level of generality, can constitute a lawyer's entire career. Many students do not enter law school simply with the goal of becoming a "lawyer," but instead perceive themselves as would-be civil rights, criminal defense, environmental, mergers-and-acquisitions, or personal injury lawyers. Specialization is a fact of life in the legal profession, and in the way lawyers think about their careers.[116] Moreover, specialization by field of law obviously implies a certain amount of specialization by client identity. Poor people do not need lawyers who specialize in asset-backed securities deals, and corporations do not hire divorce lawyers (except maybe as a benefit for their officers). A certain amount of discretion in client selection therefore exists as a byproduct of the differentiation of the legal profession into practice specialties. Some lawyers may be weakly committed to their practice specialty, perhaps having fallen into some field more or less by chance. For others, however, serving moral or political ends is an inextricable part of the motivation to become a lawyer. A union-side labor lawyer might be able to envision herself as working instead as a labor organizer, but not as a management-side labor lawyer. More broadly, "cause lawyers" are motivated by the desire to bring about social transformation, serve underprivileged clients, or pursue some other political agenda.[117] For cause lawyers, the commitment to an underlying political cause is logical prior to, and is stronger than, the commitment to being a lawyer.

In all of these cases, these specialization decisions may be justified if there are clusters of values within the legal system that support the positions of the lawyer's clients. Because the value underlying the legal system cannot be reduced to one overarching master value (say, formal instead of substantive equality), a suitably motivated lawyer has a great deal of discretion to follow a career path that is meaningful and fits well with her extra-legal projects and commitments. This is one way that lawyers can reduce the sometimes alienating effect of working within a freestanding normative system. It may be possible in many cases to bring together one's personal commitments and the values underlying one's professional role. (See chapter 5.) There may also be cases in which this happy coincidence does not happen. When this occurs, a lawyer like Anthony Griffin may justifiably believe he is obligated to act on the political values supporting the legal system and the associated role of lawyer within that system. Although these political values outweigh the moral considerations that otherwise would cause Griffin to feel nothing but revulsion at the prospect of hanging around with the Grand Wizard of the Ku Klux Klan, they do not erase them entirely. These moral values persist, and the result is that Griffin may reasonably feel like a wrongdoer, even though he acted rightly according to the principles that ought to be followed when he is acting in a professional capacity. (This possibility will also be discussed in the next chapter.) In this way, both the political and ordinary moral domains have some bearing on legal ethics, even if as a matter of reasoning toward principles of action, lawyers ought to subordinate ordinary moral considerations.

Chapter Five

From Nonaccountability to Tragedy:
The Remaining Claims of Morality

5.1   The Ideal of Innocence

People remain moral agents even while acting in a public or political role. If a morality of public roles ever lets go of this insight, it may be difficult to avoid the problem of the banality of evil, in which ordinary people occupying institutional roles work together to perpetrate monstrous horrors. One response to the problem of the banality of evil may be to insist that there is no such thing as a distinctive morality of public roles. This is David Luban's position. He wryly observes that the distinction between personal wrongs and institutional wrongs "has not been very popular since World War II."[1] His concern is that shifting the locus of evaluation from individual moral agents to institutions tends to diffuse responsibility to the point that "every agent in the institution will wind up abdicating moral responsibility."[2] In order to avoid this radical diffusion, and eventually evasion, of responsibility, Luban insists that every agent must reason from the ground up, as it were, beginning with a foundation of ordinary moral values. This is what I have called the thesis of the transparency of roles.[3] Role transparency requires an essentially direct derivation of role obligations from ordinary moral reasons—at each step of the argument, the institution, its associated roles, and particular role-prescriptions must be shown to be justified on the basis of moral considerations that would provide an excuse in the domain of ordinary morality.[4] Thus, legal ethics becomes a kind of applied moral philosophy, making use of ordinary moral considerations such as autonomy, dignity, and honesty.

I have argued that the ethics of lawyering should be understood as grounded in freestanding political considerations such as the inherent dignity and equality of all citizens, and the ideal of legitimacy. These political values are connected with ordinary moral values, but the relationship is not one of direct derivation; rather, one might say that the morality of politics stands in a more subtle kind of relationship with ordinary moral ideals, such as the inherent equality and entitlement to respect of all citizens. Things can get a bit mysterious at this point. Bernard Williams, for example, claims that political values "make sense" in terms of ordinary moral considerations, but nothing more formal can be said about this relationship.[5] For example, the ideal of procedural fairness makes sense in light of ordinary moral considerations such as the equal dignity of all persons, and the need to treat the views of those with whom we disagree with at least some measure of respect. We recognize that procedural fairness is legitimate as a normative ideal in the realm of politics in part because it reflects the importance of something being justified on the basis of something more than the exercise of naked power. Classical rule-of-law values such as the prospective announcement and evenhanded application of rules similarly make sense in light of our historical experience and moral reflection. The core ideal of the rule of law, which is constraint on the arbitrary exercise of power,[6] is not really an ideal that is found in ordinary morality, although of course it has a kinship relationship with ordinary moral ideals, as well as historical and cultural concepts. The sorts of political considerations which ground legal ethics are essentially tied to a point of view that begins with the nature of the problems and possibilities of people living together in communities, particularly in light of the nature of humans as quarrelsome but sociable beings. These problems and possibilities ground the normative evaluation of political communities.

In his defense of the Standard Conception, Tim Dare argues that it is possible to understand the connection between ordinary and political morality by distinguishing the justification of a practice from the justification of acts falling within the practice.[7] This approach has the advantage of being more rigorous than Williams's appeal to a "making sense" relationship. A practice such as promising is meant to preclude resorting to the sorts of considerations that would apply outside the practice. The normative force of a promise cannot be explained on the basis of the reasons that would have existed but for the promise. The whole point of a promise is to give someone a reason to expect that the promisor will not make an all-things-considered judgment at the time of performance concerning whether to do the thing promised. The practice of promising is justified for moral reasons (it facilitates relationships of trust and reliance, permits people to assume obligations toward each other, and so on), but notice that the function of a promise is to exclude consideration at some time in the future to reasons that otherwise would require something contrary to the promised action. Promises would not be able to perform their function if promising did not have this exclusionary effect. As Dare rightly points out, that means that the justification given for some action *within* the practice differs from the justification that would be given by someone outside the practice.[8] Professional roles work in the same way, he argues, and thus create a bifurcated structure of justification. The practice (here, the legal system and the associated role of lawyer) as a whole is justified on moral grounds, but in order for the practice to perform its function, it must exclude consideration of reasons that would apply but for the existence of the practice.

In whatever way the connection between ordinary and political normative considerations is understood, it seems clear that the political evaluative standpoint is different in kind—because of its scale, impersonality, and institutional structure—from the standpoint of ordinary morality.[9] In a vivid passage from his book *Innocence and Experience,* Stuart Hampshire contrasts the architecture of a Quaker meeting house, whose whitewashed walls and absence of decoration emphasize a moral vision of simplicity, uprightness, and "sweeping away anything contaminated or corrupted or squalid," with the corridors and warrens of the Vatican, whose "weight and splendor ... seem to overwhelm the single individuals" who act on its behalf.[10] The architecture of the Vatican, and the great cathedrals of Europe, reminds ministers that "they are not expected to see in the Church's problems an occasion for vindicating some ideal of personal integrity." Indeed, the metonymy of architecture serves as a reminder of the priority of political values over ordinary moral ideals in public life, when one is acting in an official capacity:

> In chancelleries and palaces, and in the corridors of secular power, ideals of personal integrity and of moral innocence are kept in abeyance. An overriding loyalty is owed, according to one conception of the good, to an institution of which one is part .... This loyalty provides duties which in many circumstances override the duties of personal integrity, honesty, friendship, and gentleness.[11]

As Hampshire rightly observes, and as I have been emphasizing throughout this book, there is a moral justification for what seems like an exclusion of morality from professional life. Political actors are not "subverters of morality," but display allegiance to a conception of moral responsibility with procedural justice at the foundation.[12] This is a different moral standpoint—one that takes large-scale communities and institutions as the basic objects of analysis, using evaluative concepts like legitimacy that do not have clear counterparts in ordinary morality—and it overrides what would otherwise be the morality of ordinary life, with its ideals of personal integrity and moral innocence.

It would appear that this institutional perspective (dramatized by Hampshire's imagery) simply sweeps away individual moral agency. The result would be a terrifying alienating vision of social life as "a Goffmanesque world where there are no selves, only selves-in-roles, selves who slide frictionlessly from role to role."[13] Critics of the Standard Conception sometimes talk as if lawyers inhabit this kind of existential abyss, in which one's moral personhood is relentlessly subverted to the demands of one's role.[14] However, Hampshire's point is that political morality is still morality, and good people may still engage in politics, even though ideals of personal integrity and innocence may have to yield to other ideals. This chapter considers the relationship between personal ideals and the demands of acting in a public role. It may be possible to integrate the political values associated with lawyering into one's own projects and commitments. The first section considers whether professional values may be made into a concern from the point of view of personal integrity. What I have called the "incorporationist" response has been offered as a way of integrating the two domains of value, the political and the personal. The next section takes up the possibility that it may be impossible to effect this integration, and there may be a gap between the demands of a political role and one's personal ideals. In that case, a person might be subject to feelings of having committed a wrong—sentiments of guilt and shame, for example. This possibility is known as the problem of dirty hands, and is offered as a way of making sense of the phenomenology of acting in a professional role.

The argument that has been developed in the book so far relies on political considerations like legitimacy, equality, and fairness as the foundation of a theory of legal ethics. But talking in these terms makes the problems of personal integrity and dirty hands sound a bit sterile, as if they are abstract theoretical concerns only, and would not be experienced by the lawyer as an occasion for real soul-searching. The problem is that normative considerations like legitimacy are not really part of the lived moral experience of people as individual agents. They are the property of institutions, and should be properly taken into account in structuring the ethics of actors who play a vital role in the functioning of those institutions. The difficulty is that the institutional point of view tends not to be the one from which people view their own activities, including those carried out within an institutional framework. This duality between different ways of engaging with the world, in ordinary human terms and in one's professional capacity, is that it makes these conceptual issues quite real for lawyers in practice.

5.2   Harmonizing the Demands of Role and Personal
       Integrity: The "Incorporationist" Solution

Arthur Applbaum has memorably dramatized the predicament of a public official who remains a moral agent, as he must. He imagines a dialogue between Charles-Henri Sanson, the executioner of Paris who practiced his professional craft both under the *ancien régime* and for Revolutionary governments dur-

159

ing the Terror, and the writer and former legislator Louis-Sébastien Mercier. Sanson first offers a sophisticated defense of the Principle of Neutrality, based on the value of the rule of law:

> I will start from the outside, so to speak, and show why my role is a socially useful and necessary one. A just society requires laws and their enforcement, including criminal laws and punishments. Punishments are not self-inflicting—someone must impose them. A just society also requires that the enforcement of laws not be arbitrary or capricious. People may disagree about whether criminal judgments are just, including the executioner called upon to carry them out .... But if the law is to rule, the executioner must obey a division of labor between his office and the office of the tribunal. To allow personal views about the sentences I execute to interfere with my duty is to substitute arbitrariness for the rule of law.[15]

Mercier is horrified by this defense, and after noting that a democracy may enact unjust laws (an argument Sanson deftly parries by noting that disagreement remains about the substantive justice of laws[16]), he observes that even if capital punishment is justified "from the outside," by an appeal to social utility or rule-of-law values, killing is nevertheless "odious from the inside."[17] While it may be the case that the act of execution does not exist apart from the role of executioner,[18] there is nevertheless a person inhabiting the role of executioner—a person who is subject to moral responsibility for having chosen that role, and for having taken actions within the role. "One should be *morally* good, a good man, Charles-Henri," says Mercier. "If a good professional must be a bad man, then it is immoral to be a good professional."[19]

The inside/outside distinction suggested here by the Mercier–Sanson dialogue is a different kind of criticism of role-differentiated morality and the Standard Conception. The most telling aspect of Mercier's argument is not that capital punishment and the role of executioner is unjustified on various moral and political grounds. Rather, it is that, even if a regime, institution, or role is justified from an impartial or external point of view, an agent occupying an institutional role bears an additional burden of justification, from his or her own point of view. To pick up on a distinction from moral philosophy, a lawyer may be subject to two different kinds of reasons—agent-neutral and agent-relative.[20] Agent-neutral reasons refer to considerations that are independent of the perspective, preferences, commitments, and attachments of any given person. They may refer to broad political considerations such as justice and the rule of law, or they may be moral values apart from politics, but the important feature of agent-neutral reasons is that they apply in the same way to all similarly situated agents. Agent-relative reasons, on the other hand, depend on an agent having formed attachments or made commitments that are not mandatory for all similarly situated persons. These commitments may be to impartial ethical ideals—for example, a person may make alleviating hunger or poverty into one of her most important life's goals—but the force of an agent-relative reason depends on the agent having established relationships or made commitments that are not mandatory from a moral point of view.[21]

Mercier's criticism may therefore be restated as whether one might have sufficient agent-relative reasons for performing a professional role that requires one sometimes to act "odiously from the inside." In an influential paper, Gerald Postema observes that the Standard Conception puts a lawyer in a position of needing to connect with or detach from the values associated with the role—metaphorically, like taking off or putting on her professional hat.[22] Unlike a hat, however, moral stances cannot be easily assumed or shed, at least if a person is acting in good faith. What is needed to ease the transition back and forth between ordinary and professional worlds is some kind of unifying deliberative framework that transcends the ordinary and institutional contexts. This unifying framework might be a stance of detachment from the moral convictions she had considered important in her pre-professional moral life.[23] The lawyer might avoid endorsing this attitude, believing it to be just an elaborate sham or performance, but this stance of detachment risks turning into more pervasive cynicism or skepticism about morality generally. The solution Postema recommends is for lawyers to bridge the "discontinuities in the moral landscape" with a "unified conception of moral personality."[24]

Ordinary moral considerations and the norms associated with a political role would not be in conflict for a person acting in a professional role if that person had adopted ideals and attachments that are coextensive with the social goods and values served by the role.[25] For example, if the legal system and legal profession in a society are designed to protect individual rights, and a person believes strongly in working for the protection of individual rights, then working as a lawyer creates no conflicts between personal attachments and professional obligations. A lawyer can therefore take advantage of a justification for her actions, and avoid the alienation that is created by oscillating back and forth between ordinary and political evaluative standpoints, by incorporating political values into her own set of ordinary ethical ground projects. A lawyer employing this strategy of incorporation would not face the problem that political values might require of him if he must "engage in activities, make arguments, and present positions which he himself does not endorse or embrace."[26]

Incorporation would bring along other advantages, including providing a ready source of motivation to respect professional ideals. Without getting too deep into metaethics, the trouble with moral realism, which attempts to locate moral value in natural facts such as pleasure, pain, desire, and aversion, is that moral realism gives an implausible answer to the problem of normativity. If someone asks "Why should I do such-and-such?", a moral realist is bound to give an answer that refers to normative properties in the world, which it is possible to grasp, be motivated by, and have reasons to act on. But it is hard to see how any such properties can be action-guiding, as morality is supposed to be. Morality is a branch of practical as well as theoretical reasoning. It is concerned with what people have reason to believe, but only to the extent that this bears on the ultimate question of what people have reason to do.[27] Having knowledge about some property of the world leaves an open question about why one ought to care about the property that has been discovered and act on it.[28] Even if some action is known to be "good," what reason do we have for performing good actions?

The normativity question concerns the transition from accurate perception of facts to reasons for action, so there is always an open question concerning the nature of the norm that prescribes action on the basis of the perception of facts.[29] Christine Korsgaard has offered an answer to the normativity question that also bears on the question of how one can be a good person and a good lawyer. The problem is how one can maintain a unified personality across autonomous domains of value. Korsgaard's ingenious solution to the problem of normativity is that the solution is implicit in an adequate description of the practical problem facing agents who must decide how to act. Rather than understanding ethics as seeking knowledge, she sees the problem of ethics as determining whether our reasons for action withstand the test of reflection.[30] We may have desires, incentives, and interests, but they are not yet *reasons* for action. "The normative word 'reason' refers to a kind of reflective success."[31] Our inclinations, desires, and so on only become reasons after they pass muster, so to speak, when we endorse them after a process of critical scrutiny.[32] "Reflective success" must mean endorsement from the point of view of *something*; otherwise reflection would be an empty process. But from what standpoint is one to make that determination?

Korsgaard argues that the choice-worthiness of some option must be evaluated from the point of view of the agent's *practical identity*. Practical identity is "a description under which you value yourself, a description under which you find your life to be worth living and your actions to be worth undertaking."[33] It may express itself in familiar role terms, with identity being fleshed out in terms of a person being a parent, someone's friend, a member of a religious or national community, and so on. In these cases, certain role-specific obliga-tions are built right in to the description of the role. Practical identity accord-ingly serves both as a source of normativity and of moral motivation. One does not violate the obligations associated with one's practical identity because "to violate them is to lose your integrity and so your identity, and to no longer be what you are. That is, it is to no longer be able to think of yourself under the description under which you value yourself."[34]

In ordinary moral life, we express this connection between obligation and motivation using expressions like, "I couldn't live with myself if I did that." In the context of professional roles, the practical cost of not complying with an obligation associated with that role would be giving up one of the ends for which the role is constituted, which was the reason for deciding to enter the role in the first place—this would be a kind of practical incoherence. Notice that this has the effect of closing up the gap between the sources of value that underlie a professional role and the agent's own commitments and values. Thus, the problem of alienation observed by Postema and other critics of professional role-differentiated morality does not arise for someone whose practical identity is oriented toward the demands of the role.

I have called this the "incorporationist" solution to the problem of role-differentiated morality because an agent may incorporate the values associ-ated with a professional role into her own practical identity. Then, that per-son can remain true to her own personal moral commitments while acting well within the role. The incorporation need not be an explicit, voluntary act; more commonly, a person may have preexisting commitments that happen to line up with political values. For example, a person may tend to feel empathy for disenfranchised people, and wish to support them in their struggles against injustice. Empathy, the desire to stand up on behalf of the oppressed, and perhaps even a sense of commitment to a class struggle are motivations that connect certain kinds of lawyers, such as public defenders, to the political values that underpin their role.[35] A lawyer with these commitments would therefore experience no disassociation between the requirements of her pro-fessional role and her personal moral commitments, because the ends of the role are already incorporated into her practical identity.

Integrity alone is not a sufficient condition of moral rectitude, however. The agent's projects and commitments must themselves pass muster in agent-neutral terms. Imagine the justification offered by a hypothetical public de-fender, who seeks to explain why it is ethically permissible to cross-examine (and even rudely badger) truthful witnesses, make arguments to the court with weak factual and legal support, and seek the acquittal of a factually guilty cli-ent. The lawyer may be committed to a project of defending the oppressed and struggling against injustice, and would therefore not be troubled by the harm she inflicts on third parties. Her commitments would nevertheless appear to be wanting from the standpoint of one of the victims of deception, harassment, and abuse. There may be a reason that could be offered that would justify the harm to third parties, but the public defender would be required to offer it as well, and not simply rely on her first-personal commitment to the role.

The problem of the impartial justifiability of one's projects and commitments is at the heart of a radical theory of legal ethics proposed by Daniel Markovits.[36] As Markovits sees it, the Standard Conception is justified in impartial terms. In his view, the adversary system, with its structural separation between counsel and tribunals, necessarily commits lawyers to a highly partisan scheme of duties to their clients.[37] Putting the point rather provocatively, he argues that lawyers are duty-bound to lie and cheat on behalf of clients. As he uses these terms, lying means leading a fact-finder to reach a conclusion that is at odds with what one believes to be the truth of the matter, and cheating means advancing a cause that one believes should not prevail in ordinary moral terms.[38] These duties cannot be redescribed as something else (acting, say, or playing within the rules of a game), and the limitations on partisan zeal imposed by the law of lawyering do not sufficiently constrain these acts of lying and cheating to render them morally unproblematic. Nevertheless, these duties are justified as part of a moral division of labor. The division of labor, in turn, is justified by the contribution it makes to the legitimacy of the political order in a pluralist society.[39] Political authorities stake a claim to legitimacy by establishing a "provisional, although hopefully renewable, holding-pattern," which has the effect of settling what would otherwise be persistent disagreement among citizens.[40] Adversary adjudication allows citizens to engage with the political institutions of the state, and to undergo a process of transformation, "from isolated individuals into members of a democratic *sovereign*, with which they identify and whose will they take as their own even when they have been outvoted."[41] Lawyers are a channel for this participation, which is why they have to serve as partisan representatives of clients, whose claims have yet to be transformed by engagement with the process of adjudication into the will of the sovereign.

The question remains, however, whether playing one's role in a justified division of moral labor constitutes a life worthy of commitment. Markovits thinks it does not.[42] The problem is that, while the system as a whole is justified, and lawyers play an essential role within it, lawyers continue to display personal moral vices, namely lying and cheating. There is a kind of category mistake going on here, Markovits believes, when defenders of the Standard Conception attempt to use the values underlying the legal system and the role of lawyer as the basis for an ethically appealing life for occupants of this role.[43] The problem, as he sees it, is that the impartial perspective has become hegemonic in ethics,[44] and that the hegemony of the third-personal perspective leaves no way in which to theorize the "lawyerly vices"—that is, a sense of ethical failing related to being personally involved with, or having taken authorship of, wrongdoing.[45] The actions required by the Standard Conception are incompatible with the personal ethical commitments of a person who has ethical ambitions "to be honest, to play fair, and to treat others kindly."[46] Even if, let us suppose, vigorously cross-examining a truthful witness is justified because it contributes to a process that is generally effective at finding out the truth, it still requires the lawyer to take part *personally* in lying, cheating, and possibly humiliating another person. For the lawyer to fall back on the impartial values that justify the cross-examination is for the lawyer to, in effect, see herself as merely "a cog in a causal machine,"[47] rather than an autonomous moral agent with her own commitments and values.

Instead of looking to the values that justify the legal system, Markovits proposes that lawyers commit themselves to the idea of *fidelity*. Fidelity in his account is a very different notion than fidelity to law, which I have been defending here as the central ethical obligation of lawyers. Fidelity for Markovits runs to clients, not the law, and as such is reminiscent of the much-caricatured vision of the lawyer as a hired gun or mouthpiece. The most important aspect of this kind of fidelity is self-effacement or, what Markovits calls negative capability, in an analogy with Keats's conception of the role of the poet. A negatively capable lawyer is literally a mouthpiece; she withholds judgment regarding the justice of her clients' claims, and simply assists clients in saying what they could not, due to the limitations of their expertise. The Markovitsian lawyer strives to maintain no voice and no moral commitments of her own (save for the commitment to fidelity itself) while speaking and acting on behalf of others.[48] Negative capability is a suitable ethical aspiration for lawyers because of the contribution it makes to the legitimacy of the resolution of litigated disputes. Markovits in effect proposes a reverse incorporationist solution—that is, rather than centering professional ethics around an ordinary moral ideal like struggling against oppression, his theory would mandate that lawyers incorporate the professional ideal of fidelity to clients and self-effacement into their own personal commitments.

Unlike the earlier suggestion that many lawyers may be committed to values that have some appeal in the pre-professional lives of many people, Markovits's reliance on practical identity to bridge the gap between ordinary and role-specific values depends on lawyers incorporating a highly idiosyncratic value into a central organizing principle of their moral lives. The problem with this approach is that his notion of fidelity seems to be a peculiar value for people to seek to adopt from the first-person point of view. It is easy to see the psychological attraction of the undertakings of struggling against unjust hierarchies, ministering to the friendless, or advancing the interests of one's community, and therefore the reasons why commitments of this nature might become someone's central organizing ground project. It seems less plausible that there are many people who, apart from professional roles, are moved by the idea of emptying themselves, maintaining "unusually selfless empathy,"[49] and understanding themselves as mouthpieces or hired guns.

Not only does self-effacement seem like an unlikely ideal for most people to pursue as a personal ethical commitment, but it is highly dubious as an ethical value, from the impartial point of view. Markovits recommends that lawyers in that situation "make up [their] mind about nothing," entertain all sides of the argument sympathetically, be particularly keen to see things from the client's point of view, change positions as the client requires, refuse to judge for themselves, suppress their own ideas, and "self-effacingly empathize with whatever claims the client places before [them]."[50] If lawyers do that, however, they are in no position to prevent their clients from committing serious violations of the legal entitlements of others, because they will have avoided making up their mind about the permissibility of the client's instructions.

To take one example from a high-profile legal ethics scandal, upper management in the finance and accounting departments at Enron was interested in manipulating the company's financial statements to hide substantial losses and conceal indebtedness, thereby artificially inflating the company's stock price. Lawyers worked extensively on every aspect of the transactions the company entered into, in order to realize these ends.[51] Now imagine a defrauded investor demanding to know why a lawyer assisted Enron in papering shady off-balance-sheet transactions. Markovits would have the lawyer's explanation be given in terms of the ideal of fidelity clients: "Don't you see, investors, my job is to make up my mind about nothing, and empathize with whatever claim the client puts before me." In response, surely the victims of the fraud would say to the lawyer, "Wait a second—your job is not only to understand one's client's point of view sympathetically—that may be part of it, but there are other aspects of your job, like refusing to assist your client in perpetrating serious frauds." As it happens, the investor's objection here is backed up by a great deal of tort, securities, agency, and criminal law requiring lawyers not to make up their minds about nothing, but to exercise reasonable care to protect their clients and even some non-clients who can claim the protection of the relevant law.

Not only is the argument in the voice of the hypothetical defrauded investor well supported in the law governing lawyers, but it is, I believe, a more attractive ethical ideal. It seems almost self-evident that self-effacement is a recipe for ethical disaster if followed scrupulously by lawyers. The ideal of fidelity as self-effacement means uncritically lending support to the ends of clients who may intend to cause serious harm, or at least may be indifferent to the harm resulting from their actions. In fact, much of the public outcry against lawyers, after scandals like the Enron collapse and the disclosure of legal opinions justifying the torture of detainees captured in Afghanistan and Iraq, is directed at lawyers who acted merely as facilitators of their clients' goals, without exercising judgment with respect to the legal and factual merits of their clients' positions. If they had asked hard questions, lawyers representing Enron would have realized that many of these transactions relied on aggressive interpretations of the accounting rules that virtually any independent impartial advisor acting in good faith (that is, one not receiving millions of dollars in fees from Enron) would regard as illegitimate. Reasonable people may differ over how much responsibility lawyers should have as gatekeepers, and what evidence triggers a duty to investigate and rectify client wrongdoing, but outside the context of criminal defense representation, the ideal of self-effacement seems to fail the test of impartial justification.

In fairness to Markovits, he is mostly talking about the contribution that adversary advocacy makes to the legitimacy of American democracy. The idea is that participating in the adversarial resolution of disputes legitimates the legal system on a case-by-case level, due to individual citizens having the opportunity to experience the "transformative influence of the legal process."[52] Only negatively capable lawyers can sustain the trust of clients, which is necessary to facilitate their engagement with the legal process. Even within the adversary dispute-resolution process, however, some degree of professional judgment is required to prevent the system from becoming bogged down in frivolous arguments (that is, those positions that are not cognizable under existing law). Markovits says that "lawyers who help disputants to transform their brute demands into assertions of right must not fail to assert any rights that are immanent in their clients' positions."[53] There is some ambiguity in the phrase "rights that are immanent..." If it means rights *the client believes* are immanent, then Markovits's argument is flatly inconsistent with the law of lawyering, which permits and even requires lawyers to override their clients' beliefs about what positions should be asserted in litigation.[54] The law recognizes, in essence, a responsibility on the part of partisan advocates to ensure that the effective functioning of the judicial process is not undermined. On the other hand, if Markovits means that lawyers should assert rights that are *actually* immanent in their clients' positions, then he is saying that lawyers should be partisans with due regard for their obligation of fidelity to the law, which strikes me as the right position. Outside the litigation context, the case for self-effacement becomes even more dubious. If lawyers have a responsibility to ensure the effective functioning of a system that already includes multiple procedural checks on excessive partisanship, then it would seem that the case for fidelity to law is even stronger where these checks and balances are absent. As the example of advising Enron shows, if partisan lawyers are not committed to applying the law in good faith, attempting to ascertain the content of their clients' legal entitlements (as opposed to what they can get away with), the potential exists for unscrupulous clients to engage in a great deal of unlawful activity.

For this reason, the lawyer–client relationship should be structured by the ideal of fidelity to *law*, not to clients—that is, by legal and ethical ideals of fiduciary obligations. The duty of fidelity to law arises from the essentially law-constituted nature of the lawyer–client relationship. Lawyers are agents for principals, their clients, whose lawful powers are given by their legal entitlements. Lawyers can *lawfully* do no more, and should do no less, than their clients are legally entitled to do. The question specifically considered in this chapter, starting with Mercier's challenge to Sanson and proceeding through the discussion of Markovits's position, is whether this is an appealing first-person ethical ideal. It may be the case that some people find fidelity to law appealing as an ethical commitment. An aspect of political ethics, of which legal ethics is a part, is seeking a legitimate way of ordering the relations of citizens toward their fellows, with due regard for the equality and dignity of all. This is an attractive thing to do from the ordinary moral point of view, so one can imagine people being committed to working as lawyers to serve the ends of a legitimate legal system. However, there are also less savory aspects of politics, and a theory of legal ethics must face up to the fact that sometimes political ideals may override ordinary moral considerations such as honesty, friendship, and gentleness. In those instances, the incorporationist solution will not be available, and a lawyer will have to contend with a conflict between the values associated with her political role and ordinary moral commitments.

This argument is firmly within a particular tradition in political philosophy—one indebted to Hobbes, Machiavelli, and Weber—in which politics may mean participating in activities "that honourable and scrupulous people might, *prima facie* at least, be disinclined to do."[55] Refusing on ordinary moral grounds to participate in these sorts of acts would mean that a person could not seriously pursue the morally justified ends of politics.[56] Or, to turn this point around, there may be a limit to what could be accomplished if certain social and political roles were occupied only by people who insisted on remaining virtuous by the standards of ordinary morality.[57] This is known as the problem of dirty hands. An agent gets her hands dirty when she commits an act that is justified on the grounds of political values, but would be evaluated as wrong from the standpoint of "honorable and scrupulous people"—that is, from the point of view of ordinary morality. The argument in the following section will accordingly be that, rather than seeing personal integrity as central to professional ethics, we ought to consider the problem of dirty hands as playing a significant explanatory role.

5.3   The Problem of Dirty Hands

Public institutions, and the ethics of participants (like lawyers, judges, and legislators), respond to a need for a distinctive mode in which people can relate to one another in a way that is practical, final (in the sense that people may have to be coerced into doing things that they may not believe are right), in the name of society as a whole, and yet also respectful of the diversity of beliefs and commitments of citizens.[58] These ends may be at odds with the personal ideals of people who take on public roles. Consider, for example, the contrast between the Christian conception of good as holiness with a very different conception of good, which conceives of good (at least for politicians) as cunning, strength, resoluteness, the ability to improvise unconstrained by principles, and where necessary, violence and ruthlessness.[59] Max Weber starkly articulates this latter perspective in a passage from his essay *Politics as a Vocation*:

> [H]e who lets himself in for politics, that is, for power and force as means, contracts with diabolical powers and for his action it is *not* true that good can follow only from good and evil only from evil, but that often the opposite is true. Anyone who fails to see this is, indeed, a political infant.[60]

Lawyers are not Machiavellian princes, of course, and their involvement in wrongdoing is not generally necessary to avert a catastrophe on a par with an invasion or siege. In a more modest way, however, representing clients and doing things on their behalf may involve a lawyer in what she sincerely believes to be wrongdoing, but which the client is legally entitled to do.

A person acting within a justified political role is subject to obligations that outweigh ordinary moral obligations. However a person may believe herself to have acted with dirty hands if she feels the pull of moral obligations that are outweighed by role-specific duties.[61] The "dirtiness" of the agent's hands is a function of being able to evaluate an act from multiple perspectives—such as political and ordinary moral values, or agent-neutral and agent-relative considerations. Consider how this might occur for lawyers, in the *Spaulding v. Zimmerman* case. The defendant's lawyer may be obligated by the duty of confidentiality (imposed by bar disciplinary rules as well as by the generally applicable law of agency and fiduciary duties) not to disclose the medical examination report containing the information about the plaintiff's aneurysm.[*] A moral justification for this legal rule might go something like this: "The law is highly complex, and in most cases a non-lawyer would have a hard time figuring out whether something is legal or not. Even well-meaning conscientious citizens may sometimes need to consult a lawyer to figure out how to comply with the law. In the course of that consultation, it is essential that the lawyer know everything about the client's situation, in order to provide the most reliable advice. A client, however, might understandably be wary of disclosing potentially incriminating, embarrassing, or unpleasant facts. The only way for lawyers to get full information from clients, therefore, is to give them an ironclad guarantee of confidentiality. Lawyers need to be able to reassure clients that anything they reveal will never be disclosed or used against them, and an effective way to do this is for the legal profession to establish and enforce an absolute, or near-absolute duty of confidentiality. While there may be occasional injustices that could be prevented if lawyers were permitted to disclose information learned from clients, in the long run society will be better off if lawyers respect a stringent confidentiality obligation."

From a suitably impartial point of view—call it political, institutional, or whatever—this is not a bad argument. Similar justifications may be offered for

---

[*] The equivocation here—"may" be required—is required because of variations in the duty of confidentiality in the American law governing lawyers. Arguably the rules in effect at the time of the *Spaulding* decision (based on the 1908 ABA Canons of Ethics) permitted, but did not require, the lawyer to disclose. See Cramton and Knowles (1998), p. 80. The first version of the ABA Model Rules of Professional Conduct, issued in 1983, prohibited disclosure to prevent death or bodily injury to another person in all cases except those in which the client intended to commit a *criminal* act that was likely to result in *imminent* death or serious bodily injury. Model Rule 1.6(b)(1) (1983 version). That rule subsequently went into effect in Minnesota and would have prohibited disclosure in the *Spaulding* case. Cramton and Knowles (1998), p. 81. The version of the rule now in effect in many states permits the lawyer to disclose information to the extent the lawyer reasonably believes necessary to prevent reasonably certain death or substantial bodily harm (i.e., the newer rule omits the criminal act requirement and the imminence condition). Model Rule 1.6(b)(1). Even when the 1983 version of the rules was in effect, there was quite a bit of jurisdictional variation in the bar state disciplinary rules, with many states opting for a more permissive rule that would have at least allowed disclosure in the *Spaulding* case.

pleading the statute of limitations to avoid a just debt or filing the motion to terminate benefits in the black lung benefits hypothetical. Notice, however, that it refers to considerations and values that really are not part of ordinary morality, even if they are cognizable in ordinary moral terms. As emphasized throughout this book, the lawyer's argument in justification is fundamentally about the legitimacy of a system of rules and procedures that is designed to perform a particular social function. Permitting one party's lawyer, in an adversary system of adjudication, to take corrective action where the opposing counsel, or even the judge, has made a mistake would arguably undercut the legitimacy of the process from the point of view of the client whose entitlement to confidentiality was violated. The point here is not to rehash the debate over whether confidentiality really is a good thing.[62] If it is, the argument in favor of a strong confidentiality norm will be made on the basis of political values. This leaves an uncertain connection with ordinary morality, and leaves the lawyer in this case uncertain about how her nondisclosure of the plaintiff's life-threatening medical condition should be evaluated in ordinary moral terms.

One might insist on the primacy of the ordinary moral evaluative standpoint as a ground for principles of action, but it is difficult to imagine how a system that is designed to handle moral conflict can function without the participation of officials and quasi-officials who in some sense participate in acts that may be experienced as wrongdoing from a first-person point of view. Eliminating all connection with what the lawyer believes would be wrongdoing in ordinary moral life—that is, seeking some kind of hyper-purity within an institutional role—is possible only at the expense of undermining the capacity of the institution to realize the goods for which it is constituted. This may occur because of the psychology required for acting in a professional role. Role obligations may be correlated with characteristic dispositions, which are acquired as a result of professional training and socialization. It may be the case that the dispositions associated with complying with ordinary morality coexist uneasily, if at all, with the dispositions associated with professional roles.[63] Paradoxically, a lawyer who seeks to have no authorship relationship whatsoever with wrongdoing also commits moral wrongdoing, only this time in respect of the *political* reasons for respecting a valuable social institution. If there are genuine moral obligations and genuine political obligations that require incompatible actions, there is no way to resolve this dilemma without doing wrong in virtue of one or the other evaluative domain.

The upshot of the position defended here is that the lawyer's professional obligations exclude resorting to ordinary moral considerations in deciding how to act, but that is not the end of the evaluation. There may be a "moral remainder" attached to the lawyer's decision—a bit of "uncancelled moral disagreeableness"[64] that a morally sensitive person would feel *qua* moral agent, even though she rightly believes the act was justified in political terms. The moral remainder acknowledges the perspective of the lawyer as an ordinary moral agent, despite the lawyer's justified adherence to her professional obligations while acting in a representative capacity. The lawyer may feel a sense of guilt or regret, *qua* person, while nevertheless continuing to believe that she did the right thing, all things considered. This is because of the indirect relationship between ordinary moral and political considerations. If the relationship were one of direct derivation, it would be nonsensical to talk about moral remainders, because the obligations of role, rightly understood, would create morally justifiable demands. But professionals often feel themselves to be wrongdoers in some sense, even while being rightly obligated to take some action within a professional role. What accounts for this aspect of the phenomenology of professional life? One explanation is an analysis in terms of dirty hands, which holds that the lawyer may not have made the wrong decision, but a justified belief that "something discreditable has been done" remains, *despite* the contrary decision having been reached after deliberation.[65]

Moral remainders are a species of non-action-guiding evaluative concepts. That is, they operate retrospectively, after the agent has decided what to do, and do not indicate that the agent's deliberations were mistaken as they relate to the conclusion of practical reasoning. Moral remainders are not just sentiments, although they may have an affective dimension, like feeling guilty or uncomfortable about what has been done. Beyond their affective quality, moral remainders are evaluations. They identify some action as wrongful, even though it may have been what the agent was required to do, all things considered, under the circumstances.[66] They play some role in practical reasoning, but they are differentiated from other moral considerations in not guiding action prospectively. In the case of professional ethics, there may be good reasons for considering professional obligations to exclude or outweigh ordinary moral duties. The reasons underlying ordinary moral duties do not simply disappear, however; they persist, and are the ground for the existence of moral remainders.

What follows from this is, of course, a separate question. Two possibilities are typically considered for the role of non-action-guiding evaluations. First, a political actor with dirty hands should at least feel a certain amount of anguish at the prospect of sacrificing her personal moral goodness in furtherance of the public good.[67] Suffering by itself is not enough, however. The point is not just that the actor feels lousy about having made the decision in favor of some public end, contrary to what she believes an ordinary moral agent would have done. Rather, the hope is that someone who is disinclined to act contrary to ordinary moral principles will be less likely to reach the wrong deliberative conclusion.[68] A legally permissible course of action may involve substantial and avoidable moral costs. Perhaps the client could be persuaded that although it has a legal entitlement to do something, ordinary moral considerations favor taking a different course of action. Moral remainders, if experienced as such, and internalized by the lawyer over time, may lead to a more morally sensitive style of practice in which the lawyer is better able to discern options for avoiding conflicts between legal entitlements and ordinary moral obligations. In *Spaulding*, for example, the lawyer should have made certain that Zimmerman's wishes were indeed to keep the medical examination report confidential, even with the knowledge that Spaulding was unaware of a life-threatening medical condition. Lawyers too easily assume that their clients' wishes are to maximize the advantages permitted by law, forgetting that in many cases the client may want to do the right thing in ordinary moral terms as well, even if it means giving up a legal entitlement.

The second possibility is that the interior suffering of the actor is not expressed only in a disinclination to violate ordinary moral obligations, but also in some public, socially recognized way.[69] Some price must be exacted, or some act done by way of atonement, and the punishment has to fit the nature of the wrongdoing somehow. Tim Dare has suggested that the lawyer in the statute of limitations case, who has rightly concluded that the priority of the professional role requires her to plead the defense and avoid her client's justly owed debt, must atone for the moral wrongdoing involved by lobbying for legal reform.[70] The lawyer is well positioned to understand the inadequacies of the current law, and should use her experience with the law as the basis for making an argument for reform. Similarly, David Wilkins has argued that Anthony Griffin, the African-American civil rights lawyer who represented the Ku Klux Klan, should honor the obligations he has to the black community by seeking change within the lawyering role, in a way that honors his obligations to that role.[71] As a black lawyer, Griffin must account for the moral remainder resulting from his representation of a particularly odious client.[72] One way to do this would be to focus his justification for the representation on the basis of a mistrust of state power, which is related to Griffin's experience of being African-American and having grown up in the segregated South.[73] Another response might be to ensure that a substantial proportion of his other clients were African-Americans. In both of these cases, there is a fitting act of penance or atonement. In other cases, however, it is harder to think of a fitting social expression of condemnation. The coal mining company in the black lung hypothetical may not permit its lawyer to lobby to reform the federal benefits statute, and in any event it may be highly unlikely that Congress would tinker with an old and reasonably well-functioning piece of legislation. Thus, atonement cannot be the answer across the board to the problem of dealing with moral remainders.

A final possibility for extreme cases of conflict between ordinary morality and professional roles is opting out entirely. A person may conclude that there are some things she will not do, even if the role requires them. The American law governing lawyers is actually fairly permissive in its approach to withdrawal from representation of a client. Unless there will be some material adverse effect on the interests of a client (and even if there will be, in certain cases), a lawyer may withdraw from representation, unless the lawyer is representing the client in a litigated matter, in which case the court's permission is required for withdrawal.[74] This only means that a lawyer will not be subject to discipline by the bar or a malpractice suit by the client for withdrawing. There is still an ethical question concerning the attitudes lawyers should take toward the exit option. It may be reserved for extreme cases, or considered relatively routine. In my view, exit from the relationship *on moral grounds* (as opposed to late-discovered conflicts of interest, client crimes or frauds, and similar reasons) should be an unusual event, and should be contemplated only in cases of extreme and debilitating moral conflicts between the lawyer and client. The reasons are the same at the exit stage as at the point of the client-selection decision. The legal permission lawyers have to accept or reject clients should be exercised on the basis of values that are internal to the role of lawyer, such as the ideal of the rule of law. As in the client-selection cases, however, the persistence of moral agency may result in the lawyer feeling a sense of regret about having rightly followed these role-specific obligations.

Fortunately, the most acute conflicts between the political and ordinary moral points of view do not arise with much frequency in the lives of most lawyers. A lawyer can practice her entire career without encountering a case like *Spaulding v. Zimmerman* or the hidden bodies dilemma. Nevertheless, if the overall structure of legal ethics defended here is sound, the result may be that lawyers have to deal with occasional moral remainders. I do not intend to minimize the psychological significance of these conflicts. The lawyer in the hidden bodies case said, speaking of the recognition that his silence contributed to the parents' suffering, "I caused them pain … What do you say? Nothing I could say would justify it in their minds. You couldn't justify it to me."[75] The parents' pain, and the difficult of justifying professional confidentiality in terms that spoke directly to their concerns, show the persistence of the ordinary moral perspective, despite the justified priority of the professional obligation in this case. That perspective must be acknowledged in an appropriate way, but this does not mean that the lawyer acted wrongly by keeping his clients' secret, and more generally it does not mean that action-guiding principles of legal ethics should give priority to the ordinary moral perspective. In the end, the obligation of fidelity to law is a very strong, seldom overridden one, even in cases in which morality seems to demand a different result.

Chapter Six
Legal Ethics as Craft

The basic job of the lawyer, as established by agency, contract, and tort law, is to represent her client effectively within the bounds of the law. As discussed in chapter 2, the law provides entitlements, which may be asserted in litigation, or may serve as the basis for the lawyer's advice to the client. The lawyer's role is to ascertain and protect her client's entitlements, not to be a "zealous advocate within the bounds of the law," which implies doing whatever one may get away with, as long as it is in the client's interests. If it were possible to read the meaning of the law directly from legal texts, there would not be much more to say—the client's legal entitlements would be those plainly provided for in governing documents such as cases and statutes. As any first-year law student quickly learns, however, there may be a great deal of ambiguity in the law, so that legal entitlements do not simply jump off the page at any competent inquirer, but can in many cases be discovered only with some effort and with the use of judgment. Moreover, ambiguity creates the possibility of abuse, so that a clever lawyer may be able to manipulate the law into appearing to convey an entitlement that does not actually exist. The aim of this chapter is to establish that there is enough objectivity and determinacy in the law that the set of inadequately supported legal positions is not empty, and therefore that the ethics of lawyering could, in principle, require lawyers to refrain from relying on insufficiently supported legal positions when counseling clients and structuring transactions. The stakes are high, because if there is no reliable method of interpretation that will yield sufficiently determinate, objective answers to legal questions, then the law will not be the sort of thing that is capable of possessing legitimate authority, as outlined in chapter 3. Thus, the modified Principles of Partisanship and Neutrality defended earlier stand or fall on the capacity of the law to yield moderately determinate meanings.

The argument of this chapter is that ascertaining the legal entitlements of a client is fundamentally a matter of assessing whether there are reasons that could be given in support of a conclusion that the client has a right to do such-and-such. The chapter begins, in Section 6.1, with a case study that illustrates the way ethical criticisms can be leveled against lawyers for violating the obligation of fidelity to law. Legal entitlements may be more or less well supported by reasons, but that does not imply that the law is perfectly determinate. As the case study will show, the important thing is to establish a pattern or style of ethical criticism. The point is not to convince readers that the substantive legal criticism is warranted (although I think it is), but that this is the right way to make an ethical argument that lawyers have acted wrongly in representing a client. Section 6.2 considers the way in which the lawyer's basic duty of fidelity to law can vary according to the nature of the representation. The obligation of fidelity to law must be understood in context, with some lawyers having greater latitude than others to assert less well-supported legal positions on behalf of clients. The position defended here is compatible with the thesis of moderate determinacy. Ethical lawyering is often a matter of knowing what may be done, given legal ambiguity or uncertainty. A lawyer may be permitted to argue, "the law permits X," in a brief submitted to the court in litigation, but would not be permitted to assert, "the law permits X," given the same applicable law, in an opinion letter delivered as part of a transaction, or in prospective advice given to a client about what the client may permissibly do.

Next, Section 6.3 takes up the basic jurisprudential question of the relationship between legal reasoning (and the sources of determinacy) and the political conception of legal legitimacy set out in chapter 3. The argument in that chapter was that legal reasons have a particular structure. They make reference to the underlying reasons that were up for grabs among citizens who disagreed about some matter, but they replace or outweigh those reasons in the practical deliberations of citizens subject to the law. As a result, the law is always aimed at some end—that is, it is a purposive activity. A basic constraint on a permissible interpretation of law is therefore that it be aimed at recovering the substantive meaning of some legal norm. Another important constraint is that lawyers regard the law from the internal point of view—in other words, as creating genuine obligations and not merely inconvenient obstacles to be evaded or planned around. This approach, indebted to Hart's jurisprudence, can then be used to make sense of some practical problems of legal interpretation, as discussed in the concluding Section 6.4.

6.1   The Case of the Torture Memos[1]

To frame the analysis of legal interpretation, it will be helpful to begin with a case study. The case of elite government lawyers advising on the permissibility of torture is somewhat unique in its lurid facts, but presents the very general problem of how the law, not ordinary morality, can serve as a constraint on lawyers' representation of clients. Although this is a high-profile case, and attracted sustained attention in the United States and abroad, it is actually a typical pattern for legal ethics scandals. One could conduct a similar analysis of the role of lawyers in structuring the transactions that led to the collapse of Enron, in hiding wrongdoing by principals in the savings and loan debacle in the 1980s, or in marketing bogus tax shelters.[2] These cases share a common structure, which is the assertion by lawyers of claimed legal entitlements on behalf of clients, which turn out upon closer examination to be spurious. Although superficially plausible legal arguments were offered in support of these positions by lawyers, the arguments did not withstand scrutiny. For example, an impartial investigation by a committee of the Board of Directors concluded that Enron management and outside lawyers used smoke and mirrors to obscure the lack of economic substance of several related-party transactions, with the result that the accounting treatment of these transactions on the company's financial statements amounted to fraud.[3] As one Enron employee observed, "Our job was to take advantage of the law and make as much money as we can."[4] In this case, the lawyers failed to fulfill their obligation of fidelity to law, because the positions they asserted were not adequately supported by valid legal reasons.

The trouble with making these sorts of arguments is that it is hard to go beyond assertions (e.g., that the accounting treatment of the Enron transactions was erroneous) without going into an extraordinary amount of detail. For the purposes of the arguments in this book, the important thing is not to establish that any particular legal position is inadequately supported. Making and assessing those arguments is the job of legal scholars with specialized knowledge of the relevant law.* The important thing here is to establish first that the fundamental ethical obligation of lawyers is fidelity to law, and second, that the law is the sort of thing to which one can exhibit fidelity. If the law can be made to mean anything at all, or if it is so malleable that it does not provide significant practical constraint, then the obligation of fidelity to law is an empty one. Thus, in order to show that this approach to legal ethics can do real evaluative work, this chapter begins with the predicament of lawyers working within the United States government, who were called upon to provide legal advice about the permissible treatment of detainees in the so-called War on Terror.

---

* I should note for the record that while I have made an effort to become familiar with the relevant law, real experts in these areas may have disagreements on the legal reasoning. That is all to the good, in my view. Although I stand behind my legal analysis of these cases, my goal here is less to establish those specific conclusions as it is to argue for the methodological point that legal ethics is necessarily an evaluative discourse that depends on getting the underlying law right.

The invasion of Afghanistan soon after the September 11th attacks resulted in the capture of numerous detainees with possible al-Qaeda affiliation, who might have possessed information on the structure of the organization, personnel, or even future terrorist attacks. In particular, the capture of high-ranking al-Qaeda members such as Abu Zubaydah, Mohamed al-Kahtani, and Khalid Sheikh Mohammed raised the possibility that American officials may have custody over people with extremely valuable "actionable intelligence."[5] The Bush administration was therefore faced with an urgent question regarding the limits it should impose on the interrogation techniques used by military, FBI, CIA, and other government agents and civilian contractors. Officials in the Department of Defense and advisers to the president naturally turned to lawyers to interpret and apply the domestic and international legal norms governing the treatment of prisoners. Intelligence personnel naturally made it a high priority to get these detainees to talk. Many suspected militants had proven to be skilled at resisting traditional non-coercive interrogation techniques such as promises of leniency in exchange for cooperation,[6] so American officials sought advice to see whether it would be legally permissible to use certain coercive techniques on "high value" captives.[7] For example, CIA officials wanted to know whether their field agents would be subject to criminal prosecution for using physically painful methods like "waterboarding," in which a detainee is strapped to a board and submerged until he experiences a sensation of drowning.[8] Alternatively, the Agency sought guidance on the legality of techniques not requiring direct physical contact, such as depriving prisoners of sleep, forcing them to stand for extended periods of time or assume stressful positions, bombarding prisoners with lights or sound (including, bizarrely, repetition of the jingle for Meow Mix cat food), and leaving prisoners shackled for hours.[9] One official at Guantánamo Bay believed he was permitted to authorize "a little bit of smacky-face" which would be used to give "some extra encouragement" to tight-lipped al-Qaeda suspects.[10]

It appears that the CIA was perfectly willing to take off the gloves, so to speak, but was concerned to protect its agents from future prosecution.[11] The administration had already signaled its willingness to get as tough as necessary in order to prevent terrorist attacks.[12] White House Counsel Alberto Gonzales repeatedly instructed lawyers that they were to try to be as "forward-leaning" as possible when considering how much latitude to give interrogators dealing with suspected terrorists.[13] The underlying assumption, that September 11, 2001, was a kind of normative watershed, was not lost on the lawyers advising the administration on its legal responsibilities. Subsequent disclosures have confirmed that that the treatment of detainees in Afghanistan and at Guantánamo Bay was far worse than was publicly acknowledged by Bush Administration officials.[14] For example, high-level government officials had been asked if it was permissible to subject one detainee, Abu Zubaydah, to numerous "enhanced interrogation techniques," alone or in some combination, including waterboarding, "walling" (slamming the prisoner headfirst into a wall, albeit while wearing a collar to prevent his neck from being broken), stress positions, sleep deprivation, cramped confinement, and "insects placed in confinement box" to exploit Zubaydah's fear of insects.[15] The ICRC report shows that these techniques were soon employed in the field, by CIA interrogators. Zubaydah reports, for example:

> When I was let out of the box I saw that one of the walls of the room had been covered with plywood sheeting. From now on it was against this wall that I was then smashed with the towel around my neck. I think that the plywood was put there to provide some absorption of the impact of my body. The interrogators realized that smashing me against the hard wall would probably result in physical injury.[16]

The techniques were often used in combination, with sleep deprivation, nudity, forced standing,[17] and the use of cold water being common elements in the accounts of various detainees. The goal of combining techniques was to induce a state of "learned helplessness," in which the detainee would be destroyed emotionally to the point of no longer having the will to resist.[18]

Thorough reporting confirms that torture was not an isolated occurrence, and not the work of a few bad apples, as government officials had suggested in the wake of the Abu Ghraib prisoner-abuse scandal. Instead, the United States government had constructed a torture program,[19] complete with procedures, protocols, lists of approved techniques, and safeguards to ensure that the interrogations did not go too far, resulting in the deaths of detainees.[20] Naturally, where anything becomes regularized, even bureaucratic in this way, one expects that lawyers will have been involved. Indeed, lawyers were involved from the beginning, providing legal advice to the Defense Department, the CIA, the State Department, and the uniformed military services. Throughout the development of interrogation policy, military lawyers resisted the use of coercive techniques, citing the obligations of the Geneva Conventions, the War Crimes Act, and the Uniform Code of Military Justice. Some civilian lawyers objected, too, including William H. Taft IV, the legal advisor to the State Department. However, Secretary of Defense Donald Rumsfeld rejected the advice of lawyers who expressed concerns about aggressive techniques, turning instead to a small group of lawyers in the Justice Department.[21]

The legal analysis supporting these activities was embodied in a series of memos, prepared by the Office of Legal Counsel (OLC),* which were dubbed the "torture memos" when they were leaked to the press following the revelation of prisoner abuse at Abu Ghraib. The memos consider a wide range of legal issues, from whether the Geneva Convention protections afforded to prisoners of war extend to suspected Taliban or al-Qaeda detainees, to whether the President's power as commander in chief could be limited by an act of Congress criminalizing mistreatment of prisoners. One memo excluded detainees believed to be associated with the Taliban or al-Qaeda from the protection of the international norms regarding the treatment of prisoners of war.[22] Despite forceful objections from Secretary of State Colin Powell, White House Counsel Alberto Gonzales concluded that non-state terrorism is a "new paradigm" that "renders quaint" some provisions of the Geneva Conventions imposing limitations on the questioning of captured prisoners.[23] One of the most notorious memos concluded that certain methods of interrogation might be cruel, inhuman, or degrading, yet fall outside the definition of prohibited acts of torture.[24] Even if an act were deemed torture, the memo concluded that it might be justified by self-defense or necessity. And even if an interrogation technique would otherwise be deemed wrongful, the President as Commander-in-Chief had the unilateral authority to exempt government actors from application of domestic and international legal restrictions on torture.

The position defended in this book is that the most relevant critical standpoint for evaluating the *legal* ethics of the torture memos is not the horribleness of torture from the point of view of ordinary morality. The objection to the advice given by lawyers for the Bush administration is not that it is bad moral advice; rather, it is that it is bad legal advice. The law simply does not permit what interrogators at Guantánamo Bay, Bagram Air Base, and nameless "black sites" in Eastern Europe have done to detainees. Assuming that the arguments in chapters 2, 3, and 4 are sound, there is still a potential problem, related to the indeterminacy of law. Even if lawyers have an obligation to advise clients based on their legal entitlements, not ordinary moral considerations, this may not amount to much in practice if the law can be interpreted

---

* The Office of Legal Counsel exercises power delegated from the Attorney General of the United States to advise the President (in his capacity as the head of the executive branch), and to issue legal opinions that are binding on the entire executive branch unless overruled by the Attorney General. See Goldsmith (2007), pp. 32–38. Significantly, Goldsmith describes the primary duty of the OLC as "preserv[ing] its fidelity to law while at the same time finding a way, if possible, to approve presidential actions." Ibid., p. 39.

to permit whatever the client wants to do. It is ironic, but perhaps predictable, that conservatives have appealed to the indeterminacy of the law in response to criticism of the Bush administration lawyers. Claims that legal reasoning is merely politics by other means, and that the objectivity of law is nothing more than mystification in the service of oppression, were formerly the province of the political left. After conservative lawyers were caught manipulating the law, however, it is their critics who must now defend the idea that the law really does mean something apart from whatever a clever lawyer can make it mean.

Legal indeterminacy is not a problem only for theoretically inclined legal scholars. It is very much part of the popular understanding of the legal system, as revealed by public comments made by high-ranking government officials in the course of the debate over the Bush Administration's legal response in the war on terror. For example, after the U.S. Supreme Court ruled that American personnel overseas had to comply with Common Article 3 of the Geneva Conventions, which prohibit outrages upon human dignity, President Bush noted, "[t]hat's like—it's very vague. What does that mean 'outrages upon human dignity'? That's a statement that is wide open to interpretation."[25] Similarly, Attorney General Michael Mukasey has equivocated on the question of whether waterboarding is illegal. In a letter he released in advance of a hearing on interrogation policy, he stated:

> If this were an easy question, I would not be reluctant to offer my views on this subject. But, with respect, I believe it is not an easy question. There are some circumstances where current law would appear clearly to prohibit the use of waterboarding. Other circumstances would present a far closer question.[26]

Although Bush and Mukasey do not say so explicitly, their comments suggest they would be willing to acquiesce in advice from their lawyers if the law was clear. In their view, however, the indeterminacy of the law gives them a legal permission to withhold the protections of the Geneva Conventions from detainees, and even in some cases to subject them to waterboarding.

The problem with this appeal to indeterminacy is that the law governing torture is one of those areas in which there really is not any disagreement, in good faith, about the meaning and application of core terms.[27] With respect to international law, the Third Geneva Convention, applicable to prisoners of war, prohibits the inflicting of physical or mental torture, or any form of coercion, on prisoners of war. The Fourth Geneva Convention, applicable to civilian detainees, requires the protection of civilians from all acts of violence or threats thereof. Common Article 3, which is part of all of the separate Geneva Conventions, outlaws cruel treatment and torture, as well as outrages upon personal dignity, and humiliating and degrading treatment. The Convention Against Torture prohibits not only torture, but also cruel, inhuman, and degrading treatment that does not amount to torture. The Convention contains an express nonderogation provision blocking the appeal to a national emergency as a justification of torture.[28] Moreover, the prohibition on torture is a *jus cogens* norm in international law—a peremptory standard that may not be deviated from under any circumstances. There are similar prohibitions in U.S. domestic law. These include a general federal assault statute, prohibiting assaults by striking or beating within the special maritime and territorial jurisdiction of the United States,[29] and a federal criminal statute specifically addressing torture, which prohibits anyone outside the United States to commit torture, which is defined as an act specifically intended to inflict severe mental or physical pain or suffering.[30]

As one might expect, the administration's lawyers have an explanation for why these prohibitions do not apply to prohibit the treatment inflicted upon detainees. They argue that the POW convention does not apply because al-Qaeda was not a contracting party to the Geneva Conventions, ignoring the past American practice of treating all armed combatants, not just soldiers of signatory states, as POWs under the Third Geneva Convention. With respect to the Fourth Geneva Convention on civilian detainees, the lawyers argue that the President has deemed al-Qaeda and Taliban fighters "unlawful combatants."[31] The trouble with that argument is that it may be possible for a detainee to lose POW status by being a nonprivileged or unlawful combatant, but that simply throws that detainee into civilian status, protected by the Fourth Geneva Convention. One is either a POW or a civilian detainee; it is not possible to be a kind of legal non-person, totally outside the coverage of the Geneva scheme. As the International Committee of the Red Cross has stated, "nobody in enemy hands can fall outside the law."

Regarding Common Article 3, which applies to all detainees no matter how they are categorized, the administration lawyers reasoned that the conflict with al-Qaeda is "international in scope." Common Article 3 applies to conflicts "not of an international character" and the Global War on Terrorism is, obviously enough, global. But this reasoning is simply wrong as well, because the point of Common Article 3 is to fill in the gaps in coverage created by the application of the rest of the Geneva Conventions to conflicts between nation-states. A conflict is one or the other—a war between nation states, or a conflict not of an international character—there is no such thing as an inherently non-law-governed conflict. In order to avoid the force of these arguments, the OLC lawyers backstopped them with a highly implausible "commander-in-chief override" position, claiming that the President had the authority to suspend the Geneva Conventions unilaterally.[32] This argument is untenable, however, because the President's constitutional power as commander-in-chief of the armed forces is meant to ensure only that civilian government officials play a supervisory role with respect to the military. It certainly does not mean that Congress has no coordinate role in setting legal limitations on what executive branch officials may do in the conduct of war, and it also does not mean that international legal norms are ousted by the President's authority to supervise the uniformed services.[33]

Similar arguments back and forth can be canvassed regarding other aspects of the torture memos, including the notorious limitation, in the August 1, 2002 OLC memo, defining severe pain as only that equivalent to pain accompanying organ failure or death, and the attempt to avoid the conclusion that waterboarding is torture, despite past U.S. practice of prosecuting Japanese soldiers for war crimes, specifically for waterboarding. The point here is not to exhaustively critique this specific instance of legal advising, but to suggest the difference it makes if we posit that the most basic obligation of lawyers is fidelity to law.

6.2 Interpretive Judgment

Considering the legal issues in the torture memos suggests that the evaluation of the ethical permissibility of a lawyer's advice can turn, in practice, on how well supported a legal position is. A lawyer who knew enough about international humanitarian law and the law of warfare would respond to the administration lawyers' arguments with incredulity. This incredulity is a product of participating in an activity, a *craft*, which carries with it certain internal standards of good practice—excellences, or virtues, if you like.[34] A craft grounds the possibility of normative criticism for violation of craft standards. Recognizing what it means to be a practice aimed at some end means also recognizing what it is to do well or poorly at realizing that end. This is a long tradition in ethics, going all the way back to Aristotle, but it has a contemporary application to complex institutional activities such as serving as an advisor to clients within the legal system. In the case of legal ethics, being a good lawyer means exhibiting fidelity to law, not distorting its meaning to enable the client to do something unlawful. The torture memos are lousy lawyering, and we can tell this by participating in the craft of making and analyzing legal arguments. If the political order does give the legal profession meaning, as I have been arguing in this book, then the outlines of an ethical critique of the OLC lawyers is in place.

References to craft should not be taken as appeals to some mysterious faculty of intuitive judgment, or "I know it when I see it" reasoning. An experienced lawyer may have a gut-level negative reaction to an argument, buy that intuition is only a symptom of something that has gone awry in the argument. How do we know what has gone awry? It is not easy to give a simple answer to this question, but that is not because professional craft is mysterious. Rather, it is something that takes some practice to familiarize oneself with, but with experience one can recognize good and bad legal arguments. Certain argumentative "moves" are ruled out by the existing body of law. Lawyers may not be conscious of the tacit norms regulating the exercise of interpretive judgment, but if called upon, they can generally give reasons why one interpretation is persuasive and another strikes them as implausible.[35] Going back to the torture memos example, it is well understood that the structure of the law of war is intended to create gapless coverage: There is no such thing as a person who is neither a POW nor a civilian detainee, or a war that is neither "of an international character" or "not of an international character." Someone familiar with this structure would recognize that many of the categories of non-persons and non-wars were invented by Bush administration lawyers out of whole cloth. Thus, they do not represent good-faith attempts to determine what the law means; rather, they are evasions of the law, using legal-looking arguments that do not actually hold up under scrutiny.

Lawyers frequently assess legal positions using informal judgments of plausibility. They may say an argument is solid, sensible, plausible, within the range of reasonableness, a stretch, adventurous, barely colorable, frivolous, and so on. Scholars and regulators have occasionally experimented with defining these confidence judgments in mathematical terms, for instance asking whether a position has a 10 percent chance, a 30 percent chance, and so on, of success on the merits.[36] The ABA, for example, has advised tax lawyers that they may counsel a client to take a position on a tax return as long as there is a reasonable basis in law for the position.[37] Although the ABA's ethics committee warned that a reasonable basis is more than a "colorable" claim, it also said that a lawyer may advise the taxpayer that a position is permissible even if the lawyer believes the client's position will not prevail. All that is necessary is a good-faith belief that the position is warranted by existing law. Subsequent regulations issued by the Internal Revenue Service have defined reasonable basis as approximately a one in three chance of success.[38] However, expressing judgments of plausibility in mathematical terms creates an illusion of precision that can never be obtained in legal reasoning. A lawyer may believe an argument is "pretty strong" or "not as strong, but not a complete loser," but if asked to translate those evaluations into numerical terms, will just be pulling numbers out of the air. Even worse, a lawyer may be misled into thinking that her inability to express a judgment regarding confidence in numerical terms means that the judgment is purely subjective. But one can feel strongly confident in some prediction or evaluation in certain domains without being able to quantify that judgment precisely.

Although mathematical definitions of plausibility are unlikely to be forthcoming, it may be possible to articulate an informal but nevertheless robust standard of plausibility in terms of attitudes of conviction. For example, if the lawyer could stand behind an interpretation, take pride in it, and offer it to a third party the lawyer respects for her sound judgment, then the interpretation is one that satisfies a fairly high standard of plausibility. This attitude or conviction on the part of a lawyer who offers an interpretation may be fleshed out with reference to a kind of hypothetical ideal observer. One possible heuristic using an ideal observer is that if a lawyer would be comfortable making the argument to the judge for whom she clerked, a professor she respects, or a colleague who is known for her good sense and judgment, the argument is plausible.[39] This standard is more stringent than the "laugh test" commonly employed by lawyers (i.e., whether it would be possible to make an argument in court without laughing at the ridiculousness of it). It is closer to the test proposed by Charles Fried for determining when an account of the law as given by a judge is twisted: If the lawyer offered an interpretation of law in an oral argument, or a law student offered it on an exam, would the lawyer or student be accused of being disingenuous?[40] Lawyers are comfortable making these kinds of judgments and, as we have seen, these are the sorts of arguments that have been leveled against the OLC lawyers who prepared the torture memos.

It is important not to expect the law to provide too much determinacy. In fact, in many cases, reasonable lawyers may differ on what the law permits or requires. Even if there is some indeterminacy in the law, however, it still may be possible to pick out instances in which lawyers are creating the appearance of indeterminacy where there is actually considerable certainty. To illustrate, consider this colorful quote from a former manager at Enron, describing his company's attitude toward compliance with accounting rules:

> Say you have a dog, but you need to create a duck on the financial statements. Fortunately, there are specific accounting rules for what constitutes a duck: yellow feet, white covering, orange beak. So you take the

dog and paint its feet yellow and its fur white and you paste an orange plastic beak on its nose, and then you say to your accountants, "This is a duck! Don't you agree that it's a duck?" And the accountants say, "Yes, according to the rules, this is a duck."[41]

One's intuition here is that the accountants at Enron are abusing or manipulating the applicable law. There are criteria of duck-ness and dog-ness that may not be coextensive with formal legal norms ("according to the rules," as the accountants say in the example), but there are nevertheless standards of plausibility that regulate the permissibility of asserting that something is a dog or a duck. The manipulation engaged in by the Enron lawyers depends on a spurious identification of law with formal legal norms. There may be apparent ambiguity in the governing rules, but the ambiguity is only apparent. Lawyers acquainted with the craft of making and evaluating legal arguments would recognize the duck-creation of the Enron lawyers as what it is, namely a charade.

The problem of legal interpretation is of course one that has received considerable attention from legal scholars. The problem is different in important ways, however, when considered from the point of view of lawyers, not judges. The permissibility of taking a legal position—in litigation, as the basis for a transaction, or as a ground for legal advice to a client—depends on the institutional features of the situation. Some of these features include whether there is meaningful constraint as a result of an adversarial process of briefing and argument, whether the lawyer's reasoning is public or secret, and whether the law itself contemplates flexibility in application. The most important aspect of the distinction between judges and lawyers is that, for lawyers, the obligation of fidelity to law must be understood in context. The question is, if the client "needs a duck," *when* may a lawyer say on behalf of the client, "This is a duck"? The answer is, "It depends."

To stick with the illustration (at the cost of making it a bit silly), suppose the client has been accused of the crime of possessing a dog, but wants to claim that what looks like a dog is actually a duck, which one may legally possess. It is helpful to start with this variation, because in legal ethics discourse, the criminal defense paradigm always hovers in the background, subtly informing our tacit assumptions about what a lawyer's duties ought to be.[42] It is well accepted that the criminal defense lawyer's job is to resist the application of state power to her client's case, and argue for virtually any interpretation of the law that will enable the client to avoid punishment.[43] The usual rule prohibiting lawyers from asserting claims or defenses without a good-faith basis in existing law is expressly subordinated to the constitutional entitlements of a criminal defendant, which permit (and arguably even require) the assertion of weak legal positions right up to the boundary of frivolousness.[44] Criminal-defense lawyers rightly believe that they are permitted to "put the state to its proof," requiring the prosecution to establish every element of its case beyond a reasonable doubt, even if the defense lawyer knows there is no question of the state's ability to prove its case.[45] Thus, if there is any argument, even if it is barely possible to make it with a straight face, that a dog is a duck, then the lawyer may, and arguably must, make it.

The criminal defense lawyer has virtually no obligation to ascertain that a legal argument is plausible. Lawyers may have tactical reasons not to make such laughable arguments that they lose credibility with the court and thereby diminish their effectiveness as advocates, but these are prudential reasons only, not legal or ethical obligations. Underlying this broad permission to advance practically any interpretation of the law consistent with a criminal defendant's interests is the American political tradition, emphasizing as it does the rights of the individual against the bogey of the all-powerful state.[46] The Orwellian vision of the omnipotent state may be more caricature than reality,[47] but the power differential between individuals and the state is not the whole story behind criminal defense advocacy. The real basis for the practically unlimited license of criminal defense lawyers to make creative and aggressive legal arguments is threefold. First, criminal prosecution and defense involves a substantial threat to important interests of the client, and for this reason it is situated within an institutional context that provides for fairly robust adversarial checking by partisan advocates, whose duties are oriented solely (or at least substantially) toward protecting the rights of clients. Second, permitting lawyers to argue for less well-supported conclusions of law builds some capacity for change into the legal system. For this reason, lawyers for the parties in civil litigation also have some latitude to press weaker legal arguments, subject to legal prohibitions on relying on totally unsupported positions. Finally, and most importantly, in criminal or civil litigation, one can be a zealous advocate and assume, for the most part, that the procedures and personnel of the tribunal will take care of the "bounds of the law." Adversary briefing and argument, rules of procedure and evidence, the presence of a judge and law clerks, and the possibility of appeal all serve to mitigate excesses of interpretive creativity. In other words, there is an *institutional* solution to the problem of the indeterminacy and manipulability of the law.

Where institutional checks and balances are not present, in counseling and transactional planning matters, a lawyer cannot rely on some other actor to ensure that the law is correctly interpreted and applied. In non-litigation representation, there may be no institutional mechanism to safeguard against one-sided interpretations of law. Little can be said in the abstract about all transactional practice. Some aspects, such as filing disclosures with the Securities and Exchange Commission, are quite extensively subject to procedural oversight. Lawyers in transactions also sometimes provide opinion letters on behalf of clients to third parties (lenders, guarantors, etc.)— since lawyers are exposed to civil liability for providing misleading opinion letters, there is significant constraint on lawyers' creativity in evaluating the applicable law.[48] In the absence of some effective procedural checking of the lawyer's interpretation, however, the lawyer in effect acts as a private lawgiver to the client, in that whatever interpretive judgment the lawyer renders is unlikely to be challenged by another party and tested for adequacy by a court. The law can essentially be manipulated out of existence under the guise of "zealous advocacy" if the lawyer's advice is uncoupled from the possibility that the legality of the client's actions might actually be subject to evaluation by an impartial decision-maker.

The law governing lawyers accordingly places more responsibility for getting the law right on a lawyer counseling clients, creating private ordering within the law (e.g., by contracts or incorporation procedures), or advising a government agency on its conduct. The state bar disciplinary rules provide that an attorney serving as an adviser must use independent professional judgment and render candid advice, while a lawyer representing a client in a litigated matter may assert any non-frivolous legal argument.[49] Lawyers have an obligation to use reasonable care in representing clients, and this duty may include making a reasonable evaluation of the legal basis for the client's actions, and advising the client not to do something that is legally impermissible.[50] Similarly, the Securities and Exchange Commission's regulations implementing the Sarbanes-Oxley Act require lawyers in some cases to report information "up the ladder" within a corporation where they reasonably believe their client is committing certain wrongful acts, but do not require reporting up where the lawyer is representing the client in litigation over the wrongful act.[51] Lawyers may not make materially misleading statements to third parties in the course of representing clients, and this includes statements made in documents drafted by lawyers on which third parties might reasonably rely.[52] Finally, generally applicable tort and agency law principles, as well as the rules of professional conduct, require lawyers to refuse to assist a client in an action that is not permitted by the law.[53] This requires lawyers to make an assessment of whether their clients are legally entitled to assert some right with respect to others, and to either advise the client against a course of conduct not supported by legal entitlements, or to withdraw from representing a client who wishes to do something not permitted by the law.

In transactional practice, these legal rules may mean that the lawyer is required to refuse to certify compliance with legal or accounting standards, usually in an opinion letter, where this certification would be required as a condition for the deal closing. This is the sense in which lawyers are sometimes called upon to be "gatekeepers."[54] Lawyers have a tendency to strongly overreact to the characterization of their role as gatekeepers, but this idea is far from novel or radical. Lawyers have always been potentially exposed to criminal and administrative penalties, as well as civil liability to third parties, for actively participating in their clients' fraudulent transactions. Gatekeeping liability goes beyond penalizing lawyers for knowing, active participation in client fraud, and reaches instances of what might be called—with apologies for the double negative—"failure to not-participate." Contrary to popular understanding, gatekeeping does not require lawyers to "blow the whistle" on client misdeeds, by disclosing confidential information to the authorities. The predicate for liability as a gatekeeper is not failure to disclose, but failure to timely disassociate oneself from unlawful conduct. More theoretically, lawyers who act as gatekeepers create value by serving as "transaction cost engineers."[55] Opinion letters given by counsel certify compliance with regulatory requirements, and legal liability for giving misleading opinion letters ensures that the responsibility for ensuring compliance with the law rests on the party with the best access to the facts needed to evaluate the legality of the transaction. As a result, business lawyers reduce transaction costs, reduce information asymmetries, and enable the parties to cooperate. Given that a lawyer's professional obligation is to obtain and protect legal entitlements on behalf of clients, it is hard to see how imposing liability for failure to assist a client in unlawful conduct changes the normative landscape of lawyering in any way.

Lawyers tend to react negatively to the suggestion that they should interpret the law from a quasi-judicial point of view, when acting as advisors or transactional planners. Superficially, at least, this resistance is understandable. Lawyers and judges occupy discrete roles in the legal system, and should be expected to have different responsibilities. The adversary system enacts a normative division of labor among various institutional actors, responding to political needs such as limiting government power and enhancing accountability. Lawyers in litigation need not assert only the legal positions they believe to be the best view of the law, or even those reasonably well founded. As long as a legal argument is adequately grounded, which means it has some chance of success on the merits, it is permissible to urge it to a court. While that is an accurate description of lawyers' responsibilities in litigation, it is mystifying that this argument from the adversary system is thought to prove anything about legal advising outside the litigation context. The argument that lawyers should have the same interpretive freedom in counseling as in litigation proceeds by taking the lawyer's litigation-advocacy role as the baseline, and then demanding a justification for any deviation from that baseline. But why should we take the lawyer's litigation-related duties and permissions as the baseline, and not as a special case? The normative baseline is the principal–agent relationship between clients and their lawyers. What "good lawyering" means varies by context, but it is always oriented toward the client's legal entitlements. There may be room to contest the content of those entitlements in litigation, and there may be areas of transactional practice in which it is permissible to rely on somewhat doubtful interpretations of the law, but in all cases the law sets a boundary on what lawyers justifiably may do on behalf of clients.

Even in litigation, however, the obligation of fidelity to law means that some practices by lawyers, which we take for granted, may be lacking in ethical justification. The folklore of pre-trial litigation and trial advocacy is full of stratagems for ensuring that disputes are not decided on the merits.[56] Document discovery is notoriously a shell game, with the object of ensuring that particularly probative evidence is not turned over to the adversary if at all possible.[57] Fact witnesses are prepared for their depositions by lawyers who wish to ensure that they do not inadvertently blurt out too much of the truth. Witnesses may be coached to give testimony that fits more neatly with their lawyers' theory of the case. Cross-examination techniques are designed to cast doubt on the credibility of witnesses at trial, even if the witnesses are telling the truth. (The standard example is the eyewitness identification witness who correctly identified the defendant at the scene of the crime, but was not wearing her prescription eyeglasses at the time.) Lawyers use objections to throw off the rhythm of opposing counsel's questioning, particularly when the witness is telling a compelling story. Lawyers may also make appeals to the prejudices of juries, seek to exploit racial or gender stereotypes or identification, or distract juries with inflammatory, and irrelevant evidence. Stories, perhaps apocryphal, are told of legendary trial lawyers like Clarence Darrow, who had a repertoire of tricks for distracting juries. A favorite involves a spellbinding closing argument given by opposing counsel, during which Darrow sat at counsel table impassively smoking a cigar. Anticipating the brilliant closing, he had threaded a wire into the cigar so that the ash would not fall. As his opponent's argument went on and on, the jury's attention was drawn to the miraculously long ash on Darrow's cigar. Soon they could think of nothing else, and forgot all about the other lawyer's argument.[58]

The approach to legal ethics defended here, emphasizing fidelity to law and the obligation of partisanship with respect to client entitlements, would conclude that these tactics lack ethical justification, at least *prima facie*. The only tenable justifications would apply in the special context of criminal defense, in which an argument might be made that the defendant has a procedural entitlement to put the state to its proof. Consider an example from a Michigan State Bar ethics opinion: The defendant is charged with armed robbery, and has admitted the crime to his lawyer. At the preliminary hearing, the victim testified that the crime took place at midnight, when the defendant was (truthfully) playing poker with three friends, all of whom have a good reputation in the community and will probably be believed by the jury.[59] Unfortunately, the victim was mixed up on the time, probably because the defendant had hit him on the head in the course of the robbery. The crime actually occurred at 2:00 a.m. The defendant is not going to take the stand, and thus will not falsely testify that he did not commit the robbery. The ethical question is whether the defense lawyer may call the friends to testify about the card game, knowing that the jury will draw the false inference that the defendant did not commit the robbery. The lawyer will not affirmatively state something she believes to be untrue (i.e., "My client did not commit the robbery.") but would like to argue something like the following in closing: "Ladies and gentlemen of the jury, you have heard the victim's testimony that he was robbed at midnight, but you have also heard the testimony of three upstanding citizens who were playing poker with my client at midnight. The state has an obligation to prove its case beyond a reasonable doubt, but ask yourself—is there *any* doubt that the defendant was not at the scene of the robbery at midnight?"

Without exception, every practicing lawyer (and most law students) with whom I have ever discussed the "poker game alibi" problem has concluded that it is unquestionably, unproblematically permissible to put the friends on the stand. No serious philosophical critic of the standard conception really disagrees with this conclusion.* The interesting question, though, is why there is so much agreement on the ethics of criminal defense, but so much disagreement elsewhere within legal ethics. There must be a reason to believe that criminal defense is somehow different. The standard explanation for treating criminal defense as a special case is that criminal defendants have a procedural entitlement to have the case against them proven beyond a reasonable doubt. Implementing the reasonable-doubt standard in practice requires that

---

* William Simon finds aggressive criminal defense advocacy difficult to square with his overall theoretical position, although he does come down in favor of a permission for lawyers to represent clients they know to be guilty, and to assert procedural entitlements that may result in the acquittal of a guilty client. Simon (1998), pp. 170–71. Given Simon's general commitment to legal justice, it is interesting that he supports vigorous criminal defense advocacy by appealing to the idea of nullification; he sees criminal defense representation as responding to procedural breakdowns that lead to legal *injustice*. Ibid., pp. 189–90.

defense lawyers have significant latitude to use the available evidence to construct a story inconsistent with the guilt of the accused.[60] A lawyer may cobble together, out of bits of storytelling material that are themselves true, a story that persuades the jury to draw an inference that is false. In ordinary moral terms this might count as deception, but it is consistent with the obligation of fidelity to law, because it is the only effective way for criminal defense lawyers to put the state to its proof, and require the prosecution to prove its case beyond a reasonable doubt.

Outside of the criminal defense context, however, deceptive tactics are more difficult to defend on the basis of procedural entitlements. The procedural entitlements of civil litigants are allocated differently, and except in the case of a few disfavored causes of action (like fraud and defamation), civil plaintiffs must satisfy an ordinary "preponderance of evidence" standard of proof. At the risk of overgeneralizing, civil litigation procedures are more truth-directed than criminal procedures, which are informed to a great extent by the defendant's dignitary and autonomy interests. Familiar doctrines like the exclusionary rule and the privilege against self-incrimination are not justified on the basis of ensuring the conviction of guilty defendants and the acquittal of innocent ones. Granted, civil litigants do have some entitlements that are justified on the grounds of policies other than finding out the truth. Evidentiary privileges, like the attorney–client and spousal-communication privileges, exclude probative evidence in order to protect relationships of trust and confidence against interference by third parties. Litigants can object to overly burdensome, "fishing expedition" discovery requests. And there are numerous rules, such as the statute of limitations, that protect interests such as repose, which are not related to the merits of underlying claims.

Having noted these non-truth-respecting entitlements, however, there is still a great deal of room for ethical criticism directed at lawyers who play games with the factual and legal merits of cases, outside the special context of criminal defense. A large range of practices cannot be justified ethically, even though they are routinely engaged in by lawyers. As a junior civil litigator, I learned the tricks of the trade for defending depositions, and many of them were aimed at either ensuring that one's witness did not make damaging (truthful) admissions, or at cluttering up the transcript, so that if one's witness said something damaging, it would be hard for opposing counsel to take a long excerpt from the testimony and include it as a block quote in a court filing. Similarly, some lawyers have been embarrassed by the public disclosure of documents used to prepare witnesses to testify at depositions or at trial; these documents appeared to spoon-feed the lawyers' version of the story to witnesses, to ensure they testified to facts that would be helpful at trial, whether or not the witnesses actually recalled the facts in this way.[61] These are the sorts of practices that may be conventionally accepted by practicing litigators, but cannot be justified on a conception of legal ethics that gives central importance to the legal entitlements of clients. The Standard Conception directs lawyers to protect the interests of their clients through lawful means. From that point of view, there would appear to be nothing wrong with these shenanigans unless the lawyers violated some legal prohibition, such as the rule against falsifying evidence. The obligation of fidelity to law defended here, however, would condemn these tactics as having no plausible justification in terms of protecting the legal entitlements of clients.

6.3 The Jurisprudence of Lawyering

Even if one grants that the obligation of fidelity to law should vary by context, one might nevertheless ask whether the law is the sort of thing that is capable of possessing determinacy at all, and how it would have this quality. Without getting too deep into the weeds of legal philosophy here, my suggestion would be that the nature of legal interpretation and the nature of law are related, and that law should be fundamentally understood as a practice of reason-giving, subject to certain kinds of constraints. The most basic constraint on what counts as an interpretation of law is that law must be viewed as a purposive activity, as having some point or end.[62] That is true of the law in general, and of specific areas within the law. Legal reasoning can be said to exhibit "immanent rationality," in the sense that a competent lawyer or judge working within some domain of law (such as tax, commercial, or national security law) knows how to deploy and respond to arguments using a distinctive form of reasoning, which can be differentiated from ordinary moral or political argument.[63] The rationality of each domain is, in turn, subject to the immanent rationality of law in general. The structure of legal reasoning at this level is constrained by familiar rule-of-law values, such as the necessity that legal reasons be general, public, consistent with other legal reasons, and so on.[64]

Returning to the Enron example, the law governing structured-finance transactions involving special-purpose entities may appear on its face to be subject to almost infinite manipulation. But the range of plausible interpretations of these accounting and securities-law rules narrows quite a bit if they are understood against the background of structured finance, with attention to the purpose for having and regulating this activity. Structured finance is designed to have certain economic benefits, most notably enhancing access to capital markets for institutions that are not investment banks, reducing transaction costs by eliminating certain intermediaries from the financing process, while all the while remaining relatively transparent from the point of view of managers and investors.[65] A proposed interpretation of law that would permit a transaction that does not reduce transaction costs, that does not enhance access to capital markets, and that requires transparency-reducing complexity should be viewed with suspicion, as being more likely within the zone of colorable, but not plausible interpretations. This conclusion is justified not by the text of the relevant statutes and regulations, because in many cases the language is ambiguous or susceptible to manipulation. Rather, a lawyer would regard some interpretations as implausibly aggressive because they go against the whole point of the law of structured finance—what it is "all about."[66]

When interpreting any legal norm (a case, statute, regulation, or whatever), lawyers and judges must consider the background of reasons against which the rule was established, locating it within a context and fleshing out its meaning with reference to the understandings of the players in the legal system who had a role in creating the norm in the first place and sustaining it over time. The dynamic and evolving nature of many legal norms—particularly common law rules, but also statutes and regulations as interpreted by courts and administrative agencies—links these norms with a multitude of internal legal reasons that may be relied upon as guides to interpretation. Taken together, these internal reasons structure the arguments that may be given in support of an interpretive judgment.

> [J]udges confronting an "indeterminate" norm do not simply put on their policy-making hats, even if their view is that they must make new law. They attempt to understand the meaning of the relevant norm in light of what the situation demands; they argue, by analogy, for the salience of certain facts, and they try to find principles which have some toe-hold in the existing law.[67]

The demand for a reasoned justification requires that an interpretation of legal norms be grounded in materials (texts, principles that are fairly deemed to underlie and justify legal rules, interpretive practices, hermeneutic methods, and so on) that are properly regarded in the relevant community as appropriate reasons.[68]

Of course, even if legal argumentation is structured by the immanent rationality of some domain of law, if there is a multitude of legal reasons that bear on any interesting interpretive question, it is unlikely that there will be only one obviously right answer. In the structured-finance example, the goals of reducing transaction costs and increasing the transparency of financing arrangements may conflict in many cases. (Requiring additional disclosures for the sake of transparency will almost inevitably increase transaction costs.) More generally, one might argue that every area of law is structured around oppositions between conflicting values, such as individualism and altruism.[69] For this reason, legal interpretation almost always involves the exercise of judgment, or what some scholars of statutory interpretation refer to as practical reasoning.[70] One may question whether this is enough for coordination and settlement, particularly if internal legal reasons can be plural and conflicting. There still seems to be a subjective element in interpretation if it is thrown back on judgment, which is a virtue or characteristic of a judge or lawyer, not a property of the law itself. But judgment, in turn, is not a subjective process. Judgment is not a faculty of individual interpreters, and is certainly not a matter of punting the weighing or balancing of plural factors to the subjective discretion of the decision-maker. Rather, the exercise of judgment is fundamentally a community-bound process, in that it makes reference to intersubjective criteria for the exercise and regulation of judgment.[71] "Objectivity in the law connotes standards. It implies that an interpretation can be measured against a set of norms that transcend the particular vantage point of the person offering the interpretation."[72]

This must be true in order for a judgment of the form, "The client may do such-and-such," to be a conclusion of *law*, and not something else, like politics or morality. Law is the enactment of a political community, and a legal judgment must therefore make reference to standards that transcend the individual making the judgment. The law is purposive; it is *about* something, and legal interpretation is aimed at recovering that meaning. As I have been arguing, the whole point of the law is to differentiate between something you can get away with, and something that is authorized, as a matter of right, and regulated by rules of general application. The legal system enforces that distinction by rhetorical practices that take certain considerations into account, as part of the justification of legal judgments, and exclude other considerations as irrelevant. Only considerations that are part of the law count in favor of an interpretation of law. That sounds tautological, but it is actually a significant implication of the theory of authority defended here. If citizens disagree about matters of importance to their communal life, and cannot resolve these disagreements using ordinary practical reasoning (including moral reasoning), they can fall back on the procedures made available by the legal system for establishing a communal position with respect to the matter. Determining what considerations are part of law is a task for the interpretive community, comprised of judges, lawyers, scholars, and interested citizens who have learned to differentiate between legal and nonlegal reasons. In other words, the authority of law is founded in social practices, much as H.L.A. Hart explained in *The Concept of Law*.[73]

In order for any official, institution, or practice to have authority, it must be conferred somehow—say, by a rule authorizing the subject of the rule to promulgate authoritative rules. Consider the authority of a federal statute, passed pursuant to Congressional authorization under Article I of the Constitution. Saying that the Constitution confers authority on Congress only raises the further question of where the Constitution gets its authority. In response one might point to Article VII which provides that the Constitution would be established by ratification by the conventions of nine states. However, the appeal to state ratification is either circular (because it is specified by the very document whose authority is in question) or leads to an infinite regress, as we then ask on what basis state conventions have the authority to ratify some document which can then confer authority on Congress. Without authority, one cannot confer authority, but there has to be some original source of authority—a first cause, unmoved mover, *Grundnorm*, or what have you. The nature of this original source is deeply paradoxical, however, because in order for it to claim authority it must have the power to change the normative situation of others, but it must derive this power from something other than a grant of authority, which would just get the regress rolling again. As Hart observed, law creates reasons for action that are acknowledged by citizens using the language of obligation, such as "ought," "duty," "right," and "wrong."[74] The solution to the circularity or regress of legal authority must be something that accounts for the obligatory nature of law, at a fundamental level.

The startling thing about Hart's solution to the problem of the foundation of legal authority is that he grounds the normativity of law in something empirical. Social practices validate the existence of a law and fix its content. "[A] statement about what the law is is made true by certain social facts—facts regarding the conduct and attitude of certain persons in the community."[75] This is a philosophically adventurous position—every student in an introductory ethics course learns that you cannot derive an "ought" from an "is." In order for anything to be normative—that is, to provide a justification for doing something—it is not enough for that thing simply to be practiced. Instead, it must have "ought-ness" about it somehow, in the sense that one has a duty to do what is practiced.[76] Hart seeks to locate the ought-ness of the rule of recognition in the community's practices, which seems to beg the question of how the rule of recognition creates a duty.[77] The way out of this apparent circle is to appeal to the notion of a practice as having normativity built in.[78]

For Hart, what stops the regress is the critical reflective attitude displayed by judges, who believe that certain considerations ought to be regarded as standards to be followed by other judges.[79] This is not a mere preference or hope on the part of judges, but part of a *practice* that regards deviation from these standards as an occasion for justified criticism.[80] Hart says that judges who adopt this critical reflective attitude are regarding the law from the internal point of view, not looking at it merely as observers interested in predicting behavior, but as participants in a meaningful social practice.[81] When judges regard something as a standard for deciding cases, criticize other judges for not following that standard, and accept the criticism of others as justified to the extent they do not adhere to the applicable standard, a "rule of recognition" comes into existence.[82] The rule of recognition is a standard that establishes criteria of validity or legality.[83] Primary rules governing the conduct of citizens are then validated by the rule of recognition; these rules create obligations that are backed by the authority of the legal system's master norm, the rule of recognition. "Jaywalking ... is prohibited by law in New York City even though nearly everyone ignores the rule. It is a law because it is valid, not because it is practiced."[84] The rule of recognition, on the other hand, is law only because it is practiced.

Judges' acceptance of the rule of recognition from the internal point of view is conceptually necessary in order for there to be a legal system. If judges did not acknowledge legal norms as legitimate reasons for action (indicating this by the use of words like "ought," "right," and so on), then there would be no way to differentiate an authoritative legal command, issued as part of a legitimate legal *system*, from the demand of a mugger, and the state from the gunman writ large.[85] To see Hart's point about the systematicity of official decisions, imagine some kind of strange hypothetical society in which disputes are resolved by the whim of decision-makers, but as it happens the class of decision-makers is remarkably homogeneous, in terms of socioeconomic background, ideology, education and training, and other determinants of beliefs and preferences. If these decision-makers consistently favored certain litigants—say, prosecutors or big corporations—there would be an observable regularity in their decisions, but we would not call those decisions *lawful* unless they were justified by reasons that made reference to the sorts of values that should make a difference in how legal disputes are resolved. The system would deserve the label "legal" only if the officials regarded themselves as duty-bound to make decisions on the basis of certain reasons and not others. We may disagree in some particulars over what criteria differentiate a lawful decision from one based on whim or partiality. But if we are to speak intelligibly of legality and legitimacy, there must be some criteria for distinguishing between actions that respect a regime of law and those that are responsive to other sorts of concerns.

It is important to point out that this account of the normativity of practices does not depend on the motivations of judges. Hart protests that "[t]he internal aspect of rules is often misrepresented as a mere matter of 'feelings' in contrast to externally observable physical behavior."[86] But as he emphasizes, facts about beliefs and motives "are *not necessary* for the truth of a statement that a person had an obligation to do something."[87] Judges have an *obligation* to follow the rule of recognition, which identifies the society's laws and differentiates them from other norms.[88] Nevertheless, a judge may be *motivated* by the desire to be promoted to a higher court, to win glory, or simply to continue in employment in a cushy job. Whatever specific motivations a judge may have, however, there must be something distinctive about law that provides a different sort of reason for action—otherwise there would be no such thing as a legal system as opposed to a fortuitous convergence of behavior by a bunch of people sitting on high benches wearing black robes.[89] As long as the law makes a practical difference to how a judge decides cases, in the sense that the judge accepts the legitimacy of measuring her own conduct against the standard of lawfulness articulated by the relevant community, the specific motivation a person has for being a judge is immaterial. Similarly, a citizen may not believe herself morally obligated to perform some action required by law, or may be morally indifferent yet think the law is silly. Despite having no particular motivational state toward the law, to the extent the citizen wishes to describe her conduct as lawful, she is necessarily committed to viewing the law from the internal perspective, as creating obligations.

Several points in this discussion are relevant to the jurisprudence of lawyering. The first is the difference between an obligation accepted from the internal point of view and something else. In order for a government to be characterized by the virtue of legality, legal officials must regard themselves as duty-bound to consider some reasons, and not others, as the grounds for a judgment of law. This obligation applies to lawyers as well as judges, to the extent a lawyer intends to give *legal* advice, as opposed to merely counseling on what would be moral or prudent. This is the way legal entitlements are differentiated from mere client interests. The second point is that the rule of recognition in an actual legal system may be complex and contestable. For example, judges often make reference to tacit criteria of legality.[90] There is no requirement that the rule of recognition refer only to official acts of political actors such as legislators and judges—what Dworkin refers to as pedigree criteria.[91] Moreover, the rule of recognition may have a hierarchical structure, may consist of a series of disjunctive tests, or may have a number of exceptions that are triggered by certain facts.[92] What matters from the internal point of view is whether a consideration has "been consistently invoked by courts in ranges of different cases" in support of a decision.[93] The following section considers some of the challenges these observations present for lawyers and judges trying to ascertain the content of the law. These interpretive problems arise, in part, from the process of contestation back and forth between citizens and state officials. Because lawyers play a central role in this social process of legal meaning-making, it is essential that a theory of legal ethics take account of the way the content of the law may be contestable.

6.4   Some Legal-Interpretive Puzzles

6.4.1   *Enforcement Practices and Legal Interpretation*

One way that the meaning of a legal norm may be up for grabs is if official enforcement practices appear to tolerate a certain amount of noncompliance, to the point that a new *de facto* law comes into existence.[94] A familiar example is the speed limit on a stretch of flat open highway. The posted signs may say the speed limit is 65 miles per hour, but "everyone knows" the state troopers will not pull over drivers going less than 72 m.p.h. Thus, one might come to believe that the "real" law in effect is a 72 m.p.h. speed limit. A more complex example comes from Stephen Pepper: Suppose that the Clean Water Act, associated regulations, and the client's permit allow discharges of up to 0.050 grams per liter of some pollutant into a local waterway.[95] It is quite expensive to reduce discharges to the 0.050 gram level. Now imagine that a lawyer representing the permit holder knows, from experience in similar cases, that the regional office of the EPA has a kind of triage policy, and will not commence an enforcement action unless discharges exceed 0.075 grams per liter. Is the lawyer permitted to give this kind of advice, or would providing the information tacitly encourage the client to violate the law, in violation of the lawyer's obligation not to "counsel a client to engage ... in conduct that the lawyer knows is criminal or fraudulent"?[96]

In jurisprudential terms, the community of citizens and law enforcement officials may claim to have created, by their enforcement and compliance practices, a new law permitting a higher speed limit, or discharges in excess of permit limitations. In Hart's jurisprudence it is conceptually necessary only that judges accept the rule of recognition from the internal point of view. Hart says that while judges must necessarily regard the rule of recognition from the internal point of view, "private citizens ... may obey each 'for his part only' and from any motive whatever."[97] Nevertheless, the rule of recognition is not opaque to citizens and their legal counsel. People who are interested in knowing whether the law permits or prohibits some activity can answer that question by, in effect, reasoning like a judge. The question "Is it legally permissible to do X?", where X stands for some apparently tolerated activity, can be restated more completely as follows: "If a judge were to regard X as legally permitted, or as a matter of indifference, would she be subject to legitimate criticism by her fellow judges for having acted contrary to a genuine obligation to decide this case on the basis of legal criteria?"

The effect of framing the question in these terms is subtle, but important. It shows that there is some room for flexibility in the legal system, and that judges may in effect defer to citizens' conceptions of legality. At the same time, this formulation of the inquiry shows that citizens do not have the power to unilaterally nullify the law by their practice of noncompliance. They can *propose* a different understanding of what the law requires, but courts are not bound to respect it. If other judges in the relevant community would criticize a decision to dismiss charges against a defendant for speeding, then there is no *de facto* change in the law, despite a pervasive practice of disobedience by citizens. Someone who gets a ticket for going 66 m.p.h. where the speed limit is 65 m.p.h. may feel unlucky, but she has no legitimate claim that the police officer lacked the legal authority to pull her over.

The EPA example is a bit more difficult, because the administrative agency responsible for enforcing the statutory and regulatory scheme of the Clean Water Act has a quasi-judicial role. Pepper argues that it is conceptually impossible to disentangle what can be called the conduct rule (no discharges in excess of 0.050 g/L) from the decision rule (no liability for discharges not exceeding 0.075 g/L).[98] The law governing lawyers prohibits lawyers from counseling the client to engage in *unlawful* conduct. However, breaching a contract, committing a tort and, in the environmental hypothetical, discharging effluents in excess of permit limitations are not crimes, and therefore not "unlawful" conduct if that term is understood to mean crimes. Thus, in order to give the client sufficient information about its legal rights in non-criminal cases, the lawyer must communicate something about the nature of the sanction or remedy that might attach to noncompliance, including information about the procedures courts will follow in deciding whether to impose these sanctions. The decision rule thus feeds back into the interpretation of the conduct rule, and in effect creates a new conduct rule. Pepper therefore objects strongly to the lawyer telling the client, "The law requires you to reduce discharges to 0.050 g/L," calling this advice "deception in service to obedience of the law."[99]

Stated this way, Pepper's position is simply the Holmesian bad man attitude toward compliance. By assuming that the law generates only prudential reasons for action, related to a citizen's desire to avoid the unpleasant consequences of being caught and punished, the Holmesian bad man stance simply assumes away the possibility that the law may be intrinsically reason-giving. In the hands of lawyers, the Holmesian bad man attitude is often brought to life as an exercise in interpretation. Rather than flatly denying an obligation to obey a law prohibiting something (such as discharges in excess of 0.050 g/L), a lawyer may deny that the law actually says one must not do that, or that by the terms of the governing law, the client's conduct does not constitute the prohibited conduct. In this case, the EPA enforcement practices could be a *de facto* change in the meaning of the Clean Water Act and associated regulations, but they could simply reflect the reality of budgetary limitations. Officials at the EPA might reasonably believe the law to impose penalties if a single molecule over the permit limitations is discharged, and they may fervently wish they had the resources to detect and punish all violations. On the other hand, they may believe the text of the statute and regulations are unrealistically stringent and, perhaps in cooperation with local industry, agree that more flexible limitations are permissible under a more purposive or holistic reading of the applicable legal norms.[100] Perhaps the regional office of the EPA believes that water in rural areas tends to be cleaner and more tolerant of slightly increased levels of pollution, as compared with water in urban areas; thus, this particular regional administrator might believe that a more sensible discharge limitation would be the higher level.[101] The point is, without knowing more it is impossible to say anything definite about the content of the law applicable to the discharge of pollutants.

The one thing we can say for sure is that there is a difference between regarding the law as merely a cost to be taken into account, and as intrinsically a reason for doing (or not doing) something. To emphasize a point made earlier, citizens may have a variety of motivational stances with respect to the law. The client in Pepper's example may regard the EPA permit limitations as an irritant, and would be quite happy to evade them if it were possible to do so without penalty. The internal point of view does not require that citizens be well disposed toward the law, only that they see themselves as under an obligation to accept that the law is reason-giving. Otherwise, citizens would be privileging their own view about what ought to be done, in the name of the political community, over the view actually reached by the community through established lawmaking procedures. Hart's position, as set out earlier, can be extended to provide an account of what anyone—judge, lawyer, or citizen—means when she says, "my action is legal." The claim of legality is, in essence, the avowal of having evaluated a scheme of legal entitlements and constraints from the perspective of one who regards them as creating reasons for action as such. Otherwise, it would be impossible to differentiate a claim of legal entitlement from the ability to avoid detection and punishment through power, connections, deception, or blind luck. For someone to decide that the law does not create a reason for action unless somehow it is backed by effective enforcement is to claim a kind of superior power over his fellows, or an immunity from having to abide by the same rules as others. Ignoring the law essentially takes back the respect that was extended to individuals by legal processes, and replaces it with the exercise of raw power, or with the attitude that the individual stands apart from society as a whole and is, in effect, a law unto himself.

6.4.2 Negotiated Compliance and the Endogeneity of Law

Another puzzle concerning the interpretation of law by lawyers in practice comes from the work of some legal sociologists who have investigated how organizations respond to law. On one understanding of the relationship between law and organizations, law is an exogenous factor that corporate managers have to anticipate and deal with, like the weather or shortages of supplies. As Lauren Edelman has shown, however, in practice the law actually tends to be *endogenous* in the sense that "the meaning of law is determined largely *within* (rather than outside of) the social arena that it seeks to regulate."[102] This empirical finding is a striking confirmation of Cover's vision of legal meaning as parasitic on extra-legal normative worlds. When citizens encounter the law, legal endogeneity is possible because the law as promulgated is ambiguous. Edelman, who has investigated compliance with civil rights laws, notes that federal statutes prohibiting discrimination in employment are vague when it comes to defining the operative term "discrimination." Judicial decisions and administrative regulations may help, but significant areas of uncertainty may remain. It therefore falls to lawyers, working in cooperation with managers, human resource professionals, and others, to specify what constitutes compliance in practice with anti-discrimination laws.[103] Efforts at compliance may result in the creation of formal intra-organizational structures such as grievance procedures, but the meaning of legal norms (at least as perceived by the regulated organization) may shift as the implementation of the law fuses with managerial imperatives such as efficiency and ensuring good workplace relationships. Complaints about discrimination may be reconceptualized as failures of management, resulting in additional training, counseling, or the transfer of employees, without ever really confronting the underlying claim of discrimination.

One danger associated with the endogeneity of law in the organizational context is that legal rights will be watered down by merely symbolic compliance (e.g., creating EEO offices and affirmative action plans), which tends to legitimate existing practice regardless of whether they are effective.[104] Somewhat more subtly, the translation of legal norms into managerial imperatives may weaken the force of the legal requirement. For example, translating anti-discrimination principles into exhortations to "manage diversity" in order to tap the full creative power of a diverse workforce decouples the managerial imperative from the concern for discrimination against historically disenfranchised groups.[105] "Diversity" in manager-speak may include variations in lifestyles, tastes, dress styles, geographic origin, and other concerns remote from the core civil rights value of redressing the historical disenfranchisement of protected classes.[106] In addition, because managers have assimilated the legal duty into a broader business-strategic effort to enhance productivity and market share, they may lose sight of the importance of the anti-discrimination norm.[107] This is not to say that there is anything wrong with aiming indirectly at the protection of rights—if enhancing workplace diversity has a positive impact on the organization's bottom line and also happens to improve the situation of women and people of color (as mandated by civil rights statutes), then so much the better. The point is, however, that enhancing profitability through better workplace relations may become the only goal in view for managers, so that if protecting civil rights somehow conflicts with maintaining harmonious working relationships, the need to attend to the latter may trump the duty to the former. This may happen at a subconscious level for managers, who believe they are responding to the mandates of civil rights statutes, because they had previously reinterpreted the statutory obligations as a broader (and less legally focused) mandate to improve productivity.

More generally, if the meaning of a legal norm is uncertain until it is implemented in practice, it is hard to see how the law can be used to settle disagreement. Thus, Edelman's observations of the endogeneity of law appear to challenge the settlement-based conception of legal obligation defended here. Surely the same sorts of disagreements over the weight and priority of values that necessitated the legal settlement in the first place would reenter into the contest over how the law should be interpreted in practice. Moreover, citizens whose views were taken into account in the lawmaking process, and whose views actually prevailed in that process, could become disenfranchised in the after-the-fact contestation over the "real" meaning of the law. In Edelman's case studies of anti-discrimination norms, the actors implementing the norms—managers, human resource professionals, and lawyers—have considerably greater power than employees in the workplace.[108] They are well positioned to smuggle in their own preferred interpretation of the law, under the guise of what the law "really" requires, even though they may not have been able to prevail in the legislature or the administrative rule-making process. It may happen that the conduct of institutional actors is ratified after the fact by courts who believe the conduct was in compliance with legal norms. Edelman describes how human resource managers promoted the use of internal grievance procedures, even though at the time courts were disinclined to conclude that adopting these procedures was evidence of compliance with civil rights statutes.[109] After a while, courts began to hold that an employer's adoption of effective grievance procedures might in fact constitute evidence of compliance with statutory requirements, culminating in a 1998 Supreme Court decision that an employee's failure to use a grievance procedure might be an outright defense to liability.[110]

The status of the employer's use of grievance procedures in the period prior to general acceptance by courts of this conduct as compliance is a real jurisprudential puzzle. In particular, we might ask how it is possible to identify the content of the law at some point during the period in which its meaning is emerging through the interpretive practices of managers and lawyers who advise them. A strong claim about the endogeneity of law would be that courts retrospectively ascertained and applied the "real" law that had developed previously through the efforts (let's assume they were in good faith) by lawyers and managers to comply with what they took to be the requirements of law. This sounds bizarrely circular when considered from the point of view of the managers, as if they, as the subjects of legal requirements, were aiming at some illusory target that only appeared after they hit it. There is no circularity, however, if one imagines both managers (with the assistance of lawyers) and judges as *repeatedly* aiming at the same target and adjusting their fire, so to speak, with an eye toward what other actors are doing. The legal interpretation of civil rights statutes could be understood as an ongoing dynamic process, with managers and their lawyers trying their best to hit the target of actual legal requirements, and judges refining the law based on the inputs of the parties in a series of disputes. Maybe the first lawyer to suggest using grievance procedures was picking up on a suggestion in a judicial opinion or ambiguous language in EEOC regulations that provided an arguable basis for this approach to compliance. Subsequent judges may have agreed with that interpretation, but that does not mean the law did not exist until someone tried out the use of grievance procedures and had that approach ratified by a court. The law existed and had meaning to the extent that members of an interpretive community, consisting of lawyers, judges, subjects of legal regulation, and knowledgeable observers, could agree on what it required, to a sufficient degree of objectivity. On this dynamic view, the meaning of a legal norm cannot be divorced from its application in practice.

It seems like a curious ontological claim to say that the law existed as some kind of potential but as-yet unrecognized notion in the minds of members of the interpretive community, but this is perfectly consistent with—and indeed may be implied by—a theory of law that emphasizes its basis in shared social practices. Private actors, such as managers, lawyers, and other compliance professionals, may take into account certain reasons that they believe bear on the content of the legal entitlements of organizational actors. These entitlements are then subjected to challenge by employees in litigation. In the process of deciding these cases, judges may cite the reasons given by the organization as reasons in support of a conclusion that the organization has an entitlement to do something (e.g., employ internal grievance procedures to resolve claims of discrimination). Thus, the reasons given by citizens, when thinking about what the law means *for them*, may eventually feed back into the legal system and become aspects of what the law actually means. Putting this possibility in Robert Cover's terms, one might posit a diversity of normative visions—a plurality of "laws"—offered by various communities that coexist within one overarching polity.[111] The resulting law, in the sense of "the thing to which respect is owed" is not imposed from above, by some official state actor, but emerges from a process of contestation among these competing normative visions, only one of which is the state's.

Cover's vision has a great deal of power. There often is a struggle to define the meaning of central normative notions like equality or dignity, and the victor in this struggle may be a social movement or a dissident community. Certainly the transition from the separate-but-equal regime of *Plessy* to the desegregation decisions of *Brown* and later cases can be understood as a process by which one community's vision of equality became the dominant one, replacing the state law that had existed previously. Moreover, the legitimacy of the resulting law—the Civil Rights Act and cases upholding it against constitutional challenges—is bolstered by the vigorous contestation that surrounded its adoption; no one can claim that his or her voice was not heard in the cacophonous national debate about the meaning of racial equality. But it does not follow from this broad historical account of legitimacy that the micro-level ethics of lawyering should necessarily be understood as a process of enabling citizens to contest the meaning of law in application. The inference from a Cover-style conception of jurisgenerative law-in-action to a conception of legal ethics requires careful attention to the variety of institutional settings of lawyers' practices. This is true even if we hold constant the idea that there is ambiguity in the applicable legal texts—cases, statutes, regulations, and the like—as well as nontextual sources of guidance such as canons of statutory construction, that bear on the content of a legal entitlement in any given case. As emphasized throughout this book, the ethics of lawyering must be understood in context, and what may be true of advocacy in pursuit of legal change (as in the example of civil rights litigation) may not carry over into the different institutional context of legal advising.

The most significant fact about the lawyers in Edelman's study is that they did see themselves as attempting to discern the substantive meaning of the law, as it applied to their particular situation. The process of attempting to work out legal meaning in practice may have led to a change in the meaning of law as interpreted by courts, but the lawyers did not view themselves as having no obligation of fidelity to law. The observed fact that legal meaning can take shape through the process of application of law does not provide license to conclude that evasion of the law is ethically permissible. How to differentiate between evasion and attempting to discern legal meaning? The answer to that question brings us back, full circle, to the case study that began this chapter. A critic who wishes to establish that any lawyer is behaving unethically must engage with the nature of the legal reasoning given by the lawyer in support of her conclusion that the client has a legal entitlement to do something. If that reasoning passes muster, by the standards of the interpretive community, then the lawyer is justified in ethical terms. Otherwise, we can criticize the lawyer for failing to comply with the obligation of fidelity to law.

Conclusion

As I have argued throughout this book, lawyers should not aim directly at justice, and should not make decisions in the same way that morally reflective people make any ethical decision. This sounds like a strange, even perverse way to end a book on legal ethics, but I think it is the unavoidable implication of understanding the values that infuse the ethics of lawyering as fundamentally political, as related to considerations like democratic legitimacy and the rule of law. To emphasize a point I have made throughout the book, the institutions and procedures that make up the legal system do not exist in isolation from considerations of morality and justice; rather, they reflect a moral stance that we take toward powerful actors. If the rule of law means anything, it is that arbitrary power is intolerable, and claims of right must be justified in a way that accords respect to all affected citizens. When lawyers work within a reasonably well-functioning legal system, their actions have value that derives from these ideals. By orienting legal ethics around these values, we can see more clearly what is wrong when lawyers manipulate the law in the service of powerful clients. The ethical failing is not violation of ordinary moral obligations, but failure to exhibit the fidelity to law that is the basic duty of all lawyers.

Public criticism of lawyers seems to be a permanent feature of our discourse. As a noted legal historian observes, large Wall Street law firms have been criticized at least since the nineteenth century for "serv[ing] rich, evil clients rather than the public; and ... pervert[ing] the legal profession, turning free, independent craftsmen into workers in factories of law."[1] Prior to the American Revolution, attorneys were regarded as an adjunct to an unpopular and corrupt government, in a conspiracy to suppress the rights of the colonists, and obstacles to peace or godly government.[2] Lawyer jokes, many of which have remained remarkably constant over time, show that the public has always harbored the suspicion that lawyers are fomenters of strife, economic parasites who profit from the troubles of others, untrustworthy characters who can espouse positions they do not personally believe in, and people with power by virtue of having access to the arcane mysteries of law.[3] The arguments in this book are meant to be a way of responding to this sort of criticism, by showing that there is something worthwhile about playing a role within a system that serves valuable social ends.

Some readers may see this as making a fetish of legality, forgetting that the form of the rule of law can be used by some pretty horrific governments. As Judith Shklar has observed, "procedurally 'correct' repression is perfectly compatible with legalism."[4] Legality is only one virtue of government, and a rule-of-law regime can commit gross injustices. This does not mean, however, that the normative significance of the rule of law—and therefore the lawyer's role—does not reside in qualities such as the capacity of legal systems to safeguard against the abuse of power, and to enable people to give a justification for their actions that refers to considerations that have been adopted using tolerably fair procedures, in the name of the community as a whole. The argument here has been that to the extent the lawyer's role is morally justified, the justification will depend on political ideals related to the rule of law. If that is the right way to approach the ethics of lawyering, it is not a sufficient objection to point out the possibility of defects in the legitimacy of a legal system. Simply saying "Nazi Germany" is no more sufficient to tag legality with a negative value than citing some utopian legal system would be sufficient to associate legality with a positive value. The hard work of arguing for the value of a legal system is in the details.

One might also object that the theory defended here places too much trust in the determinacy of law, thinking that there is something for lawyers to be faithful to, when in fact we all (smart academic lawyers, that is) know that the law is too manipulable to serve as a meaningful constraint. I sometimes wonder whether anyone actually believes this, because nothing could be more ordinary and unremarkable than criticizing lawyers for getting the law wrong. For example, David Luban has noted that American lawyers object to the establishment of the law-free zone at Guantánamo Bay as a "standing affront to a political order that gives their profession meaning."[5] To make sense of that objection, one must both appreciate the normative significance of the political order underlying the legal profession and presuppose that the law is sufficiently determinate that one can criticize government lawyers for working around the law, rather than exhibiting fidelity to law. One is certainly entitled to respond that the lawyers' reasoning was correct, and the critics of the Bush Administration are merely playing politics. Like the illegitimacy critique, making this response stick requires getting into the details. Someone who wishes to argue that John Yoo and others did nothing wrong cannot avoid engaging rigorously with the governing law and the legal reasoning employed by the lawyers in question. As long as we are doing that, I contend, we are doing legal ethics the right way.

The implication is that a theory of legal ethics cannot aim directly at considerations of morality, justice, or the public interest. The reason for this is not that there is no such thing as justice or the public interest (i.e. that it is nothing more than the aggregation of individual preferences), as public-choice theorists maintain. Rather, it is that disagreement over normative notions like justice or the public interest is what gives rise to the need for law in the first place. Calling upon lawyers to interpret the content of law with respect to the public interest has the effect of reintroducing the normative controversy that the law is meant to settle. Permitting lawyers to evade the law in the public interest manifests disrespect for the procedures of law-making and law-interpreting, which in turn means disrespecting the equality and dignity of other citizens. The law is not some alien excrescence, but is an institutional practice we have created for a reason.[6] That reason is to enable us all to live together as peacefully and harmoniously as possible, consistent with the recognition that we are all autonomous beings who disagree about the terms of this framework of cooperation. Lawyers do serve the public interest, but they do so indirectly, by treating the law with respect when representing and advising clients. This is the sense in which the lawyer is a quasi-public official — an "officer of the court" as that term is generally understood in legal ethics.[7] Lawyers are nevertheless not fully political officials because they have obligations of loyalty and partiality to clients. The traditional role of attorney as wise counselor reflects both the obligation of fidelity to the law and the duties of care, confidentiality, candor, communication, diligence, and loyalty that are owed to clients.

I have no illusions that a book about philosophical legal ethics will be able to counteract the pressures lawyers sometimes feel to do what their clients want, even if that means finding a way to work around inconvenient legal restrictions. Similarly, the effects of structural changes in the practice of law on lawyers' ethics is a subject deserving its own booklength treatment.[8] The goal here is merely to establish a way of thinking about legal ethics that explains why lawyers justifiably believe they have obligations of loyal client service and, at the same time, are *lawyers* and not hired guns or mouthpieces in a pejorative sense. The ideal of fidelity to law explains the ethical significance of both partiality to clients and independence from clients to the extent required by law. It also explains why legal ethics is not simply the application of the ethics of ordinary persons, but requires careful attention to the political and institutional context of legal practice. The position set out here is particularly suitable for an occupational group whose professional expertise consists of reasoning about the legal entitlements of clients. From the point of view of lawyers, there is nothing mysterious about what this book recommends. In the end, being an ethical lawyer means doing well at the craft of lawyering. This is not an elitist vision, like the "lawyer–statesman" ideal[9]; nor does it demand cultural conditions that may no longer exist in order to flourish.[10] Fidelity to law may on occasion be a demanding obligation, but all lawyers have the capacity to comply with it, and thus to satisfy the ethical requirements of their profession.

Notes

In the notes that follow, I hope to avoid the practice familiar to readers of American law reviews of continuing arguments from the main body of text into the notes, so that a reader has to constantly flip back and forth between text and notes to get the flow of the discussion. Beyond a purely bibliographical function, the notes here are intended to deal with peripheral or technical matters that can safely be ignored by most readers but which may be of occasional interest.

Notes to Introduction

1. This question became one of the canonical formulations of a central problem in legal ethics after a decision by U.S. District Judge Stanley Sporkin, ruling on a case arising out of the massive series of savings and loan failures in the 1980s. *Lincoln Savings & Loan Association v. Wall*, 743 F. Supp. 901, 920 (D.D.C. 1990). See also Langevoort (1993). Susan Koniak has given Judge Sporkin's question a nicely ironic echo in her congressional testimony on the late 1990s financial accounting scandals. Susan P. Koniak, "Where Were the Lawyers? Behind the Curtain Wearing Their Magic Caps," in *Accountability Issues: Lessons Learned from Enron's Fall—Senate Judiciary Committee Hearing* (Feb. 6, 2002).

2. Eric Posner and Adrian Vermeule, "A 'Torture' Memo and Its Tortuous Critics," *The Wall Street Journal* (July 6, 2004), at A22.

3. Rhode (2000a), pp. 66–67 (arguing that lawyers should be prepared to "accept personal responsibility for the moral consequences of their professional actions"); Simon (1988), p. 1090 ("Lawyers should take those actions that, considering the relevant circumstances of the particular case, seem likely to promote justice.").

4. Fuller (1958), p. 631 ("Law, as something deserving loyalty, must represent a human achievement; it cannot be a simple fiat of power or a repetitive pattern discernable in the behavior of state officials."). Although many ideas in this book are indebted to H.L.A. Hart, I also drew a great deal of inspiration from Lon Fuller's jurisprudence. In fact, the title *Lawyers and Fidelity to Law* was inspired by the very Fullerian idea that the moral goodness inherent in the practice of lawyering is related to the social achievement of governing with due respect for the value of legality. See Fuller (1969), pp. 200–224.

5. Simon (2001).

6. The former Lord Chief Justice of England and Wales gives a striking example of this attitude from Britain during the 1956 Suez crisis. Prime Minister Anthony Eden directed that the government not consult with the Legal Adviser to the Foreign Office, Sir Gerald Fitzmaurice, who had advised against the government's actions. Eden said,

"The lawyers are always against us doing anything. For God's sake, keep them out of it. This is a political affair." Quoted in Bingham (2007), p. 83. Eden's words could have been spoken by many officials within the Bush Administration as the government considered responses to the September 11th attacks and the ongoing "war on terror." See Lichtblau (2008).

7. Yoo (2006), p. x.

8. Ibid., p. xii.

9. Ibid.

10. Bob Gordon and Bill Simon have long advocated for taking this question seriously within legal ethics. In a jointly authored paper, from which I have learned a great deal, they write: "Serious reflection about legal ethics has to be grounded in theoretical understanding of the nature of legality and the goals of the legal system, and of how lawyers' practices may serve or subvert those goals." Gordon and Simon (1992), p. 238. This book is one attempt at such a theoretical understanding.

11. Rawls (1993), pp. 55–58.

12. See, e.g., Galston (2003), p. 30 ("Value pluralism is offered as an account of the actual structure of the normative universe .... So value pluralism is not to be confused with emotivism, noncognitivism, or Humean arguments against the rational status of moral propositions."). Hobbes, for example, was a moral realist. See Hobbes (1994), xv, 17, p. 95 ("[T]here is, in men's aptness to society, a diversity of nature rising from their diversity of affections, not unlike to that we see in stones brought together for the building of an edifice.").

13. Wong (2006), p. 44 (a naturalistic account of morality "generates significant constraints on what could count as an adequate morality, given its functions and given human nature"); Hampshire (1983), pp. 142–43 (listing several biological features of human life, such as the dependence of very young children on adults and the comparative helplessness of the old, "which may be appealed to as imposing some limits on moral requirements in all times and in all places").

14. Hampshire (1983), pp. 141–42. For example, both American and classical Chinese Confucian cultures acknowledge the importance of family relationships, the obligations of gratitude and respect, and the need to reciprocate for gifts received. Chinese ethics, however, which places a significantly greater emphasis on the duty of filial piety, includes an aesthetic component in its conception of the worthwhile life, and stresses social harmony. Wong (2006), pp. 17–20. Alasdair MacIntyre has argued that secular philosophical ethics in the West is an incoherent mishmash of fragments of past ethical traditions that once flourished, but have since died out. Moral disagreement is due to the survival of moral concepts apart from the traditions that gave them meaning. See MacIntyre (1984), pp. 6–10. One of the strengths of Wong's theory of pluralistic relativism is that it shows how traditions and cultures can be differentiated by priorities among ethical value commitments, but rational disagreement can still be possible. Different cultures select from among a plurality of basic values, which are also present in the ethical traditions of other cultures. The values emphasized by other

cultures are intelligible as paths that our own culture might have taken. Wong (2006), pp. 19–20.

15. Rawls (1993), pp. 39, 94, 147, 150–54.

16. Schwartz (1978); Postema (1980), pp. 73–74; Luban (1988), p. xx. The Standard Conception is generally summarized with two principles governing the lawyer's action and one additional principle stating an inference that observers are expected to draw. These are (1) partisanship—the justified preference of one's client's interests over the interests of others; (2) neutrality—the lawyer's agnosticism about the moral worth of the client's projects and the ends by which they are to be achieved; and (3) nonaccountability—preclusion of observers' negative moral evaluation of the lawyer for acting on principles (1) and (2).

17. See, e.g., Wasserstrom (1975), p. 1 ("the lawyer–client relationship renders the lawyer at best systematically amoral and at worst more than occasionally immoral in his or her dealings with the rest of mankind."). Stephen Pepper nicely inverted this critique by seeking to capture the label of "amoral ethics" for his own ethical theory. See Pepper (1986).

18. "Freestanding" is a term borrowed from Rawls. See John Rawls, "Reply to Habermas," in Rawls (1993), pp. 374–75. Another way to put the same point is to stress the autonomy of political values, relying on distinctively political notions like citizenship and legitimacy to do the evaluative work. See, e.g., Bernard Williams, "Realism and Moralism in Political Theory," in Williams (2005), p. 1. Martin Stone nicely summarizes Kant's conception of political obligation (see also Waldron [1996]), as follows: "The object of civic association ... is well-being, only not that kind of well-being ... which is already in reach in a state of nature. Civic association brings about a new kind of human good that is not just an operation (maximizing, equalizing, etc.) on more basic goods; it makes it possible for persons to live in a new way—in conformity with 'principles of Right.'" Stone (2001), p. 142. The idea of a new kind of human good that comes into being only in civic and political associations is central to the structure of value defended here.

19. Joseph Raz argues that the most normatively attractive conception of the rule of law is one whose core idea is "principled faithful application of the law," by which he means that legal decisions (he is thinking of those made by judges, but I would include legal advice by lawyers representing clients as well) are reasoned and public, and which are responsive and responsible to a common legal culture in the society. See Joseph Raz, "The Politics of the Rule of Law," in Raz (1994), p. 374.

20. Waldron (1999a), pp. 86, 101, and *passim*.

21. P.L. 105-298 (1998).

22. Model Rules, Rule 1.16(b)(4) (permitting withdrawal where lawyer has fundamental disagreement with client's action or considers it repugnant), Rule 2.1 (permitting counseling on the basis of "moral, economic, social and political factors" if they are relevant to the client's situation).

23. Simon (1998), p. 1.

24. Bernard Williams, "Politics and Moral Character," in Williams (1981), p. 64. For other prominent contributions to the literature on dirty hands, see Weber (1946); Walzer (1973); Thomas Nagel, "Ruthlessness in Public Life," in Nagel (1979); Thompson (1987); Gowans (1994).

25. Bernard Williams, "Politics and Moral Character," in Williams (1981), p. 63.

26. Gowans (1994), pp. 233–34; Bernard Williams, "Politics and Moral Character," in Williams (1981), p. 64 ("only those who are reluctant or disinclined to do the morally disagreeable when it is really necessary have much chance of not doing it when it is not necessary").

27. Walzer (1973), pp. 178–79.

28. Wilkins (1990), pp. 475–76 ("If ... it is possible to provide a 'legal' justification for virtually any action, it is hard to see how the requirement that zealous advocacy must occur within the bounds of the law meaningfully restrains a lawyer's decisionmaking."). See also Luban (1988), p. 16 (noting that the notion of a "good faith" interpretation of law is itself open to manipulation in pursuit of client objectives); Levinson (1987), p. 368 (arguing that when one is attentive to the way lawyers think about the law in action, "one will discover the *genuinely* important emphasis on the inherent indeterminacies within the law and the concomitant ability to distinguish practically any case or construe practically any statute in a way that will count at least as a 'good faith argument for the extension, modification or reversal of existing law.'").

29. Luban (2007), p. 23; Sarat (1998), p. 818.

30. Even in litigation, fidelity to law is one of the fundamental obligations of the lawyer, along with loyalty to the client. Lawyers may not assert constructions of law that are not adequately grounded, either in existing law or in a good faith argument for the extension, modification, or reversal of existing law. Fed. R. Civ. P. 11; Model Rules, Rule 3.1. Lawyers have an obligation to disclose controlling legal authority not cited by their adversary, an obligation that does not extend to factual evidence not discovered by opposing counsel. Model Rules, Rule 3.3(a)(2). Advocates have been severely sanctioned for stretching legal arguments too far, and for not candidly informing the court of the limitations of their position. See, e.g., *Precision Specialty Metals, Inc. v. United States*, 315 F.3d 1346 (Fed. Cir. 2003).

31. Timothy Endicott argues that no one, not even deconstructionists and critical legal studies scholars, really makes radical indeterminacy claims. Endicott (2000), pp. 16–17.

32. Being constrained by something external to the decision-maker is all that I mean by objectivity. The word "objectivity" tends to provoke set readers off, possibly because of the influence of Critical Legal Studies, which repeatedly criticized liberal conceptions of the rule of law and legal legitimacy for failing to deliver on the promise of *necessary* guarantees that a "decision-maker's ideology played no role in the choice of an outcome." Kennedy (1997), p. 32. But that is much too strong. No method of legal reasoning can necessarily guarantee that a particular decision was not tainted by ideology; requiring decision-makers to articulate reasons can, however, narrow the role

of subjective preferences—what Kennedy refers to as ideology—to the point that ideology does not threaten the content-independence of legal judgments.

Rawls says something important and general about how objectivity is a property of a discipline of reasoning, not something "outside" which can be used as a yardstick:

> [W]e assert a judgment and think it correct because we suppose we have correctly applied the relevant principles and criteria of practical reasoning. This parallels the reply of mathematicians who, when asked why they believe there are an infinity of primes, say: any mathematician knows the proof. The proof lays out the reasoning on which their belief is based .... [B]eing able to give the proof, or to state sufficient reasons for the judgment, is already the best possible explanation of the beliefs of those who are reasonable and rational.

Rawls (1993), p. 120. The notion of legal craft defended here is similar to what Rawls invokes to explain why the judgment "there is an infinity of primes" is warranted—one who is competent in the relevant craft can give the proof, and that is all the objectivity that is needed.

33. The problem originated in the Hart–Fuller debate, and has become a staple of jurisprudence scholarship. See Fuller (1958), p. 663; Hart (1958), p. 607. For a modern overview, see Schauer (2008).

34. Hart (1994), p. 127.

35. Marty Lederman, "Sorry, Ben, but Judge Mukasey Can (and Should) Answer the Question," *Balkinization* (Oct. 29, 2007), <http://balkin.blogspot.com/2007/10/sorry-ben-but-judge-mukasey-should.html>. Waterboarding has been described as follows, by a former instructor at the U.S. Navy's Survival, Evasion, Resistance, and Escape (SERE) School:

> Waterboarding is controlled drowning .... It does not simulate drowning, as the lungs are actually filling with water. There is no way to simulate that. The victim is drowning .... A team doctor watches the quantity of water that is ingested and for the physiological signs which show when the drowning effect goes from painful psychological experience, to horrific suffocating punishment to the final death spiral. Waterboarding is slow motion suffocation with enough time to contemplate the inevitability of black out and expiration—usually the person goes into hysterics on the board .... When it is done right it is controlled death.

The full article can be found in an online magazine called *Small Wars Journal*, <http://smallwarsjournal.com/blog/2007/10/waterboarding-is-torture-perio/>, and excerpts appeared in various newspapers, including the *Independent* (UK) and the *New York Daily News*. For a similar description, by a former Navy flight crew member who attended SERE training, see Richard E. Mezo, "Why It Was Called 'Water Torture,'" *The Washington Post* (Feb. 10, 2008), at B07.

36. The call for a jurisprudence of lawyering is from Levinson (1987).
37. See Daniels (1979); Scanlon (2003).
38. Daniels (1979), pp. 258–59.

Notes to Chapter One

The Standard Conception, For and Against

1. See, e.g., Williams (1985), p. 12 ("we have a conception of the ethical that understandably relates to us and our actions the demands, needs, claims, desires, and, generally, the lives of other people"); ibid., p. 188 (defining ethical obligation in terms of not taking action that would be "associated with others' expectations, or with blame for failure"); Scanlon (1998), p. 189 (taking the position that justifiability to others is basic to ethics). In this book, I will take the idea of being able to offer a justification for one's actions, and thus not be subject to blame by others, as essential to the subject matter of ethics.

2. When I speak of lawyers or the legal profession, I have in mind an occupational group in a common-law system like the United States. The structure of the ethical problems facing lawyers is broadly similar in the U.S., the United Kingdom, Canada, Australia, and New Zealand, although lawyers arguably play a more prominent role in American political life generally, as compared with lawyers in other common-law systems, and there are other subtle differences that may be obscured by my emphasis on the American system. See Woolley (1996). Members of professions in civil-law countries, such as Continental European, Latin American, and East Asian systems, conceive of their obligations to clients, the law, and society as a whole in very different terms. The education, training, and socialization process for lawyers is also very different in these systems. Thus, many of the ethical dilemmas we will consider here do not arise in the same way for civilian lawyers. See generally Hazard and Dondi (2004); Lasser (2004); Kagan (2001); Leubsdorf (2001); Barceló and Cramton (1999); Merryman (1985), pp. 101–10; Luban (1984).

3. Legal sociologist Marc Galanter has traced many of these themes in the public image of lawyers through the evolving corpus of lawyer jokes. See Galanter (2005). Galanter identifies recurring themes in these jokes, which he organizes into nine clusters, including:

Discourse: Lawyers lie incorrigibly. They corrupt discourse by promoting needless complexity, mystifying matters by jargon and formalities, robbing life's dealings of their moral sense by recasting them in legal abstractions, and offending common sense by casuistry that makes black appear white and vice versa.

Economic Predators: Lawyers are ... parasitic rent-seekers who don't really produce anything, but merely batten on the productive members of society, often in alliance with the undeserving...

Enemies of Justice: Lawyers are indifferent to justice and willingly lend their talents to frustrate it.

Ibid., p. 17.

4. Luban (1984), p. 246.

5. For the "freestanding" terminology, see John Rawls, "Reply to Habermas," in Rawls (1993), pp. 374–75. Rawls calls this a political conception, to distinguish it from metaphysical doctrines. See Rawls (1993), pp. 29–35. For a succinct overview of the distinction between ordinary and political morality, see Simmons (2008), pp. 2–3. For a powerful defense of the autonomy of political morality, see Bernard Williams, "Realism and Moralism in Political Theory," in Williams (2005).

6. Cf. Rawls (1993), p. 93 (noting that political constructivism begins with a "rather complex conception of person and society"—that is, with a conception of persons as citizens).

7. See, e.g., Nelson (1998), p. 775. One of the law-firm associates who participated in a study by the ABA litigation section noted that "we can all pretty much spot an ethical issue and we know that we have a duty to take it up with those who are responsible and discuss it and take appropriate action." It is clear from context, however, that this lawyer meant "ethical issue" as "conduct potentially violating the rules of professional conduct."

8. See Wolfram (1986) § 2.2, pp. 22–27. For an ambitious assertion of the inherent power to regulate, see *Birbrower, Montalbano, Condon & Frank v. Superior Court*, 949 P.2d 1 (Cal. 1998) (denying a law firm's claim for payment under its contract with the client, because the contract was unenforceable due to the firm's unauthorized practice of law in California).

9. American Bar Association, Standards for the Approval of Law Schools, Standard 302(a)(5). This curricular mandate dates back to the Watergate scandal, and the public's outrage at the fact that many of the participants in the cover-up were lawyers.

10. Most academic philosophers use the terms ethics and morality interchangeably, as I will here. See David Copp, "Introduction," in Copp (2006), p. 4.

11. Fried (1976), p. 1060. Similarly, Gerald Postema picks up on the distinction between persons-qua-persons and persons acting in a professional capacity, and notes that "lawyers ... claim special warrant for engaging in some activities which, were they performed by others, would be likely to draw moral censure." Postema (1980), p. 63; see also Gewirth (1986), p. 283 ("The separatist thesis is invoked ... in transactions between professionals and their clients or other affected persons where this or some other general moral requirement of rights is not fulfilled, so that a moral right of the client or someone else is infringed."); Wasserstrom (1975), p. 1 ("the lawyer–client relationship renders the lawyer at best systematically amoral and at worst more than occasionally immoral in his or her dealings with the rest of mankind.").

12. For the contrary view, see Luban (2007), pp. 59–61 (arguing that what look like the duties of professionals are only weakly pragmatically justified, and should

be seen as having no moral weight than other conventional norms, such as rules of etiquette).

13. Wasserstrom (1975), p. 3.

14. Postema (1980), p. 65 ("For many professional roles the moral universe of the role is considerably narrower than that of ordinary morality...").

15. Applbaum (1999), p. 46 ("are roles merely shorthand for a nexus of obligations, values, and goods that have moral weight without appeal to role as a moral category?"); Luban (1988), p. 125 ("the appeal to a role in moral justification is simply a shorthand method of appealing to the moral reasons incorporated in that role"). The aim of Richard Wasserstrom's classic article is to establish that roles should be understood as a nexus of ordinary moral values or, as he puts it, that "we might all be better served if lawyers were to see themselves less as subject to role-differentiated behavior and more as subject to the demands of the moral point of view." Wasserstrom (1975), p. 12.

16. Joseph Raz, "On the Autonomy of Legal Reasoning," in Raz (1994), p. 328.

17. See, e.g., Dare (2009), p. 34 ("Role-obligations ... are moral requirements whose content is fixed by the function of the role, whose normative force flows from the role, and that apply to an individual by virtue of their status as a role-occupant.").

18. See Goldman (1980), pp. 2–3 (distinguishing strongly and weakly differentiated role obligations).

19. See Raz (1979), pp. 17, 22, 27; Raz (1986), p. 33.

20. Applbaum (1999), pp. 56–57.

21. Pileggi (1985). The film version is *GoodFellas*, directed by Martin Scorcese. I am using wiseguys here, but similar examples are a staple of the jurisprudence literature. David Luban cites numerous philosophers of law who note that there are internal standards regulating the practice of poisoning, blackmail, genocide, and lynching. Luban (2007), p. 112 n.29. But I like the wiseguy example, because the norms in question are so colorful, and have been so effectively dramatized by actors like Robert De Niro, Joe Pesci, and Paul Sorvino.

22. Pileggi (1985), p. 39.

23. Luban (1988), p. 130.

24. MacCormick (2007), p. 4.

25. See Dare (2009), ch. 3 (making a similar argument for an indirect relationship between ordinary morals and the role-specific obligations of lawyers).

26. John Rawls, "Reply to Habermas," in Rawls (1993), p. 380.

27. See, e.g., Michelman (1988), p. 1500.

28. Joseph Raz, "The Politics of the Rule of Law," in Raz (1994), pp. 371, 374. In this article, Raz argues that the rule of law is essentially a requirement of public reason-giving, with a view toward "breed[ing] a common understanding of the legal culture of the country, to which in turn [public decisions] are responsive and responsible."

29. See generally Joseph Raz, "Authority, Law and Morality," in Raz (1994).

30. This example is based on the description of the Dalkon Shield products liability litigation in Rhode (1994), p. 669. Some details are also discussed in Luban (2007), pp. 35–36.

31. Richard Wasserstrom cites an example, to similar effect, of a California procedure whereby the defendant in a rape case can compel the victim to submit to a psychiatric examination. Wasserstrom (1975), pp. 6–7. There is no similar procedural entitlement for other crimes, suggesting very strongly that the right reflected at the time the sexist bias of the criminal justice system.

32. I made this argument, using the Dalkon Shield hypothetical, in a review of Applbaum (1999). See Wendel (2001).

33. Compare Bernard Williams's claim that a freestanding normative domain may be connected with ordinary morality if its central concepts are those that have moral salience—that is, if there is a legitimation that can be offered for the practice that speaks in terms of reasons that make sense to us as part of a whole cluster of "political, moral, social, interpretive and other concepts." Bernard Williams, "Realism and Moralism in Political Theory," in Williams (2005), p. 11.

34. See the similar arguments in Dare (2009).

35. Simon (1998), p. 53.

36. Luban (1990), pp. 430–31.

37. This problem is based on the classic case of *Zabella v. Pakel*, 242 F.2d 452 (7th Cir. 1957), although I have embellished the facts in some places and simplified them in others. *Zabella* is a bona fide classic, appearing in many leading works of legal ethics theory. See, e.g., Dare (2009), pp. 2–3; Hazard and Dondi (2004), p. 175; Simon (1998), p. 29; Pepper (1999), p. 189; Luban (1988), pp. 9–10; Postema (1980), p. 66; Fried (1976), p. 1064.

38. Daniel Markovits contends that the lawyer in this case is cheating, in ordinary moral terms. Markovits (2008), p. 65.

39. See Dare (2009), pp. 5–12; Luban (2007), p. 20; Simon (1998), p. 7; Luban (1988), pp. xx–xxi; Schwartz (1983), pp. 150–51; Postema (1980), p. 73; Simon (1978), pp. 36–37.

40. The Model Rules have a peculiar "rule," which can have no binding effect, announcing that "[a] lawyer's representation of a client ... does not constitute an endorsement of the client's political, economic, social or moral views or activities." Model Rules, Rule 1.2(b).

41. The hidden bodies case, or Lake Pleasant Bodies case as it is sometimes called, is a staple of professional responsibility casebooks and academic scholarship. For an excellent summary of the case, see Zitrin and Langford (1999), pp. 7–26. For the attempt to prosecute the lawyers involved for violating a statute respecting the treatment of bodies, see *People v. Belge*, 83 Misc. 2d 186, 372 N.Y.S.2d 798 (Onondaga County Ct. 1975), *aff'd*, 50 A.D.2d 1088, N.Y.S.2d 711 (1975), *aff'd*, 41 N.Y.2d 60, 359 N.E.2d 371, 390 N.Y.S.2d 867 (1976).

42. As a general statement about the duty of confidentiality, that is incomplete; lawyers in most jurisdictions have discretion to disclose confidential information to prevent, rectify, or mitigate certain types of harm. Model Rules, Rule 1.6(b). In the hidden bodies case, however, it remains an accurate statement to say that the lawyer had no discretion to reveal the location of the bodies to the authorities or the parents.

43. Quoted in Zitrin and Langford (1999), p. 19.

44. Ibid.

45. Gordon (1998a), p. 732; Suchman (1998), p. 845 ("Large-firm partners ... tended to deny the moral dimensions of their work entirely, and to reduce most issues to either ethical rules [i.e., the state bar disciplinary rules] or pragmatic strategies.").

46. Nelson (1998), p. 780; see also Gordon (1998a), p. 711 (quoting lawyers in the same study who stated: "You're not hired to give moral advice"; "we're not moral judges of our clients"; and "there is morality, but it is not the domain of lawyers"); Sarat (1998), pp. 819–20 (quoting another lawyer in the same study, who said, "I don't want to have a moral dialogue. The client didn't hire me to be a philosopher. If he wants that kind of advice he can go to a priest.").

47. Nelson (1998), pp. 788–89.

48. Gordon (1998a), p. 714 ("To a very large extent ... the choice of approach will be dictated by the instructions or, in the absence of instructions, by the perceived situation, interests, and desires of their clients."); Suchman (1998), p. 849 (quoting one lawyer who said, "if executives [of the client] tell the in-house counsel that there's nothing morally wrong, you can't go against that").

49. Sarat (1998), pp. 820–21; Suchman (1998), pp. 850–51. Participants in the study had a hard time stating criteria to differentiate permissible manipulation of the rules of the game from impermissible bad behavior. They were sometimes able to define the boundary ostensively; there was agreement, for example, that "it is okay to make repeated objections as to form or to use breaks to throw off questioners in depositions ... [but] it is not okay to threaten routinely to seek sanctions or to call the opposing counsel or party names." Sarat (1998), p. 820. Gordon interprets this example as standing for the principle that as long as some tactic has "some more-than-minimal relation to an arguably legitimate purpose," it is permissible. Gordon (1998a), p. 712.

50. Gordon (1998a), p. 710; Nelson (1998), p. 781; Suchman (1998), p. 850.

51. Restatement § 16(1).

52. Pepper (1986), pp. 616–17.

53. See Raz (1986), pp. 372–73.

54. Pepper (1986), p. 617.

55. Ibid.

56. See Luban (1986), pp. 638–40.

57. Pepper (1986), p. 617.

58. Luban (1986), p. 638.

59. Raz (1986), p. 381. David Luban rightly points out that autonomy entered the vocabulary of ethics via Kant, but autonomy for Kant is something very different from freedom of choice. Kantian autonomy is about acting on moral laws, rather than acting "heteronomously" according to inclinations. See Luban (2007), pp. 75–76. See also Schneewind (1998), for a magisterial history of the vicissitudes of the notion of autonomy in ethics.

60. Raz (1986), p. 388.

61. Luban (1986), p. 638.

62. See, e.g., Pepper (1986), p. 630 ("an injection of ethical constraint [is contrary to] the moral values that inhere in the premises of the first-class citizenship justification").

63. See John Rawls, "Reply to Habermas," in Rawls (1993), pp. 374–75.

64. Pepper (1986), p. 617.

65. Luban (1986), p. 641.

66. Ibid., p. 642.

67. Pepper (1986), p. 660.

68. Ibid., p. 617

69. See Waldron (1989), p. 74 ("a justification for liberal neutrality should explain why neutrality is a *political* not a universal requirement").

70. Another way of putting this point is that the state may intervene in some activity if it has an impartially justifiable goal—that is, some end that all affected persons can, in principle, agree with. In private relationships, whether families, friendships, or civic associations, the persons affected by a decision made on behalf of the group are more likely to agree with the reasons given. In a larger-scale pluralistic society, however, it is more difficult to find consensus. That is why "neutrality as a political ideal governs the *public* relations between persons and the state, not the *private* relations between persons and other institutions." Larmore (1987), p. 45.

71. Ronald Dworkin, "Political Judges and the Rule of Law," in Dworkin (1985), p. 11.

72. Ibid. ("[S]ubstantive justice is an independent ideal, in no sense part of the ideal of the rule of law."). It should be noted that Dworkin goes on to criticize this conception of the rule of law, what he calls the "rule-book conception," for not insisting that the rule of law incorporate (true) moral rights. Dworkin's notion of the rule of law is rather idiosyncratic. Most legal theorists take the rule of law to be a formal conception only, having nothing to do with substantive justice, or the content of the rights of citizens. See, e.g., Joseph Raz, "The Politics of the Rule of Law," in Raz (1994), pp. 371–78; Joseph Raz, "The Rule of Law and Its Virtues," in Raz (1979), p. 214. Even Lon Fuller, who confusingly refers to the inner *morality* of law, has in mind certain formal features like generality and prospectivity. See Fuller (1969), p. 39. For Fuller, the essence of the rule of law is "subjecting human conduct to the governance of rules," ibid., p. 46, not doing justice. As Raz reminds us, however, formal conceptions of the rule of law have some real bite, and exclude many systems of governance from being regarded as lawful. If the law is to be capable of guiding behavior (which must be true if the law is the sort of thing that can claim practical authority over its subjects), then the law must be relatively general, open, clear, stable, and public. *See* Joseph Raz, "The Rule of Law and Its Virtues," in Raz (1979), pp. 213–16.

73. Ibid., p. 220 ("We value the ability to choose styles and forms of life, to fix long-term goals and effectively direct one's life toward them. One's ability to do so depends on the existence of a stable, secure framework for one's life and actions.").

74. Dershowitz (1996), p. 166.

75. Quoted in a number of sources, with both approval and disapproval; see, e.g., Dare (2009), p. 6; Luban (2007), p. 22; Markovits (2003), pp. 213–14; Freedman and Smith (2002), pp. 79–80; Luban (1988), pp. 54–55; Fried (1976), p. 1060 n.1. Dare's account is a particularly lively and concise summary of the case.

76. For this understanding of the context of Brougham's speech, see Shaffer (1985), pp. 204–6.

77. Model Code, EC 5-1.

78. Model Rules, Rule 1.7 (simultaneous-representation conflicts), Rule 1.8(a) (business transactions with clients), Rule 1.8(j) (sexual relations with clients), Rule 1.9 (successive-representation conflicts).

79. Applbaum (1999), pp. 65–65; Luban (1988), pp. 12, 155–56; Postema (1980), p. 73.

80. See Fletcher (1993).

81. Bernard Williams, "Persons, Character, and Morality," in Williams (1981), pp. 11–12.

82. Ibid., p. 18.

83. Fried (1976), p. 1061.

84. Ibid., p. 1062.

85. Ibid., p. 1066.

86. Ibid., p. 1069.

87. Ibid., p. 1071.

88. Simon (1978), p. 108.

89. Finnis (1980), p. 142.

90. Fletcher (1993), pp. 179–80 n.46.

91. Dauer and Leff (1977).

92. Ibid., pp. 578–79.

93. Ibid., p. 581.

94. Fried (1976), p. 1073.

95. Finnis (1980), p. 142.

96. Fried (1976), p. 1066.

97. Ibid., p. 1077 (italics in original removed).

98. Luban (2007), Ch. 2.

99. See Korsgaard (1996b); Johnston (1994), pp. 79–83.

100. Luban (2007), p. 71.

101. Korsgaard (1996b), p. 133.

102. Luban (2007), p. 76.

103. Ibid., pp. 73–74, 77–79. The quotation is from ibid., p. 89.

104. Ibid., pp. 83–85.

105. Luban has made this argument in connection with the corporate attorney–client privilege, and has concluded that the value of human dignity does not justify the privilege in the organizational context. Luban (2007), p. 88; Luban (1988), pp. 220–33.

106. Luban (2007), pp. 102–3 (citing Fuller [1969], p. 106).

107. Ibid., pp. 106–9. Here Luban picks up the Aristotelian idea of the internal normativity of some object or practice:

[T]o recognize something as a steam engine or a light switch is already to recognize what it ought to do, to recognize a built-in standard of success or failure. Success or failure at what? At being a steam engine or a light switch—at being what it is, one might say. Purposive concepts are *aspirational* concepts—and now we recognize that Fuller's morality of aspiration is intimately connected with his analysis of purposive concepts, and hence with the is/ought distinction.

Ibid., pp. 109.

108. Ibid., pp. 110, 112.

109. Ibid., pp. 118.

110. Ibid., pp. 111–12.

111. Dare (2004).

112. Simon (1998), p. 138; Simon (1988), p. 1090.

113. Simon (1998), p. 27.

114. See, e.g., *Boomer v. Atlantic Cement Co.*, 257 N.E.2d 870 (N.Y. 1970).

115. Simon (1998), p. 30.

116. Rawls (1971), p. 7.

117. See Fed. R. Civ. P. 1 ("These rules ... shall be construed and administered to secure the just, speedy, and inexpensive determination of every action.").

118. See Dworkin (1985), p. 165 ("If we accept justice as a political virtue we want our legislators and other officials to distribute material resources and protect civil liberties so as to secure a morally defensible outcome.").

119. Simon (1998), p. 56.

120. Ibid., p. 138.

121. Dare (2009).

122. Schneyer (1984).

123. Simon (1988), p. 1091; Simon (1998), p. 9 (distinguishing the Contextual View from the Dominant View).

124. See Simon (1998), p. 82 (distinguishing a substantive conception of law, in contrast with positivism, which is committed to an interpretation of "specific legal norms as expressions of more general principles that are indissolubly legal and moral").

125. Ibid., p. 62 (noting the divergence between the "technical" rules respecting confidentiality and the intuitions of lawyers and clients regarding what justice requires).

126. Simon (1988), pp. 1091–94 (directing lawyers to consider "the relative merits of the client's goals and claims and the goals and claims of others whom the lawyer might serve").

127. Simon (1998), p. 145.

128. Simon (1988), pp. 1092, 1103–4 (instructing lawyers not to interpret statues and regulations in accordance with "problematic" purposes that "pose an especially

grave threat to fundamental legal values"); Simon (1998), p. 106 (referring to a hierarchy of legal norms, with some being more "basic" than others).

129. Simon (1998), pp. 139–40, 143–44.

130. Simon (1988), pp. 1098–102; Simon (1998), p. 107 (giving examples of institutional dysfunction, including small but organized minorities who block repeal of anachronistic statutes), p. 141 (duty on lawyer to aim directly at justice is "triggered by the fact that, without some assistance from defense counsel, the procedure cannot be relied on to produce a just resolution").

131. Simon (1988), pp. 1113–14.

132. Ibid., pp. 1116; see also Simon (2001) (arguing that popular-culture portrayals valorize lawyers who are willing to dispense with legal niceties in the pursuit of substantive justice).

133. Simon (1988), p. 1114.

134. H.L.A. Hart argued that for any legal system, there is a master rule for distinguishing law from non-law; this is the rule of recognition. Hart (1994), pp. 100–110. He further insisted that the existence and content of the law can be determined without reference to moral criteria. H.L.A. Hart, "Postscript," in Hart (1994), p. 269. Hart stressed the content-independence of law in papers written after the first edition of *The Concept of Law*. See H.L.A. Hart, "Commands and Authoritative Legal Reasons," in Hart (1982), p. 243.

135. Ronald Dworkin, "The Model of Rules I," in Dworkin (1977), pp. 40–41, 43; Ronald Dworkin, "Hard Cases," in Dworkin (1977), p. 90.

136. Dworkin (1986), p. 240; Ronald Dworkin, "Hard Cases," in Dworkin (1977), pp. 87–88.

137. Ronald Dworkin, "The Model of Rules II," in Dworkin (1977), pp. 65–68.

138. Dworkin (1986), p. 248.

139. Ronald Dworkin, "The Model of Rules I," in Dworkin (1977), p. 30; Ronald Dworkin, "Hard Cases," in Dworkin (1977), p. 81.

140. Ibid., pp. 52, 90, 225, 256.

141. Ibid., pp. 255–56.

142. Postema (1987).

143. See, e.g., Simon (1998), pp. 151–56 (arguing that lawyers for a wealthy private university should not take advantage of a procedural irregularity in a union election; the reason for the irregularity was mere carelessness that did not prejudice anyone; and the university's demand for a new election does not comport with the purpose of the NLRA, which is to ensure that unions are genuinely representative of the bargaining unit); Simon (1988), pp. 1105–7 (arguing that a lawyer is justified in "planning around" a provision of a public assistance program that reduces cash grants in proportion to in-kind income received by the grantee, including housing provided at no cost; even though there is no textual exception in the statute applicable to the client's situation, reducing the beneficiary's cash grant in this case would be "problematic" in that it "endangers fundamental values" such as the interest in a minimally adequate income). In both of these cases, I think a fair reading of the applicable law goes

squarely against Simon's proposed interpretation. There are at least plausible reasons why the university would be justified in demanding an election that complies with the formal requirements of the NLRA. To his credit, Simon sets out these reasons fairly—see Simon (1998), p. 153—but he concludes in the end that they are not sufficiently weighty. Maybe not, but they are weighty enough to justify the lawyers in following the instructions of their client to insist on the new election. In the welfare-rights case, Simon is making an argument for the fundamental importance of a right to a minimally adequate income that is normatively attractive, but clearly against the grain of modern Supreme Court caselaw. See Simon (1988), p. 1107 n.55.

NOTES TO CHAPTER TWO

From Partisanship to Legal Entitlements: Putting the Law Back into Lawyering

1. See, e.g., Applbaum (1999), p. 6.
2. Wasserstrom (1975), p. 2.
3. The principle of loyalty to clients is one of the central norms in the law of lawyering, and is expressed in numerous provisions in the Model Rules, including Rule 1.2(a) (permitting client to define the scope of representation), 1.4 (requiring communication of relevant information to client), 1.7–1.9 (prohibiting certain conflicts of interest), and 1.16 (regulating withdrawal from representation).
4. For the analysis of the relationships of (claim-) rights and duties, and privileges and "no-rights," see Hohfeld (1923). The term "entitlement," which I use throughout this book, was made prominent in legal scholarship by Calabresi and Melamed (1972).
5. *Spur Industries v. Del E. Webb Development Co.*, 494 P.2d 700 (Ariz. 1972). A similar and much-discussed example involving a cement plant and neighboring landowners is *Boomer v. Atlantic Cement Co.*, 257 N.E.2d 870 (N.Y. 1970).
6. Restatement § 16(1).
7. Model Rule 1.2(d).
8. Restatement § 23(1).
9. *Upjohn Corp. v. United States*, 449 U.S. 383 (1981).
10. Restatement § 82.
11. The law governing lawyers has specific rules governing identification of arguments as statements about what the law ought to be, as opposed to what the law is. For example, Model Rule 3.3(a)(2) requires lawyers to disclose legal authority in the controlling jurisdiction known to be directly adverse to the position taken by the lawyer. Rule 11 of the Federal Rules of Civil Procedure permits lawyers to make nonfrivolous arguments for the extension, modification, or reversal of existing law or the establishment of new law. A well-known case from the U.S. Court of Appeals for the Ninth Circuit declined to impose sanctions on a lawyer for not specifically flagging an argument as one for the modification of law, as opposed to the application of existing law, but this conclusion was based on the absence of any textual basis for the duty in Rule 11, not a conclusion about the ethical obligations of lawyers more generally. See *Golden Eagle Distrib. Corp. v. Burroughs Corp.*, 801 F.2d 1531 (9th Cir. 1986).

12. Waldron (1996), pp. 1548–50; Gray (1996), p. 43 (*"each* of these goods or values is internally complex and inherently pluralistic, containing conflicting elements, some of which are constitutive incommensurables"); Rawls (1993), p. 56.

13. Jeremy Waldron links value pluralism in this sense with the authority of law. See Waldron (1999a), p. 112 ("On any plausible account, human life engages multiple values and it is natural that people will disagree about how to balance or prioritize them.").

14. See, e.g., Isaiah Berlin, "The Pursuit of the Ideal," in Berlin (1990), pp. 10–11.

15. Hampshire (1983), p. 146.

16. See Robert Audi, "Intuitionism, Pluralism, and the Foundations of Ethics," in Audi (1997); Larmore (1987), pp. 131–34; Thomas Nagel, "The Fragmentation of Value," in Nagel (1979). David Ross famously listed categories of *prima facie* moral obligations, arising from different circumstances of human existence, including duties of loyalty, gratitude, beneficence, non-maleficence, and perfectionist duties. See Ross (1930), pp. 20–21. *Prima facie* obligations should be distinguished from what one has all-things-considered reason to do. A *prima facie* obligation is one that would be obligatory, in the absence of reasons to do otherwise. *Prima facie* obligations can be outweighed by other considerations, however, and determining an all-things-considered obligation requires some kind of weighing or balancing of *prima facie* obligations. See Brink (1994), pp. 216–17.

17. Jonsen and Toulmin (1988), pp. 250–63. The authors, who praise the method of classical casuistry as a solution to moral disagreement, note that "[i]n law and morals ... what matters most is an ability to recognize, in full subtlety and detail, the relevant features of any particular case—both 'circumstances of the action' and 'conditions of the agent'—and to present them as bearing on the present issue in terms that 'speak to the conditions' of the current audience." Ibid., p. 258. See also Rawls (1993), p. 56 ("To some extent all our concepts, and not only moral and political concepts, are vague and subject to hard cases; and this indeterminacy means that we must rely on judgment and interpretation ... within some range ... where reasonable persons may differ").

18. Rawls (1993), pp. 54–58. Waldron argues that Rawls does not carry through the implications of the burdens of judgment. In his view, they must affect judgments about public reason as well. See Waldron (1999a), p. 152.

19. Finnis (1980), p. 231.

20. Isaiah Berlin, "Two Concepts of Liberty," in Berlin (1997), pp. 218–19.

21. Ibid., p. 220.

22. Ibid., p. 225.

23. Ibid., pp. 221–22 ("The sage knows you better than you know yourself, for you are the victim of your passions, a slave living a heteronomous life, purblind, unable to understand your true goals. You wish to be a human being. It is the aim of the State to justify your wish.... [H]umanity is the raw material upon which I impose my creative will; even though men suffer and die in the process, they are lifted by it to a height to which they could never have risen without my coercive—but creative—violation of their lives. This is the argument used by every dictator, inquisitor, and bully who seeks

some moral, or even aesthetic, justification for his conduct."); see also Pogge (2007), p. 187 (explicating Rawls) ("A democratic society engenders an abundance of competing and mutually incompatible values; a society whose members would all accept the same rich array of community values cannot be realized without substantial governmental regimentation and repression.").

24. Stephen Pepper overstates the case a bit when he argues that lawyers who refuse to represent clients, or refuse to take action on behalf of existing clients, on the grounds of ordinary moral considerations tend toward "rule by an oligarchy of lawyers." Pepper (1986), p. 617. Granting Pepper a bit of hyperbole, however, his point remains sound, that a lawyer bears the burden of justifying to a client the legitimacy of actions taken in a professional role. Ordinary moral considerations, if not shared by the client, would not be a legitimate basis for limiting the client's access to legal entitlements.

25. See, e.g., *Osterlind v. Hill*, 160 N.E. 301 (Mass. 1928).

26. *Hustler Magazine v. Falwell*, 485 U.S. 46 (1988).

27. *Collin v. Smith*, 578 F.2d 1197 (7th Cir. 1978).

28. See, e.g., *West Virginia Board of Education v. Barnette*, 319 U.S. 624 (1943).

29. *Strickland v. Washington*, 466 U.S. 668 (1984).

30. Hart (1994), pp. 82–83, 88–89.

31. I owe this formulation to Yasutomo Morigiwa.

32. Thompson (1975), p. 261.

33. Among many other sources, this quotation can be found in a commencement address delivered by U.S. Supreme Court Justice Stephen Breyer at Boston College Law School. The Supreme Court decision in question was *Worcester v. Georgia*, 31 U.S. [6 Pet.] 515 (1832).

34. Quoted in Clayton (1992), p. 18.

35. See Dudziak (2000), pp. 115–18.

36. Holmes (1897), pp. 459–62. For a similar usage of the Holmesian bad man metaphor, see Gordon and Simon (1992), p. 249.

37. The use of the term "bad" here is almost unavoidable given the prominence of Holmes in these debates, but note that the bad citizen need not be morally vicious. Holmes's notion is perhaps better captured by Fred Schauer's stipulation that the bad citizen is "disinclined to obey stupid laws just because they are the law." Schauer (1994), p. 500. Sanford Levinson describes Holmes's character in a way that emphasizes the analytic distinction between law and morality when he says the bad man is someone who may yield to superior force, but won't let the law tell him right from wrong. Quoted in Luban (1997), p. 1562. David Luban equates the bad man with "the economists' rational calculator," who weighs the costs of potential sanctions and benefits of noncompliance when deciding whether to follow the law. Ibid., p. 1571. Finally, it should be noted that I use the term bad *man* to invoke Holmes's image, but I have in mind both men and women as citizens, officials, and lawyers.

38. Karl Llewellyn probably did not intend it to be taken as a definition of law when he said to a group of entering law students that "[w]hat these officials [judges, lawyers, court personnel, etc.] do about disputes is, to my mind, the law itself." Llewellyn

(1930), p. 3. Nevertheless, Llewellyn is often associated with this cartoon version of legal realism.

39. See Hart (1994), pp. 136–47.

40. Luban (1986), p. 647.

41. These arguments are developed in greater detail in Wendel (2006).

42. Hart uses the term "puzzled man" to describe what I would call the good citizen. In his critique of Holmes, Hart asks "Why should not law be equally if not more concerned with the 'puzzled man' or 'ignorant man' who is willing to do what is required, if only he can be told what it is?" Hart (1994), p. 40.

43. Ibid., p. 116.

44. Ibid., p. 117.

45. Ibid., pp. 137–38 ("it cannot be doubted that ... in relation to some spheres of conduct in a modern state individuals do exhibit the whole range of conduct and attitudes which we have called the internal point of view.... They ... look upon [the law] as a legal standard of conduct, refer to it in criticizing others, or in justifying demands, and in admitting criticism and demands made by others.").

46. See Luban (2007), ch. 4, particular pp. 138–39, for an argument along these lines. Luban notes that a legal system in which only officials adopt the internal point of view would simply reproduce the situation of the gunman writ large, which Hart was so keen to reject. In Luban's view, a necessary condition for there to be a functioning legal system, as opposed to an ersatz legal system like a mafia, is that most citizens, most of the time, adopt the internal point of view toward most of the laws.

47. Hart (1994), p. 195.

48. In this regard, the normativity of law is not distinctive, but is similar to the normativity of any other social practice that is constituted and regulated by rules or other standards internal to the practice. Lon Fuller makes a similar point in defending his conception of the "inner morality of law," where he notes that the natural law regulating "the enterprise of subjecting human conduct to the governance of rules" is really no different from the natural law of carpentry, as perceived by a carpenter who is interested in a building not falling down. See Fuller (1969), p. 96.

49. Finnis (1980), p. 14 ("Hart's man who is moved by ... self-interest ... waters down any concern he may have for the function of law as an answer to real social problems.... [H]e dilutes his allegiance to law and his pursuit of legal methods of thought with doses of that very self-interest which it is an elementary function of law (on everybody's view) to subordinate to social need").

50. I owe this useful phraseology to Daniel Markovits. See Markovits (2006), p. 1385. Raz makes a similar point with a hypothetical dystopian society:

[T]ry to imagine a situation in which the political authorities of a country do not claim that the inhabitants are bound to obey them, but in which the population does acquiesce to their rule. We are to imagine courts imprisoning people without finding them guilty of any offense. Damages are ordered, but no one has a duty to pay them. The legislature never claims to impose duties of care or of contribution to common services. It merely pronounces that people who behave in certain ways will be made to suffer.

Raz (1985), p. 6. Being made to suffer for doing something is not the same thing as having a duty to do it. Conceptually, it is impossible to talk about rights, duties, and obligations without having in mind the *legitimacy* of political authorities. And, as we will see in chapter 3, legitimate authorities are those who issue directives on the basis of reasons, not merely those who exercise power or whose commands are habitually obeyed by their subjects.

51. I use the term "practice" here in the sense (developed by Alasdair MacIntyre) of "any coherent and complex form of socially established cooperative human activity through which goods internal to that form of activity are realized in the course of trying to achieve those standards of excellence which are appropriate to, and partially definitive of, that form of activity." MacIntyre (1984), p. 176.

52. MacIntyre (1984), at p. 190.

53. Rawls argues that it does not make sense to regard oneself as acting within a practice while at the same time refusing to accept the regulative standards of the practice. Rawls (1955), pp. 25–26.

54. Tyler (2006).

55. Edelman and Suchman (1997), p. 488.

56. Ibid., pp. 493, 495–98.

57. Suchman (1998), p. 852.

58. See, e.g., United States Senate, Permanent Subcommittee on Investigations, Committee on Governmental Affairs, "U.S. Tax Shelter Industry: The Role of Accountants, Lawyers, and Financial Professionals" (2003), pp. 14, 102 (describing the netting of gains and artificially generated tax losses in grantor trusts, in order to obfuscate massive losses created by tax shelters). Striking anecdotes abound about the opacity of disclosures made by Enron, including the remark of a prominent Houston financial advisor who did not recommend Enron stock because he couldn't make sense of its financial statements, and Warren Buffet's statement that he never understood how Enron made money. See Swartz and Watkins (2003), pp. xi–xiii, 331. James Chanos, a sophisticated Wall Street hedge fund manager, stated in his congressional testimony that he and colleagues at his fund "read the footnotes in Enron's financial statements about these transactions over and over again, and ... we could not decipher what impact they had on Enron's overall financial condition." James Chanos, Testimony, in "Lessons Learned from Enron's Collapse: Auditing the Accounting Industry—Report of the House Committee on Energy and Commerce," H.R. Doc. No. 107-83, at 73 (Feb. 6, 2002). The complexity of some of the SPE transactions, such as the "Raptor" hedges, made it difficult even for internal Enron managers to know how a given business unit was performing. Baird and Rasmussen (2002), pp. 1802–4. For a discussion of the problem of drafting standard-form contracts with onerous provisions, see Hazard and Dondi (2004), pp. 70–71.

59. Moss (2000), p. 1322.

60. This problem is based on a case handled by students and faculty at the Washington and Lee Law School Legal Practice Clinic. The inspiration for Cole Minor is pictured in an article on the black lung clinic in the W&L law alumni magazine. See Wendy Lovell, "David v. Goliath," *Washington and Lee School of Law Magazine* (Fall 2005), p. 23. I have taken some liberties with the facts to make the problem more interesting, but the overall narrative of the actual case is essentially as described.

61. 30 U.S.C. § 901(a).

62. Quoted in Galanter (2005), p. 44.

63. See Simon (1988), p. 1103. Although Simon doesn't use the term "loophole," his reference to cases in which "lawyers have an opportunity to shape an activity or a transaction in a way that seems consistent with a plausible surface interpretation of a rule but that appears to undermine its purpose," is a pretty good working definition of a loophole. He goes on to refer to the notorious case of *Walkovszky v. Carlton*, 223 N.E.2d 6 (1966), in which the owner of a fleet of taxicabs was permitted to create dozens of separate corporations, each owning one cab, and severely undercapitalize the corporations, thus shielding what would otherwise be corporate assets of the fleet owner from liability for personal injuries. This is a case that many readers intuitively feel involves loophole lawyering.

64. Timothy Endicott argues that no one, not even deconstructionists and critical legal studies scholars, really makes radical indeterminacy claims. Endicott (2000), pp. 16–17.

65. Stone (1995), pp. 53–55.

66. See Lawrence B. Solum, "Indeterminacy," in Patterson (1996), p. 490, for this helpful distinction. I am using the term "legal sources" here for reasons that should be clearer in chapter 6. Briefly, identifying "the law" with legal texts, such as statutes and judicial decisions, downplays the significance of tacit interpretive principles that are an essential aspect of legal reasoning. Judgments of relevant similarity, for example, are absolutely essential to common-law reasoning, but extremely difficult to formalize, and in any event non-textual.

67. Hart (1994), pp. 126–29. It is not really central to the arguments in the text at this point, but readers who are familiar with Anglo-American jurisprudence will associate the claim that there is a right answer to every question of law with Dworkin. See, e.g., Ronald Dworkin, "Is There Really No Right Answer in Hard Cases?", in Dworkin (1985).

68. The discussion in this paragraph is indebted to many conversations with Alice Woolley about legal interpretation.

69. The case is *MacPherson v. Buick Motor Co.*, 111 N.E. 1050 (N.Y. 1916). Arguably, the result in *MacPherson* was foreshadowed by English cases such as *Heaven v. Pender*, 11 Q.B.D. 503 (1883), and American cases like *Thomas v. Winchester*, 6 N.Y. 397 (1852) and its progeny, including cases that applied the principle of *Thomas* to products like coffee urns and scaffolding. (See *Statler v. Ray Manufacturing* and *Devlin v. Smith*, cited in the *MacPherson* opinion.) On the other hand, some scholars

have argued that Cardozo was such a brilliant rhetorician that the result in his opinion seems foreordained, even though it was a fairly tendentious reading of the existing law. For a thorough analysis of the law prior to *MacPherson* and Cardozo's opinion, see Levi (1949), pp. 8–27.

70. 116 N.W.2d 704 (Minn. 1962). For further historical research on the case, see Floyd and Gallagher (2008); Cramton and Knowles (1998).

71. Cramton and Knowles (1998), p. 74. Cramton and Knowles argue that many lawyers in Minnesota were unfamiliar with the then relatively new discovery rules. Ibid., p. 81. Although Spaulding's lawyer was inexperienced, even lawyers who had been in practice for many years might not have known to request a copy of the medical examination report, or might not have realized that making the request would not have the effect of waiving the physician–patient privilege covering the plaintiff's treating physician's records.

72. To make the problem difficult, when I teach this case I ask students to assume that Zimmerman is a mean-spirited person who is completely indifferent to Spaulding's welfare and refuses to consent to the lawyer disclosing the information. In reality, however, Zimmerman was 19 years old at the time of the accident; Spaulding was 20, and riding in Zimmerman's car, so it is fair to infer that they were friends. Cramton and Knowles (1998), p. 88. I also hypothesize that Zimmerman could be financially ruined if he is hit for a judgment for the full amount of Spaulding's damages, taking the aneurysm into account. In fact, the parties never contemplated damages in excess of the limits of the various insurance policies, for reasons relating to substantive tort law then in effect. Ibid., pp. 69–70.

73. See, e.g., Simon (1988), pp. 1098–99 (discussing a case arising out of the negotiation of a personal-injury settlement, in which the lawyer for the insurance company realizes that the plaintiff's lawyer is unaware of a recent statute abolishing contributory negligence as a defense, and is therefore substantially under-valuing the plaintiff's claim). Thanks to Greg Cooper for pressing me to clarify my response to these cases.

74. Simon (1998), pp. 58–59.

75. Model Rules, Rule 1.6(b)(2), (b)(3); Restatement § 67.

76. The Supreme Court has cautioned that courts considering claims by criminal defendants of ineffective assistance of counsel should be fairly deferential to the decisions made by trial counsel. "Representation is an art, and an act or omission that is unprofessional in one case may be sound or even brilliant in another." *Strickland v. Washington*, 466 U.S. 668 (1984). While this dictum has been taken too far by lower federal courts, particularly by the Fifth Circuit in a case involving a defense lawyer who slept through substantial portions of a capital murder trial, *Burdine v. Johnson*, 262 F.3d 336 (5th Cir. 2001) (en banc), it is nevertheless true in some cases that it is difficult to judge the wisdom of a lawyer's decision without being subject to the distorting effects of hindsight.

77. This is not an unrealistic estimate of the potential downside risk to Zimmerman's lawyer. A lawyer in Washington State who disclosed client confidences, leading

to the successful prosecution of a corrupt judge, was suspended for six months. See the description of the Doug Schafer case in Hazard (2005), pp. 385–88. On the other hand, in the absence of aggravating factors (present in the Schafer case) and with the presence of the mitigating factor of saving Spaulding's life, it is likely that the actual discipline meted out to Zimmerman's lawyer would be less severe.

78. Fed. R. Civ. P. 26(b)(1).

79. Fed. R. Civ. P. 26(c).

80. I am grateful to Arthur Applbaum for pressing me on this point.

81. This brilliant variation on the Dalkon Shield case was invented by Shawn Copeland, a North Carolina lawyer and a regular participant in the Washington and Lee Legal Ethics Institute.

82. Model Code, Canon 7 ("a lawyer should represent a client zealously within the bounds of the law").

83. Model Rules, Preamble ¶ [2].

84. See Gordon (1998a), pp. 727–28, 733 (identifying "zealous" advocacy as the "master norm" of practicing lawyers). See also Smith (2000), for a vigorous defense of the ideal of zealous advocacy, although here in the core context of criminal defense representation. Canadian lawyers tend to use the term "zealous" as well, to describe the basic obligation of lawyers. See, e.g., Hutchinson (1999), pp. 89–91; Woolley (1996).

85. Charles Wolfram argues that it is an idiosyncrasy of the American legal profession that lawyers believe themselves to need some kind of strong emotional identification with the client in order to be effective representatives. See Charles W. Wolfram, "A Lawyer's Duty to Represent Clients, Repugnant and Otherwise," in Luban (1983), p. 224. Many other legal professional traditions appear not to value psychological virtues like "zeal" on behalf of clients; indeed, the traditions of the French profession demand that *avocats* exercise independence from their clients, which demands a psychological state of detachment and disinterestedness, the diametric opposite of zeal. Leubsdorf (2001), p. 19.

86. Restatement § 16(1).

87. See, e.g., Fed. R. Civ. P. 11.

88. Model Rule 3.3.

89. See, e.g., Blumberg (1967). Kenneth Mann summarizes the sociological research on defense lawyers who represent street criminals:

[T]he criminal defense attorney ... substantially compromises zealous advocacy of his client's interest to attend to other independent or conflicting interests. The defense attorney in the plea bargain model is not a Perry Mason craftily guiding a case through a dramatic criminal trial. Rather, he is an "operator" concerned with currying the favor of the prosecutor or judge, restraining adversariness in order to finish cases efficiently. The defense attorney puts a high premium on helping the court organization run smoothly because it helps him maintain an economically viable practice in which a sufficient number of cases are handled at a low enough cost.

Mann (1985), p. 230. The story is very different with respect to a lawyer representing white collar criminal defendants. In that case, it is much closer to the paradigm of representing large corporate clients in civil litigation.

90. Dare (2004).

91. Ibid., p. 27.

92. Ibid., p. 30.

93. See, e.g., *In re Zawada*, 92 P.3d 862 (Ariz. 2004) (suspending prosecutor for trying to discredit opinion of psychological experts at trial by accusing them of fabricating their testimony and arguing that the mental health professions "create excuses for criminals").

94. Dare (2004), p. 34.

95. I owe this example to Arthur Applbaum.

96. Koniak (1992).

97. See the narrative of the facts of the Kaye Scholer matter in the introduction to Symposium, "In the Matter of Kaye, Scholer, Fierman, Hayes, and Handler: A Symposium on Government Regulation, Lawyers' Ethics, and the Rule of Law," *Southern California Law Review* 66: 977–84. See also Hazard (2005), pp. 161–63 (citing scholarly commentary on the case).

98. Gordon (1998b), p. 318.

99. Model Code, EC 7-3.

100. Ibid., EC 7-4.

101. Ibid., EC 7-19.

102. Ibid., EC 7-5.

103. See Model Rules, Rule 3.8, cmt. [1] ("A prosecutor has the responsibility of a minister of justice and not simply that of an advocate."); ABA Standards Relating to the Administration of Criminal Justice, Prosecution Function, Standard 3-1.2(c) ("The duty of the prosecutor is to seek justice, not merely to convict."); *Brady v. Maryland*, 373 U.S. 83 (1963) (requiring prosecutors, as a matter of constitutional due process, to turn over potentially exculpatory evidence to the defendant). For a thorough discussion of these principles in the context of a high-profile instance of prosecutorial misconduct, see Mosteller (2007).

104. A leading law school casebook on professional responsibility makes this point in the context of transactional counseling and providing legal opinion letters: "[T]he range of legal interpretation that is considered legitimate when a lawyer is providing a client with a legal justification for action before the action has occurred is much narrower than the range of legal argument that would be considered legitimate in defending a client in an adversary proceeding alleging the client's past actions constituted a violation of law." Hazard (2005), p. 105. See also Hazard and Dondi (2004), pp. 164–65; Gordon and Simon (1992), p. 248 (reporting the "respectable view" of

corporate lawyers that the lawyer's role in counseling clients is the "affirmative one of promoting compliance with the regulation's purposes").

105. Hodes (1999), p. 1366. I am grateful to John Gaal, with whom I taught a lively continuing legal education session on witness coaching, for reminding me of this passage from Hodes's article.

106. Waldron (1994), pp. 535–36 n.66.

107. See Moon (1994), p. 100 (arguing that a legitimate political order "must be open to consider[ing] the values and aspirations, the needs and attachments, that any particular formulation of a framework of justice appears to suppress").

108. Fed. R. Civ. P. 11.

NOTES TO CHAPTER THREE

From Neutrality to Public Reason: Moral Conflict and the Law

1. David Luban makes this point using a quotation from William Whewell, the author of a widely used nineteenth century treatise on ethics:

> "[e]very man is ... by being a moral agent, a Judge of right and wrong .... This general character of a moral agent, he cannot put off, by putting on any professional character"

Quoted in Luban (2007), p. 19.

2. Burton Dreben, "On Rawls and Political Liberalism," in Freeman (2003); John Rawls, "Reply to Habermas," in Rawls (1993).

3. Christiano (2004); Waldron (1999a).

4. Rawls (1993), pp. 53–54, 60–61, 94, 133–37, 168–69.

5. For this way of drawing the distinction, see John Rawls, "Reply to Habermas," in Rawls (1993), p. 421, taken in turn from Stuart Hampshire's review of *Political Liberalism*. See Stuart Hampshire, "Liberalism: The New Twist," *New York Review of Books* 40:14 (Aug. 12, 1993).

6. The argument throughout is influenced by Hampshire (1989). The image of reasonable pluralism driving a wedge between substantive and procedural conceptions of justice is from Cohen (1994), which is critical of Hampshire's position.

7. Markovits (2006), p. 1385. Compare Thomas Nagel, "Ruthlessness in Public Life," in Nagel (1979), pp. 87–88 (arguing that state coercion can be legitimate if it is "impersonally imposed by an institution designed to promote certain results").

8. I have borrowed J. B. Schneewind's useful term, the "Grotian problematic," to describe this fundamental presupposition of politics, as seen by Hugo Grotius. See Schneewind (1998), pp. 70–72, and *passim*. In particular, Grotius was concerned to find a standpoint independent of contested religious points of view, from which to justify legal principles. He thus stands in the tradition of Hobbes and Locke, as thinkers who see liberal political institutions as a way of moving beyond intractable (and often violent) conflict over ultimate principles of value.

9. Rawls (1993), pp. 3–4.

10. Finnis (1980), pp. 86–90.

11. Gray (1996), p. 43 ("*each* of these goods or values is internally complex and inherently pluralistic, containing conflicting elements, some of which are constitutive incommensurables").

12. Waldron (1996), pp. 1548–50.

13. Waldron (1999a), pp. 86, 101–2, 160, and *passim*.

14. See, e.g., Gutmann and Thompson (1996).

15. See Rawls (1993), Lecture IV ("The Idea of an Overlapping Consensus"), especially pp. 147–50, for the argument that citizens can endorse the political conception of legitimacy as true or reasonable from within their own comprehensive doctrines, whatever they may be. The ideal of public reason is explained in Rawls (1993), Lecture VI. The liberal principle of legitimacy, for Rawls, is connected with the ideal of public reason in the following way: "[O]ur exercise of political power is fully proper only when it is exercised in accordance with a constitution the essentials of which all citizens as free and equal may reasonably be expected to endorse in the light of principles and ideals acceptable to their common human reason." Ibid., p. 137.

16. See Cohen (2003); Joshua Cohen, "For a Democratic Society," in Freeman (2003).

17. Many readers have pressed me to explain how a theory of legal ethics founded on procedural justice can withstand the actual injustice that pervades real legal systems. I am particularly grateful to Kate Kruse, Steve Shiffrin, and Christian Williams for their persistent and vigorous criticism on this point.

18. As one progressive critic of the legal system observed, "case-by-case injustice is not what poor people face; they confront a host of unjust institutions, acting for and within an unjust society." Wexler (1970), p. 1050. A modest version of the "pervasive injustice" claim is that the law is not a tool used by the powerful to entrench their dominance and resist social change, but a dumb, intentionless, utterly amoral agglomeration of special-interest legislation with no rationality (let alone nefarious rationality) beyond the desire of some organized lobby to capture economic rents.

19. See, e.g., Bingham (2007); Joseph Raz, "The Rule of Law and Its Virtue," in Raz (1979); Fuller (1969).

20. The fact of reasonable pluralism is a significant theme of Rawls's *Political Liberalism*. See Rawls (1993), pp. 36–37, 136–38, 153.

21. See the line of cases beginning with *Buckley v. Valeo*, 424 U.S. 1 (1976), including *Nixon v. Shrink Missouri Government PAC*, 528 U.S. 377 (2000); *Colorado Republican Federal Campaign Committee v. FEC*, 518 U.S. 604 (1996).

22. See generally Murphy (2000); Phillips (1985).

23. Rawls (1993), pp. 55–58.

24. Ibid., p. 36 and n.37.

25. Hampshire (1989), p. 90.

26. Finnis (1980), pp. 86–90. Assertions about self-evident values are likely to strike some readers as the worst kind of armchair empiricism. It may strike others as ob-

jectionably essentialist, neglecting historical and cultural differences. Finnis provides only a few supporting citations to the work of anthropologists, but he relies primarily upon the lists assembled by other philosophers of the "sorts of things it is rational to desire for their own sakes." Ibid., p. 98n. Martha Nussbaum defends a similar list—although she calls it a list of capabilities, not basic values—grounded in summaries of "empirical findings of a broad and ongoing cross-cultural inquiry." Nussbaum (1999), p. 40. Nussbaum's list is aimed at finding "activities characteristically performed by human beings [that] are so central that they seem definitive of a life that is truly human." Ibid., p. 39. (Interestingly, there is a substantial overlap between Finnis's list and Nussbaum's.) All of these capacities can be understood to entail rival conceptions of ethical value; thus, no one should assume that these sorts of lists of capacities are intended as a framework for settling moral conflict. See Moon (1994), pp. 27–28. They do, however, set boundaries on what constitutes an acceptable reason in the domain of private and public ethics.

Nussbaum elsewhere defends this method as the only way to prevent a slide into vacuous subjectivism, where the notion of value collapses into a mere preference, and there is nothing that can be said of any ethical position beyond "that's just your opinion." See Nussbaum (1992). Her method is unabashedly normative—there is no claim that this is some sort of value-neutral set of data "read off" the world by anthropologists. Ibid., pp. 214–15. As a result, any objection to her list would have to be similarly descriptive and normative (i.e., it would claim that such-and-such is not actually a distinctive human capability). For the purposes of my argument (and Finnis's, for that matter), it is necessary only to establish that some list of basic values can be arrived at by some procedure of reasoning (both empirical and a priori), and that this list cannot be objectively prioritized.

27. Wong (2006), pp. 37, 39, 47, and ch. 4. For a functional approach to basic moral constraints, which is indebted to Hume, see Blackburn (1998), p. 308 ("We are social animals, with certain biological needs. We have to coordinate our efforts; we have to establish systems of property and promise-keeping and sometimes even government. We can then comfort in reflecting that there are not so many admirable, coherent, mature, livable ethical systems on offer...").

28. Waldron (1999a), p. 102. Elsewhere Waldron is clear that the need for law to settle disagreement is not a matter of the sentiments or motivations of citizens, but is an a priori truth about ethical reasoning. See Waldron (1996), pp. 1546–47.

29. Hobbes (1994), xiii, 13; p. 78.

30. Finnis (1980), p. 139.

31. Baird, Gertner, and Picker (1994), pp. 191–92.

32. This example is intended to illustrate *moral* disagreement, not the application of equal protection principles from American constitutional law, such as the "strict scrutiny" applied to government actions that base decisions on "suspect classifications." For the most recent cases from the U.S. Supreme Court applying the Equal Protection Clause to university admissions programs, see *Grutter v. Bollinger*, 539 U.S.

306 (2003); *Gratz v. Bollinger*, 539 U.S. 244 (2003). In other contexts, the Court has sided with the citizens who argue that all racial classifications are suspect, regardless of whether they are employed with a benign motive. See *Shaw v. Reno*, 509 U.S. 630 (1993) (redistricting on the basis of race for the purpose of increasing minority representation); *City of Richmond v. J. A. Croson Co.*, 488 U.S. 469 (1989) (affirmative action plans in government contracting).

33. See, e.g., Ronald Dworkin, "Bakke's Case: Are Quotas Unfair," in Dworkin (1985).

34. Again, this example should be taken at face value, without trying to work through the law respecting end-of-life medical care, advance directives, family decision-making authority, and the like. Most of the governing law here is at the state level, and the U.S. Supreme Court has held that there is no constitutional prohibition on a state enacting a ban on physicians assisting patients in committing suicide. See *Washington v. Glucksberg*, 521 U.S. 702 (1997). The Court has held, however, that competent individuals have a constitutional right to refuse life-prolonging treatment. See *Cruzan v. Director, Missouri Department of Health*, 497 U.S. 261 (1990).

35. For an excellent overview of these arguments, see Beauchamp and Childress (1994), pp. 215–49. Another helpful article, although it is difficult to disentangle the moral arguments from the analysis of constitutional law, is Ronald Dworkin, "Do We Have a Right to Die?," in Dworkin (1996).

36. John Rawls, "Reply to Habermas," in Rawls (1993), pp. 421–22.

37. Ibid., pp. 428–29 ("A legitimate procedure is one that all may reasonably accept as free and equal when collective decisions must be made and agreement is normally lacking. The burdens of judgment lead to that even with reasons and good will on all sides."). Note that this is not Rawls's own view—he goes on to express serious doubts about this idea of procedural legitimacy.

38. Fuller (1958). One of the distinctive features of Fuller's jurisprudence is the so-called "internal morality of law," which asserts that law does not possess legitimate authority over the practical reasoning of citizens if its adoption and application is flawed in certain formal ways. See Fuller (1969), pp. 33–41.

39. See Gutmann and Thompson (1996), pp. 52–63 (arguing that politics should aim at deliberative agreement, in which people are able to justify their claims to others in terms they can accept); cf. Luban (1988), p. 35 (considering the idea that "disobedience to the law is morally disrespectful of other people").

40. See Amy Gutmann, "Rawls on the Relationship Between Liberalism and Democracy," in Freeman (2003), p. 169 (defining the fundamental ideal of democracy as ensuring the equal political liberty of citizens); Raz (1979), p. 280 (arguing that valuing pluralism leads to the recognition that people ought to have avenues for developing their talents and projects, "subject to the constraints imposed by the necessities of social co-operation and of securing similar opportunities to all").

41. See Walzer (1981), p. 262.

42. Barry (1995), p. 7.

43. See Waldron (1996), pp. 1546–47 (reading Kant as explaining normative conflict on the basis of something other than contingent motivations). Compare Scanlon's discussion of Mill, who appeals to "the social *feelings* of mankind; the *desire* to be in unity with our fellow creatures." Scanlon (1998), p. 154 (citing J. S. Mill, *Utilitarianism*, ch. 3) (emphasis added). I think Waldron and Scanlon are right that a moral theory should not appeal to a psychological or motivational element. The foundation of a moral theory is what people have a *reason* to do, not a desire to do. Reason, in turn, is a matter of what can be justified to others.

44. Larmore (1987), p. 62.

45. Ibid., pp. 63–64; see also Korsgaard (1996b), pp. 121–23.

46. Byron (1998); Schmidtz (1992).

47. Rawls (1971), p. 358.

48. Phillips (1985), p. 554.

49. Waldron (1999a), p. 30; see also Greenawalt (1987), p. 166.

50. Michael Crowley, "Oppressed Minority: The Misery of Being a House Democrat," *The New Republic* (June 23, 2003), at 18. The amendment to an appropriations bill would have removed a provision stripping civil-service protection from 700,000 Defense Department employees.

51. Ibid. at 20 (quoting Rep. Barney Frank).

52. David S. Broder, "Time Was GOP's Ally on the Vote," *The Washington Post* (Nov. 23, 2003), p. A1.

53. Charles Babington, "Ethics Panel Rebukes DeLay," *Washington Post* (Oct. 1, 2004), p. A1.

54. Waldron (1999a), p. 236.

55. Steve Shiffrin has raised this objection with me on many occasions, and nothing I say about the process doing "well enough" will convince him that the legal system is, by and large, legitimate.

56. Cohen (2003), p. 23. Cohen sensibly understands the ideal of respect for competing viewpoints as entailing a requirement that political majorities offer reasons the minority can accept.

57. Taking an example almost at random from the Citizens Against Government Waste 2009 "Pig Book" of earmark spending, three members of the Michigan congressional delegation secured $951,000 in funding for energy-efficient street lamps for downtown Detroit. See www.cagw.org/site/PageServer?pagename=reports_pigbook2009. If the federal government makes funding available for state and local governments to adopt energy-efficient technologies, however, it is easy to see how any given municipality's interests would be matter of indifference to other senators and representatives, but of great interest to the local congressional delegation. Maybe it is wasteful in general for the federal government to subsidize the transition by state and local governments to energy-efficient lighting, but it also may be a very good thing for the federal government to do in view of the long-term economic and environmental benefits and the inability of some poorer states and local governments (like Detroit) to

fund the transition on their own. All this to say, the ascription "pork-barrel spending" is a contestable one.

58. My former colleague Trevor Morrison would call this a "turtles all the way down" problem.

59. Alexander and Schauer (1997), p. 1383. The "famous violinist" allusion in the text is to Judith Jarvis Thomson's famous thought experiment meant to illustrate the rights at stake when forcing a woman to carry a pregnancy through to term.

60. John Rawls, "Reply to Habermas," in Rawls (1993), p. 431.

61. As the Supreme Court has said: "If there is any fixed star in our constitutional constellation, it is that no official, high or petty, can prescribe what shall be orthodox in politics, nationalism, religion, or other matters of opinion or force citizens to confess by word or act their faith therein." *West Virginia Board of Education v. Barnette*, 319 U.S. 624, 642 (1943). For cases protecting insulting or offensive speech, see, e.g., *R.A.V. v. City of St. Paul*, 505 U.S. 377 (1992) (cross burning); *Texas v. Johnson*, 491 U.S. 397 (1989) (flag burning); *Hustler Magazine v. Falwell*, 485 U.S. 46 (1988) (offensive parody ad); *Cohen v. California*, 403 U.S. 15 (1971) (jacket bearing the words "fuck the draft"). Cases distinguishing obscenity from protected sexually explicit expression include *Renton v. Playtime Theatres*, 475 U.S. 41 (1986); *Young v. American Mini Theatres*, 427 U.S. 50 (1976). There are of course myriad exceptions for things like "fighting words," *Chaplinsky v. New Hampshire*, 315 U.S. 568 (1942); speech that is likely to be overheard by children, *FCC v. Pacifica Foundation*, 438 U.S. 726 (1978) (George Carlin's "seven dirty words" routine); and some expressive conduct, e.g., *Barnes v. Glen Theatre, Inc.*, 501 U.S. 560 (1991) (nude dancing); *United States v. O'Brien*, 391 U.S. 367 (1968) (burning draft card). The analysis of these cases under constitutional law protecting freedom of expression is therefore a matter of determining which underlying values are served by a law and which cut against the enforceability of the law. It is a richly normative analysis, and it is rare to encounter a law that has no plausible normative case that can be made for it. The point of this little digression is that one should be hesitant to conclude that disagreement over the justice of a law is not in good faith.

62. Waldron (1999a), p. 160.

63. Rawls (1993), pp. 36–38, 63–64 (distinguishing reasonable pluralism and pluralism as such).

64. Ibid., p. 37.

65. Forst (2002), pp. 38–42, 184–85, is extremely helpful on this aspect of Rawls's theory.

66. Ibid., p. 38 (emphasis in original).

67. David Luban's position is representative of the attitude of many critics of the Standard Conception:

Lawyers do not lie under an obligation to obey the law simply because it is the law. In my view, we have an obligation to obey the law only when (1) the legal requirement corresponds with a moral requirement, in other words, when violating the legal requirement would be *malum in se*, or else (2) when the law establishes a fair and reasonable scheme of social cooperation

Luban (1996), p. 258. Luban is not a philosophical anarchist. Rather, he is skeptical of claims that the law generally establishes a fair and reasonable scheme of social cooperation. To the extent he believes that a legally established framework is fair and reasonable, our positions may not diverge substantially. See, e.g., Luban (2007), ch. 5, on "the torture lawyers of Washington," which presupposes that "rule-of-law societies generally prohibit torture." Ibid., p. 205.

68. Wolff (1990), p. 28 (emphasis in original).

69. See Korsgaard (1996b), especially Lecture 3, "The Authority of Reflection."

70. See Scanlon (1998).

71. Wolff (1990), p. 28 (emphasis in original).

72. Applbaum (1999), ch. 6; Greenawalt (1987); Simmons (1979); Raz (1979), pp. 233–49; Nozick (1974), pp. 90–95; Smith (1973); Wasserstrom (1973). Larry Alexander and Emily Sherwin argue the law has authority only insofar as it makes it more likely that citizens will comply with the requirements of morality:

> [W]e are interested in more than coordination. The controversies Lex [their personified lawgiver] addresses can be settled in better or worse ways, and one of the benefits the community seeks from his rules is avoidance of moral error through the application of Lex's superior expertise. Members of the community presumably have selected Lex because they have confidence in his moral expertise.

Alexander and Sherwin (2001), pp. 98–99. See also Hurd (1995), p. 425 ("[T]he intentions of lawmakers are, on this view, a heuristic guide to determining the content of the law, which is itself a heuristic guide to determining the content of morality"); Moore (1985), p. 286 ("the interpretive premises necessary to decide any case can and should be derived in part by recourse to the dictates of ... moral reality").

The Hurd–Alexander–Sherwin position, that the law serves as a heuristic or a proxy for determining the content of morality, would underwrite only a weak defeasible claim of legitimacy, and invite citizens to re-balance the underlying reasons to see whether the directives of law did, in fact, track the requirements of morality. Hurd (1995), p. 418. Once this is applied to actual legislatures, instead of an idealized Lex-the-lawgiver, the case for the legitimacy of law does not look very good. Most actual legislatures would have a hard time successfully guiding anyone a block down the street, let alone in the direction of morality. As discussed at length in the text, however, the Hurd–Alexander–Sherwin objection relies on a tacit assumption that the nature of compliance with the demands of morality is the same in communities as it is for individuals acting in relative isolation.

73. The term is Finnis's. See Finnis (1980), p. 318.

74. For a good summary of these arguments against a general obligation to obey the law, see Simmons (2008), ch. 3.

75. See Joseph Raz, "The Problem of Authority: Revisiting the Service Conception," in Raz (2009).

76. Joseph Raz, "Authority, Law and Morality," in Raz (1994); Raz (1979), pp. 22–27.

77. Raz (1986), p. 23.

78. Raz defines authority this way: "A man, or body of men, has authority if it follows from his saying 'Let X happen' that X ought to happen." See Raz (1979), p. 11. See also Smith (1990), p. 89 ("basic to most persons' attitude towards the law is a conviction that, in a reasonably just society, government enjoys not only the power to rule, but the right").

79. Sartre (1956), pp. 86–112.

80. Raz sees his conception of authority as a response to Wolff's argument that following the directives of authority entails giving up the right (and the responsibility) to act on one's own best understanding of what reason requires. See Raz (1979), pp. 26–27; Joseph Raz, "Authority, Law, and Morality," in Raz (1994), p. 212.

81. See Raz (1986), p. 53; Joseph Raz, "Introduction," in Raz (1990), p. 13; Joseph Raz, "Authority, Law, and Morality," in Raz (1994), p. 214.

82. See Raz (1979), pp. 21–22, for the analogy with the authority of experts.

83. Cf. Isaiah Berlin, "Two Concepts of Liberty," in Berlin (1997), p. 213 ("For the musician, after he has assimilated the pattern of the composer's score, and has made the composer's ends his own, the playing of the music is not obedience to external laws, a compulsion and a barrier to liberty, but a free, unimpeded exercise. The player is not bound to the score as an ox to the plough, or a factory worker to the machine. He has absorbed the score into his own system, has, by understanding it, identified it with himself, has changed it from an impediment to free activity into an element in that activity itself.").

84. Raz (1986), p. 29. I am indebted to a questioner (whose name I unfortunately did not learn) at the Society of Legal Scholars conference in 2003, at St. Catherine's College, Oxford, for pressing me with what I have come to think of as the Problem of the Annotated Cookbook. After I had used the Jacques Pépin analogy to explain the authority of law, the questioner pointed out that most cooks gain experience with a recipe and end up altering it to improve it, or at least to suit their own preferences. My response was that the authority of cookbooks was different from the authority of law, in that one can annotate one's cookbook without losing the benefit of the authority. Upon re-reading Raz it became clear that he would make that distinction in terms of theoretical authorities and practical authorities, as discussed here.

85. Hurd (1991), p. 1615.

86. The "no difference thesis" holds that "the exercise of authority makes no difference to what its subjects ought to do, for it ought to direct them to do what they ought to do in any event." Raz (1986), p. 48. The no difference thesis holds for theoretical, or recognitional, authorities like Jacques Pépin, but not for practical authorities such as the legal system.

87. For the distinction between theoretical and practical authorities, see Joseph Raz, "Authority, Law, and Morality," in Raz (1994), p. 211: "The directives of a person or

institution with practical authority are reasons for action for their subjects, whereas the advice of a theoretical authority is a reason for belief for those regarding whom that person or institution has authority." For a discussion of the distinction between practical and theoretical reasoning in ethics, see Darwall, et al. (1992), pp. 131–37; Korsgaard (1996b), pp. 45–47; cf. Rawls (1993), p. 93 (distinguishing moral realism and constructivism, in part, on being rooted in theoretical and practical reasoning, respectively).

88. Raz (1986), pp. 29–30, 42, 47.

89. Joseph Raz, "Authority, Law, and Morality," in Raz (1994), p. 214.

90. These examples are from Raz (1986), p. 75.

91. Raz (1986), pp. 41–42.

92. Ibid., pp. 47–48.

93. Ibid., p. 35.

94. Ibid., p. 61 ("If every time a directive is mistaken ... it were open to challenge as mistaken, the advantage gained by accepting the authority as a more reliable and successful guide to right reason would disappear."); Joseph Raz, "Authority, Law, and Morality," in Raz (1994), p. 218 ("[T]he subjects of any authority ... can benefit by its decisions only if they can establish their existence and content in ways which do not depend on raising the very same issues which the authority is there to settle."). There is an intriguing parallel here with Hobbes's argument that the judgments of the sovereign are to be taken by citizens as their own judgments—that is, to create exclusionary reasons for action. In the institution of the commonwealth, citizens effectively will themselves adopt the will of another in their practical reasoning:

> The only way to erect such a common power ... is [for citizens] to confer all their power and strength upon one man, or upon one assembly of men, that may reduce all their wills, by plurality of voices, unto one will ... and every one to own and acknowledge himself to be author of whatsoever he that so beareth their person shall act, or cause to be acted, in those things which concern the common peace and safety, and therein to submit their wills, every one to his will, and their judgments, to his judgment.

Hobbes (1994), xvii, 13; p. 109. In comparison with the alternative of the state of nature, it is rational for individuals to act *as if* the common basis of action settled upon by the sovereign (which can be an assembly) is the result of their own exercise of will. In order for an unruly collection of individuals competing for honor and advantage to form a stable peaceful society, it is necessary to confer the power on an authority to exercise judgment on behalf of citizens—that is, to recognize a power in a person or institution to create exclusionary reasons.

95. Raz (1986), pp. 41, 44, 59. The dependence thesis is the claim that "authoritative directives should be based on reasons which already independently apply to the subjects of the directives and are relevant to their action in the circumstances covered by the directive." Ibid., p. 47; see also Joseph Raz, "Authority, Law, and Morality," in Raz (1994), p. 214.

96. Raz (1986), pp. 47, 55–59. One might also employ the distinction between first-order reasons, which are reasons for doing something or refraining from doing something, and second-order reasons, which are reasons to act on or refrain from acting on reasons. See Raz (1979), pp. 17, 22, 27; Raz (1986), p. 33.

97. Raz (1986), pp. 58–59.

98. Ibid., pp. 42, 48, 58–61 (using the term "preemptive" reason); Joseph Raz, "Authority, Law, and Morality," in Raz (1994), p. 213 (also using "preemptive"); Raz (1979), p. 17 (using the term "exclusionary" reason). For some reason the term "exclusionary" seems to have caught on in the literature to a greater extent than "preemptive," so I will adopt it here. See, e.g., Finnis (1980), p. 269.

99. Larmore (1987), pp. 53, 59.

100. To be clear, Raz would almost certainly not accept the extension of his views in this way. He denies that there is a general obligation to obey the law. Raz (1986), pp. 99–104; Raz (1979), pp. 233–49. In this argument, I am following Waldron's "woollier and less well defined" appropriation of the Razian Normal Justification Thesis as a way of explaining why legal texts, which "stand for the time being in the name of the whole community" can create exclusionary reasons upon which citizens should act. See Waldron (1999a), p. 101. My argument must be understood as Razian-in-flavor, or Raz-inspired, not as an account of Raz's views.

101. See Waldron (1999b), p. 173 (making a similar appeal to the normative significance of Hart's account of the transition from a pre-legal society to one with a legal system).

102. Finnis (1980), p. 134.

103. Ibid., p. 83 (listing the things that "all human societies" reveal as basic ethical concerns such as the prohibition on killing other human beings with justification, the maintenance of some regulation of sexual activity and family structures, seeking after truth, treating the dead with respect, and so on). These basic ethical values may be objectively incommensurable. Ibid., p. 115. See also Isaiah Berlin, "The Pursuit of the Ideal," in Berlin (1990), pp. 10–11; Gray (1996), p. 144. The argument here relies on value pluralism, without necessarily committing to a position one way or the other on whether these values are incommensurable.

104. Finnis (1980), pp. 147–50. For a similar functional approach to basic moral constraints, which is indebted to Hume, see Blackburn (1998), p. 308 ("We are social animals, with certain biological needs. We have to coordinate our efforts; we have to establish systems of property and promise-keeping and sometimes even government. We can then take comfort in reflecting that there are not so many admirable, coherent, mature, livable ethical systems on offer...."). The coincidence between Rawls, Finnis, and the neo-Humean Simon Blackburn suggests that the need to coordinate compliance with the demands of morality in communities is something common to the morality of politics.

105. Rawls (1993), pp. 55–58.

106. Finnis (1980), pp. 246–48.

107. Ibid., p. 154.

108. Greenawalt (1987), pp. 161–63, reads Finnis as making an appeal to the benefits that the existence of law confers on members of a community. I think Finnis is better understood as arguing that, in communities, the law replaces the practical reasoning of individuals, which is aimed in turn not only at good consequences, but at the requirements of practical reasonableness in general. See Finnis (1980), p. 318; see also ibid., p. 125 (arguing that it is a basic requirement of practical reasonableness that people foster the good of their communities).

109. Joseph Raz, "Authority, Law and Morality," in Raz (1994), pp. 214–15.

110. Waldron (1999a), p. 282 ("The identification of someone as a right-bearer expresses a measure of confidence in that person's moral capacities—in particular his capacity to think responsibly about the moral relation between his interests and the interests of others.").

111. Waldron (1999a), p. 101.

112. Okay, I'll admit that "I Fought the Law" isn't really a Clash song—it was written by Sonny Curtis, and has been recorded by dozens of artists—but the Clash did it the best.

113. Waldron (1999a), pp. 114–17. Dworkin also emphasizes the connection between legality and mutual respect, although he derives from it a much different conception of the nature of law—namely law as integrity. Dworkin (1986), p. 190 ("the expressive value is confirmed when people in good faith try to treat one another in a way appropriate to common membership in a community governed by political integrity and to see each other as making this attempt, even when they disagree about exactly what integrity requires in particular circumstances").

114. See Rawls (1971), pp. 354–55 (discussing natural duties to support just institutions).

115. See Rhode (2000a), pp. 77–80; Simon (1998), ch. 4; Applbaum (1999), ch. 6; Luban (1988), ch. 3. Luban argues that the structure of role morality depends on a process of justification that assesses the importance of social institutions, roles, and role obligations. At each step of the justification process, one must inquire into the strength of the justification, and thus the weight of the reason generated. Luban (1988), pp. 133–35.

116. Luban (1986), p. 638.

117. See, e.g., Jeremy Waldron, "Normative (or Ethical) Positivism, in Coleman (2001), p. 410.

118. Ibid., p. 421.

119. The quoted language, "creative and aggressive," is often used as a term of approval by lawyers. It is highly ironic, and suggestive of how backwards some lawyers have gotten the understanding of their professional obligations, that the firm hired to conduct an internal investigation of allegations of accounting improprieties at Enron concluded that the transactions in question were "creative and aggressive" but not improper. See letter from Vinson and Elkins to Enron (Oct. 15, 2001), excerpted in Hazard (2005), pp. 217–18. One might cynically observe that the firm conducting the investigation had billed millions of dollars to Enron, mostly for structuring these transactions. Cramton (2002). In the words of a subsequent investigative report,

"[t]he result of the [outside law firm's] review was largely predetermined by the scope and nature of the investigation and the process employed. The scope and process of the investigation appear to have been structured with less skepticism than was needed to see through these particularly complex transactions." Powers (2002), pp. 176–77.

120. Quoted in Graber (2006), p. 1. President Andrew Jackson is said to have warned his Attorney General that he had better help Jackson disestablish the national bank. When the Attorney General balked at providing the advice Jackson sought, Jackson said, "You must find a law authorizing the act or I will appoint an Attorney General who will." Quoted in Clayton (1992), p. 18. For a contemporary example, consider the reaction of Enron Chief Financial Officer Andy Fastow when advised by an in-house lawyer that he was required to disclose income from related-party transactions: "Let's figure out a way not to disclose it." See McLean and Elkind (2003), p. 328.

121. See Benjamin Weiser, "Doubting a Case, a Prosecutor Helped the Defense," *The New York Times* (June 23, 2008). Luban's analysis first appeared on the *Balkinization* blog. See http://balkin.blogspot.com/2008/06/when-good-prosecutor-throws-case.html. Details in this discussion and quotations from Luban and Stephen Gillers are from the *Times* article and Luban's blog post. Many of these sources are reprinted in Gillers (2009), pp. 489–501.

122. Model Rules, Rule 3.8. Most of the duties stated in this rule have counterparts in the constitutional law of criminal procedure. See, e.g., *Brady v. Maryland*, 373 U.S. 83 (1963) (obligation to disclose exculpatory evidence). See Mosteller (2007) for a thorough analysis of the unlawful conduct of Mike Nifong, the prosecutor who pursued sexual assault charges against several members of the Duke lacrosse team.

123. I owe this way of putting the point to Alice Woolley.

124. See Luban (2007), ch. 7 ("The Ethics of Wrongful Obedience") and ch. 8 ("Integrity: Its Cause and Cures"); Zimbardo (2007); Regan (2004); Doris (2002).

125. Woolley (2009). One approach might be to consider professional discipline of law firms, to create incentives to respond to dysfunctional organizational cultures. See Schneyer (1991).

126. David Luban, "The Adversary System Excuse," in Luban (1983). This essay was republished as ch. 1 of Luban (2007), indicating that Luban's skepticism about the adversary system is undiminished.

127. The quote is from Luban's blog post, cited earlier, and refers to lawyers who ascribe responsibility for unjust outcomes to the system, rather than taking personal moral responsibility.

Notes to Chapter Four

Legal Entitlements and Public Reason in Practice

1. Norman Spaulding puts it nicely when he says "the lawyer's role is grounded in a logic of *service*, not identification." Spaulding (2003), p. 6.

2. Stuart Hampshire, "Liberalism: The New Twist," *New York Review of Books* 40:14 (Aug. 12, 1993).

3. See Fuller (1958). Fuller's argument, in brief, is that substantively evil legal systems are unlikely to exhibit procedural virtues like coherence so, a legal system that is coherent is unlikely to be evil. *See* ibid., p. 636. In terms of logical form, this argument is plainly flawed (it commits the fallacy of affirming the consequent). However, it is apparent that Fuller really intends this as an empirical argument, not one of conceptual necessity. He suggests that "when men are compelled to explain and justify their decisions, the effect will generally be to pull these decisions toward goodness." Ibid. He also says it is his impression that "even in the most perverted regimes there is a certain hesitancy about writing cruelties, intolerances, and inhumanities into law." Ibid., p. 637. See also ibid., p. 645, where he argues that the external and internal moralities of law "reciprocally influence one another." As discussed in the text, however, examples abound of open, written, public laws embodying intolerance and inhumanity. The Nazi Nuremberg Laws are as clear a case of intolerance and inhumanity as one is likely to encounter, yet they conform to the formal requirements of writtenness, publicity, generality, prospectivity, and so on.

4. Fuller (1958), pp. 644–46 (discussing what he calls either the morality of order or the internal morality of law). This notion is central to Fuller (1964).

5. Rawls (1971), pp. 363–68, 371–77.

6. Greenawalt (1987), pp. 233–34; Rawls (1971), pp. 382–83.

7. Rawls (1971), p. 365.

8. King (1963).

9. Greenawalt (1987), p. 232.

10. See, e.g., Raz (1979), pp. 263–64; Rawls (1971), pp. 368–71.

11. Rawls (1971), p. 369.

12. Terrell (2003), p. 835 (criticizing this broad-brush approach).

13. Model Rules, Rule 1.2(a)

14. Ibid., Rule 1.2, cmt. [2].

15. Ibid., Rule 1.4(a)(2).

16. Fed. R. Civ. P. 1.

17. Bingham (2007).

18. With apologies to Stanley Fish.

19. Cf. Williams (1985), p. 133 ("Disagreement does not necessarily have to be overcome. It may remain an important and constitutive feature of our relations to others").

20. See, e.g., 42 U.S.C. § 1988 (providing fees to the prevailing party in actions to redress violations of the U.S. constitution, brought under 42 U.S.C. § 1983).

21. Fed. R. Civ. P. 11.

22. *NAACP v. Button*, 371 U.S. 415 (1963); Model Rules, Rule 7.3 (prohibiting in-person solicitation of prospective clients only "when a significant motive for the lawyer's doing so is the lawyer's pecuniary gain").

23. Sarat (1998), p. 322.

24. Markovits (2008); Michelman (1988). Antecedents of this view can be found in the influential work of Robert Cover. See Cover (1983).

25. Cover (1983), pp. 11–16.

26. Ibid., p. 18.

27. Thompson (1975).

28. Austin Sarat and Stuart Scheingold, "Cause Lawyering and the Reproduction of Professional Authority," in Sarat and Scheingold (1998).

29. See, e.g., Smith (2000), p. 952 ("It is difficult, if not impossible, to zealously represent the criminally accused and simultaneously tend to the feelings of others. This is ... even more so in a time when criminal punishment is regarded as the answer to almost all of our social problems.").

30. Duncan Kennedy, "Rebels from Principle: Changing the Corporate Law Firm from Within," *Harvard Law School Bulletin* (Fall 1981), p. 36 (reprinted in Rhode [1994], p. 86).

31. Bolt (1966), Act I, sc. 6.

32. Gordon (2003), pp. 1198–99. Kenneth Arrow similarly points out that contracts, markets, and transactions depend on relationships of trust and confidence. Arrow (1973). "Every contract depends for its observance on a mass of unspecified conditions which suggest that performance will be carried out in good faith without insistence on sticking literally to its wording." Ibid., p. 314. It is impossible to draft contracts with sufficient specificity to handle every situation that could conceivably arise in the course of a commercial relationship. Thus, the parties depend on one another not to behave opportunistically. Because the parties in most complex commercial relationships act through lawyers, lawyers' practices can play a vital role in sustaining the conditions needed for stable markets, but they can also undermine them if they do not understand themselves as having an obligation to maintain respect for the framework of legal rights and duties that set limits on what parties permissibly may do.

33. See Rhode (2000a), pp. 76–79; Simon (1998), pp. 148–49.

34. Rhode (2000a), p. 79.

35. Ibid., p. 76.

36. Ibid., p. 77.

37. Ibid., p. 79.

38. Simon (1998), pp. 151–56.

39. See McLean and Elkind (2003), p. 151 ("In business terms, it was as if the company had discovered a way to defy the laws of gravity. Using off-balance-sheet vehicles and other complex transactions, Enron seemed to be able to make money magically appear without either adding debt or issuing stock. And that's precisely how many Enron executives felt, especially those who worked directly for Fastow: they thought they *were* magicians, reinventing corporate finance, rewriting the rules of the game, thumbing their nose at the way business had always been done.").

40. See, e.g., Goldsmith (2007), pp. 88–89, 210–11, 215 (describing and criticizing the attitude of many within the Bush administration); Yoo (2006) (vigorously defending the administration's approach to executive power).

41. See Wendel (2005b).

42. See, e.g., Feldman (1996); Postema (1980); Simon (1978), pp. 39–41.

43. Shaffer (1987a).

44. Ibid., pp. 968–70.

45. See, e.g., Pepper (1999), p. 188 ("The client comes in with a human problem .... Because the lawyer is in the business of providing legal assistance, it is very likely he or she will define the problem in legal terms .... This will often tend to distill out, or disguise, the moral dimension and the more complex human elements from the situation."). See also Freedman and Smith (2002), p. 70; Shaffer (1987b); Pepper (1986), pp. 630–32.

46. Shaffer and Cochran (1994), pp. 44–54.

47. Ibid., p. 51.

48. Jonsen and Toulmin (1988).

49. Model Rules, Rule 2.1.

50. Sarat and Felsteiner (1995), pp. 85–107.

51. Ibid., p. 95.

52. Ibid., pp. 96–101.

53. Ibid., p. 102.

54. The discussion of *Spaulding* is greatly indebted to conversations with Kate Kruse, and her unpublished paper, "Beyond Cardboard Clients in Legal Ethics."

55. Smith (1990), p. 76.

56. Cramton and Knowles (1998), pp. 69–71, 91–94. Cramton and Knowles argue convincingly that the lawyers never discussed disclosure with their clients because insurance-defense lawyers at the time were accustomed to thinking of the liability carrier as the real client, at least if it was likely that the case would settle or result in a judgment within policy limits, and often had little meaningful interaction with the insureds. Ibid., pp. 92–93. The modern law governing lawyers more clearly establishes that an insurance-defense lawyer's primary client is the insured, with only secondary obligations owed to the insurer. See, e.g., *Paradigm Insurance Co. v. The Langerman Law Offices*, 24 P.3d 593 (Ariz. 2001).

57. Cramton and Knowles (1998), pp. 87–88, 94–95.

58. Ibid., p. 95 ("Lawyers have a terrible habit of fitting client objectives into a simplified moral framework—assuming that clients are governed only by selfish concerns—and then deciding matters for them as if the clients were moral ciphers."). See also Kruse (2006), p. 382; Simon (1978), pp. 52–55.

59. Model Rules, Rule 1.2(a); Restatement § 21(3).

60. Wendel (2008b).

61. The "shocks the conscience" standard is from *Rochin v. California*, 342 U.S. 165 (1952).

62. Joseph Raz, "The Problem About the Nature of Law," in Raz (1994), pp. 202–4, 214–15; Coleman (1982). H.L.A. Hart accepted this "inclusive" variety of legal positivism in the posthumously published postscript to *The Concept of Law*. H.L.A. Hart, "Postscript," in Hart (1994), pp. 247–48. Inclusive, or "soft" positivism is the thesis that "morality can be a condition of legality: that the legality of norms can sometimes depend on their substantive (moral) merits, not just their pedigree or social source." Jules

Coleman, "Incorporationism, Conventionality, and the Practical Difference Thesis," in Coleman (2001), p. 100. Different flavors of legal positivism exist, but in all cases the essential positivist claim is that the legal validity of a norm is a matter of locating it within the sources specified by the relevant rule of recognition. The rule of recognition specifies binding criteria for legal officials to use in deciding whether a given norm is a rule that is part of a legal system. See, e.g., Hart (1994), pp. 94–95, 100. A rule of recognition could conceivably specify that a judge consider, for example, whether a particular punishment is genuinely cruel or unusual.

Siding against this flavor of positivism, Raz has objected that incorporating moral judgments is incompatible with the law's claim to authority. Joseph Raz, "Authority, Law and Morality," in Raz (1994). The trouble, as Raz recognizes, is that the law may make a conventional practice of referring to norms outside the law:

> The law itself quite commonly directs the courts to apply extralegal considerations. Italian law may direct the courts to apply European Community law, or International law, or Chinese law to a case. It may direct the court to settle a dispute by reference to the rules and regulations of a corporation, or an unincorporated association, or by references to commercial practices or moral norms.

Joseph Raz, "On the Autonomy of Legal Reasoning," in Raz (1994), p. 333. In these "incorporation" cases, legal rules specify that a decision-maker can evaluate the conduct of citizens with reference to something outside the law. The critical point is that nothing in the law *requires* the decision-maker to evaluate whether the extra-legal norms are true, attractive, valid, or whatever. Judicial decision-making can be purely empirical. For example, a judge in the United States today might conclude that capital punishment does not violate the Eighth Amendment's prohibition on cruel and unusual punishment, because there is an apparent consensus among a majority of Americans that the death penalty is not cruel and unusual. This conclusion would be a valid proposition of law even though one might argue (as I would) that capital punishment is cruel and unusual, as a matter of critical, not conventional, morality. Whether it is *really* true as a matter of morality that capital punishment is not cruel, it would be impossible to ascertain the law of the United States on this point without discovering the morality of the community.

Although the law could, in theory, require judges to determine whether it is really (morally) the case that capital punishment is cruel, if it did so it would lose its capacity to coordinate in the face of disagreement. This is not precisely Raz's view, by the way. His authority argument appeals to the notion of dependent reasons, and the way authorities function in practical reasoning. As Coleman summarizes the authority argument: "Law's claim to authority entails ... that one cannot determine the law's identity or content by appealing to the dependent reasons that would justify it." Jules Coleman, "Incorporationism, Conventionality, and the Practical Difference Thesis," in Coleman (2001), p. 134. Coleman and Raz differ over whether it is a necessary condition, as well as a sufficient condition, that the content of law be determinable without recourse to moral argument. Coleman posits a moral/legal expert who could be consulted to learn the content of the law, who herself engaged in moral reasoning to determine what the law should be; the law understood in this way retains its capacity to mediate between persons and the reasons that apply to them, which is all that is necessary for the law to be an authority. Ibid. at 139–41. For the purposes of the argument set out here, it is not necessary to resolve jurisprudential debates at this level of detail. In most of the cases that are interesting problems for legal ethics, there is no confusion between what the law is and what some lawyer believes it ought to be. Rather, the question is which set of reasons should ground the lawyer's duties. The apparent incorporation by law of morality is not a reason to believe that the lawyer's role is moralized directly, rather than responding indirectly to the needs of citizens in the circumstances of politics.

63. Shaffer (1987a), pp. 977–79.

64. Pepper (1999), pp. 189–90.

65. Ibid., p. 190.

66. Ibid., p. 191.

67. Shaffer (1987a), p. 982.

68. Ibid., p. 983 (quoting Robert Bellah, et al., *Habits of the Heart* (1985)).

69. Ibid., p. 985.

70. Wolfram (1986) § 10.2.2, p. 571. The rule is the same in Canada. See Hutchinson (1999), p. 73 ("there are no prohibitions on lawyers refusing to represent particular clients or causes").

71. Model Rules, Rule 6.2.

72. Ibid., Rule 6.2(c).

73. Boon and Levin (1999), pp. 27–29. The cab-rank rule is followed in other common-law jurisdictions. In New Zealand, for example, it extends to all lawyers, not just in-court advocates. See Webb (2000) § 6.1, p. 153.

74. Boon and Levin (1999), pp. 181–82. John Flood's research describes how clerks, who serve as intermediaries between solicitors and barristers, steer cases toward particular barristers for career-development reasons, and how solicitors and clerks negotiate to find the "right" solicitor for a given case, without respecting the cab-rank principle. See Flood (1983), pp. 54–59, 65, 69–76. As Flood notes, "this sifting of the solicitors effectively nullifies the impact of the cab-rank rule of the Bar." Ibid., p. 71.

75. *Rondel v. Worsley*, [1969] 1 AC 191. I am grateful to Duncan Webb for this reference. See also Boon and Levin (1999), p. 29.

76. Hazard and Hodes (2001) § 51.5, pp. 51–57.

77. Model Rules, Rule 1.16(b)(4).

78. Ibid., Rule 1.16(d).

79. Ibid., Rule 1.16(c).

80. Restatement § 32, cmt. j ("An action is imprudent ... only if it is likely to be so detrimental to the client that a reasonable lawyer could not in good conscience assist it .... A client's intended action is not imprudent simply because the lawyer disagrees with it.").

81. Model Rule 1.2(b).

82. See, e.g., the Washington State attorneys' oath, reproduced at *http://www.courts .wa.gov/court_rules/*.

83. Cf. Spaulding (2003), pp. 1, 20–21, 25, 30 (2003) (arguing that the lawyer disciplinary rules, interpreted in light of their underlying structure and purpose, are intended to shape the lawyer's attitudes toward prospective clients and current clients, and that lawyers are urged to work toward an attitude of detachment from their clients and their causes).

84. Dershowitz (1996), p. 157.

85. Ibid., p. 160.

86. Tigar (1995), pp. 104–5.

87. Ibid., p. 108.

88. Editorial, "Unveiled Threats," *The Washington Post* (Jan. 12, 2007), p. A18. See also Neil A. Lewis, "Official Attacks Top Law Firms Over Detainees," *The New York Times* (Jan. 13, 2007).

89. In all likelihood, these comments were not Stimson's private viewpoint, but represented the position of the Bush Administration. An editorial in *The Wall Street Journal* quoted an unnamed official as saying that "this information [the identity of the law firms] might cause something of a scandal, since so much of the pro bono work being done to tilt the playing field in favor of al Qaeda appears to be subsidized by legal fees from the Fortune 500." Robert L. Pollock, "The Gitmo High Life," *The Wall Street Journal* (Jan. 12, 2007), p. A12.

90. Charles Fried, "Mr. Stimson and the American Way," *The Wall Street Journal* (Jan. 16, 2007), p. A21.

91. Freedman (1995).

92. Ibid., p. 114.

93. Simon (1988), pp. 1094–96.

94. See also Collett (1999).

95. Freedman (1995), p. 115 (citing Michael E. Tiger, "Setting the Record Straight on the Defense of John Demjanjuk," *Legal Times* (Sept. 6, 1993), p. 22.).

96. See, e.g., Farah Stockman, "Potshot at Guantanamo Lawyers Backfires," *Boston Globe* (Jan. 29, 2007). For the quote about tilting the playing field in favor of Al Qaeda, see Robert L. Pollock, "The Gitmo High Life," *The Wall Street Journal* (Jan. 12, 2007), p. A12.

97. See Dare (2009), p. 9.

98. Described and analyzed with great subtlety in Wilkins (1995).

99. Ibid., p. 1031.

100. Ibid., p. 1032.

101. Ibid., pp. 1032–33.

102. Applbaum (1999), ch. 5 ("Are Lawyers Liars?") for an extended argument for the persistence of description. See also Williams (1995). Williams notes that it is hard to say when "the same act" is done in both professional and non-professional contexts, because some acts can only be done in a professional context. The morally relevant distinction, he argues, is that acts done in a professional context are often accompa-

nied by particular professional dispositions, and these can also be the object of moral evaluation. We can also understand subtle conflicts on this two-level structure, such as the possibility that ordinary morality carries with it characteristic dispositions, which are not identical with the dispositions encouraged by (or presupposed by) professional morality. Ibid., p. 195.

103. Applbaum (1999), p. 91.

104. Ibid., p. 81.

105. I am grateful to Alice Woolley for some extremely helpful conversations that clarified my thinking on this point.

106. Applbaum (1999), p. 92.

107. Murray Schwartz, "The Zeal of the Civil Advocate," in Luban (1983), p. 151. Schwartz argues: "[I]n our legal system no lawyer need accept any client who seeks his or her legal assistance; accordingly, voluntary acceptance of a client carries with it moral accountability for means and ends employed in that representation."

108. For arguments like this in the legal ethics literature, see, e.g., Freedman and Smith (2002), chs. 2–4; Dershowitz (1996), chs. II and VIII; Ogletree (1993); Luban (1988), pp. 58–66; Bellows (1988); Wishman (1981).

109. Wolfram (1986) § 10.2.3, at 576 (citing *NAACP v. Virginia ex rel. Button*, 371 U.S. 415, 443 [1963]).

110. *Guam Soc'y of Obstetricians and Gynecologists v. Ada*, 100 F.3d 691 (9th Cir. 1996); *Schneider v. Colegio de Abogados de Puerto Rico*, 917 F.2d 620, 640 (1st Cir. 1990). I owe these references to Collett (1999).

111. Rhode (2000a), pp. 207–9.

112. Wilkins (1998); Levinson (1993), p. 1578.

113. The case is *Stropnicky v. Nathanson*, 19 MD.L.R. 39 (M.C.A.D. Feb. 25, 1997).

114. Spaulding (2003); Markovits (2003).

115. See, e.g., Charles W. Wolfram, "A Lawyer's Duty to Represent Clients, Repugnant and Otherwise," in Luban (1983).

116. Abel (1989), pp. 202–5; Heinz and Laumann (1982).

117. Carrie Menkel-Meadow, "The Causes of Cause Lawyering: Toward an Understanding of the Motivation and Commitment of Social Justice Lawyers," in Sarat and Scheingold (1998).

NOTES TO CHAPTER FIVE

From Nonaccountability to Tragedy: The Remaining Claims of Morality

1. Luban (2007), p. 50.

2. Ibid., p. 46; see also Luban (2008), p. 1441 ("we cannot simply wave a wand and make our extralegal moral agency, and therefore moral accountability, disappear").

3. Wendel (2008a), p. 1423.

4. Luban (2007), pp. 57–58. This is essentially the fourfold root structure from *Lawyers and Justice*. See Luban (1988), pp. 129–39.

5. Bernard Williams, "Realism and Moralism in Political Theory," in Williams (2005), pp. 10–11 ("The idea is that a given historical structure can be ... an example of the human capacity to live under an intelligible order of authority. It makes sense (MS) to us as such a structure .... The question is whether a structure MS as an example of authoritative order. This requires, on the lines already explained, that there is a legitimation offered which goes beyond the assertion of power; and we can recognize such a thing because in the light of the historical and cultural circumstances, and so forth, it MS to us as a legitimation."). See also Bernard Williams, "Professional Morality and Its Dispositions," in Luban (1983), p. 260.

6. Joseph Raz, "The Rule of Law and Its Virtue," in Raz (1979), p. 219.

7. See Dare (2009), ch. 3, relying on Rawls (1955). The example of promising is from Rawls's influential paper.

8. Dare (2009), p. 43.

9. Thomas Nagel, "Ruthlessness in Public Life," in Nagel (1979), p. 89.

10. Hampshire (1989), pp. 172–74.

11. Ibid., pp. 174–75.

12. Ibid., pp. 175–76.

13. Luban (2007), p. 281.

14. See, e.g., Postema (1980), pp. 64–72; Wasserstrom (1975), pp. 14–15.

15. Applbaum (1999), pp. 30–31.

16. Ibid., pp. 32–33.

17. Ibid., p. 35.

18. For Sanson's argument to this effect see ibid., p. 39.

19. Ibid., p. 40.

20. See, e.g., Christine M. Korsgaard, "The Reasons We Can Share: An Attack on the Distinction between Agent-Relative and Agent-Neutral Reasons," in Korsgaard (1996a); Nagel (1986), p. 170, for this distinction.

21. Samuel Scheffler, "Projects, Relationships, and Reasons," in Wallace (2004), pp. 251–52.

22. See, e.g., Postema (1980).

23. Ibid., p. 78.

24. Ibid., p. 82.

25. Ibid. ("Each lawyer must have a conception of the role that allows him to serve the important functions of that role in the legal and political system while integrating his own sense of moral responsibility into the role itself.")

26. Ibid., p. 77.

27. Korsgaard (1996b), pp. 44–47.

28. Darwall, Gibbard and Railton (1990), pp. 116–19 (discussing the continuing centrality of G. E. Moore's open question argument to ethical theory).

29. Korsgaard (2003), pp. 110–12.

30. Korsgaard (1996b), p. 47.

31. Ibid., p. 93.

32. Ibid., p. 97.

33. Ibid., p. 101.
34. Ibid., p. 102.
35. See, e.g., Ogletree (1993).
36. See Markovits (2008); Markovits (2006); Markovits (2003).
37. Markovits (2008), pp. 25–26, 44, 67, 81–88.
38. Ibid., pp. 3–4, 25, 36–41.
39. Ibid., pp. 174–87.
40. Ibid., p. 177.
41. Ibid., p. 180.
42. Ibid., pp. 103–6.
43. Ibid., pp. 107–11.
44. Markovits (2003), p. 242.
45. Nagel (1986), p. 176; Markovits (2003), pp. 226–27.
46. Markovits (2003), pp. 261, 270.
47. Ibid., p. 262.
48. Markovits (2008), pp. 92–96.
49. Ibid., p. 93.
50. These quotes are from Markovits (2003), pp. 273–74.
51. See, e.g., McLean and Elkind (2003); Coffee (2004); Gordon (2003); Koniak (2003).
52. Markovits (2008), pp. 195–96.
53. Ibid., p. 199.
54. This is true even in the criminal defense context, and even with respect to appointed counsel. See, e.g., *Jones v. Barnes*, 463 U.S. 745 (1983).
55. Bernard Williams, "Politics and Moral Character," in Williams (1981), p. 57.
56. Ibid., p. 60.
57. Williams (1995), p. 197.
58. Williams (2005), pp. 126–27.
59. Hampshire (1989), pp. 162–65; Weber (1946).
60. Weber (1946), p. 123.
61. Walzer (1973); Thomas Nagel, "Ruthlessness in Public Life," in Nagel (1979).
62. The argument given by the hypothetical defender of the strict confidentiality rule is offered in Model Rule 1.6, cmt. [2] and Restatement § 60, cmt. b. It is frequently recited by courts in the related context of justifying the attorney–client (evidentiary) privilege. See, e.g., *Upjohn Corporation v. United States*, 449 U.S. 383 (1981) (the purpose of the privilege is to "encourage full and frank communication between attorneys and their clients" because the lawyer's advice "depends on the lawyer's being fully informed by the client"). A powerful justification for the privilege was given by a federal court of appeals:

> The attorney–client privilege is essential to preservation of liberty against a powerful government. People need lawyers to guide them through thickets of complex

government requirements, and, to get useful advice, they have to be able to talk to their lawyers candidly without fear that what they say to their own lawyers will be transmitted to the government.

Much of what lawyers actually do for a living consists of helping their clients comply with the law. Clients unwittingly engage in conduct subject to civil and even criminal penalties. This valuable social service of counseling clients and bringing them into compliance with the law cannot be performed effectively if clients are scared to tell their lawyers what they are doing, for fear that their lawyers will be turned into government informants.

United States v. Chen, 99 F.3d 1495 (9th Cir. 1996) (Kleinfeld, J.). Among legal ethics scholars, Monroe Freedman is well known for his vigorous defense of the duty of confidentiality, see Freedman and Smith (2002), pp. 127–28, 135–37, and Stephen Pepper is also a prominent defender of a strong confidentiality obligation, see Pepper (1998). In general, however, academic support for confidentiality is considerably weaker than the allegiance of practicing lawyers to the duty. For academic criticism, see, e.g., Rhode (2000a), pp. 106–15; Simon (1998), pp. 54–62; Fischel (1998); Zacharias (1989); Luban (1988), pp. 189–92, 201–5, 213–20; Bruce M. Landesman, "Confidentiality and the Lawyer–Client Relationship," in Luban (1983).

63. Williams (1995), pp. 194–95.

64. Bernard Williams, "Politics and Moral Character," in Williams (1981), p. 63 ("In some cases the claims of the political reasons are proximate enough, and enough of the moral kind, to enable one to say that there is a moral justification for that particular political act, a justification which has outweighed the moral reasons against it. Even so, that can still leave the moral remainder, the uncancelled moral disagreeableness I have referred to.").

65. Ibid., p. 61.

66. Gowans (1994), p. 132.

67. Walzer (1973), pp. 176–77. Here I am blending Walzer's summaries of the positions of Machiavelli and Weber, which I think are best represented by the "suffering servant" ideal. As Walzer writes, "a sign of our own conscientiousness ... [is that] personal anguish sometimes seems the only acceptable excuse for political crimes." Ibid., p. 176. See also Williams (1995), p. 196.

68. Bernard Williams, "Politics and Moral Character," in Williams (1981), p. 64.

69. Walzer (1973), pp. 177–79.

70. Dare (2008), pp. 149–50.

71. Wilkins (1998), pp. 1549–50.

72. Ibid., p. 1570.

73. Ibid., p. 1571.

74. Model Rules, Rule 1.16.

75. Quoted in Zitrin and Langford (1999), p. 19.

1. The arguments in this section, and the example of the torture memos, were presented as part of the 2008 F. W. Wickwire Memorial Lecture in Legal Ethics and Professional Responsibility, at Dalhousie Law School, see Wendel (2008b), and also formed the core case study in Wendel (2005b). Some of this discussion is drawn from a review of several books about the treatment of detainees and the legal analysis in the torture memos. See Wendel (2009).

2. I have written about the Enron and tax shelter cases in Wendel (2005a); see also Gordon (2003). For an analysis of the role of lawyers in the savings and loan crisis, see Gordon (1998b).

3. Powers (2002), pp. 4–5.

4. David Streitfeld and Lee Romne, "Enron's Run Tripped by Arrogance, Greed; Profile: A Lack of Discipline and a Drive to Bend the Rules Were Key Factors in the Meltdown," *Los Angeles Times* (Jan. 27, 2002), p. A1.

5. See, e.g., Neil A. Lewis, "Fresh Details Emerge on Harsh Methods at Guantánamo," *The New York Times* (Jan. 1, 2005).

6. See R. Jeffrey Smith and Dan Eggen, "Gonzales Helped Set the Course for Detainees," *The Washington Post* (Jan. 5, 2005), at A1 (noting that Abu Zubayda "refused to bend to CIA interrogations" and that the Agency was "determined to wring more from" him); Jess Bravin and Gary Fields, "How Do U.S. Interrogators Make a Suspected Terrorist Talk?," *The Wall Street Journal* (Mar. 4, 2003), at B1.

7. See Eric Lichtblau, "Gonzales Says '02 Policy on Detainees Doesn't Bind C.I.A.," *The New York Times* (Jan. 19, 2005), at A1. One memorandum, from a commander of an interrogation team at Guantánamo Bay, sought approval for a variety of euphemistically named interrogation methods including stripping detainees ("[r]emoval of clothing"), taking away their scriptures ("[r]emoval of comfort items, including religious items"), hooding, stress positions, forced shaving, and threatening detainees with dogs ("[u]sing detainees individual phobias"). See Memorandum from Lt. Col. Jerald Phifer to Commander, Joint Task Force 170, "Request for Approval of Counter-Resistance Strategies," in Greenberg and Dratel (2005), p. 227.

8. See David Johnston, et al., "Nominee Gave Advice to C.I.A. on Torture Law," *The New York Times* (Jan. 29, 2005), at A1; Douglas Jehl and David Johnston, "White House Fought New Curbs on Interrogations, Officials Say," *The New York Times* (Jan. 13, 2005), at A1. Regarding waterboarding, see #36 in the Introduction's endnotes. An extensive account of the use of water torture by Japanese, North Korea, and North Vietnamese forces against American service personnel, and in many cases the subsequent prosecution for war crimes, can be found in Wallach (2007). The Bush administration has admitted that waterboarding had been used in several cases, insisted that it was legal, and intimated that it could be used in the future. See Jennifer Loven, "White House Defends Interrogation Method," *Associated Press* (Feb. 6, 2008); Scott Shane, "CIA Chief Doubts Tactic to Interrogate is Still Legal," *The New York Times* (Feb. 8,

2008); Philip Shenon, "Mukasey Offers View on Waterboarding," *The New York Times* (Jan. 30, 2008).

9. See, e.g., Neil A. Lewis, "Fresh Details Emerge on Harsh Methods at Guantánamo," *The New York Times* (Jan. 1, 2005).

10. Jess Bravin and Gary Fields, "How Do U.S. Interrogators Make a Suspected Terrorist Talk?," *The Wall Street Journal* (Mar. 4, 2003), at B1. Euphemisms like "smacky-face" are common in the apologetics of torture offered by the administration and its supporters. For example, Sen. Jim Talent (R-Mo.) said, "If our guys want to poke somebody in the chest to get the name of a bomb maker so they can save the lives of Americans, I'm for it." Jackie Northam, "Army Probes Deaths of Iraq, Afghanistan Detainees," *All Things Considered*, NPR Broadcast (Mar. 16, 2005). U.S. Supreme Court Justice Scalia later picked up this strategy of minimizing torture in an interview with BBC radio, where he said:

Is it really so easy to determine that smacking someone in the face to determine where he has hidden the bomb that is about to blow up Los Angeles is prohibited in the constitution? It would be absurd to say you couldn't do that. And once you acknowledge that, we're into a different game.

See "U.S. Judge Steps into Torture Row," <http://news.bbc.co.uk/2/hi/americas/7239748.stm>.

11. See Mike Allen and Dana Priest, "Memo on Torture Draws Focus to Bush," *The Washington Post* (June 9, 2004), at A3 (quoting former administration official saying that the CIA "was prepared to get more aggressive and re-learn old skills, but only with explicit assurances from the top that they were doing so with the full legal authority the president could confer on them"); Jane Mayer, "Outsourcing Torture," *The New Yorker* (Feb. 14, 2005) (reporting testimony by head of counter-terrorism operations for the CIA, who told Congressional committees that "there was a 'before 9/11' and there was an 'after 9/11.' After 9/11, the gloves came off.").

12. See, e.g., Amanda Ripley, "Redefining Torture," *Time* (June 13, 2004) (quoting Vice President Dick Cheney's post-9/11 interview in which he said it would be "vital for us to use any means at our disposal, basically, to achieve our objective").

13. See, e.g., Michael Isikoff, et al., "Torture's Path," *Newsweek* (Dec. 27, 2004/Jan. 3, 2005); R. Jeffrey Smith and Dan Eggen, "Gonzales Helped Set the Course for Detainees," *The Washington Post* (Jan. 5, 2005), at A1; Tim Golden, "After Terror, A Secret Rewriting of Military Law," *The New York Times* (Oct. 24, 2004), at A1.

14. Journalist Mark Danner obtained a confidential copy of a 2007 report by the International Committee of the Red Cross ("ICRC Report"), detailing the treatment of fourteen "high-value detainees" in U.S. custody. See Mark Danner, "U.S. Torture: Voices from the Black Sites," *New York Review of Books* (April 9, 2009). The full ICRC Report is available at the NYRB web site: http://www.nybooks.com/icrc-report.pdf. Also, on April 16, 2009, the Justice Department released four previously classified memos prepared by lawyers in the Office of Legal Counsel (OLC) during the Bush

Administration. The memos are available at the web site of the American Civil Liberties Union, which had sued to force their disclosure. http://www.aclu.org/safefree/general/olc_memos.html.

15. See Memo from Assistant Attorney General Jay S. Bybee to John Rizzo, Acting General Counsel of the Central Intelligence Agency (Aug. 1, 2002).

16. ICRC Report, *supra*, p. 30.

17. One detainee, who had lost a leg fighting in Afghanistan, was forced to stand, with his arms shackled above his head, for two weeks. His interrogators soon figured out that they could remove his artificial leg to "add extra stress to the position." He was stripped naked while being forced to stand and made to wear a diaper. On occasions when the diaper was not replaced, he had to urinate and defecate on himself. See Danner, *supra*, quoting ICRC Report. Public discussion of the Bush Administration's torture regime has often focused on waterboarding, and features arguments back and forth over whether it is torture. (For example, a conservative talk radio host in Chicago subjected himself to the technique, lasted six or seven seconds before insisting that it be discontinued, and reported, "[i]t's way worse than I thought it would be ... and I don't want to say this: absolutely torture." See Ryan Pollyea, "Mancow Waterboarded, Admits It's Torture," *NBC Chicago* (May 22, 2009), http://www.nbcchicago.com/news/local/Mancow-Takes-on-Waterboarding-and-Loses.html. While it is useful to get clear on whether waterboarding by itself constitutes torture, one must not lose sight of the fact that American interrogators used these techniques in concert, and the cumulative effect was much worse than the effect of using them singly.

18. See Scott Shane and Mark Mazzetti, "In Adopting Harsh Tactics, No Look at Past Use," *The New York Times* (April 21, 2009); Scott Horton, "Six Questions for Jane Mayer, Author of The Dark Side," *Harpers* (July 14, 2008).

19. See Executive Summary, *Senate Armed Services Committee Inquiry Into the Treatment of Detainees in U.S. Custody*, available at http://levin.senate.gov/newsroom/supporting/2008/Detainees.121108.pdf. The first page of the summary concludes, "[t]he abuse of detainees in U.S. custody cannot simply be attributed to the actions of 'a few bad apples' acting on their own. The fact is that senior officials in the United States government solicited information on how to use aggressive techniques, redefined the law to create the appearance of their legality, and authorized their use against sdetainees."

20. A quote was widely reported, and is also referenced in the Senate Armed Services Committee Report (see Executive Summary, *supra*, p. xvii), from the chief counsel to the CIA's Counterterrorism Center. This lawyer noted that the definition of torture is "basically subject to perception. If the detainee dies you're doing it wrong."

21. See Executive Summary, *supra*, p. xxi, for this history.

22. See Memorandum from Jay S. Bybee, Assistant Attorney General, to Alberto R. Gonzales, Counsel to the President, and William J. Haynes II, General Counsel of the Department of Defense (Jan. 22, 2002), in Greenberg and Dratel (2005). The relevant international treaties are the Geneva Convention [III] Relative to the Treatment of Prisoners of War (Aug. 12, 1949), 75 U.N.T.S. 135, 6 U.S.T. 3517, as well as the protec-

tions contained in so-called Common Article III, which apply in all contexts covered by any of the four Geneva Conventions for the Protection of Victims of War.

23. Memorandum for the President, from Albert R. Gonzales (Jan. 25, 2002), in Greenberg and Dratel (2005). According to sources at the State Department, Powell "hit the roof" when he read the analysis prepared by Justice Department lawyers. See John Barry, et al., "The Roots of Torture," *Newsweek* (May 24, 2004). For additional reporting on Secretary Powell's reaction, see R. Jeffrey Smith and Dan Eggen, "Gonzales Helped Set the Course for Detainees," *The Washington Post* (Jan. 5, 2005), at A1. Powell's objections are succinctly presented in a memo to Alberto Gonzales. *See* Memorandum from Colin L. Powell, Secretary of State, to Counsel to the President (Jan. 26, 2002), in Greenberg and Dratel (2005).

24. See Memorandum from Jay S. Bybee, Assistant Attorney General, to Alberto R. Gonzales, Counsel to the President (Aug. 1, 2002), in Greenberg and Dratel (2005).

25. Press Conference of the President (Sept. 15, 2006), available at <http://www.whitehouse.gov/news/releases/2006/09/20060915-2.html>. The unedited comment is reported in Richard Leiby, "Down a Dark Road: Movie Uses Afghan's Death to Ask Tough Questions About U.S. and Torture," *The Washington Post* (April 27, 2007), at C01.

26. Quoted in Scott Horton, "'Reasonable Minds Can Differ'," *Harpers* (Jan. 31, 2008), available at <http://www.harpers.org/archive/2008/01/hbc-90002285>. The letter is available online at <http://i.a.cnn.net/cnn/2008/images/01/29/letter.to.senator.leahy.pdf>.

27. See the discussion in Luban (2007), ch. 5 ("The Torture Lawyers of Washington"); and Bruff (2009), pp. 237–39.

28. Convention Against Torture and Other Cruel, Inhuman or Degrading Treatment or Punishment, G.A. Res. 39/46, 39 U.N. GAOR, Supp. (No. 51), U.N. Doc. A/39/51 (1984), Art. 2(2) ("No exceptional circumstances whatsoever, whether a state of war ... or any other public emergency, may be invoked as a justification of torture.").

29. 18 U.S.C. § 113.

30. 18 U.S.C. §§ 2340-2340A. The "severe pain" language of this statute became notorious when the OLC analysis leaked showing that government lawyers used a federal health-benefits statute as an analogy to support the definition of severe pain as only that pain equivalent to pain accompanying organ failure or death. The benefits statute actually defined "emergency," not "severe pain." See 42 U.S.C. § 1395w-22(d)(3)(B). Emergency is, in turn, defined in the alternative as a situation involving severe pain or one associated with organ failure or death. Former OLC head Jack Goldsmith, among many others, criticized this reasoning. Goldsmith (2007), pp. 144–50. The OLC subsequently expressly repudiated its reliance on this statute. See Memorandum from Daniel Levin, Acting Assistant Attorney General, to James B. Comey, Deputy Attorney General (Dec. 30, 2004), available at http://www.usdoj.gov/olc/18usc23402340a2.htm.

31. See Executive Order of George W. Bush (Feb. 7, 2002); Executive Order of George W. Bush (July 20, 2007), <http://www.whitehouse.gov/news/releases/2007/07/20070720-4.html> (reaffirming "unlawful combatant" determination).

32. See Memorandum from Jay S. Bybee, Assistant Attorney General, to Alberto R. Gonzales, Counsel to the President (Aug. 1, 2002), in Greenberg and Dratel (2005).

33. For a magisterial analysis, see the booklength two-part article on the commander-in-chief power, Barron and Lederman (2008), written by two former OLC lawyers who have since rejoined the OLC in the Obama Administration.

34. David Luban, "Natural Law as Professional Ethics: A Reading of Fuller," in Luban (2007), 107–8.

35. Fiss (1982); Schön (1983).

36. See D'Amato (1983), pp. 1–3, for an example of definitions of legal determinacy given in mathematical terms. See also the proposal by U.S. Circuit Judge Frank Easterbrook, quoted in Levinson (1987), p. 375:

> [S]omething is frivolous only when (a) we've decided the very point, and recently, against the person reasserting it, or (b) 99 of 100 practicing lawyers would be 99 percent sure that the position is untenable, and the other 1 percent would be 60 percent sure it's untenable.

37. ABA Standing Comm. on Prof'l Ethics, Formal Op. 85-352 (July 7, 1985).

38. Treasury Dept. Circular 230, 31 C.F.R., Subtitle A, Part 10, § 10.34(a), (d)(1). This regulation uses the language of "a realistic possibility of being sustained on the merits."

39. Mark Suchman reports one finding of the ABA Litigation Section's study of the ethics of large-firm lawyers is that associates "frequently discussed morality in terms of how an action would appear in a newspaper or to a judge or jury." At least associates employed this heuristic; Suchman reports that partners tended not to see ethical issues at all, and analyzed the case studies used by the investigators solely in terms of considerations like reputation and strategy. Suchman (1998), pp. 844–45.

40. Fried (2004), p. 1232.

41. Quoted in McLean and Elkind (2003), pp. 142–43.

42. Luban (1988), pp. 58–66.

43. For a strong defense of the idea that criminal defense lawyers have no obligation at all to respect the law, see Smith (2003). Smith argues that criminal defense lawyers are only prudentially (she says "pragmatically") required to respect the bounds of the law, which is an untenable position. However, a lawyer's belief that she does not have a genuine nonprudential obligation to respect the law would entail the belief that other actors within the legal system, including the prosecutor and judge, also do not have an obligation to respect the law. There would be a practical contradiction if the criminal defense lawyer held that belief while simultaneously demanding compliance by prosecutors and judges. Nevertheless, Smith's conclusion, that a criminal defense lawyer should "engage in advocacy that is as close to the line as possible, and, indeed, should test the line," ibid., p. 90, is supportable on the basis of a reasonable division of labor among prosecutors, defense lawyers, and judges, who collectively aim at a plurality of competing ends.

44. Model Rules, Rule 3.1, cmt. [3] ("The lawyer's obligations under this Rule are subordinate to federal or state constitutional law that entitles a defendant in a criminal matter to the assistance of counsel in presenting a claim or contention that otherwise would be prohibited by this Rule."). The Supreme Court has held that a lawyer does not have a constitutional duty to present every arguable legal issue potentially assertable on appeal, even if the client insists that the claims be briefed and argued. *Jones v. Barnes*, 463 U.S. 745 (1983). However, if the lawyer seeks the court's permission to withdraw from representing the client, because the client's appeal would be legally frivolous, the lawyer must bring to the court's attention anything that arguably might support the appeal. *Anders v. California*, 386 U.S. 738 (1967), held to be non-mandatory by *Smith v. Robbins*, 528 U.S. 259 (2000). The Court in *Jones* tried to distinguish *Anders*, by stating that the federal constitution required a lawyer to "support his client's appeal to the best of his ability," but part of lending effective support to the client's appeal was winnowing out weak arguments to concentrate on those with a higher likelihood of success. For the purposes of the argument here, however, the important point is that *Jones* and *Anders* involve client challenges to their lawyers' judgments of frivolousness, *not* restrictions imposed by courts or bar authorities on the assertion of frivolous arguments.

45. Restatement § 110(2) ("a lawyer for the defendant in a criminal proceeding ... may so defend the proceeding as to require that the prosecutor establish every necessary element."). The criminal defense lawyer's right, and even duty, to put the state to its proof is derived from several constitutional rights enjoyed by the defendant, including the presumption of innocence and the evidentiary requirement that the state prove its case beyond a reasonable doubt, *In re Winship*, 397 U.S. 358 (1972), *Mullaney v. Wilbur*, 421 U.S. 684 (1975), and the due process requirement that the jury find all elements of the state's case beyond a reasonable doubt, *Apprendi v. New Jersey*, 530 U.S. 466 (2000).

46. See Freedman and Smith (2002), §§ 2.03, 2.04.

47. Simon (1998), pp. 173–79.

48. See the analysis in Hazard (2005), chs. 2 and 3.

49. Compare Model Rules, Rule 2.1 (advisor) and Rule 3.1 (advocate).

50. See, e.g., *FDIC v. O'Melveny & Myers*, 969 F.2d 744 (9th Cir. 1992), *rev'd*, 512 U.S. 79 (1994), *aff'd in relevant respects on remand*, 61 F.3d 17 (9th Cir. 1995).

51. Compare 17 C.F.R. § 205.3(b)(2)-(3) (duty to report where representing issuer in non-litigation context) with 17 C.F.R. § 205.3(b)(7)(ii) (no duty to report up where lawyer retained "[t]o assert, consistent with his or her professional obligations, a colorable defense on behalf of the issuer ... in any investigation or judicial or administrative proceeding relating to such evidence of a material violation").

52. See, e.g., *Klein v. Boyd*, Fed. Sec. Rep. ¶ 90,136 (3d Cir. 1998), *vacated on grant of rehearing en banc* (reprinted in Hazard [2005], p. 191).

53. The Model Rules provide that "[a] lawyer shall not counsel a client to engage, or assist a client, in conduct that the lawyer *knows* is criminal or fraudulent." Model Rules, Rule 1.2(d) (emphasis added). The knowledge requirement here may cause

lawyers to believe they are permitted to advise clients on the basis of weakly supported interpretive judgments. The idea would be that if there were any plausibility at all to the interpretation, a lawyer does not know it is frivolous, and therefore that the client is acting without an adequate legal basis. Notice, further, that the Model Rules formulation does not talk in terms of the client acting "unlawfully" but rather engaging in conduct that is "criminal or fraudulent." This language may tempt lawyers to think they can advise clients to engage in conduct that is not defined as a crime or a civil fraud under the law of the relevant jurisdiction. The Model Code did permit, but not require, the lawyer to refuse to engage in conduct that the lawyer "believes to be unlawful." Model Code, DR 7-101(B)(2). Although lawyers sometimes forget the limited scope of the disciplinary rules, they are only the bar's vision of ethically sound legal practice; they are legally enforceable in grievance proceedings, but they do not trump generally applicable legal rules prohibiting conduct, which can be enforced by courts despite a bar disciplinary rule apparently permitting it. See Koniak (1992). Thus, if a state bar disciplinary rule permits a lawyer to counsel a client to engage in unlawful (but not criminal or fraudulent) conduct, the lawyer runs the risk of being held liable to the client for malpractice if the client's unlawful conduct exposes the client to legal liability. See, e.g., *FDIC v. O'Melveny & Myers*, 969 F.2d 744 (9th Cir. 1992), *rev'd*, 512 U.S. 79 (1994), *aff'd in relevant respects on remand*, 61 F.3d 17 (9th Cir. 1995).

The Restatement, which was designed to take generally applicable law into account, would not permit lawyers to engage in the evasion of advising the client on the basis of weakly supported interpretive judgments. Referring to agency and contract law, it states that "a lawyer retains authority that may not be overridden by a contract with or an instruction from the client to refuse to perform, counsel, or assist future or ongoing acts in the representation that the lawyer *reasonably believes* to be *unlawful*." Restatement § 23(1) (emphasis added).

54. See Coffee (2003); Coffee (2004); Coffee (2006).

55. Gilson (1984).

56. See, e.g., Luban (2007), pp. 32–40; Gillers (2005), pp. 360–96; Rhode (2000a), pp. 81–105; Frankel (1975).

57. See, e.g., *Washington State Physicians Insurance & Exchange v. Fisons Corp.*, 858 P.2d 1054 (Wash. 1993).

58. I have heard this story on numerous occasions, but have been unable to ascertain its veracity. It is offered here as a bit of folklore about good lawyering, not as a historically accurate event.

59. Michigan Bar Association Ethics Op. CI-1164 (1987).

60. Mitchell (1987).

61. See Rhode (2000a), p. 97.

62. Hart and Sacks (1994), pp. 143–50. Hart and Sacks are talking about attributing a single purpose to a piece of legislation, but their legal process materials have come to be understood as embodying the more general point that the law should be understood as a purposive activity. As David Luban shows in an insightful discussion, Lon Fuller is another legal theorist who emphasizes the purposive nature of law. See Luban (2007),

pp. 108–9. Outside the specific context of law, Alasdair MacIntyre relies on the concept of a *practice*, as "any coherent and complex form of socially established cooperative human activity through which goods internal to that form of activity are realized in the course of trying to achieve those standards of excellence which are appropriate to, and partially definitive of, that form of activity." MacIntyre (1984), p. 187. The theory of interpretation I defend here is indebted substantially to the idea that the purposiveness or goal-directedness of any practice—what it is all about, so to speak—is a non-circular source of obligations internal to the practice, because it would be incoherent to claim to be engaging in any activity without caring about the goods that are internal to that form of activity. Ibid., pp. 190–91. Cf. Bingham (2007), p. 78 (arguing that an aspect of the rule of law is that officials must exercise power that has been conferred on them for the purpose for which those powers were conferred).

63. Weinrib (1988), pp. 953–54 (borrowing this analysis from Roberto Unger, who of course is a critic of the idea of legal formalism). On the idea of internal or immanent rationality, Rawls says something important and general about how objectivity is a property of a discipline of reasoning, not something "outside" that can be used as a yardstick:

> [W]e assert a judgment and think it correct because we suppose we have correctly applied the relevant principles and criteria of practical reasoning. This parallels the reply of mathematicians who, when asked why they believe there are an infinity of primes, say: any mathematician knows the proof. The proof lays out the reasoning on which their belief is based .... [B]eing able to give the proof, or to state sufficient reasons for the judgment, is already the best possible explanation of the beliefs of those who are reasonable and rational.

Rawls (1993), p. 120.

64. Joseph Raz, "The Politics of the Rule of Law," in Raz (1994); Raz (1979), pp. 213–14.

65. I am indebted here to Steven Schwarcz's work on asset securitization and structured finance transactions. See Schwarcz (1994); Schwarcz (2002).

66. Cf. Siegel (2001), p. 316 (using the idea that the venue statute is "all about" convenience to flesh out the meaning of the statutory text).

67. Stone (2002), p. 192.

68. Wendel (2005a).

69. See Kennedy (1976).

70. Farber (1992); Eskridge and Frickey (1990).

71. Postema (1987); Fiss (1982).

72. Fiss (1982), p. 744.

73. The discussion in this paragraph is drawn from two careful and helpful articles on Hart's practice conception of rules. See Shapiro (2001); Zipursky (2001).

74. Hart (1994), p. 57.

75. Zipursky (2001), p. 225.

76. Dworkin (1977), p. 51.

77. Shapiro (2006), p. 1166.

78. Jules Coleman, "Incorporationism, Conventionality, and the Practical Difference Thesis," in Coleman (2001), pp. 110–11.

79. Hart (1994), p. 56 ("[I]f a social rule is to exist some at least must look upon the behavior in question as a general standard to be followed by the group as a whole.").

80. Hart writes: "What is necessary is that there should be a critical reflective attitude to certain patterns of behavior as a common standard, and that this should display itself in criticism (including self-criticism), demands for conformity, and in acknowledgments that such criticism and demands are justified, all of which find their characteristic expression in the normative terminology of 'ought,' 'must,' and 'should,' 'right' and 'wrong.'" Ibid., p. 57. He returns later to the idea that the legitimacy of a norm is bound up with the acceptance by others of the norm as a standard for justified criticism: "[W]here rules exist, deviations from them are not merely grounds for a prediction that hostile reactions will follow or that a court will apply sanctions to those who break them, but are also a reason or justification for such reaction and for applying the sanctions." Ibid., p. 84.

Fred Schauer has cited Brian Simpson's insight that Hart really should have talked about a "practice of recognition," with "practice" being understood in the Wittgensteinian sense, rather than a *rule* of recognition. Simpson (1986). I owe this citation, and appreciation of its significance, to Schauer's plenary lecture at the IVR World Congress in Krakow. See Schauer (2007) for the written version of this lecture, which does not, however, cite Simpson. (The discussion of Hart's practice conception of rules may have come up during the questions and answers.) I think Schauer and Simpson are absolutely right that the notion of a practice, as developed by Wittgenstein and Alasdair MacIntyre, is crucial to understanding what legal reasoning and argumentation is all about, beyond solving the theoretical problem of how social facts can create obligations.

81. Hart (1994), p. 89.

82. Ibid., p. 116 ("if [the rule of recognition] is to exist at all, [it] must be regarded from the internal point of view as a public, common standard of correct judicial decision, and not as something which each judge merely obeys for his part only.").

83. Ibid., pp. 100–101.

84. Shapiro (2001), p. 155.

85. Hart draws the distinction in terms of acting out of obligation from acting because one feels obliged. Hart (1994), pp. 82–83, 88–89. Giving up one's wallet at gunpoint reveals a sense of being obliged to act, for fear of experiencing the consequences of inaction. When someone acts out of obligation, by contrast, the explanation of the person's action makes reference to normative standards, not merely the desire to avoid harm.

86. Ibid., p. 57.

87. Hart (1994), p. 83.

88. Ibid., p. 116. Hart insists that "if [the rule of recognition] is to exist at all, [it] must be regarded from the internal point of view as a public, common standard of correct judicial decision, and not as something which each judge merely obeys for his part only." And since he further argues that the rule of recognition is necessary for there to be a legal system at all, *see* ibid., p. 100, it is clear that the recognition by judges that the law is a reason as such for making decisions is the conceptual heart of legality.

89. Ibid., p. 116.

90. See Zipursky (2001), p. 228.

91. Shapiro (2007), p. 8. For Dworkin's term "pedigree," see Ronald Dworkin, "The Model of Rules I," in Dworkin (1977), p. 17.

92. Zipursky (2001), p. 235.

93. H.L.A. Hart, "Postscript," in Hart (1994), p. 265.

94. Discussions of this problem with Ted Schneyer and Sarah Cravens were quite helpful. I'm pretty sure they still disagree with me, but at least I think I've avoided making some of the mistakes they warned me against.

95. See Pepper (1986), pp. 627–28.

96. Model Rules, Rule 1.2(d).

97. Hart (1994), p. 116.

98. Pepper (1995), pp. 1567, 1570–71. The terminology of conduct rules and decision rules is from Dan-Cohen (1984).

99. Pepper (1986), p. 629; see also Pepper (1995), pp. 1564–71.

100. See Simon (2006).

101. Pepper (1995), p. 1570.

102. Edelman (2002), p. 192 (italics in original); see also Edelman (2004), p. 238; Edelman (2005).

103. Edelman (2002), pp. 196–97. Edelman refers to lawyers, managers such as human resources personnel and EEO compliance officers, consultants, and other specialists, both inside and outside organizations, as "compliance professionals." Edelman (2004), p. 239. These professionals act as "filters through whom legal ideas must pass on their way to organizations." Ibid.

104. Edelman (2002), p. 198.

105. Ibid.

106. Edelman (2004), p. 242.

107. Edelman (2002), p. 202 ("The professions will continue to take strong legal principles and infuse them with managerial values so that they take on a meaning more consistent with the traditional managerial prerogatives of efficiency, control, and profit.").

108. Ibid., p. 201 ("Legal endogeneity allows patterns of injustice that become institutionalized in the organizational realm to be incorporated into—and legitimated by—public legal rules and norms.").

109. Ibid., pp. 199–200.

110. *Faragher v. City of Boca Raton*, 118 S. Ct. 1115 (1998).
111. Cover (1983), p. 42.

Notes to Conclusion

1. Friedman (1985), p. 639.
2. Ibid., pp. 94–97.
3. Galanter (2005).
4. Shklar (1964), p. 17.
5. David Luban, "Tales of Terror: Lessons for Lawyers from the 'War on Terrorism,'" Keynote Presentation at Third International Legal Ethics Conference, Gold Coast, Australia.
6. Gordon (1998b), p. 321.
7. Gordon (2009), pp. 1173–74.
8. One excellent contribution is Regan (2004).
9. Kronman (1993).
10. Markovits (2008).

Bibliography

Citations to primary legal sources conform to the standards of *A Uniform System of Citation*, the so-called Bluebook published by the law reviews of Harvard, Yale, Columbia, and Penn, except for references to frequently cited sources for the law governing lawyers. The 2003 version of the American Bar Association's *Model Rules of Professional Conduct*, with the most current amendments, is cited as "Model Rules, Rule xx," the ABA's now superseded *Model Code of Professional Responsibility* is cited as "Model Code, Canon [or EC, or DR] xx," and the American Law Institute's *Restatement (Third) of the Law Governing Lawyers*, officially published in 2001, is cited as "Restatement § xx."

In addition to the traditional sources cited here, I was assisted from time to time by the emerging medium of legal weblogs, or blogs. Although posting on blogs does not generally rise to the level of "real" scholarship, at least one exception should be made for the tireless and extremely high-quality legal commentary posted by Marty Lederman at the "Balkinization" blog (http://balkin.blogspot.com/). My understanding of the law of warfare, executive power, and the specific legal issues surrounding torture and the treatment of detainees was greatly enhanced by these posts. Of course, I do not agree with Lederman on all points, but he should be acknowledged as having essentially produced a major work of scholarship, in electronic form, on the state of post-9/11 national security law in the United States, from which I learned a considerable amount while working on the ethical issues pertaining to the torture memos.

*

Abel, Richard L. (1989) *American Lawyers* (New York: Oxford University Press).

Alexander, Larry and Emily Sherwin. (2001) *The Rule of Rules: Morality, Rules, and the Dilemmas of Law* (Durham, N.C.: Duke University Press).

Alexander, Larry and Frederick Schauer. (1997) "On Extrajudicial Constitutional Interpretation." *Harvard Law Review* 110: 1359–87.

Applbaum, Arthur Isak. (1999) *Ethics for Adversaries* (Princeton, N.J.: Princeton University Press).

Arrow, Kenneth. (1973) "Social Responsibility and Economic Efficiency." *Public Policy* 21: 303–17.

Audi, Robert. (1997) *Moral Knowledge and Ethical Character* (New York: Oxford University Press).

Baird, Douglas G., Robert H. Gertner, and Randall C. Picker. (1994) *Game Theory and the Law.* (Cambridge, Mass.: Harvard University Press).

Baird, Douglas G. and Robert K. Rasmussen. (2002) "Four (or Five) Easy Lessons from Enron." *Vanderbilt Law Review* 55: 1787–812.

Barceló, John J., III and Roger C. Cramton, eds. (1999) *Lawyers' Practice and Ideals: A Comparative View* (The Hague: Kluwer Law International).

Barron, David J. and Martin S. Lederman. (2008) "The Commander in Chief at the Lowest Ebb" Parts I and II. *Harvard Law Review* 121: 689–804.

Barry, Brian. (1995) *Justice as Impartiality* (New York: Oxford University Press).

Beauchamp, Tom L. and James F. Childress. (1994) *Principles of Biomedical Ethics* (4th ed.) (New York: Oxford University Press).

Berlin, Isaiah. (1990) *The Crooked Timber of Humanity* (Henry Hardy, ed. Princeton, N.J.: Princeton University Press).

———. (1997) *The Proper Study of Mankind* (Henry Hardy and Roger Hausheer, eds. New York: Farrar, Straus and Giroux).

Bingham, Thomas (Baron of Cornhill). (2007) "The Rule of Law." *Cambridge Law Journal* 66: 67–85.

Blackburn, Simon. (1998) *Ruling Passions: A Theory of Practical Reasoning* (New York: Oxford University Press).

Blumberg, Abraham. (1967) "The Practice of Law as a Confidence Game." *Law and Society Review* 1: 15–39.

Bolt, Robert. (1966) *A Man for All Seasons* (New York: Vintage Books).

Boon, Andrew and Jennifer Levin. (1999) *The Ethics and Conduct of Lawyers in England and Wales.* (Oxford: Hart Publishing).

Brink, David O. (1994) "Moral Conflict and Its Structure." *Philosophical Review* 103: 215–47.

Bruff, Harold H. (2009) *Bad Advice: Bush's Lawyers in the War on Terror* (Lawrence, Kan.: University Press of Kansas).

Byron, Michael. (1998) "Satisficing and Optimality." *Ethics* 109: 67–93.

Calabresi, Guido and A. Douglas Melamed. (1972) "Property Rules, Liability Rules, and Inalienability: One View of the Cathedral." *Harvard Law Review* 85: 1089–128.

Christiano, Thomas. (2004) "The Authority of Democracy." *Journal of Political Philosophy* 12: 266–90.

Clayton, Cornell W. (1992) *The Politics of Justice: The Attorney General and the Making of Legal Policy* (Armonk, N.Y.: M.E. Sharpe).

Coffee, John C., Jr. (2003) "The Attorney as Gatekeeper: An Agenda for the SEC." *Columbia Law Review* 103: 1293–316.

———. (2004) "What Caused Enron? A Capsule Social and Economic History of the 1990s." *Cornell Law Review* 89: 269–309.

———. (2006) *Gatekeepers: The Professions and Corporate Governance* (New York: Oxford University Press).

Cohen, Joshua. (1994) "Pluralism and Proceduralism." *Chicago-Kent Law Review* 69: 589–618.

———. (2003) "Procedure and Substance in Deliberative Democracy," in *Philosophy and Democracy* (Thomas Cristiano, ed.) (New York: Oxford University Press).

Coleman, Jules. (1982) "Negative and Positive Positivism." *Journal of Legal Studies* 11: 139–64.

———. (1996) "Authority and Reason," in George (1996).

———, ed. (2001) *Hart's Postscript: Essays on the Postscript to* The Concept of Law. (New York: Oxford University Press).

Coleman, Jules and Scott Shapiro, eds. (2002) *The Oxford Handbook of Jurisprudence and Legal Philosophy*. (New York: Oxford University Press).

Copp, David, ed. (2006) *The Oxford Handbook of Ethical Theory* (New York: Oxford University Press).

Cover, Robert M. (1983) "The Supreme Court 1982 Term—Foreword: *Nomos* and Narrative." *Harvard Law Review* 97: 4–68.

Cramton, Roger C. (2002) "Enron and the Corporate Lawyer: A Primer on Legal and Ethical Issues." *Business Lawyer* 58: 143–88.

Cramton, Roger C. and Lori P. Knowles. (1998) "Professional Secrecy and Its Exceptions: *Spaulding v. Zimmerman* Revisited." *Minnesota Law Review* 83: 63–127.

D'Amato, Anthony. (1983) "Legal Uncertainty." *California Law Review* 71: 1–55.

Dan-Cohen, Meir. (1984) "Decision Rules and Conduct Rules: On Acoustic Separation in Criminal Law." *Harvard Law Review* 97: 625–77.

Daniels, Norman. (1979) "Wide Reflective Equilibrium and Theory Acceptance in Ethics." *Journal of Philosophy* 76: 256–82.

Dare, Tim. (2004) "Mere-Zeal, Hyper-Zeal and the Ethical Obligations of Lawyers." *Legal Ethics* 7: 24–38.

———. (2009) *The Counsel of Rogues?: A Defense of the Standard Conception of the Lawyer's Role* (Aldershot: Ashgate).

Darwall, Steven, Allan Gibbard, and Peter Railton. (1990) "Toward *Fin de siècle* Ethics: Some Trends." *Philosophical Review* 101: 115–89.

Dauer, Edward A. and Arthur Alan Leff. (1977) "Correspondence: The Lawyer as Friend." *Yale Law Journal* 86: 573–84.

Dershowitz, Alan M. (1996) *Reasonable Doubts: The Criminal Justice System and the O. J. Simpson Case* (New York: Touchstone).

Doris, John M. (2002) *Lack of Character: Personality and Moral Behavior* (New York: Cambridge University Press).

Dudziak, Mary L. (2000) *Cold War Civil Rights: Race and the Image of American Democracy* (Princeton, N.J.: Princeton University Press).

Dworkin, Ronald. (1977) *Taking Rights Seriously*. (Cambridge, Mass.: Harvard University Press).

———. (1985) *A Matter of Principle* (Cambridge, Mass.: Harvard University Press).

———. (1986) *Law's Empire*. (Cambridge, Mass.: Harvard University Press).

———. (1996) *Freedom's Law*. (Cambridge, Mass.: Harvard University Press).

Edelman, Lauren B. (2002) "Legality and the Endogeneity of Law," in Robert A. Kagan, et al., eds., *Legality and Community: On the Intellectual Legacy of Philip Selznick* (Lanham, Md.: Rowman & Littlefield).

Edelman, Lauren B. (2004) "The Legal Lives of Private Organizations," in Sarat (2004).

——. (2005) "The Endogeneity of Law: Civil Rights at Work," in Laura Beth Nielsen and Robert L. Nelson, eds., *Handbook on Employment Discrimination Research: Rights and Realities* (Dordrecht: Springer).

Edelman, Lauren B. and Mark C. Suchman. (1997) "The Legal Environments of Organizations." *Annual Review of Sociology* 23: 479–515.

Endicott, Timothy A. O. (2000) *Vagueness in Law* (New York: Oxford University Press).

Eskridge, William N. and Philip P. Frickey. (1990) "Statutory Interpretation as Practical Reasoning." *Stanford Law Review* 42: 321–84.

Eskridge, William N., Jr. (1994) *Dynamic Statutory Interpretation* (Cambridge, Mass.: Harvard University Press).

Farber, Daniel A. (1992) "The Inevitability of Practical Reason: Statutes, Formalism, and the Rule of Law." *Vanderbilt Law Review* 45: 533–48.

Feldman, Heidi Li. (1996) "Codes and Virtues: Can Good Lawyers Be Good Ethical Deliberators?" *Southern California Law Review* 69: 885–948.

Finnis, John. (1980) *Natural Law and Natural Rights*. (New York: Oxford University Press).

Fischel, Daniel R. (1998) "Lawyers and Confidentiality." *University of Chicago Law Review* 1–33.

Fiss, Owen M. (1982) "Objectivity and Interpretation." *Stanford Law Review* 34: 739–63.

Fletcher, George P. (1993) *Loyalty* (New York: Oxford University Press).

Flood, John A. (1983) *Barristers' Clerks: The Law's Middlemen*. (Manchester, UK: Manchester University Press).

Floyd, Timothy W. and John Gallagher (2008). "Legal Ethics, Narrative, and Professional Identity: The Story of David Spaulding." *Mercer Law Review* 59: 941–61.

Forst, Rainer. (2002) *Contexts of Justice: Political Philosophy Beyond Liberalism and Communitarianism* (John M. M. Farrell, trans.) (Berkeley: University of California Press).

Frankel, Marvin E. (1975) "The Search for Truth: An Umpireal View." *University of Pennsylvania Law Review* 123: 1031–59.

Frankfurt, Harry. (2005) *On Bullshit* (Princeton, N.J.: Princeton University Press).

Freedman, Monroe H. (1975) *Lawyers' Ethics in an Adversary System*. (Indianapolis: Bobbs-Merrill).

——. (1995) "The Lawyer's Moral Obligation of Justification." *Texas Law Review* 74: 111–18.

Freedman, Monroe H. and Abbe Smith. (2002) *Understanding Lawyers' Ethics*. (Newark, N.J.: Matthew Bender & Co., 2d ed.).

Freeman, Samuel, ed. (2003) *The Cambridge Companion to Rawls* (New York: Cambridge University Press).

Fried, Charles. (1976) "The Lawyer as Friend: The Moral Foundations of the Lawyer–Client Relation." *Yale Law Journal* 85: 1060–89.

———. (2004) "A Meditation on the First Principles of Judicial Ethics." *Hofstra Law Review* 32: 1227–44.

Friedman, Lawrence M. (1985) *A History of American Law* (New York: Touchstone) (2d ed.).

Fuller, Lon L. (1958) "Positivism and Fidelity to Law: A Reply to Professor Hart." *Harvard Law Review* 71: 630–72.

———. (1969) *The Morality of Law* (New Haven: Yale University Press) (rev'd ed.).

Galanter, Marc. (1998) "The Faces of Mistrust: The Image of Lawyers in Public Opinion, Jokes, and Political Discourse." *University of Cincinnati Law Review* 66: 805–46.

———. (2005) *Lowering the Bar: Lawyer Jokes and Legal Culture* (Madison, Wis.: University of Wisconsin Press).

Galston, William A. (2002) *Liberal Pluralism* (New York: Cambridge University Press).

George, Robert P., ed. (1996) *The Autonomy of Law: Essays on Legal Positivism* (New York: Oxford University Press).

Gewirth, Alan. (1986) "Professional Ethics: The Separatist Thesis." *Ethics* 96: 282–300.

Gillers, Stephen. (2005) *Regulation of Lawyers: Problems of Law and Ethics* (New York: Aspen Publishers, 7th ed.).

———. (2009) *Regulation of Lawyers: Problems of Law and Ethics* (New York: Aspen Publishers, 8th ed.).

Gilson, Ronald J. (1984) "Value Creation by Business Lawyers: Legal Skills and Asset Pricing." *Yale Law Journal* 94: 239–313.

Goldman, Alan H. (1980) *The Moral Foundations of Professional Ethics* (Savage, Md.: Rowman & Littlefield).

Goldsmith, Jack. (2007) *The Terror Presidency* (New York: Norton).

Gordon, Robert W. (1998a) "The Ethical Worlds of Large-Firm Litigators: Preliminary Observations." Fordham Law Review 67: 709–38.

———. (1998b) "A Collective Failure of Nerve: The Bar's Response to *Kaye, Scholer*." *Law and Social Inquiry* 25: 315–22.

———. (2003) "A New Role for Lawyers?: The Corporate Counselor After Enron." *Connecticut Law Review* 35: 1185–216.

———. (2009) "The Citizen-Lawyer—A Brief Informal History of a Myth with Some Basis in Reality." *William & Mary Law Review* 50: 1169–206.

Gordon, Robert W. and William H. Simon. (1992) "The Redemption of Professionalism?" in Nelson, Trubek, and Solomon (1992).

Gowans, Christopher. (1994) *Innocence Lost: An Examination of Inescapable Moral Wrongdoing* (New York: Oxford University Press).

Graber, Mark A. (2006) *Dred Scott and the Problem of Constitutional Evil* (New York: Cambridge University Press).

Gray, John. (1996) *Isaiah Berlin* (Princeton, N.J.: Princeton University Press).

Greenawalt, Kent. (1987) *Conflicts of Law and Morality.* (New York: Oxford University Press).

Greenawalt, Kent. (1996) "Too Thin and Too Rich: Distinguishing Features of Legal Positivism," in George (1996).

Greenberg, Karen J. and Joshua L. Dratel. (2005) *The Torture Papers: The Road to Abu Ghraib* (New York: Cambridge University Press).

Gutmann, Amy and Dennis Thompson. (1996) *Democracy and Disagreement* (Cambridge, Mass.: Harvard University Press).

Hampshire, Stuart. (1983) *Morality and Conflict* (Cambridge, Mass.: Harvard University Press).

———. (1989) *Innocence and Experience* (Cambridge, Mass.: Harvard University Press).

Hart, H.L.A. (1955) "Are There Any Natural Rights?" *Philosophical Review* 64:175–91.

———. (1958) "Positivism and the Separation of Law and Morals." *Harvard Law Review* 71: 593–629.

———. (1982) *Essays on Bentham: Studies in Jurisprudence and Political Theory.* (New York: Oxford University Press).

———. (1994) *The Concept of Law*. (New York: Oxford University Press, 2d ed.).

Hart, Henry M., Jr. and Albert M. Sacks. (1994) *The Legal Process: Basic Problems in the Making and Application of Law* (William N. Eskridge, Jr. and Philip P. Frickey eds.) (Westbury, N.Y.: Foundation Press).

Hazard, Geoffrey C., Jr. and Angelo Dondi. (2004) *Legal Ethics: A Comparative Study* (Stanford, Cal.: Stanford University Press).

Hazard, Geoffrey C., Jr., and W. William Hodes. (2001) *The Law of Lawyering*. (Gaithersburg, Md.: Aspen Law and Business, 3d ed.).

Hazard, Geoffrey C., Jr., et al. (2005) *The Law and Ethics of Lawyering*. (New York: Foundation Press, 4th ed.).

Heinz, John P. and Edward O. Laumann. (1982) *Chicago Lawyers: The Social Structure of the Bar* (Chicago: Northwestern University Press) (rev'd ed.).

Hobbes, Thomas. (1994) *Leviathan*. (Edwin Curley, ed. Indianapolis: Hackett Publishing Co.).

Hodes, W. William. (1999) "The Professional Duty to Horseshed Witnesses—Zealously, Within the Bounds of the Law." *Texas Tech Law Review* 30: 1343–66.

Hohfeld, Wesley N. (1923) "Some Fundamental Legal Conceptions as Applied in Judicial Reasoning." *Yale Law Journal* 23: 16–59.

Holmes, Oliver Wendell, Jr. (1897) "The Path of the Law." *Harvard Law Review* 10: 457–78.

Hurd, Heidi M. (1991) "Challenging Authority." *Yale Law Journal* 1611–77.

———. (1995) "Interpreting Authorities," in Marmor (1995).

Hutchinson, Allan C. (1999) *Legal Ethics and Professional Responsibility* (Toronto: Irwin Law).

Johnston, David. (1994) *The Idea of a Liberal Theory* (Princeton, N.J.: Princeton University Press).

Jonsen, Albert R. and Stephen Toulmin. (1988) *The Abuse of Casuistry: A History of Moral Reasoning* (Berkeley: University of California Press).

Kagan, Robert A. (2001) *Adversarial Legalism: The American Way of Law* (Cambridge, Mass.: Harvard University Press).

Kennedy, Duncan. (1976) "Form and Substance in Private Law Adjudication." *Harvard Law Review* 89: 1685–778.

———. (1997) *A Critique of Adjudication {fin de siècle}* (Cambridge, Mass.: Harvard University Press).

King, Martin Luther, Jr. (1963) "Letter from Birmingham Jail," in Hugo Adam Bedau, ed., *Civil Disobedience in Focus* (New York: Routledge 1991).

Koniak, Susan P. (1992) "The Law Between the Bar and the State." *North Carolina Law Review* 70: 1389–487.

———. (2003) "When the Hurlyburly's Done: The Bar's Struggle with the SEC." *Columbia Law Review* 103: 1236–80.

Korsgaard, Christine M. (1996a) *Creating the Kingdom of Ends* (Cambridge: Cambridge University Press).

———. (1996b) *The Sources of Normativity* (New York: Cambridge University Press).

———. (2003) "Realism and Constructivism in Twentieth-Century Moral Philosophy." *Journal of Philosophical Research* 99–121.

Kronman, Anthony T. (1993) *The Lost Lawyer: Failing Ideals of the Legal Profession* (Cambridge, Mass.: Harvard University Press).

Kruse, Katherine R. (2006) "Fortress in the Sand: The Plural Values of Client-Centered Representation." *Clinical Law Review* 12: 369–440 (2006).

Langevoort, Donald C. (1993) "Where Were the Lawyers? A Behavioral Inquiry into Lawyers' Responsibility for Clients' Fraud." *Vanderbilt Law Review* 46: 75–119.

Larmore, Charles E. (1987) *Patterns of Moral Complexity* (New York: Cambridge University Press).

Lasser, Mitchel de S.-O.-l'E. (2004) *Judicial Deliberations: A Comparative Analysis of Judicial Transparency and Legitimacy* (New York: Oxford University Press).

Leubsdorf, John. (2001) *Man in His Original Dignity: Legal Ethics in France.* (Aldershot: Ashgate).

Levi, Edward H. (1949) *An Introduction to Legal Reasoning* (Chicago: University of Chicago Press).

Levinson, Sanford. (1987) "Frivolous Cases: Do Lawyers Really Know Anything at All?" *Osgoode Hall Law Review* 24: 353–78.

———. (1993) "Identifying the Jewish Lawyer: Reflections on the Construction of Professional Identity." *Cardozo Law Review* 14: 1577–612.

Lichtblau, Eric. (2008) *Bush's Law: The Remaking of American Justice* (New York: Pantheon Books).

Llewellyn, Karl N. (1930) *The Bramble Bush: On Our Law and Its Study* (New York: Oceana).

Luban, David. (1984) "The Sources of Legal Ethics: A German-American Comparison of Lawyers' Professional Duties." *Rabels Zeitschrift für ausländisches und internationales Privatrecht* 48: 245–88.

Luban, David. (1986) "The Lysistratian Prerogative: A Reply to Stephen Pepper." *American Bar Foundation Research Journal* 1986: 637–49.

———. (1988) *Lawyers and Justice: An Ethical Study* (Princeton, N.J.: Princeton University Press).

———. (1990) "Freedom and Constraint in Legal Ethics: Some Mid-Course Corrections to *Lawyers and Justice*." *Maryland Law Review* 49: 424–62.

———. (1996) "Legal Ideals and Moral Obligations: A Comment on Simon." *William and Mary Law Review* 38: 255–67.

———. (1997) "The Bad Man and the Good Lawyer: A Centennial Essay on Holmes's *The Path of the Law*." *New York University Law Review* 72: 1547–83.

———. (2007) *Legal Ethics and Human Dignity* (New York: Cambridge University Press).

———. (2008) "The Inevitability of Conscience: A Response to My Critics." *Cornell Law Review* 93: 1437–65.

———, ed. (1983) *The Good Lawyer: Lawyers' Roles and Lawyers' Ethics* (Totowa, N.J.: Rowman & Allanheld).

Lyons, David. (1977) "Principles, Positivism, and Legal Theory." *Yale Law Journal* 87: 415–35.

———. (1984) *Ethics and the Rule of Law* (New York: Cambridge University Press).

MacCormick, Neil. (2007) *Institutions of Law: An Essay in Legal Theory* (Oxford: Oxford University Press).

MacIntyre, Alasdair. (1984) *After Virtue* (Notre Dame, Ind.: University of Notre Dame Press, 2d ed.).

Mann, Kenneth. (1985) *Defending White-Collar Crime* (New Haven: Yale University Press).

Markovits, Daniel. (2003) "Legal Ethics from the Lawyer's Point of View." *Yale Journal of Law and the Humanities* 15: 209–93.

———. (2006) "Adversary Advocacy and the Authority of Adjudication." *Fordham Law Review* 75: 1367–95.

———. (2008) *A Modern Legal Ethics: Adversary Advocacy in a Democratic Age* (Princeton, N.J.: Princeton University Press).

McLean, Bethany and Peter Elkind. (2003) *The Smartest Guys in the Room: The Amazing Rise and Scandalous Fall of Enron* (New York: Portfolio).

Merryman, John Henry. (1985) *The Civil Law Tradition* (Stanford, Cal.: Stanford University Press, 2d ed.).

Michelman, Frank. (1988) "Law's Republic." *Yale Law Journal* 97: 1493–537.

Mitchell, John. (1987) "Reasonable Doubts Are Where You Find Them: A Response to Professor Subin's Position on the Criminal Lawyer's 'Different Mission'." *Georgetown Journal of Legal Ethics* 1: 339–61.

Moon, J. Donald. (1994) *Constructing Community: Moral Pluralism and Tragic Conflicts* (Princeton, N.J.: Princeton University Press).

Moore, Michael S. (1985) "A Natural Law Theory of Interpretation." *Southern California Law Review* 58: 277–398.

——. (1989) "Authority, Law, and Razian Reasons." *Southern California Law Review* 62: 827–96.

Moss, Randolph D. (2000) "Executive Branch Legal Interpretation: A Perspective from the Office of Legal Counsel." *Administrative Law Review* 52: 1303–30.

Mosteller, Robert P. (2007) "The Duke Lacrosse Case, Innocence, and False Identifications: A Fundamental Failure to 'Do Justice'." *Fordham Law Review* 76: 1337–412.

Murphy, Liam B. (2000) *Moral Demands in Nonideal Theory* (New York: Oxford University Press).

Nagel, Thomas. (1979) *Mortal Questions.* (Princeton, N.J.: Princeton University Press).

——. (1986) *The View from Nowhere* (New York: Oxford University Press).

Nelson, Robert L. (1998) "The Discovery Process as a Circle of Blame: Institutional, Professional, and Socio-Economic Factors that Contribute to Unreasonable, Inefficient, and Amoral Behavior in Corporate Litigation." *Fordham Law Review* 67: 773–808.

Nelson, Robert L., David M. Trubek, and Rayman L. Solomon. (1992) *Lawyers' Ideals / Lawyers' Practices: Transformations in the American Legal Profession* (Ithaca, N.Y.: Cornell University Press).

Nozick, Robert. (1974) *Anarchy, State, and Utopia* (New York: Basic Books).

Nussbaum, Martha C. (1992) "Human Functioning and Social Justice: In Defense of Aristotelian Essentialism." *Political Theory* 20: 202–46.

——. (1999) *Sex and Social Justice* (New York: Oxford University Press).

Ogletree, Charles, Jr. (1993) "Beyond Justifications: Seeking Motivations to Sustain Public Defenders." *Harvard Law Review* 106: 1239–94.

Patterson, Dennis, ed. (1996) *A Companion to Philosophy of Law and Legal Theory.* (Malden, Mass.: Blackwell).

Pepper, Stephen L. (1986) "The Lawyer's Amoral Ethical Role: A Defense, A Problem, and Some Possibilities." *American Bar Foundation Research Journal* 1986: 613–35.

——. (1995) "Counseling at the Limits of the Law: An Essay in the Jurisprudence and Ethics of Lawyering." *Yale Law Journal* 104: 1545–610.

——. (1998) "Why Confidentiality?" *Law and Social Inquiry* 23: 331–37.

——. (1999) "Lawyers' Ethics in the Gap Between Law and Justice." *South Texas Law Review* 40: 181–205.

Phillips, Michael. (1985) "Reflections on the Transition from Ideal to Non-Ideal Theory." *Noûs* 19: 551–70.

Pileggi, Nicholas. (1985) *Wiseguy: Life in a Mafia Family* (New York: Simon & Schuster).

Pogge, Thomas. (2007) *John Rawls: His Life and Theory of Justice* (Oxford: Oxford University Press).

Postema, Gerald J. (1980) "Moral Responsibility in Professional Ethics." *New York University Law Review* 55: 63–89.

——. (1987) "'Protestant' Interpretation and Social Practices." *Law and Philosophy* 6: 283–319.

Postema, Gerald J. (2002) "Philosophy of the Common Law," in Coleman and Shapiro (2002).

Powers, William C., Jr. (2002) "Report of the Special Investigative Committee of the Board of Directors of Enron Corp."

Rawls, John. (1955) "Two Concepts of Rules." *Philosophical Review* 64: 3–32.

———. (1971) *A Theory of Justice*. (Cambridge, Mass.: Harvard University Press).

———. (1993) *Political Liberalism*. (New York: Columbia University Press) (paperback edition).

Raz, Joseph. (1979) *The Authority of Law*. (New York: Oxford University Press).

———. (1985) "Authority and Justification." *Philosophy and Public Affairs* 14: 3–29.

———. (1986) *The Morality of Freedom*. (New York: Oxford University Press).

———. (1994) *Ethics in the Public Domain*. (New York: Oxford University Press).

———. (2006) "The Problem of Authority: Revisiting the Service Conception." *Minnesota Law Review* 90: 1003–44.

———. (2009) *Between Authority and Interpretation* (Oxford: Oxford University Press).

———, ed. (1990) *Authority*. (New York: New York University Press).

Regan, Milton C., Jr. (2004) *Eat What You Kill: The Fall of a Wall Street Lawyer* (Ann Arbor: University of Michigan Press).

Rhode, Deborah L. (1994) *Professional Responsibility: Ethics By the Pervasive Method* (New York: Aspen Publishers).

———. (2000a) *In the Interests of Justice: Reforming the Legal Profession*. (New York: Oxford University Press).

———, ed. (2000b) *Ethics in Practice: Lawyers' Roles, Responsibilities, and Regulation*. (New York: Oxford University Press).

Ross, W. D. (1930) *The Right and the Good* (Indianapolis: Hackett Publishing Co., reprint edition).

Sarat, Austin. (1998b) "Enactments of Professionalism: A Study of Judges' and Lawyers' Accounts of Ethics and Civility in Litigation." *Fordham Law Review* 67: 809–35.

———, ed. (2004) *The Blackwell Companion to Law and Society* (Malden, Mass.: Blackwell).

Sarat, Austin and Stuart Scheingold, eds. (1998) *Cause Lawyering: Political Commitments and Professional Responsibilities*. (New York: Oxford University Press).

Sarat, Austin and William L. F. Felsteiner. (1995) *Divorce Lawyers and Their Clients* (New York: Oxford University Press).

Scanlon, T. M. (1998) *What We Owe to Each Other*. (Cambridge, Mass.: Harvard University Press).

———. (2003) "Rawls on Justification," in Freeman (2003).

Schauer, Frederick. (1994) "Critical Notice." *Canadian Journal of Philosophy* 24: 495–509.

———. (2007) "Is There a Concept of Law?" Plenary Lecture at IVR World Congress of Philosophy of Law, reprinted in *Law and Legal Cultures in the 21st Century: Diversity and Unity* (Tomasz Gizbert-Studnicki and Jerzy Stelmach, eds.) (Warsaw: Oficyna).

Scheffler, Samuel, ed. (1988) *Consequentialism and Its Critics* (New York: Oxford University Press).

Schmidtz, David. (1992). "Rationality Within Reason." *Journal of Philosophy* 89: 445–66.

Schneewind, J. B. (1998) *The Invention of Autonomy: A History of Modern Moral Philosophy* (New York: Cambridge University Press).

Schneyer, Ted. (1984) "Moral Philosophy's Standard Misconception of Legal Ethics." *Wisconsin Law Review* 1984: 1529–72.

———. (1991) "Professional Discipline for Law Firms?", *Cornell Law Review* 77: 1–46.

Schön, Donald. (1983) *The Reflective Practitioner: How Professionals Think in Action* (New York: Basic Books).

Schwarcz, Steven L. (1994) "The Alchemy of Asset Securitization." *Stanford Journal of Law, Business, and Finance* 1: 133–54.

———. (2002) "Enron and the Use and Abuse of Special Purpose Entities in Corporate Structures." *University of Cincinnati Law Review* 70: 1309–18.

Schwartz, Murray L. (1978) "The Professionalism and Accountability of Lawyers." *California Law Review* 66: 669–98.

———. (1983) "The Zeal of the Civil Advocate," in Luban (1983).

Shaffer, Thomas L. (1985) *American Legal Ethics: Text, Readings, and Discussion Topics* (New York: Matthew Bender).

———. (1987a) "The Legal Ethics of Radical Individualism." *Texas Law Review* 65: 963–91.

———. (1987b) "Legal Ethics and the Good Client." *Catholic University Law Review* 36: 319–30.

———. (1990) "Legal Ethics After Babel." *Capital University Law Review* 19: 989–1007.

Shaffer, Thomas L. and Robert F. Cochran. (1994) *Lawyers, Clients, and Moral Responsibility.* (Minneapolis: West Publishing Co.).

Shapiro, Scott J. (2001) "On Hart's Way Out," in Coleman (2001).

———. (2006) "What Is the Internal Point of View?" *Fordham Law Review* 75: 1157–70.

———. (2007) "The 'Hart-Dworkin' Debate: A Short Guide for the Perplexed," in Arthur Ripstein, ed., *Ronald Dworkin* (New York: Cambridge University Press).

Shklar, Judith N. (1964) *Legalism.* (Cambridge, Mass.: Harvard University Press).

Siegel, Jonathan R. (2001) "What Statutory Drafting Errors Teach Us About Statutory Interpretation." *George Washington Law Review* 69: 309–66.

Simmons, A. John. (1979) *Moral Principles and Political Obligations.* (Princeton, N.J.: Princeton University Press).

———. (2008) *Political Philosophy.* (New York: Oxford University Press).

Simon, William H. (1978) "The Ideology of Advocacy: Procedural Justice and Professional Ethics." *Wisconsin Law Review* 1978: 29–144.

———. (1988) "Ethical Discretion in Lawyering." *Harvard Law Review* 101: 1083–145.

Simon, William H. (1996) "Should Lawyers Obey the Law?" *William & Mary Law Review* 38: 217–54.

———. (1998) *The Practice of Justice: A Theory of Lawyers' Ethics.* (Cambridge, Mass.: Harvard University Press).

———. (2001) "Moral Pluck: Legal Ethics in Popular Culture." *Columbia Law Review* 101: 421–47.

———. (2006) "Toyota Jurisprudence: Legal Theory and Rolling Rule Regimes," in Gráinne de Búrca and Joanne Scott, eds., *Law and New Governance in the EU and the US* (Oxford: Hart Publishers).

Simpson, A.W.B. (1986) "The Common Law and Legal Theory," in William Twining, ed., *Legal Theory and Common Law* (Oxford: Blackwell).

Smith, Abbe. (2000) "Defending Defending: The Case for Unmitigated Zeal on Behalf of People Who Do Terrible Things." *Hofstra Law Review* 28: 925–61.

———. (2003) "The Difference in Criminal Defense and the Difference it Makes." *Washington University Journal of Law and Policy* 11: 83–140.

Smith, M.B.E. (1973) "Is There a Prima Facie Obligation to Obey the Law?" *Yale Law Journal* 82: 950–76.

———. (1990) "Should Lawyers Listen to Philosophers About Legal Ethics?" *Law and Philosophy* 9: 67–93.

Soper, Philip. (1977) "Legal Theory and the Obligation of a Judge: The Hart/Dworkin Dispute." *Michigan Law Review* 75: 473–518.

Spaulding, Norman W. (2003) "Reinterpreting Professional Identity." *Colorado Law Review* 74: 1–104.

Stone, Martin J. (1995) "Focusing the Law: What Legal Interpretation is Not," in Marmor (1995).

———. (2001) "The Significance of Doing and Suffering," in Gerald J. Postema, ed., *Philosophy and the Law of Torts* (Cambridge: Cambridge University Press).

———. (2002) "Formalism," in Coleman and Shapiro (2002).

Suchman, Mark C. (1998) "Working Without a Net: The Sociology of Legal Ethics in Corporate Litigation." *Fordham Law Review* 67: 837–74.

Swartz, Mimi and Sherron Watkins (2003). *Power Failure: The Inside Story of the Collapse of Enron.* (New York: Doubleday).

Terrell, Timothy P. (2003) "Toward Duty–Based Lawyering?: Rethinking the Dangers of Lawyer Civil Disobedience in the Current Era of Regulation." *Alabama Law Review* 54: 831–52.

Thompson, Dennis. (1987) *Political Ethics and Public Office* (Cambridge, Mass.: Harvard University Press).

Thompson, E. P. (1975) *Whigs and Hunters: The Origin of the Black Act* (New York: Pantheon Books).

Tigar, Michael. (1995) "Defending." *Texas Law Review* 74: 101–10.

Tyler, Tom R. (2006) *Why People Obey the Law.* (Princeton, N.J.: Princeton University Press).

Waldron, Jeremy. (1989) "Legislation and Moral Neutrality," in Goodin and Reeve (1989).

―――. (1994) "Vagueness in Law and Language: Some Philosophical Issues." *California Law Review* 82: 523–40.

―――. (1996) "Kant's Legal Positivism." *Harvard Law Review* 109: 1535–66.

―――. (1999a) *Law and Disagreement.* (New York: Oxford University Press).

―――. (1999b) "All We Like Sheep." *Canadian Journal of Law and Jurisprudence* 12: 169–86.

Wallace, R. Jay, et al. (2004) *Reason and Value: Themes from the Moral Philosophy of Joseph Raz* (New York: Oxford University Press).

Wallach, Evan. (2007) "Drop By Drop: Forgetting the History of Water Torture in U.S. Courts." *Columbia Journal of Transnational Law* 45: 468–506.

Waluchow, W. J. (1994) *Inclusive Legal Positivism.* (New York: Oxford University Press).

Walzer, Michael. (1973) "Political Action: The Problem of Dirty Hands." *Philosophy and Public Affairs* 1: 160–80.

―――. (1981) "Philosophy and Democracy." *Political Theory* 9: 379–99.

Wasserstrom, Richard. (1973) "The Obligation to Obey the Law." *UCLA Law Review* 10: 780–807.

―――. (1975) "Lawyers as Professionals: Some Moral Issues." *Human Rights* 5: 1–24.

Webb, Duncan. (2000) *Ethics, Professional Responsibility and the Lawyer.* (Wellington, New Zealand: Butterworths).

Weber, Max. (1946) "Politics as a Vocation," in *From Max Weber: Essays in Sociology* (H. H. Gerth and C. Wright Mills, eds.) (New York: Oxford University Press).

Weinrib, Ernest J. (1988) "Legal Formalism: On the Immanent Rationality of Law." *Yale Law Journal* 97: 949–1016.

Wendel, W. Bradley. (2001) "Professional Roles and Moral Agency." *Georgetown Law Journal* 89: 667–718.

―――. (2004) "Civil Obedience." *Columbia Law Review* 104: 383–425.

―――. (2005a) "Professionalism as Interpretation." *Northwestern University Law Review* 99: 1167–233.

―――. (2005b) "Legal Ethics and the Separation of Law and Morals." *Cornell Law Review* 91: 67–128.

―――. (2006b) "Lawyers, Citizens, and the Internal Point of View." *Fordham Law Review* 75: 1473–99.

―――. (2008a) "Legal Ethics as 'Political Moralism' or the Morality of Politics." *Cornell Law Review* 93: 1413–36.

―――. (2008b) "Executive Branch Lawyers in a Time of Terror." *Dalhousie Law Journal* 31: 247–65.

―――. (2009) "The Torture Memos and the Demands of Legality." *Legal Ethics* 12: 107–23 (book review).

Wexler, Stephen. (1970) "Practicing Law for Poor People." *Yale Law Journal* 79: 1049–68.

Wilkins, David B. (1990) "Legal Realism for Lawyers." *Harvard Law Review* 104: 468–524.

———. (1995) "Race, Ethics, and the First Amendment: Should a Black Lawyer Represent the Ku Klux Klan?" *George Washington Law Review* 63: 1030–70.

———. (1998) "Identities and Roles: Race, Recognition, and Professional Responsibility." *Maryland Law Review* 57: 1502–94.

Williams, Bernard. (1981) *Moral Luck.* (New York: Cambridge University Press).

———. (1985) *Ethics and the Limits of Philosophy* (Cambridge, Mass.: Harvard University Press).

———. (1995) "Professional Morality and Its Dispositions," in Bernard Williams, *Making Sense of Humanity* (New York: Cambridge University Press).

———. (2005) *In the Beginning Was the Deed* (Geoffrey Hawthorn, ed.) (Princeton, N.J.: Princeton University Press).

Wolff, R. P. (1990) "The Conflict Between Authority and Autonomy," in Raz (1990).

Wolfram, Charles W. (1986) *Modern Legal Ethics.* (Minneapolis: West Publishing Co.).

Wong, David B. (2006) *Natural Moralities: A Defense of Pluralistic Relativism* (New York: Oxford University Press).

Woolley, Alice. (1996) "Integrity in Zealousness: Comparing the Standard Conceptions of the Canadian and American Lawyer." *Canadian Journal of Law and Jurisprudence* 9: 61–100.

———. (2009) "Regulating Dignity: A Review of *Legal Ethics and Human Dignity,*" *Legal Ethics* 11: 261–72.

Yoo, John. (2006) *War by Other Means: An Insider's Account of the War on Terror* (New York: Atlantic Monthly Press).

Zacharias, Fred C. (1989) "Rethinking Confidentiality." *Iowa Law Review* 74: 351–411.

Zimbardo, Philip. (2007) *The Lucifer Effect: Understanding How Good People Turn Evil* (New York: Random House).

Zipursky, Benjamin C. (2001) "The Model of Social Facts," in Coleman (2001).

Zitrin, Richard and Carol M. Langford. (1999) *The Moral Compass of the American Lawyer* (New York: Ballantine).

Index